Development Delusions and Contradictions

David Sims

Development Delusions and Contradictions

An Anatomy of the Foreign Aid Industry

palgrave
macmillan

David Sims
Economist and Urban Development
Specialist
Cairo, Egypt

ISBN 978-3-031-17769-9 ISBN 978-3-031-17770-5 (eBook)
https://doi.org/10.1007/978-3-031-17770-5

This Palgrave Macmillan imprint is published by the registered company Springer Nature Switzerland AG.
The registered company address is: Gewerbestrasse 11, 6330 Cham, Switzerland

Acknowledgments

This book is made up of ideas that come from many colleagues, but most of these still pursue careers in the development industry and thus should probably remain incognito. On the other hand, David B. Allen, who is retired, has no reservations being mentioned as an important inspiration to the author. Also, much credit must go to my wife Sonja for her invaluable support. Thanks must also be extended to Wyndham Hacket Payne, Paul Smith Jesudas, and Balaji Padmanaban at Palgrave Macmillan for their great help in pushing this manuscript to publication.

Contents

Abbreviations

ADB	Asian Development Bank
AfDB	African Development Bank
AFD	Agence française de développement
AIIB	Asian Infrastructure Investment Bank
ASEAN	Association of Southeast Asian Nations
BBC	British Broadcasting Corporation
BDS	Business Development Services
BMZ	Federal Ministry for Economic Development and Cooperation (Germany)
BRIC	Brazil, Russian, India, and China
CDC	Colonial Development Corporation (now British International Investment)
CDC	Centers for Disease Control and Prevention (USA)
CDF	Country Development Framework
CEO	Chief executive officer
CGD	Center for Global Development
CGIAR	Consultative Group for International Agricultural Research
CHF	Swiss Francs
CNRS	Centre national de la recherche scientifique
CV	Curriculum Vitae
DAC	Development Assistance Committee (of the OECD)
DFAT	Department of Foreign Affairs and Trade (Australia)
DfID	Department for International Development (now part of FCDO)
DoC	Drivers of Change
DRC	Democratic Republic of Congo
DSA	Daily Subsistence Allowance
EBRD	European Bank for Reconstruction and Development

EC	European Commission
ECR	Executive Vice Presidency
EIB	European Investment Bank
EPRDF	Ethiopian People's Revolutionary Democratic Front
EU	European Union
FAO	Food and Agriculture Organization
FCDO	Foreign, Commonwealth, and Development Office
FDI	Foreign Direct Investment
FMO	Dutch Development Bank
FY	Fiscal Year
GBP	British pound
GDP	Gross Domestic Product
GEF	Global Environment Facility
GIZ	Gesellschaft für Internationale Zusammenarbeit (formerly GTZ)
GIZ IS	GIZ International Services
GNI	Gross National Income
GSDRC	Governance and Social Research Centre
IBRD	International Bank for Reconstruction and Development (WBG)
ICB	International Competitive Bidding
IDA	International Development Association (WBG)
IDB	Inter-American Development Bank
IFAD	International Fund for Agricultural Development
IFC	International Finance Corporation (WBG)
IFI	International Finance Institution
IMF	International Monetary Fund
INGO	International Non-Governmental Organization
IOM	International Organization for Migration
IQC	Indefinite Quantity Contract
IT	Information Technology
JICA	Japanese International Development Agency
KfW	Kreditanstalt für Wiederaufbau (German development bank)
KWH	Kilowatt Hour
MCC	Millennium Challenge Corporation (USA)
MDB	Multilateral Development Bank
MfDR	Management for Development Results
MIGA	Multilateral Investment Guarantee Agency
MMS	Money Moving Syndrome
NCB	National Competitive Bidding
NGO	Non-governmental Organization
OCHA	UN Office for the Coordination of Humanitarian Affairs
ODA	Official Development Assistance
ODI	Overseas Development Institute

OECD	Organization for Economic Cooperation and Development
O&M	Operations and Maintenance
PBR	Payment by Results
PEA	Political and Economic Analysis
PMS	Performance Measurement Systems
PIU	Project Implementation Unit
PMU	Project Management Unit
PPP	Public Private Partnership
PPPa	Purchasing Power Parity
PRAG	Procurement and Grants for EU External Actions – A Practical Guide
PfR	Program for Results
PRSP	Poverty Reduction Strategy Paper
R&D	Research and Development
RFP	Request for Proposal
RBM	Results-based Management
SDGs	Sustainable Development Goals
SIDA	Swedish International Development Agency
SME	Small and Medium Enterprises
SOAS	School of Oriental and African Studies
S&S	Sites and Services
SWOT	Strengths, Weaknesses, Opportunities, Threats
TA	Technical Assistance
ToR	Terms of Reference
TVE	Town and Village Enterprises
TVET	Technical and Vocational Education and Training
TWP	Thinking and Working Politically
UAE	United Arab Emirates
UN	United Nations
UNCDF	United Nations Capital Development Fund
UNDB	United Nations Development Business
UNDP	United Nations Development Programme
UN-Habitat	United Nations Human Settlements Programme
UNHCR	United Nations High Commissioner for Refugees
UNOPS	United Nations Office for Project Services
UNEP	United Nations Environment Programme
UNESCO	United Nations Educational, Scientific and Cultural Organization
UNFCCC	United Nations Framework Convention on Climate Change
UNIDO	United Nations Industrial Development Organization
UNCTAD	United Nations Conference on Trade and Development
UNV	UN Volunteers
USAID	United States Agency for International Development

VAT	Value Added Tax
VfM	Value for Money
VIP	Very Important Person
WB	World Bank
WBG	World Bank Group
WDR	World Development Report
WEF	World Economic Forum
WHO	World Health Organization
ZOPP	Zielorientierte Projektplanung (goal-oriented project planning)

Introduction

Around 1700 almost everyone on earth was poor or destitute, and Thomas Hobbes' phrase about life as "poor, nasty, brutish and short" certainly hit the mark. Perhaps only one-tenth of the world's population was living what could be considered anywhere near comfortable lives. At least, this is what most economic historians will tell you.

Jumping ahead 250 years, one could definitely say two completely different worlds had emerged—a prosperous West and a definitely lagging Rest. The reasons for this ascendency of the West were due to processes and factors that, even today, are not well understood, but this huge West–Rest economic divide led to the realization that this gap was one of the great issues of the times, one that needed to be addressed as part of any new world order. Thus, by 1950 it could be said that the Development Era began. Some 70 years later, after untold machinations and lots and lots of money, the West is still very much at it.

Western nations and institutions constructed increasingly sophisticated systems to redress this divide, based originally on the idea that transposed expertise and capital was what was needed to help nations build modern economies, to prosper, and eventually to be self-sustaining. Not only would these 'emerging' nations become partners in global prosperity; they would become great consumers as well and, through the miracles of free trade, economies of scale and comparative advantage, the West as well as the Rest would benefit. Yet what sounded so clear and noble back at the start of the Development Era, and what has remained, at least ostensibly, the philosophical bedrock of helping poor nations, has had to face a very rocky road, to say the least.

There is not much to brag about. The poorest nations then are still the poorest nations now, and the ascendency of the 30-some countries of the West over the 160 or so countries of the Rest remains very, very clear. There are only five small countries that have unequivocally joined the ranks of the advanced nations, and there may be a handful of other countries that are—with a lot of luck in say 30 or 40 years—within reach of joining the club. (China, as this book shows, is hard to classify.) Yes, since the 1990s most measures show a marked decline in absolute poverty and generally improved livelihoods (as well as the rise of small middle classes and a marked increase in income inequality), but this hardly constitutes a changing world order.

How does foreign assistance from the West to the Rest fit into this picture? As will be seen, its effects are underwhelming. There are those who say development aid has had a small measurable impact on economic growth and poverty alleviation, but others say it hasn't, and some say, considering all the other factors in play, that trying to assess its impact is pretty much a fool's errand. In any event, this questionable value of foreign aid is underscored by the fact that almost no one is satisfied with its performance, and the need to improve, reform, and reinvent it and its modalities is a constant refrain.

In other words, stimulating 'development' has been much more difficult than Western optimists had originally thought. Aid processes have been buffeted by ideologies, un-enlightened self-interest, some very ineffective and petulant governments on the receiving end, and hugely powerful global markets that no one could have imagined in the early halcyon days of Development. And the road has not been helped by a one-size-fits-all arrogance that has conveniently ignored the unique historical trajectories of poor countries and that constantly reinforces a fairy-tale perception that outside money, plus Western technical and managerial knowhow are what is needed.

So, how did such a situation come about? Why, in spite of seven decades of the Development Era, with some very smart people in control, with committed technical cadres, with endless discussions and initiatives, and with lots of funds to fertilize the landscape, has it not been possible to get things right? And why, peering into the future, does it seem that there will be More of the Same? These are questions that this book answers. To do so, it looks in detail at the impressive number of aid structures and modalities that have been set up by the 'development community' as well as the considerable posturing in poor countries that has evolved to accommodate them. Collectively, these can be called the development industry. This is a behemoth that is very much an 'industry' in the sense that it has a quantifiable turnover (to the tune of over $200 billion per year in 2021), employs or otherwise occupies a cast of hundreds of thousands, and makes lots of money for companies, INGOs, and individuals. Also, more than any other global industry, it includes inordinate numbers of conceptualizing' organizations that track the flow of funds, that measure development results and outcomes, that talk about the need for innovative approaches and, above all, that must justify the industry's many activities. Finally, it can be considered an industry because it is treated as such by a whole raft of players—by donors, academics, foundations, journalists, politicians, think tanks, private contractors, and NGOs.

To understand this industry, a substantial enquiry or anatomy of its many aspects and how they interrelate and have evolved is needed, since the overall malaise in the industry is definitely more than the sum of its parts. Only by stripping away extensive posturing and political correctness, by looking at the systemic motivations that underpin the behaviors of industry players, and by identifying what drives the many obsessional themes that riddle the industry, can the contradictions and pathologies of the industry be laid bare. This is what this book aims to do, something that is long overdue.

Of course, there is a long history, practically as long as aid itself, of those who have looked askance at aspects of the industry and its foibles. Especially over the last two decades some of these critics—even some who could be considered mainstream development experts—have scored very good points, and the author is much beholden to them and the reasoning behind their critical stances. Yet most aid critiques have for the most part delivered partial messages, usually concentrating on certain aspects—looking at particular institutions, particular economic approaches, particular modes of aid delivery, or particular regions (often Africa these days). Plus, many of the industry's ills have become so commonplace that they are simply considered unfortunate facts of life. Thus, it is high time that a comprehensive treatment is put forth, since our thesis is that there are behaviors, structures, and dynamics that are found with surprising consistency throughout the development industry that need to be catalogued, dissected, and, especially, interconnected. In other words, this is a huge subject that needs to large canvas to show *both* how delivering anything like effective development assistance has become extremely difficult, ***and*** how at the same time it has made anything like real, endogenous development in the Rest well-nigh impossible.

This book carefully looks at some twenty root themes or traits found in the business, to see how they evolved, to uncover their operating characteristics, and to chart their pernicious impacts. In so doing it is hoped that paths of enquiry will have been carved out for others. The arguments found in this book offer a wealth of entry points for academic, technical, and journalistic research. Much more work needs to be done to illuminate how the industry's behaviors were created, how they have become imbedded, and how they reinforce each other. The idea is to stimulate others and thus bring into the mainstream of development thought what should have been there all along. After all, it is ironic that the Development Beast, which spares no effort at analyzing economies and societies in the Rest, never turns its efforts towards analyzing itself, except in the most superficial ways. Were even the tiniest fraction of the industry's energies and resources turned inward and devoted to questioning the structures and motivations that drive it, there might be some very surprising conclusions.

This book is divided into three parts: Part I first provides an introductory chapter that simply charts the scope and nature of the Development Industry and the complex world of donors, their many operations and imperatives, and their many henchmen and pilot fish. It then moves on to identify traits or imperatives that riddle donor behavior, and these are grouped into eleven thematic chapters. These chapters help tease out the contradictions operating and the real motivations and incentives that keep the development train running on its tracks, however ineffective or irrelevant it may be.

Part II looks at the receiving end of the industry—the effects of donor operations within the countries they are ostensibly meant to help, the ways these countries react, and the consequent (mostly negative) posturing. It starts with a background chapter that gives a straightforward analysis of the predictably weak governments found in most development countries and how they got that way. There are then seven chapters that illustrate how the good intentions of donors have tended to unravel in the Rest, and where the unintended consequences, rarely if ever considered, have kicked in.

Putting the two sides together, Part III first presents a summing up chapter that shows how collectively the problems of the development industry are more than the sum of its individual parts, and it identifies eleven main conclusions for readers to take away. Part III concludes with a chapter about the probable future of the Development Industry and possible if very difficult ways its activities and structures could be changed, and changed fundamentally.

Something for Readers to Keep in Mind: Donor Self-interest

Readers of this book should keep in mind that donor governments provide development assistance for a number of reasons that have nothing to do with helping countries develop economically or with alleviating the poverty of their citizens.

First, there are what could be called strategic interests, something pursued by the more powerful donor countries. These are totally un-subtle forms of self-interest, where the donor country wishes to advance its diplomatic and security interests in particular countries or regions by offering aid programs of various kinds as sweeteners. Frequently these aid programs are intertwined with military assistance and weapons sales. The aim is to buy goodwill from others or to encourage them to take up positions they might otherwise reject, and as such aid can be considered a classic tool of statecraft.

Second, there are commercial interests on the part of rich countries, where aid programs are seen as a means to promote trade, exports, and investment opportunities for their own companies. The promotion of commercial interests is a very old and well-established kind of diplomacy, and it can be found, in some form or other, as part of almost all bilateral aid programs. This commercial dimension can be considered intrinsic to almost any bilateral aid, since it serves the important function of gaining political backing for a country's aid program from its corporate sector.

Third, there are donor self-interests that are imbedded within aid delivery structures themselves. Most obvious are what is called tied aid, that is, stipulations that a donor country's aid programs must procure national goods, firms, and experts. There have been some successful efforts since 2005 to reduce this form of aid, but the practice persists. And what could be called 'informally tied aid,' remains rampant. Due to pressure from businesses and due to years of chummy relations, a large majority of contracting for development services goes to firms in the donor country. Even international agencies tend to procure most of their services from firms and individuals located in Western countries.

Attempts to reign in these particular donor interests have had little effect, and some pessimists might even say that these self-interests are so dominant that development itself is simply an elaborate sideshow. They certainly color how aid is financed and delivered, and as this book trolls through the many structural contradictions imbedded in the ways the development industry operates, it is important to keep in mind this background of donor country self-interest. In fact, one needs to be particularly vigilant, and in looking at new paradigms and initiatives that are frequently spun out by the industry, it well behooves the observer to ask: Who will end up getting the work, and who ultimately benefits?

A Long Time in the Making

This book has been an idea for a long time. The author has spent his entire life living or working in development contexts, and he has gone from junior specialist to senior expert to 'dinosaur in demand' over some 50 years in the business. He has worked in many Asian, African, and Middle Eastern countries for a plethora of both bilateral and multilateral agencies or the consulting firms they hire and has seen the operations of the development industry from close up. It did not take very long to realize that this industry embodied serious contradictions, generated little positive impact, wasted tons of money, was pompously self-important and, to put icing on the cake, in many cases had a serious negative impact for countries on the receiving end.

This realization crystalized during a long stint by the author in Nepal in the early 1990s, where even then the weight of donors in practically everything that could be considered developmental was causing counterproductive overload and confusion in Kathmandu and around the country, but somehow donors couldn't see this (or more likely, simply didn't care). This eye-opener led the author to begin to explore more and more about the paradoxes found in the development industry, both those at the fine-grained project level and also in the wider literature. But it seemed that little could be found about what really mattered—the contradictions and unintended consequences *of the development industry itself*—and these little snippets were obscured under immense quantities of mind-numbing technical and prescriptive output. Over the decades it became very apparent to the author that donors thrived on objectifying the Rest as something detached and out there, justifying new paradigms and warmed-over agendas to further the business of development while studiously avoiding any look inward at the industry *itself* as part of the problem.

A Certain Focus on Egypt

Since half of the author's professional life has involved working in Egypt, it is inevitable that Egypt (and with it the Arab region) takes a certain pride of place in this book. Many other countries of the Rest are also covered, but there is value in having a deep grounding in one single place, especially one with a long history of international aid from a plethora of donors, and it is useful to have a point of reference to avoid scattered generalizations and to allow a teasing out of concrete examples of how the aid system—and the 'partnership' principles upon which it is based—was largely counterproductive.

Egypt is a good choice for these purposes. Since the mid-1970s Egypt has been a major target for Western development initiatives ranging over practically anything that needs 'developing' and even some things that don't. At various periods Egypt has been the single largest recipient of economic assistance, almost every paradigm of development thinking has been tried out, and the list of Egypt's 'development partners' represents a near complete roll-call of those prominent in the business. Egypt is also a good case because, over the last 60 years, its development trajectory has been less than impressive; for example, in 1964 Egypt and South Korea had exactly the same GDP per capita, whereas by 2019 South Korea's exceeded Egypt's by a factor of ten. What went wrong? Egypt has suffered from many external factors that could be said to partly explain some of this dismal record, yet one cannot help but wonder why so much aid has had so little effect, and examples from Egypt help illuminate both how the development industry is ineffective and also how it continues to pour out its beneficence in spite of practically nothing to show for it.

A Certain Focus on Things Urban

The author's expertise in the development business has been as an economist and urban development specialist—sometimes as part of a consultant team, sometimes leading a team, and sometimes as an individual. Most of the development initiatives seen up close have had to do with things urban—housing, urban expansion and plans, industry, urban poverty, slum and informal settlement upgrading, local area development, land administration, municipal finance, and urban infrastructure, transport and services, not to mention fashionable cross-cutting issues. One of the advantages of 'things urban' is that they encompass practically every development issue one can think of. Thus, while no claim is made that this book covers the whole range of development issues, to be specialized in the urban dimension is one way to become familiar with most of them.

What Is Not Covered in This Book

Not specifically covered are humanitarian or emergency aid (responding to disasters, conflict, and refugees), something that is an enormous and expanding sub-industry in its own right. Unlike development assistance, humanitarian aid does not usually pretend to put people or nations on paths of self-sustaining growth. Instead, it mainly aims to save lives, alleviate suffering, and to return people to normal life. The kinds of humanitarian operations and the specialists involved are usually different from those of mainstream development efforts, since they tend to be more straightforward in what they deliver, and they rarely involve host governments directly as 'partners.'

Even so, the borders between humanitarian and development efforts are frequently blurred. More and more, humanitarians will claim to have expertise in development issues—particularly those surrounding poverty alleviation—and at the same time classic development agencies are becoming more involved with the effects of disasters and conflicts and ways to make populations more resilient to them. And to a very large extent humanitarian aid *is* a business, and this makes it a close cousin to the development industry. There is a large overlap in the extensive use of large service contractors, specifically INGOs, and, moreover, there is also overlap in terms of sources of funding, bureaucratic processes, market promotion, and institutional self-preservation.

How to Use This Book

The chapters are presented in a logical order (with contextual chapters found at the beginning of Parts I and II), but each subsequent chapter can be read as stand-alone thematic treatments. The chapter subheadings can be useful guides.

This book covers much territory and many themes, and there are sometimes causes and effects that link up the behaviors or phenomena described in individual chapters. Thus, embedded in the text are occasional references to other chapters, and these provide the reader a way to follow up these linkages, should he or she so wish.

Nomenclature

There are numerous ways to refer to the world's few advanced countries versus the many that are less developed. This book uses the terminology of *the West* versus *the Rest* (thanks to William Easterly, who popularized the phrase). Others prefer the dichotomy North versus South. Other dichotomies include First World versus Third World (with the second world having dropped out of history), or rich versus poor nations, or industrialized versus industrializing nations. The West (and its counterfoil, the Rest) is preferred, since it encapsulates the history and the dominant economic, cultural, and political senses of power embedded in Western countries.

So, what countries are considered Western? Obviously, the countries of Western Europe, North America, plus Japan, Australia, and New Zealand. And to these must be added South Korea, Singapore, Hong Kong, Taiwan, and Israel. But what about Russia and Eastern Europe? Here one is in somewhat of a grey area, since these countries do not conform to the classic 'developing' country, yet still exhibit some of their characteristics (including lots of people with miserable incomes). And what about resource-rich countries? These may have extremely high GDP per capita but, as most people in the aid business would agree, are anything but 'developed.'

Most other countries are almost all firmly part of the Rest, whether they are categorized as 'emerging' or 'frontier' economies, or 'fragile' or 'conflict' countries, or whether they can be termed, as the World Bank does, as 'low income' or 'low middle-income' or 'high middle-income.' Some of the high middle-income countries (e.g., Turkey, Chile, Mexico, Costa Rica, Thailand, and Malaysia) might be considered by some to be on their way to join the West, but this is very debatable. And China, with its enormous population, has become somewhat an anomaly, acquiring a hugely and sophisticated economy but which is still middle-income poor, at least in GDP/capita terms.

In this book the generic term '*donors*' is used as shorthand for all government agencies or international institutions or development foundations in the West that dispense funds, advice, or knowledge aimed at the Rest. Some may say that multinational financial institutions such as the World Bank are not strictly donor agencies, since most of their funding is through loans that need to be paid back at some point, they should definitely be included as donors since their funds come ultimately from Western country pledges, their goals are similar to those of the bilaterals, they all use similar development-speak, and they frequently coordinate with each other and often co-fund programs. Similarly, the dozens of UN agencies are included as donors, even though many are little more than specialized talk shops and conduits for funds from other donors. I also include private foundations and charities with activities in the Rest as donors, almost all of which are based in the West.

PART I

Inside the Donor World

CHAPTER 1

Background: A Sketch of the Development Industry

This first chapter presents a survey of the development industry, something to provide context before the reader takes up the analytical chapters of Part I. This cannot be considered an exhaustive treatment of what is a very large, complex, and little understood industry (or 'community' as it is sometimes called, to give it a cuddly glow), and the reader can refer to a small number of sources that struggle to describe the subject from different points of view. These include books by Arjan de Haan (2009), Degnbol-Martinussen and Engberg-Pedersen (2003), and Sogge (2002), although these miss many aspects and are somewhat out-of-date. There is also a very short introduction (Wickstead, 2015) and a 32-chapter anthology (Arvin & Lew, 2015).

Why Call It an Industry?

The development or 'development cooperation' industry is very much an industry in the sense that it has a quantifiable size or turnover, employs or otherwise occupies a cast of hundreds of thousands, and makes lots of money for companies, NGOs, and individuals. Also, it commands the attention of a host of organizations and individuals who monitor, study, or otherwise conceptualize development and the ways that those in the industry try to promote it. In other words, it can be considered an industry because it is treated as such by a whole raft of players—by academics, foundations, journalists, politicians, think tanks, contractors, and NGOs.

D. Sims, *Development Delusions and Contradictions*,
https://doi.org/10.1007/978-3-031-17770-5_1

That it is an industry or a "concept of a community of interested parties" (Dichter, 2003, 98) is underscored by the existence of a number of professional associations, career services, trade publications, and trade fairs that cluster around it, as well as the nonstop roll-out of conferences, workshops, colloquiums, forms, and other events sponsored and well-attended by main players. In fact, there are probably few other industries of global reach that are surrounded by such strong and increasing ancillary activities.

However, development assistance is a peculiar type of industry. Its 'product' or 'markets' are not at all obvious—unlike classic industries such as say the steel, oil, automotive, or tourist industries. Such industries are all first measured by what are final global sales and the changing market shares within it, numbers that are analyzed to death both inside private corporations to assess divisional and managerial performance and outside by the legions of financial analysts who feel they need to tell you how to invest. But the development industry mainly processes donor government funds for spending on what could be called intermediary markets (like contracting, materials and equipment, consultants, grant awards to INGOs, and various other professional services), which are in turn supposed to carry out development efforts directly or indirectly in non-donor countries, teaming up in most cases by partners found in local markets. To a lesser extent the industry also processes funding coming from private foundations and charity organizations whose expenditures at least ostensibly support the same development and poverty reduction goals.

Donor countries or multilaterals sometimes transfer funds directly to recipient governments in the form of budget support or policy lending or, what is much the same, structural adjustment loans. These, the simplest of development flows, do not pass directly through the industry's intermediaries, yet they are also part of it, since the same donor institutions are involved, the 'development' aims and justifications are the same, and many of the same people and institutions are involved. This straightforward and direct flow of funds came very much in vogue in the 1990s (peaking in 2002), but budget support has since declined, representing only a small fraction, less than 6 percent, of the total development industry's annual value in 2014 (Kennard & Provost, 2016). Thus for the other ninety-some percent of development funding, there is definitely an 'industry' composed of those competing for slices of these varied flows.[1]

So, these days practically all aid industry expenditures go through competitive procurement processes of one sort or another. These flows are what can be considered the core of the 'industry,' in the sense that they generate intense interest and competition on the part of the businesses who want to grab some of these flows. A UK government publication glowingly summed up the advantages (Department for International Trade, 2014): "Aside from the usual payoffs of international trade, aid funded business means orders are always backed by funds, is a secure way to do business in new markets, which can provide lucrative long-term opportunities, allows business to establish a local presence, provides valuable international trade experience, (and) is useful to have in your company experience history and references when bidding for future projects."

Private businesses—mainly large engineering firms, management companies, and specialized consulting groups—have always played a role in the development industry, but since the turn of the century, and particularly since the 2007–2008 financial crisis, the visibility and activities of very large corporations have become more pronounced. According to Kennard and Provost (2016), "(t)he 21st century has witnessed a corporate takeover of aid: US and European corporations not only making millions off foreign aid budgets, but use aid and global development institutions to break into new markets and influence public policy in the developing world.... Now, CEOs of major multinationals sit on UN panels charting the future of global development; USAID is partnering with Walmart and Chevron; and NGOs like Oxfam and Save the Children have joined hands with corporate behemoths Unilever and GlaxoSmithKline. With traditional aid budgets under pressure, donors are increasingly turning to the private sector to fill the gap."

A Strange Industry Indeed

There are a couple of conceptual difficulties with the 'industry' approach to analyzing foreign assistance. First, one should say (and donors increasingly do) that their funding is only an intermediate step, and that the final

[1] The administrative budgets of donor agencies and IFIs do not normally go through competitive procurement processes, but these are miniscule compared to the development funds they manage.

result or 'product' is development of the receiving country writ large, something much more difficult to measure, although small armies of aid evaluators and impact analysts make livings out of doing precisely that. This conceptual problem comes back time and time again and is one of the most discussed aspects of development—that its aims and results are messy and that success or market impact cannot be measured in any straightforward way, except over a very long term through abstract macroeconomic data such as GDP per capita and its variants, which conveniently makes it impossible to ascribe either economic development or poverty alleviation impacts to any particular interventions. This 'lack of market feedback' makes the development industry extremely self-referential, one that has had to construct its own convoluted, expensive, and mostly self-congratulatory systems to try to fill this gap. It is hard to think of another industry with such a strange arrangement, except perhaps defense spending.

Second, some might say that development is hardly an industry but simply another form of public expenditures where funds are allocated and spent on service providers through a bureaucracy in order to, say, improve health or education or some other public pursuit. Cannot development aid simply be seen, and analyzed, as such, a collection of monopolistic public enterprises that procure services and try to develop means, in the absence of market feedback, to assess good performance and citizen satisfaction? The "new public management" paradigm, popular since the early 1990s, has had its influence in Western public enterprises, in which quantitative performance indicators are supposed to substitute for non-existent market feedback (Streeck, 2017, 105). But such an approach is extremely problematic when applied to development assistance, since instead of one or a small cluster of monopolistic/oligopolistic agencies in a particular country, one is talking about scores and scores of more or less independent international agencies, each with their own rules and internal cultures doing their work in parallel with each other. And these agencies operate in scores if not hundreds of individual countries and in a bewildering and ever-expanding number of economic sectors and subsectors. And each donor agency has to consider as its ultimate 'consumers' the general public (or the poor) for which there is no direct access or even straightforward way of reading 'consumption.' The irony is that donors have been reduced to relying on feedback mechanisms that work more or less in their own advanced countries (where sophisticated statistical systems have been built up over time and where there is also pervasive accountability through electoral mechanisms), but that for the most part fail miserably in developing countries. These are countries that are data-challenged and have imperfect democratic feedback (if any at all).

The Size of the Industry

The most used and detailed source for the annual flow of development funds globally is official development assistance (ODA) compiled by the Development Assistance Committee (DAC) of the Organization for Economic Cooperation and Development (OECD), even though it is not comprehensive and has its acknowledged methodological weaknesses.[2] ODA is reported as coming mostly from thirty-some DAC countries—all the usual industrialized countries, plus 20 other countries that report to it and from ten more countries that do not but for which estimates are made. The money is net allocated amounts *as reported by* the donor.[3] It also includes funds provided by donor countries and allocated through international finance institutions (IFIs), such as the World Bank, as we will see below.

Official OECD-monitored ODA amounted to $ 157.0 billion in 2016,[4] and by 2020 the figure had reached $161.2.[5] (ODA figures for 2021 were significantly higher, but these were largely due to Covid-related expenditures.) These official amounts include most humanitarian aid but not China's aid program,[6] nor aid to Israel or Russia, nor does it include private foundation funding (e.g., the Bill and Melinda Gates, Ford, or Rockefeller foundations), nor does it include the considerable number of

[2] The definition of official development assistance is given by OECD in http://www.oecd.org/dac/stats/officialdevelopmentassistancedefinitionandcoverage.htm. Accessed 10 May 2022.

[3] All donor government transfers are included, but loans are recorded only if the loan includes at least a 25% at concessional value (measured by net present value discounted at 10 percent).

[4] http://stats.oecd.org/qwids

[5] https://www.developmentaid.org/#!/news-stream/post/92614/foreign-aid-and-top-donor-countries-in-2020?utm_source=Newsletter&utm_medium=Email&utm_campaign=NewsDigest&token=d8190b86-06e8-11ea-8cc5-52540068df95

[6] Over the 2010–2014 period, China's total foreign aid that met ODA criteria (grants plus concessionary loans) averaged about $10 billion per year. China's government also extends a huge amount of more or less commercial loan to recipient governments, equal to about $40 billion annually over the same period, called Other Official Flows, using the funny acronym OOF (Taylor, 2017).

private charity initiatives aimed at developing countries. There are no hard estimates for these various 'off-DAC' aid flows, but one can hazard a guess that they might have added some $35 billion to the ODA total in 2017, and probably more in 2020. There are no hard figures on how much of declared DAC actually reaches developing countries, although there is much to indicate it is much lower. In other words, as in all numbers dealing with the development industry, there is considerable confusion and conflicting data. In addition, the ODA figures, as a measure of international aid resources flowing to developing countries, are weakened by the inclusion of several categories of expenditures that are disbursed within specific donor countries, particularly refugee and training costs. Finally, additional commitments to debt relief or to climate finance cannot be reliably measured due to frequent double counting.

In any event, let us take the $160 billion as a rough approximation of the size of the official development industry in 2019, add some $40 billion to account for all nonofficial flows, and compare this $200 billion to some other global industries. In one sense, it doesn't really amount to much. For example, the global market value for bottled water was about the same, valued at $157bn in 2013, and this industry is growing rapidly (Elmhirst, 2016). Then there is the global fitness and mind-body industry estimated at $595 billion per year, and trumping them all, the personal care, beauty, and anti-aging industry at a whopping $ 1083 billion.[7] And don't forget that global military expenditures, the mother of all global industries that depend on government budgets, topped $ 1.7 trillion dollars in 2016, or some 11 times that of the development industry.[8]

The point is that the development industry is large in terms of money flows, but these flows are insignificant compared to global consumer industries and Western governments expenditures on their own citizens and their own defense.

[7] These are all global figures for 2018 based on 'industry research' by the Global Wellness Institute, which claims to cover all aspects of "the $4.2 trillion global wellness economy." See https://globalwellnessinstitute.org/press-room/statistics-and-facts/. Accessed 25 May 2022.

[8] https://www.statista.com/topics/1696/defense-and-arms/

Growth of the Industry

As far as can be determined from DAC statistics, the sum of net official development assistance flows has been growing slowly but rather steadily, albeit with some peaks and troughs. Looking back over the period 2000–2015, development assistance increased by 2.26 times or 5.6 percent annually, again in real terms. The 2018–2020 period has seen a leveling and even a tiny dip in total ODA, but Chinese and private foundation aid has probably more than compensated for this.

In any event, it should be clear that the development industry financial flows have been growing steadily for decades. In fact, over the long term it is one of the most steady growth industries in constant dollar terms, even discounting stagnation in the 'lost' 1990s and an earlier dip in 1979–1981. Foreign aid tracked by the OECD increased 5.7 times since 1960—from $32 billion to $158 billion, in constant 2015 prices, which translates into an average annual increase of 3.3 percent. Yet over the same period net ODA fell from 1.6 percent of the total GDP of developing countries to only 0.6 percent. This fact has led some to see not only the increasing irrelevance of development assistance (and its replacement by commercial lending), but also the demise of the development industry itself. One observer even said (Gill, 2018): "I won't be encouraging my children to go into the aid industry. The next decade may be its last."

Well, we shall see. Our own take is that, in ten or twenty years, things will remain much the same, with development expenditures probably slightly higher in real terms, and with more ostensible reform, more new paradigms, and new funding arrangements, in spite of the fact that the industry is becoming less relevant when compared to recipient country GDP or to other external flows such as private sector investment and remittances.

The Money, Its Sources, and Its Management

It is certainly money that drives the development industry, and most of this comes from the budgets of donor governments, either through annual allocations to bilateral development agencies or, in the case of multinational banks, from periodic replenishing by member countries, or in the case of UN agency core funds, from annual country contributions. In fact, the OECD sometimes computes official donor contributions simply by country, omitting multilaterals and UN agencies, since they compute such money as originating from country contributions. So, ultimately, almost all official development funding comes from taxpayers in rich countries, either directly or indirectly. This is where it could be said that the existential threat to the development industry lies, and those who live off the industry know it well. For decades there has been considerable lobbying by the industry aimed at taxpayers and various citizen and parliamentary forums, using a whole range of arguments from the moralistic (shocking poverty and starvation), to the semi-altruistic (a prosperous third world is a safer world for us) to the pure self-interest: (creating new markets for Western corporations).

This existential angst about securing continued funding is one factor that confirms that the aid industry is an industry. Those within the 'development community' feel the need to come together to preserve the flow of funds and to defend this flow from those who would divert this money elsewhere. It is an unending fight played out in Western capitals between aid skeptics on the one hand and aid champions on the other. One industry observer, Pablo Yanguas (2018) wrote about how it is time for the aid community to abandon its defensive, siege mentality and to, as it were, come out swinging. Yanguas bemoans the fact that there "are very few people left, outside the aid industry proper, who are either willing or able to articulate and communicate the moral value of foreign aid," and that the unbridled critics of the industry have a field day talking about the waste, the arrogance, and the cozy relationship between donors and private firms. So Yanquas calls for "a new discourse around aid that makes taxpayers proud of what they fund, and that is honest with them about the enormity of the task, but also about the intrinsic moral value of the payoffs."

The ranking of countries according to how much aid they disburse is a favorite development topic, one that comes around time and again. In what could be called the Moral Superiority Sweepstakes, the OECD annually publishes how much a country's aid budget represents as a percentage of national GDP. Inevitably this shows that some countries—currently Denmark, Luxemburg, Norway, Sweden, Germany, and the UK (until 2021)—are great donors, all of which contribute over 0.7 percent of annual GDP to development. For some reason, back in 1972, this became the target adopted by developed countries, a kind of shame game. And of course, according to this metric the USA consistently and impressively underperforms, and in 2016 it only coughed up the equivalent of 0.17 percent of GDP. (The DAC average was 0.32 percent.)

Main Types of Development Funding

For the uninitiated, and even for some of those firmly established in the business, it is worth setting out the main types of official development assistance. For clarity, these are grouped into six categories:

Project Grants: These are cash grants, and they mostly come from bilateral donors, almost always for specific projects. Recipient governments prefer this kind of funding, even though, as we point out below, the actual disbursements are phased and are anything but straightforward.

Project and Program Loans: These come mainly from multilateral development banks (MDBs). They are soft or concessionary loans, with interest rates normally significantly below commercial rates and with long maturities and generous repayment grace periods. In almost all cases these are sovereign loans, meaning that their repayment is guaranteed by the recipient country's government. Thus, the ministry or implementing agency that directly benefits from the project loan does not itself need to pay it back, and there is the strange situation where the institutional benefactor itself mainly feels no pain if the project goes soar. And since repayment for most project loans do not begin for years, in the minds of officials there is no financial squeeze and any problems can be conveniently 'kicked down the road.' Most MDBs also offer a variety of guarantee instruments associated with portfolio loans, covering a portion of possible losses.

Policy Loans and Budget Support: This kind of funding is theoretically aimed to convince recipient governments to adopt the right sectoral policies and major economic reforms. As a policy loan, it is disbursed in trances upon the recipient formally adopting the desired policy and performing according to milestones or indicators that are carefully spelt out. In spite of the sometime onerous 'policy' conditionality that is either attached or implied, poor countries like these policy loans/grants since (1) the money itself is completely fungible and (2) many are the ways to cleverly sidestep the conditionality on down the line.

Technical Assistance (TA): Also called 'technical cooperation' in UN- and EU-speak, these are inevitably grants, mainly for the hiring of experts and in-house advisors, but also for training and capacity building programs, conferences and study tours, and bits of related hardware. In other words, technical assistance is a kind of catchall used extensively by all donors for all sorts of purposes, including for hiring outside expertise to do the work the donor staffer simply hasn't the time or competence to undertake her/himself. In most cases the technical services are completely designed, commissioned, managed, and paid for by the donor (or his captive trust fund, see below), with only minimal management functions devolved to the recipient through, say, a steering committee set up for the purpose. In the spirit of 'ownership,' donors are allowing more and more technical assistance services to be contracted out by the recipient ministry or agency itself out of earmarked funds, but always with tight supervision by the donor. Technical assistance grants have often been widely criticized as being wasteful and unproductive, not to mention supply driven and insensitive, but at a level of some 20 to 35 percent of all official development assistance funds, it is hardly going to wither away soon.[9]

Financing the Private Sector: The idea of extending loans to private entities to spur development has a long history. The International Finance Corporation (IFC) was established in 1956 as the private sector arm of the World Bank Group, and it provides both cheap loans and equity stakes to private companies in the Rest. By 2011 the IFC's total investments amounted to $18.7 billion with another $820 million to advisory services for 642 projects. A number of other financial institutions have become similar players, as we list below. The IFC and other such institutions have come under criticism for being non-transparent, for working mainly with large companies or wealthy individuals and families who hardly need help from public institutions, and for investing in projects with dubious development impact.[10]

Debt Swaps and Debt Cancellation: Prominent in the 1980s, debt swaps are agreements between a debt-strapped recipient government and its creditors whereby some or all of its debt need not be repaid but is converted to local currency as long as it is used by the government for agreed development projects. Debt cancellation is simply a situation where the overhang of outstanding sovereign loans is so great that a country simply cannot repay, and for either charitable or geopolitical reasons a portion of the overhang is simply cancelled. Extensively used in the 1990s and 2000s, especially in Africa and Latin America, such debt forgiveness may well become needed again as some emerging economies become overexposed to debt due to the ravages of Covid-19 and slide towards disaster.

[9] In 2019 an exhaustive review of technical assistance estimated that TA made up between 25 and 40 percent of total ODA (Cos & Norrington-Davies, 2019, 3).

[10] One infamous example in 2010 was the IFC helping a Saudi prince (the billionaire Alwaleed bin Talal) to finance a sumptuous five-star hotel in Accra (Einhorn, 2013).

The Recent Surge in Multi-Actor Financing Mechanisms

Since the late 1990s bilateral and multilateral donors have been coming up with ever more complicated multi-actor financing mechanisms, special funds, and facilities. These are briefly described below. Not only are there virtually scores of such initiatives, they combine what are mostly the same multilateral development banks (MDBs), bilateral donors, and foundations in astounding permutations of arrangements. Although the rationale for these new mechanisms are usually to allow more focus and streamlined financing, one can imagine the amounts of time and effort are required to negotiate these setups, mobilize donors, and manage procurement and flows of funds over many years. Given that the administrative structures and their staff are perceived as constantly under pressure with never enough time to attend to all the demands put upon them, piling up these new financing facilities would seem counter-intuitive. But evidently not, as the following paragraphs will show.

Co-financing has been around in the development industry for decades. Based mainly on agreements between multilateral and bilateral development agencies and sometimes with the lending windows of export credit agencies, official co-financing simply combines these funds under an agreed administrator with a common timeline. Such co-financing is usually sourced from official development assistance, and grants or loans may be earmarked for individual projects on a case-by-case basis or for regional or sectoral programs. The ADB is a leader in co-financing, and its website enthusiastically endorses the arrangements, since it "focuses on strong partner and client coordination for easy access and efficiency in processing, low transaction costs, and harmonized and transparent mechanisms in reporting to financing partners on the development impact of their contributions."[11] That is, as long as everything goes smoothly.

Trust funds enable development partners to apply smaller, mostly TA grants aimed at a group of countries or specific focus areas. Usually, an MDB administers the funds provided by bilaterals as trustee or sub-trustee. The main advantage is that a single agreement can cover a number of projects, reducing the need for case-by-case negotiations. Trust funds are much appreciated by MDBs, as they can fund preparations or technical studies for a large concessional loan project that the MDB itself may not

[11] See ADB webpage https://www.adb.org/site/cofinancing/official-cofinancing (no date). Accessed 18 May 2022.

easily be able to finance. For example, the ADB acts as a trustee for at least 48 trust funds established by one or more development partners (usually bilateral agencies but also independent foundations).

Blended finance is yet another financial mechanism used in the industry, one that has grown in importance in the last few years. The practice refers to combining development funds (bilateral or multilateral) with those of private capital flows. This approach has become almost a mantra in the World Bank and other key donors, since it implies tapping into the huge world of private equity and foreign direct investment (FDI) flows that can be somehow steered or cajoled towards financing development projects by using relatively smaller donor funds as catalysts and leverage (for risk reduction, e.g.). This sounds like sweet words to private corporations and financial managers seeking more penetration in emerging markets, and blended finance by 2018 had already created a $50 billion market and was set to expand rapidly (Harvey, 2018). But besides the obvious requirement that such blended finance make an acceptable return to private investment without high risk, there are other issues: "Blending can be problematic: it does not necessarily support pro-poor activities, often focuses on middle-income countries, and may give preferential treatment to donors' own private-sector firms" (Pereira, 2017).

Thematic Funds and Facilities: The development industry has set up what could be called 'thematic' funds or facilities that are supposed to address specific global development issues and finance efforts to address them. One of the first was the Global Environment Facility (GEF) established on the eve of the 1992 Rio Earth Summit to help tackle the planet's most pressing environmental problems. Since then, the GEF has provided $14.5 billion in grants and mobilized $75.4 billion in additional financing for almost 4000 projects, and at least four other global facilities have been set up recently which echo the environmental theme. Other thematic funds have been set up; the World Bank is trustee for the Global Agricultural and Food Security Program (2010), the Global Partnership for Education (2002), and the Public Private Infrastructure Advisory Facility (1999). The ADB is the trustee for other thematic funds, such as the ASEAN Infrastructure Fund, the Credit Guarantee and Investment Facility, and the Pakistan Economic Corridors Programme. Of particular note is China's Regional Cooperation and Poverty Reduction Fund, one of China's first moves into the development field. The ADB collaborates with this fund, and China is increasingly active in such regional cooperation efforts, particularly in the Greater Mekong Sub-region and the Central Asia Regional Economic Cooperation countries.

Deciding How to Spend the Money

How a bilateral donor or IFI allocates its funds by policy, sector, mechanism, and country is pretty opaque, and it occurs very much at the highest, command-and-control levels of these aid agencies. Of course, there is much talk about themes, comprehensive strategies, priority sectors, alignment with foreign policy objectives, etc. But in spite of all the discussion around lessons learned, feedback, policy and program reviews, allocation formulae, and innovative financing mechanisms, the decisions to expand existing project clusters, to launch new programs, or to expand geographically are something that the development industry's foot soldiers and hired experts know little about. Something goes on at the directorate-general level (EC speak) or global practice level (World Bank speak) or deputy director level (USAID speak) that is very hush-hush. Of course, much lip service is paid to a donor's strategic approach in a particular country or region, to other country-specific analyses and strategies, and to the outcomes of project identification missions. This gives the appearance of reasoned and rational budget decisions that are built on previous experiences and on assessments of a recipient country's absorption capacities and development strategies. But the reality is quite different, and grants and loans to a particular country have more to do with continuing—or slightly tweaking—previous levels of funding of budget line items and resolving the inevitable colossal bureaucratic delays and recipient country tantrums than anything else. In bilateral funding, things are further confused when Western legislatures pressure for special interests. (In the USA this has become an art form in itself.) Yet once a donor agency has added its new budget to old flows, what one is presented with are well-crafted announcements that imply consistent programmatic approaches, ones that are always in perfect step with overarching strategic goals and reasoned new initiatives.

The Short-Leash and Time-Bound and Nature of Development Moneys

Someone might naively think, having read the glowing words about development 'partnerships' and recipient 'ownership,' that agreed levels of funding for specific programs or projects are simply transferred to the relevant ministry for them to manage. Nothing could be further from the truth. All grants and loans allocated by donor governments are strictly time-bound, with detailed sequencing and completion dates prominently displayed both in donor documentation and in their financial agreements with recipient governments, and with complicated conditions specified before each tranche is disbursed or 'triggered.' Whether it is for extremely short technical studies and project design, or for huge infrastructure projects that may extend over five years or more, the donor keeps allocations on a very short leash, dribbling the funds out through byzantine bureaucratic dances that leave little space for project officers, their consultants, and their local counterparts to get on with the real business of executing a project efficiently. Even the simplest of payments will normally require a coveted 'no objection' from the donor agency and, if disbursed by a partner agency, dozens of signatures. Mechanisms that would allow independent management and retention of allocations over multiple years basically don't exist, except for a few ventures such as the USA's Millennium Challenge Account and some tiny NGO endowment funding by USAID.

Who's Who in the Industry?

The industry depends on Western governments and MDBs coughing up money regularly—and these funds are administered by a bewildering number of actors. As a former chairman of a DAC committee put it in 2007, "The last time the OECD counted, there were more than 200 bilateral and multilateral organizations channeling official development assistance" (De Haan, 2009, 60). And the numbers of institutions, their various programs, and the multiples of approaches are constantly expanding. Rough estimates of the number of people working in these donor organizations put the global total at about 200,000 persons in 2014, about half of which were international (Koch & Schulpen, 2018).[12] In addition, as we shall see, there were a huge and diverse set of other

[12] According to this study, in 2014 there were some 218,000 employees in donor agencies, of which just over half were national staff working in donor offices overseas. In addition, there were about 457,000 employees of development INGOs, all but 40,000 of which were national staff.

people—guesstimated at over 400,000 active in the business in 2015—that have managed to enjoy a slice of the flow of development funds.[13]

It is possible to distinguish four main types of donors. The largest, in terms of total disbursements, continue to be bilateral donors, made up of national agencies in developed/rich countries that administer their governments' funds. Multilateral organizations represent the second largest, and these are international organizations such as UN agencies, the World Bank, the IMF, other international and regional development banks, and the European Union. Third, there are international and national NGOs. Finally, there are private philanthropic organizations and foundations that administer their own funds.

Whereas traditionally bilateral aid represented the bulk of ODA—some 70 percent in 2005 (De Haan, 2009, 23)—over the subsequent decade multilaterals became more important, and in 2016 the OECD estimated that the share of multilateral aid to bilateral aid was roughly half and half (OECD, 2017). Much of this shift was simply that donor countries are increasingly co-funding with multilaterals, and, as we have seen in the previous section, multilateral banks may join together to fund a single large project, bilaterals may pool contributions under multilateral banks, and international NGOs are being increasingly used to administer funds and can thus increasingly be seen as contractor-like service providers. Philanthropic institutions and private foundations are a system apart, since they raise and administer their own funds mainly from private donations or from their own endowments. However, these foundations are also known to co-fund both bilateral and multilateral operations in particular countries, and they too often have recourse to INGOs as contractors.

Before going through our list of who's who, it must be pointed out that there is only one entity that could be considered anything like an apex organization, and this the OECD's Development Cooperation Directorate (DCD), which supports the Development Assistance Committee (DAC). The DAC provides donors a forum for various kinds of development issues, and it is the technical arm that collects and published copious amounts of statistics about DAC members, non-DAC donors, development projects and programs, and it maintains an exhaustive database about ODA official Development funds and flows. There are various UN

[13] In 2002 Thomas Dichter tossed out a "conservative global estimate" of roughly half a million people who make their living out of the industry (Dichter, 2003, 37). It is probably a much larger number now.

agencies that sometimes function as overall coordinators within the 'development community' (such as UNDP and WHO) and the World Bank, given its huge weight and multilateral nature, also often has an apex voice, as could also be said of the IMF. But only the OECD's DAC represents an intersection at the top of the industry.

Bilateral Donors

There were 30 countries in 2017 that, according to the OECD-DAC, provided development assistance to some 146 developing countries. This total is up from 22 a decade or so earlier, due to the arrival of several smaller countries, mainly Eastern European, to the DAC club. A country will usually have one prominent development agency (such as the former DfID in the UK, USAID in America, or JICA in Japan) with annual budgets that run to the billions of dollars and employ thousands. Yet, confusingly, a donor government may also channel development funds through a number of other agencies, departments, or ministries—in the USA alone there are some twenty that administer international development or humanitarian aid of some sort.

The main bilateral agencies are large, well-established, and with considerable presence in scores of developing countries. Their home offices are very structured, as a look at any organogram will show, and the phrase 'overly bureaucratic' is one commonly used by aid critics and even by former donor staffers to describe how these agencies function. These bureaucratic strictures extend to the country offices and result in a whole additional set of tensions, with a trend for always more standardization to improve 'effectiveness' from headquarters, with an inevitable loss of in-country dynamism. Yes, ostensible reforms (including decentralization) are common among bilaterals, and there is a penchant for exhibiting managerial dynamism. Yet these organizations are, without a doubt, bureaucracies supreme.

How big and entrenched are the main bilateral agencies? In 2016 USAID, the largest bilateral worldwide, had about 3000 staff at the Washington headquarters, 2000 foreign service officers abroad, and 5000 local staff in USAID country offices. At the end of 2017 the German Cooperation Agency (GIZ) had roughly 3500 staff in Eschborn and other sites in Germany, 2300 assigned abroad, and 6000 local staff in their country offices. In contrast, DfID counted a total of 3600 staff both in London and abroad. These samplings show that, while substantial, such organizations are not particularly huge in numbers of staff, especially compared to domestic public agencies in the West or to multinational corporations. In fact, most bilateral aid agencies have cut staff numbers substantially since the heady 1970s, and slimming down has continued to be a management mantra, and to compensate, agencies have for the most part increasingly outsourced tasks and contracted consultants, something that has raised eyebrows (House of Commons, 2016–2017).

Program funds flowing through these agencies will normally be disbursed as grants, although all the larger bilateral donors will also have soft loan windows (similar to those of the multilateral development banks, see below) that may be administered by the main prominent donor agency or by a specialized institution. Almost all established donor countries also contribute significantly to multilateral banks and the UN system, usually through multi-annual pledges, and EU countries pay into the development budget of the European Commission as part of their annual assessments.

It is hard to generalize across scores of bilateral development agencies, but professional staff both at headquarters and 'in the field' are always extremely busy, or at least give the appearance of being so. They are well paid, especially once the various perks for overseas assignments and holidays and retirement benefits are included in calculations (Chap. 17). But morale has often been mentioned as a problem (as have difficulties in recruiting for overseas positions, especially in difficult places like Afghanistan and the Sahel), and, to outsiders, bilateral donor administrators can seem to be quite arrogant, acting as if the money they manage is their own.

Multilateral Development Banks (MDBs)

These institutions, sometimes known in the development industry as International Finance Institutions (IFIs), operate like investment banks and mainly advance soft, long-term loans to the governments of developing countries. These MDBs rely on funding pledges and replenishments from their country members and are governed by boards of directors who represent these countries.

The largest, most prominent, and oldest of these MDBs is of course the World Bank. One of the 1944 Brenton Woods institutions, the Bank (as it is simply called among its staff and consultants) had in 2019 a full-time professional staff of 12,300 persons (of which about 4500 were in 119 country offices), and it contracts untold thousands of consultants every year (Edwards, 2019). The World Bank has top notch development research capacities and generates hundreds of publications each year. The World Bank Group includes the International Finance Corporation, its lender to the private sector (see also below).

The International Monetary Fund (IMF) is another of the Bretton Woods institutions whose mandate is "to ensure the stability of the international monetary system—the system of exchange rates and international payments that enables countries (and their citizens) to transact with each other."[14] It has a total of one trillion dollars to call upon to advance structural adjustment and emergency loans to countries in trouble, and it has been very active in many poor countries and emerging economies when the need for economic stability becomes paramount.

Quite a number of regional MDBs have been formed since the 1950s that more or less following the model of the World Bank, sometimes slavishly. These include the African Development Bank, the Asian Development Bank (some 3000 employees), the European Bank for Reconstruction and Development, the European Investment Bank, the Inter-American Development Bank, the Islamic Development Bank, and, most recently, the Asian Infrastructure Investment Bank (set up by China) and the New Development Bank (set up by the BRIC countries). A number of smaller multilateral development funds and banks have also been created, and in Arab countries alone at least eleven such funds have been listed. Most established bilateral donor countries also have development banks of one sort or the other, such as KfW in Germany and the Dutch Development Bank. Not all of these MDBs lend just to developing countries, and in fact for some the main business remains in advanced or Eastern European countries.

Unlike bilateral donors who only employ their nationals, the management and staff of MDBs are very international, with increasing numbers of those who were originally from developing countries themselves. This provides these banks with a welcome diversity and international flavor not normally found in bilateral agencies. For these MDBs, recruitment focuses on those with prestige Western academic backgrounds, and, furthermore, the internal culture of these banks ensures that loyalty is to the institution,

[14] International Monetary Fund, "About the IMF" no date. https://www.imf.org/en/About. Accessed 10 May 2022.

its neoliberal market values, and its financial mechanisms as prime game changers.

Other Multilateral Donors: UN Agencies and the EU

The UN specialized agencies are some of the oldest institutions in the development game, since most of these were formed shortly following the establishment of the United Nations itself in 1947. (The International Labour Organization is even older, having been formed as an outcome of the 1919 Treaty of Versailles.) There are 32 of these agencies that work on international development issues and belong to the UN Development Group. They include well-known sectoral agencies such as WHO, FAO, UNIDO, UNEP, IFAD, and UNESCO; multisectoral agencies such as UNDP, UNOPS, UNCTAD, UNCDF, and UNHCR; plus lesser known thematic agencies such as UN-Habitat, UNAIDS, and UN-Women. There are so many of these UN agencies that duplication and uncoordinated actions are recognized problems. In fact, in 2005 and 2006 the concept of 'One UN' was heavily promoted, and the Secretary-General set up a High-Level Panel on UN System-Wide Coherence in the Areas of Development, Humanitarian Assistance and the Environment. A key recommendation of this Panel was that the UN system should "Deliver as One" at the developing country level. Yet after several years of pilot efforts, little has been achieved, and the One UN idea has had little impact on operations.[15]

It is important to realize that—ever since the 1980s—core funding levels for UN development agencies have stagnated, and that presently none have much money to play with. Staff expenses, administrative costs, and events eat up almost all core funds. As a consequence, these agencies spend inordinate amounts of time in raising funds themselves and in pitching co-funding schemes with better-endowed bilateral and multilateral donors, and oftentimes it is the politically neutral aura of the UN that convinces bigger spenders to partner with UN agencies. UNDP, the largest UN agency, is a case in point. Although in 2020 it had a total budget of $5.60 billion, only $696 million was from core or 'regular resources' for which UNDP had discretionary control, and the remainder came from pledges

[15] One change to come out of these One UN efforts was to establish the position of UN Resident Coordinator in many countries, *but still maintaining* the UN Resident Representative position.

and commitments from UN member countries and MDBs for a variety of programs (UNDP, 2021, 6).

Funding problems bedeviled UN agencies during the coronavirus epidemic, and even the WHO, whose visibility skyrocketed, found it necessary in 2021 to tackle its funding woes by formulating a forceful, long-term strategy. Unfortunately, the only solution it could come up with, after lengthy debates, was (typically) to set up a special commission to study the problem.

It should be noted that UN funding to developing countries is, except for the very sleepy UNCDF, all grant based, and most of UN disbursements to the Rest go to support a hodgepodge of technical assistance and training and awareness activities (which the UN calls 'technical cooperation').[16]

In contrast to the UN system, development assistance from the EU (or more accurately, from the European Commission primarily through three of its directorates) is very well funded. Funding comes from the general EU budget or through the European Development Fund. The ultimate source of all EU development funds is through annual contributions from EU member states, which is over and above what these European donors allocate through their bilateral aid programs and their contributions to MDBs.

Although some of the European Commission's development programs are welcomed by both recipient countries and aid observers, there is a general perception that the institutional setup is absurdly bureaucratic and rule-bound, wasteful, and obtusely managed. Brussels, where the EU aid administration is located, has become synonymous with red tape and tight collusion with service contractors. In 2000 the UK international development secretary Claire Short famously said, "Anyone who knows anything about development knows that the EU is the worst agency in the world, the most inefficient, the least poverty-focused, the slowest, flinging money around for political gestures rather than promoting real development" (Black, 2000). Almost two decades later, many still have this opinion, although it should be said that there has been a noticeable improvement in on-time disbursement.

[16] The United Nations Capital Development Fund is unique among UN agencies in providing seed capital exclusively in least-developed countries. Some 70 percent of its funds go to Sub-Saharan Africa.

Private Sector Lending Windows

Lending money (and contributing equity) to private businesses that operate in the Rest is almost as old as the development industry itself. The idea is that there are development benefits such as job creation, enhanced productivity, new economic sectors, increased exports, etc. that are attached to such investments beyond their purely commercial returns, and this has spurred a number of Western donors and specialized institutions to assist private entities with investment loans, equity contributions, investment risk guarantees, and technical advice.

MDBs have had an early and visible role in supporting private corporations, first by the World Bank's International Finance Corporation in 1956, and later by the ADB, the AfDB, the IDB, the EIB, and the EBRD. The IFC is seen by most as the lead in this kind of financing. It uses money from the IDA, the World Bank Group's huge soft lending fund, and also raises capital on international markets; then it lends these money either directly to private businesses or through financial intermediaries, mainly local banks, to a large number of smaller customers. Overall multilateral lending windows have seen their portfolios grow impressively over time; for example, their volumes increased ten-fold from 1990 to 2010. And their overall objective of creating "the right business climate for investment" has often led them to finance global corporations operating in developing countries (Bretton Woods Project, 2010, 4).

There are also a surprising number of specialized bilateral agencies who also lend and provide equity to private companies in the Rest, sometimes called 'bilateral development finance institutions.' There is a long history of these; Britain's CDC Group was formed in 1948 and Germany's Deutsche Investitions und Entwicklungsgesellschaft (part of KfW) was set up in 1962. In the 1970s and 1980s the Netherlands, Belgium, the USA, France, Finland, Sweden, and Spain formed similar financial entities, and, in the post-2000 period, Switzerland, Portugal, Austria, and Canada have added their own. In 2018 the United States, with great fanfare, transformed its Overseas Private Investment Corporation into the International Development Finance Corporation.

It must be stressed that the vast bulk of this private lending is in providing capital that must be repaid with interest, thus only a tiny portion of this can be categorized as 'grant equivalent' aid. Thus, for example, in 2019 ODA totaled USD 152.8 billion, but only USD 1.4 billion in grant equivalents was lent to private companies in the form of net loans and equities (OECD, 2020).

So, it is a funny world. For decades huge sums have been lent to private companies by donor institutions through these private sector windows. These have shown positive impact on selected private corporations, a few SMEs, and some local banks, but there are criticisms about how effective this support is in terms of wider development impacts (Kenny, 2020). There are also criticisms of their extreme risk aversion (and consequent shying away from poorest countries and local businesses who most need their help), their undercutting of commercial lenders, and their less-than transparent style of operations.

Research About Development

Research in development issues is imbedded in many donor activities, and even more research is outsourced to universities and institutes. The World Bank has a small army of experts present in its Development Research Group, and it is considered by many to dominate the field. Other donor agencies carry out their own in-house research, with examples including former DfID's Central Research Department, the research department of the Swedish International Development Agency (SIDA), and the ADB's Economic Research and Regional Development Department. Bilateral donor agencies also frequently outsource specific studies and analysis, mainly to home country institutes, think tanks, universities, and consultants. In Canada's case there is the International Development Research Centre (IDRC), which operates separately from the Canadian International Development Agency and has a 50-year history of research and training activities in cooperation with universities and institutes worldwide.

There are also a number of independent research institutes and networks that focus on particular sectors, such as the International Food Policy Research Institute, the International Rice Research Institute, the UK-based International Institute of Environment and Development, and the Consultative Group on International Agriculture Research (CGIAR). There are even some fully independent research centers to be found in developing countries, such as the African Economic Research Consortium, based in Nairobi and founded in 1988, which includes efforts to raise research capacities in Africa through collaborative degree programs.

Efforts have been made by Western research entities and their donor agency godfathers to support more research and training centered in developing countries themselves. Both IDRC and CGIAR are long-running examples of this approach. After all, it would seem logical that the locus of effective and relevant research should progressively be shifted to the countries that are, after all, the object of such research. But overwhelmingly, it is in the West where almost all development research takes place, and it is from the West that almost all funding for such research flows. Even CGIAR and the African Economic Research Consortium continue to rely exclusively on funding from Western institutions. Hardly any funding for development research comes from governments in the Rest, except for certain prestige science and engineering studies that have little or no relevance to the country's development but that demonstrate they can successfully mimic the West.

New Bilateral Donors and the Rise of China

Besides the 29 countries (plus the EU) who are currently members of the OECD's Development Assistance Committee, there are a handful of other countries that report their development funding to the OECD, such as Arab Gulf countries, Taiwan, Turkey, and Israel. In addition, Brazil, India, China, and others have become important donor players.

According to a research paper (Gulrajani & Swiss, 2017) that looked at 26 newer donors over the 2010–2014 period, most of the aid programs of these countries are tiny in financial terms. Also, their contributions through multilateral agencies are almost non-existent, much of their aid is tied, and their selection of recipients is partly driven by geopolitical self-interest. In other words, according to the paper, these newer donors have yet to reach the stature or maturity of the traditional Western ones.

Why should there be a rush among nations to become donors? As the authors of an Overseas Development Institute (ODI) research report suggest, "becoming a donor is muscle-flexing on the world stage, a display of a state's financial wealth and bureaucratic capacity to assist weaker nations. This is an important reason why western democratic liberal countries are donors, why new EU members must become donors, and why even states that continue to receive aid increasingly provide it as well." In other words, world history has ingrained 'donorship' as something that is good, desirable, and appropriate for all modern states, a marker that they have joined the enviable club of advanced nations.

The one exception to the anemic performance of new donors is, of course, China, especially since 2000. The country has managed to change from recipient to donor in a pronounced way; according to a BBC report (Hatton, 2021), between 2005 and 2017 China's ODA averaged from $4 to $8 billion annually. This would put it slightly higher than ODA from say Canada or Sweden, and this amount is totally eclipsed by at least $550 billion in loans from China that were made over the same period for mostly big-ticket infrastructure projects in developing countries. These loan agreements carried commercial interest rates and very tough conditions for repayment, and most of them (since 2013) fell under the One Belt One Road Initiative. These loans, which were advanced by Chinese state banks and often were off-the-books, have often been criticized as funding super-modern showcase projects beloved by local autocrats. They have also been criticized for sending recipient governments into bottomless debt holes and for the non-competitive ways project implementation has been directly commissioned to Chinese companies (almost always accompanied with Chinese labor). News reports about China's strong-arm tactics in poor countries have become common. The Chinese-financed, built, and leased port of Hambantota in Sri Lanka is an excellent example of how Chinese state companies and banks, always supported by their government, have leveraged a ruler's penchant for splashy projects that buries his country under yet further debt and, in this case, provided China with a geopolitical and military opening (Abi-Habib, 2018). Other examples have been reported, such as dubious Chinese investments to Malaysia, the resulting debt overhang, and attempts by the Malaysian government to squirm out of these (Beech, 2018, 1 and 8).

Whatever the merits of its economic penetration in these regions, parts of China's development actions have recently evolved into more institutionalized and classic donor structures. In January 2016 it formed the Asian Infrastructure Investment Bank (AIIB), a regional multilateral bank headquartered in Beijing that has 87 countries so far on its board of directors. If its early programs and procurement mechanisms are any indication, it will operate much as do, for example, the World Bank or the ADB. And in 2018 the Chinese government announced that it was setting up a new dedicated and high-level aid agency to be called the National Development and Cooperation Agency. One can only wait and see how these two new structures evolve. But with increasing economic clout, and with a hard-to-deny excellence in its own economic development, China may at some point represent a colossus in the development industry.

NGOs and Civil Society, or the 'Third Sector'

The presence of NGOs in the aid business has expanded rapidly over the last two to three decades and now represents a truly vast and complex subsector. Already by 1989 some 4000 of these organizations could be counted in OECD countries alone, and in 2008 roughly 15 percent of DAC aid flows were spent through nongovernmental channels (De Haan, 2009, 49). It has become received wisdom that nongovernmental partners have key roles in implementing aid programs, mainly because they are adept at mobilizing and have local knowledge and capacities. They are particularly useful in humanitarian, relief, and refugee work, and they often represent to the Western public the most visible face of development efforts.

Some civil society organizations perform important services as watchdogs and critics of the development industry, uncovering some of its most egregious practices and lobbying for more poverty alleviation focus. However, the idea of NGOs being small, locally based, dedicated, altruistic, and pro-poor organizations is hardly the real story. Such organizations do exist, but it is INGOs who have come to dominate the sector. These, with few exceptions, are very large global organizations that provide services to donors and aggressively seek more and more such business. Some of these INGOs raise money from charitable contributions, but the bulk of their funds come from donor agencies and philanthropic foundations grants. Some are faith based, especially those from the USA. Examples of prominent INGOs include Oxfam (UK, USA), CARE International, Save the Children, Christian Aid, World Vision, and Catholic Relief Services. Almost all are headquartered in Western countries, and they have substantial annual budgets and staff numbering in the thousands.

Local development NGOs operating in poorer countries are an important part of the scene, mostly having been formed to respond to the funds made available by international development agencies in their rush to support civil society. But, except for rare exceptions, none of these have expanded in other countries to capture even a fraction of the global work that prominent INGOs have garnered. For the most part, they remain useful but secondary actors, mainly sub-contracted by INGOs, and mostly do the humdrum dirty work, especially in relief operations.

One important exception is BRAC (formerly Bangladesh Rural Advancement Committee), which has been ranked first worldwide by NGO Advisor from 2016 to 2020. It is based in Dhaka, it started as a microfinance operator but soon expanded and diversified into a wide range of activities across a number of developing countries. SEWA, the Self-Employed Women's Association in India, is another NGO firmly grounded in the Rest. It is a union of women, it operates on principles of self-reliance and Gandhian thought, and it has become very successful, expanding from Gujarat into all of India.

Generally, civil society development organizations in the Rest and their networks and federations and advocacy work have considerable visibility both in international forums and in their own countries, and they have a self-appointed function of independent moral consciences to the industry. But these kinds of organizations also serve a very useful purpose, beyond their Doing Good posturing; by their presence in high-level events and their extensive production of reports, blogs, etc., they help legitimize the mainstream development donors who hire them and allow such donors to claim that they are listening to civil society.

Philanthropic Foundations

An untold number of foundations and charities—again mainly Western—work wholly or partly on aspects of international development, advocate policy changes, and contribute serious funding to development efforts. Some operate with their own funding (from fundraising, endowments, or both) and some are funded by yet other foundations, mainly from those setup by the extremely wealthy, especially in the USA. Some could be called 'philanthropic,' such as the Ford, MacArthur, Mellon, Soros, and Rockefeller foundations, and their main role is providing grants, sometimes partnering with donors. Since its establishment in 2000 by far the wealthiest of these has been the Bill and Melinda Gates Foundation. These foundations fund wide ranging social, health, environmental, and anti-poverty initiatives, some of which are found in rich countries. Anand Giridharadas (2018) dissects the behavior of (mostly American) philanthropic foundations run by the super-rich, and how by tossing "symbolic scraps to the forsaken," these high flyers can continue to accumulate unimagined wealth and resist any control or oversight over their operations. Most of these concentrate on sprinkling bits of money at good causes in the West, but they also love to bestow their beneficence on the Rest.

The flows of funds from these foundations and charities towards developing countries has, since the 2000s, become quite substantial. For example, those based in the United States increased their spending three-fold between 2002 and 2015, to reach a new annual high of $9.3 billion (Council on Foundations, 2018, 3). Moreover, in the 2011–2015 period, just twelve percent of international grant dollars from these U.S. foundations were contracted to organizations actually based in the countries where programs were implemented. The remaining eighty-eight percent was channeled through organizations based almost exclusively in Western countries.

Another characteristic of these foundations is their very strong fear of taking on anything that could be considered risky or perceived as damaging to their reputations, as pointed out forcefully by Dichter (2019a, b). It might seem that these organizations, which rely mostly on their own endowments and are free from the constraints posed by parliaments and nosey aid watchdogs, would be able to go boldly and tackle some of the most intractable problems facing the poor in developing countries. But evidently not. Over and over these philanthropies have funded the usual mainstream INGOs and humanitarian organizations on classic humanitarian and health sector work.

The Armies of Consultants, Experts, and Service Contractors

The development industry simply could not function without private consultants, contractors, and service providers. They come in the form of various specialists who provide their knowledge, advice, and capacity building knowhow to donor agencies, either as part of firms or as individuals. There are no hard figures, but globally one is probably looking at hundreds of thousands of international experts and specialists either working for hundreds of firms or as independent consultants either hired directly by donors or included by consulting firms for specific bids. And although one would have thought that such expertise would by now be found in abundance in recipient countries themselves, and although there has recently been a modest rise in non-Western firms that have made the leap into international competition, they still represent only a tiny fraction of the overall business.

Large development firms or consultancies with global reach increasingly dominate the development business scene. In the early days there were smaller, leaner, and more specialized operations, some little more than ma-and-pa shops. But a number of factors have inexorably led to industry consolidation and large corporate management structures. First, faced with the increasingly bureaucratic demands of their donor agency clients and ever-stiffer competition, these firms needed to build considerable capacities to seek out bids, write proposals, assemble expert teams, and work towards contract signing.[17] More staff were needed for marketing, product development, and, increasingly, the management of these large operations. And they also needed extensive rosters of independent consultants they could call on for particular bids. They also needed to have their own considerable financial resources to cover the substantial costs of preparing for scores or even hundreds of tenders per year (of which they might land a handful if they're lucky). Thus, ever since the 1980s smaller firms have been eaten up through mergers, buy-outs, and attrition. Most of what remains are now behemoths clustered conveniently near donor agencies in Washington, Brussels, London, Frankfurt, Paris, Tokyo, etc. Chasing ever more work is a constant preoccupation for them (Chap. 5).

Although a firm will try to land contracts from anywhere, most large Western consulting companies will naturally concentrate on their home country's bilateral agencies. Providing services for USAID is a good example, and data compiled on funding for the October 2010 through March 2011 period shows that the ten top firms were all American (or were American subsidiaries of UK firms). Half of these have headquarters in the Washington area and the rest on the Eastern Seaboard (Villarino, 2011). In 2015, USAID contractors secured a total of $4.68 billion in work, and *half* of this went to just three firms—Chemonics, Tetra Tech ARD, and Abt Associates (Orlina, 2017).

Other big service providers to Western donors include huge management and accounting firms whose core business is services to large multinational corporations, but who have also increasingly taken on development agencies as clients. Examples include KPMG, Deloitte, McKinsey, and PricewaterhouseCoopers (PwC). In fact, in 2017 PwC managed to top DfID's list of consulting firms.

It is important to realize that almost all of the development work in the consulting world is contracted directly from Western donor agencies or through host governments implementing their projects. Developing

[17] The need for consolidation has been exacerbated by the introduction in the 1990a of 'indefinite quantity contracts' (USAID) and 'framework contracts' (EC and DfID) whereby firms and consortiums are first vetted to be accepted on multi-year 'on call' sector-specific arrangements, in theory to reduce the time and cost of procuring consulting services. Inevitably, these are typically led by well-established development consultancies.

countries themselves almost never purchase such services with their own money, and why should they? So much is being spent by donors to developing countries that the idea of spending their own scarce funds on expensive advice hardly ever catches on. But in the rare cases when it does, it tends to be for design work and feasibility studies for a ruler's pet scheme or for prestige megaprojects. And these consulting firms duly oblige without qualms.[18]

It is also important to realize that, although there are large numbers of consulting firms in developing countries that have managed to carve out work, with few exceptions these remain second-level technical providers, usually as subcontractors forming part of consortium bids led by the large international consulting firms. In spite of many calls for more local firms with native capacities to take the lead on projects, little has changed. It seems that donors simply prefer the established, well-known Western firms for which they have had dealings over decades.

Academia and Affiliated Institutes

Universities and their associated institutes and research centers have long played important roles in the development industry. Weighty scholarly papers on various aspects of third world economic development and on dimensions of poverty have been produced ever since 'development' became a mainstream concept, largely the product of university economists but also with differing takes coming from sociologists, anthropologists, geographers, agronomists, political scientists, etc. In the early days of development, universities were the refuges for serious critics of development aid, including *dependencia* theorists (from the left) and less-government-is-better neoliberals (from the right).

One of the more impressive examples of the academia-development nexus can be seen in the number or scholarly journals that are devoted to some aspect of poverty or development in the Rest, often looking at the impacts of aid programs. These journals usually appear several times a year and, collectively, represent an outpouring of thousands of peer-reviewed articles each year.

[18] Examples of a developing country itself paying for such expensive advice can be found in Egypt for decidedly splashy projects. McKinsey was contracted in 2007 for re-inventing and branding the new town of Sixth of October, and Skidmore, Owings, and Merrill was commissioned to make the master plan for the new administrative capital in 2015.

Originally, this interest in development among academics was part of classic academic pursuits, funded by university departments. However, with the rise of development funding by various donors, it didn't take long for academia to respond, and over the decades the roles of Western universities have become more complex and nuanced, and more imbedded in what has become a bewildering symbiosis with the development industry itself. In the last couple of decades, a handful of universities in the Rest, especially in India, Southeast Asia, and China, have joined in.

One of the first roles was for universities to offer training courses to technicians and professionals coming from developing countries, mainly financed through scholarship programs setup by Western governments. These remain one of the mainstays, but progressively universities have undertaken more and more prominent advisory functions. These have included taking on specific donor-commissioned studies (both technical work such as representative household surveys and agricultural field trials, and sectoral work of a more policy nature), offering specialized courses and degrees in development-related subjects and providing a convenient home for former donor bureaucrats and development experts.

Further cementing the symbiosis has been the rise of the university as contractor/consultant. Faced with financial crunches, university departments—again almost exclusively in the West—have discovered that a convenient source of additional revenue could be derived from bidding—either alone or part of a consortium—for juicy consultant work spun out by donors. Not only would having an academic aura increase chances of winning, the proposed academic experts would in most cases allow cheaper bids, since overheads were already subsumed.

Academia has also become more and more a way for students to prepare for careers in some aspect of development. Universities offer an ever-expanding list of both undergraduate and graduate degrees, mostly in multi-disciplinary development studies of one sort or another. By 2016 there were over 100 universities worldwide offering courses in development studies. According to the Top Universities website, in 2016 of the top ten universities in development studies, five were located in the UK, three in the USA, one in Australia, and one in South Africa. The only Third World universities offering such studies in the top fifty were Delhi University at number 18 and the Universidad Nacional Autónoma de

México at number 29.[19] In the USA alone there are over 50 such degree programs, and every year between 4000 and 7000 people graduate (Dichter, 2016).

Think Tanks and Policy Institutes

Think tanks and development institutes play important roles as policy forums and research platforms, commenting on and sometimes influencing donor development approaches. Most of these are very visible, churning out weighty policy papers and analyses of hot topics. They have also functioned as sinecures for ex-donor professionals, academics, and aid officials who just might at some point recycle back into the business. They tend to have diverse sources of funding, but most depend in part on research and study grants from donor agencies themselves.

The Overseas Development Institute, established in 1960 and located in London, is probably the oldest. It has 240 staff including researchers and communicators, and it produces useful research papers and analyses. It depends on a bewildering number of funders, from donors to foundations to NGOs, the largest of which is DfID. Another policy institute is the Institute for Development Studies at the University of Sussex, which was set up in 1977. The German Development Institute (Deutsches Institut für Entwicklungspolitik), located in Bonn, partly government-owned, and with a staff of over 100 professionals, is also prominent. Yet another development research institute is the University of Oslo's Centre for Development and Environment, founded in 1990 and with a focus on aspects of sustainable development. Across the Atlantic, the Center for Global Development (CDG), founded in 2001 and located in Washington D.C., has become America's main forum for development policy, calling itself a 'think-and-do tank.' In 2018 it had dozens of funding agreements with donors and other institutes and foundations, of which the Bill and Melinda Gates Foundation was the most prominent.

It should be added that there are many more think tanks and institutes whose scope is wider than just development studies but who carry out some of research on Third World economic and social issues. These include the Royal Institute of International Affairs in London (founded with a royal charter in 1926 and also known as Chatham House), the Council on

[19] For a complete listing, see https://www.topuniversities.com/university-rankings/university-subject-rankings/2016/development-studies

Foreign Relations in New York, the Brookings Institute in Washington, the French Institute of International Relations, the AD Institute in Tokyo, and several others—mostly found in the USA.

Voluntary Organizations

Voluntarism has been a feature of the development landscape almost from the word go. The most prominent and most organized approaches are those of UN Volunteers, the Peace Corps (USA), the UK's Voluntary Service Organization, the European Voluntary Service, and the Japanese Overseas Cooperation Volunteers (JOCV). For all but UNVs it seems that the main purpose of most of these organizations is to promote international relations and, unabashedly, to give the home country volunteer an experience that will make him or herself a better person. Helping others in poor countries is also mentioned, but it seems almost incidental to the main task of widening the Western volunteer's own horizons. There are also a wide number of other types of voluntary programs and activities that Westerners can join, some of which are unabashed joy rides which have come to be called 'voluntourism,' many of which are pay-to-help systems with only the smallest impact (if any) on those who are ostensibly being helped.

Pilot Fish of the Development Industry

No description of the development industry would be complete without mentioning some of the sundry players that attach themselves to it and that help it define itself. These are a surprisingly diverse group of organizations, many of which are not well known even to industry players themselves. And, it must be underlined, most of these entities are staffed by Westerners and headquartered in the West. Here are listed the most prominent.

The Development Assistance Committee of the OECD can be considered the main apex organization of the Development World, as we have pointed out above. It might as well be called the Donors' Own Club, since its membership and reporting are made up of the 30 main donor countries. Most multinational development banks and the UNDP are DAC observers, as are some newer donor countries that are classified as 'participants' or 'observers' but not full members. The DAC was formed in 1961 and is headquartered in Paris (in the definitely upscale sixteenth arrondissement).

Increasingly important on the outsourcing and procurement side of the development industry are international organizations that function as business opportunity networks and job posting sites. The oldest and largest is UN Development Business or DevBus, another is DevelopmentAid, and third is Devex International (Chap. 5). Another network—the Society for International Development—should be mentioned, since it is both an industry talk-shop and a development career advisory, with weekly events and webinars coming out of its Washington DC chapter. It is unabashedly closely associated with ex-USAID officials.

For more than a decade there have been at least two global trade fairs that serve the development and humanitarian industries: AidEx, with an annual flagship conference in Brussels plus another in Nairobi, and the Aid and International Development Forum, with an annual event taking place in Washington D.C. (at the Ronald Reagan Office Building, coincidentally where the headquarters of USAID is located). Both of these are mainly occasions for companies to promote themselves and sell products and services, although both have dozens of speakers and discussion groups about trending topics. Humanitarian aid and disaster relief figure prominently, and a look at speakers and sponsoring companies will show that logistics, food security, health, IT, technology, media, and procurement have dominant positions. Each event claims to be the central market place for the industry, and each also has an innovation award.

The development industry has been frequently criticized for being opaque and un-transparent, especially after this was identified as one of the four issues of aid effectiveness in Paris in 2005. Thus, the International Aid Transparency Initiative was set up at the Accra Forum in 2008. It has become part of the aid landscape, with its 'Aidstandard' data reporting and publishing system and an aid transparency index. Called 'Publish-What-You-Fund,' this index, which ranks 45 development agencies by how open they are about their funding activities, showed that in 2018 the most transparent were the ADB, UNDP, and DfID, and the most abysmal were China's Ministry of Finance and Commerce, the UAE's Ministry of Finance and International Cooperation, Japan's Ministry of Foreign Affairs, and the UN's Office of Coordination of Humanitarian Affairs.[20]

[20] See http://www.publishwhatyoufund.org/the-index/2018/. Accessed 20 May 2022.

No review of the pilot fish of development would be complete without at least mentioning the rise of development industry blogs. These mostly personal blogs can be entertaining and interesting, if somewhat strident and opinionated. William Easterly managed a popular development blog called Aid Watch from 2008 to 2011 when it was discontinued, probably out of shear fatigue. By 2020 scores of blogs had been set up that comment about aspects of the development industry, including some critical ones such as Aidnography, From Power to Poverty, Fifty Shades of Aid, Development Policy, Bank Information Center, the Bretton Woods Project, and Eurodad. Others, such as *Stuff Expat Aid Workers Like* or Shotgun Shack focus more on the NGO and humanitarian sides of the business, how aid workers are treated, how they are conflicted, and other self-interest issues. It seems that many url-based personal blogs on development are shifting towards newsletters and podcasting.

Towards What Sectors Does Development Aid Go?

There is no hard and fast way to categorize aid into economic sectors, as many aid projects and programs tend to be multisectoral and the ultimate destinations of flows hard to pin down. However, the OECD Creditor Reporting System makes valiant efforts to do this. These figures on sectoral allocations show that there are a wide variety of ways that donor funds end up in recipient countries. But one factor stands out—the traditional economically productive sectors (manufacturing, agriculture, productive infrastructure, transport, tourism, etc.) are becoming eclipsed by funds going to governance, civil society, basic public services, human rights, humanitarian crises, and other 'soft' sectors. Productive sectors received much more funding in the earlier decades of the Development Era (especially the 1950s to 1980s), but since the 1990s the 'menu' of target sectors (and subsectors) has grown much more diverse. As Thomas Dichter (2019b) has commented: ".... looking at how our foreign aid money is allocated today it seems as if we've pretty much forgotten about development. We devote surprisingly little of our aid money to Truman's array of interventions: industry and science, technical knowledge transfer, capital investment, and overall 'economic life.'" He is talking about American bilateral aid in 2001, but the comment is equally valid today for all development assistance.

Similarly, it could be said that there is another parallel shift that global development aid has progressively become less about 'development' per se and more about 'poverty alleviation.' Whether talking about social safety nets, cash transfers, microfinance, or other schemes designed to reach and help the poorest in Third World countries, this emphasis on poverty alleviation has almost totally eclipsed earlier approaches that worked towards *transforming* the economies of latecomer countries to become engines of rapid, dynamic, and self-sustained growth. This was forcefully argued in a paper (Ghosh, 2015) in which she concluded that the miasma created by the emphasis on poverty alleviation conveniently avoids asking the more important question of why people are poor (and assetless) in the first place and what factors keep them so. It keeps the imperative focused on just 'lifting them up' enough so they can be classified as non-poor.

What Countries Are the Beneficiaries of All This Development Aid?

A total of 142 countries were classified by OECD's DAC in 2020 as recipients of development assistance.[21] A rather rigid system of categorizing these countries has been employed for years, and in 2020 they were as follows: There were 49 Less Developed Countries (with nominal GNI/capita/year less than $1005 in 2016), 37 Lower Middle-Income Countries (with GNI/capita/year between $1006 and $3955 in 2016), and 56 Upper Middle-Income Countries (with GNI/capita/year between $3955 and $12,235 in 2016). This system may sound reassuringly logical, but it manages to lump together in each category countries whose average per capita incomes differ by a huge factor of three or four. And in these classifications are large countries like China, India, and Indonesia, middle sized countries like Egypt, Thailand, Myanmar, and Kenya, and tiny countries like Saint Helena, Samoa, and Tuvalu. These artificial categorizations are often used by donors to determine under what terms their moneys are allocated to individual countries.[22]

Not content with this categorization, development institutions also classify ODA-recipient countries into a number of other categories, such

[21] The OECD list of ODA recipients effective for 2020 flows can be found at https://www.oecd.org/dac/financing-sustainable-development/development-finance-standards/DAC-List-of-ODA-Recipients-for-reporting-2020-flows.pdf. Accessed 20 May 2022.

[22] For example, the World Bank only allows countries classified as Less Developed Countries to access very soft loans and advantageous technical assistance grants provided through its International Development Association (IDA). Once a country 'graduates' to Lower-Middle Income status, it must rely on IBRD loans under stiffer terms.

as fragile states (the preferred moniker since 2014 is a kinder 'states of fragility'), conflict states, small states, small island states, and even land locked states. These can be further classified, and diligently are, into specific continents or regions, and these tend to echo regional divisions within donor bureaucracies.

What countries get the most aid these days? In 2018 the top ten recipients of ODA were, in descending order, Afghanistan, Syria, Bangladesh, India, Ethiopia, Jordan, Iraq, Nigeria, Colombia, and Kenya (Ipati, 2020). These rankings have been remarkably consistent over the 2009–2018 period, except that aid to Syria and Jordan only became significant in 2013 and 2014. Besides these two anomalies, the most consistently increasing ODA flows were to Bangladesh, who went from $717 million in 2009 to $2.35 billion in 2018. And of course, in 2021 Afghanistan dropped out of the ODA ranking.

Summing Up: Does Anything Ever Change?

This short survey of the development industry hopefully orients the reader to be able to comprehend the several themes that are found in subsequent chapters. As he or she reads on, it will be important to keep in mind the sheer complexity, the variety, and the little oddities of the industry and the large and diverse number of people who populate it.

As will be seen, one feature of this industry over its lifetime is a seeming constant ferment and change, with new initiatives, new partnerships, new paradigms, new analytics and new funding mechanisms constantly being bantered about and receiving immense interest. The word 'reform', especially as it relates to donor agencies, is rarely off the table, and even the awful phrase 'doing development differently' has become common. These phenomena of cosmetic change and fads and fashions are described in Chaps. 10 and 11 below.

References

Abi-Habib, M. (2018, June 25) How China got Sri Lanka to cough up a port. *New York Times*. Accessed May 20, 2022, from https://www.nytimes.com/2018/06/25/world/asia/china-sri-lanka-port.html

Arvin, B. M., & Lew, B. (Eds.). (2015). *Handbook on the economics of foreign aid*. Edward Elgar.

Beech, H. (2018, August 23). We cannot afford this. *International New York Times*.

Black, I. (2000, May 18). Short labels EU the worst aid agency in the world. *The Guardian*. Accessed May 26, 2022, from https://www.theguardian.com/world/2000/may/18/eu.politics1

Bretton Woods Project. (2010, March). *Bottom lines or better lives? – Rethinking multilateral financing to the private sector in developing countries*. Accessed May 15, 2022, from https://www.brettonwoodsproject.org/doc/private/privatesector.pdf

Cos, M., & Norrington-Davies, G. (2019, January). *Technical assistance: New thinking on an old problem*. Agulhas Applied Knowledge for Open Society Foundations. Accessed May 15, 2022, from https://www.shareweb.ch/site/DDLGN/Documents/OSF-Technical%20Assistance-Jan-2019-Edited.pdf

Council on Foundations. (2018). *The state of global giving by US foundations 2011-2015*. Accessed May 27, 2022, from https://www.issuelab.org/resources/31306/31306.pdf

De Haan, A. (2009). *How the aid industry works: An introduction to international development*. Lynne Rienner Publishers Inc.

Degnbol-Martinussen, J., & Engberg-Pedersen, P. (2003). *Aid: Understanding international development cooperation*. Zed Books Ltd.

Department for International Trade. (2014, April 14). *Guidance: Aid Funded Business, Item 2*. last updated 1 September 2021. Accessed May 10, 2022, from https://www.gov.uk/guidance/aid-funded-business#commercial-opportunities-in-international-aid-and-development

Dichter, T. (2003). *Despite good intentions: Why development assistance to the third world has failed*. University of Massachusetts Press.

Dichter, T. (2016, November 15) Opinion: Is it right to expect a career in development? *Devex*. Accessed May 20, 2022, from https://www.devex.com/news/opinion-is-it-right-to-expect-a-career-in-development-88753

Dichter, T. (2019a, March 1). Trained incapacity: The risk avoidance of U.S. Philanthropies' global giving is bad for the world. *Forbes Magazine*. Accessed May 20, 2022, from https://www.forbes.com/sites/thomasdichter/2019/03/01/trained-incapacity-the-risk-avoidance-of-u-s-philanthropies-global-giving-is-bad-for-the-world/?sh=1d49689c17ef

Dichter, T. (2019b, March 25). Foreign aid drift: Whatever happened to development aid? *Forbes Magazine*. Accessed May 20, 2022, from https://www.forbes.com/sites/thomasdichter/2019/03/25/foreign-aid-drift-whatever-happened-to-development-aid/?sh=79819862ebc8

Edwards, S. (2019, October 25). In decentralization push, World Bank to relocate hundreds of DC staffers. *Devex*. Accessed May 26, 2022, from https://www.devex.com/news/in-decentralization-push-world-bank-to-relocate-hundreds-of-dc-staffers-95875

Einhorn, C. (2013, January 2). Can you fight poverty with a five-star hotel? *Foreign Policy*. Accessed May 15, 2022, from https://foreignpolicy.com/2013/01/02/can-you-fight-poverty-with-a-five-star-hotel/

Elmhirst, S. (2016, October 6). Liquid assets: how the business of bottled water went mad. *The Guardian*. Accessed May 20, 2022, from https://www.theguardian.com/business/2016/oct/06/liquid-assets-how%2D%2Dbusiness-bottled-water-went-mad

Ghosh, J. (2015, September 4). From 'development' to 'poverty alleviation': What have we lost? *The Frontline*, Print edition.

Gill, I. (2018, January 19). The end of aid. *Brookings blog*. Accessed May 10, 2022, from https://www.brookings.edu/blog/future-development/2018/01/19/the-end-of-aid/

Giridharadas, A. (2018). *Winners take all: The Elite Charade of changing the world*. Alfred A. Knopf. Accessed May 20, 2022, from https://quotefancy.com/anand-giridharadas-quotes

Gulrajani, N., & Swiss, L. (2017, March 14). *Why do countries become donors? Assessing the drivers and implications of donor proliferation*. Overseas Development Institute. Accessed April 1, 2022, from https://www.odi.org/publications/10747-why-do-countries-become-donors-assessing-drivers-and-implications-donor-proliferation

Harvey, F. (2018, January 23). 'Blended finance' is key to achieving global sustainability goals says report. *The Guardian*. Accessed May 25, 2022, from https://www.theguardian.com/environment/2018/jan/23/blended-finance-is-key-to-achieving-global-sustainability-goals-says-report

Hatton, C. (2021, September 29). *China: Big spender or loan shark?* BBC.com. Accessed May 20, 2022, from https://www.bbc.com/news/world-asia-china-58679039

House of Commons. (2017). *International Development Committee, "DFID's use of private sector contractors," Eighth Report of Session 2016–17*. Accessed from https://publications.parliament.uk/pa/cm201617/cmselect/cmintdev/920/920.pdf

Ipati, S. (2020, March 21). Top ten ODA recipients in 2018. *Developmentaid*. Accessed from https://www.developmentaid.org/#!/news-stream/post/59556/the-top-10-oda-recipients-in-2018

Kennard, M., & Provost, C. (2016, May 8). How aid became big business. *Los Angles Review of Books*. Accessed May 27, 2022, from https://lareviewofbooks.org/article/aid-became-big-business/

Kenny, C. (2020, March 10). Lending practices of the private sector window: How effective are they? *Blog post*. Center for Global Development. Accessed May 26, 2022, from https://www.cgdev.org/blog/lending-practices-private-sector-window-how-effective-are-they

Koch, D.-J., & Schulpen, L. (2018, June). An exploration of individual-level wage effects of foreign aid in developing countries. *Evaluation and Program Planning, 68*, 233–242. Accessed May 26, 2022, from https://www.sciencedirect.com/science/article/pii/S0149718917302811#sec0045

OECD. (2017). *Development co-operation report 2017: Data for development.* Accessed May 20, 2022, from https://www.oecd-ilibrary.org/development/development-co-operation-report-2017_dcr-2017-en

OECD. (2020, April 16). *Aid by DAC members increases in 2019 with more aid to the poorest countries.* Accessed May 15, 2022, from https://www.oecd.org/dac/financing-sustainable-development/development-finance-data/ODA-2019-detailed-summary.pdf

Orlina, E. C. (2017, May 12). Top USAID contractors for 2016. *Devex.* Accessed May 20, 2022, from https://www.devex.com/news/top-usaid-contractors-for-2016-90202

Pereira, J. (2017, February 13). Blended finance: What it is, how it works and how it is used. *Oxfam International.* Accessed May 18, 2022, from https://www.oxfam.org/en/research/blended-finance-what-it-how-it-works-and-how-it-used

Sogge, D. (2002). *Give and Take: What's the Matter with Foreign Aid?* London and New York, Zed Books.

Streeck, W. (2017). *How will capitalism end? Essays on a failing system.* Verso.

Taylor, A. (2017, October 11). China treats its foreign aid like a state secret. New research aims to reveal it. *Washington Post.* Accessed May 20, 2022, from https://www.washingtonpost.com/news/worldviews/wp/2017/10/11/china-treats-its-foreign-aid-like-a-state-secret-new-research-aims-to-reveal-it/?utm_term=.ff7befecca06

UNDP. (2021). *Funding compendium 2020.* Accessed May 10, 2022, from https://www.undp.org/sites/g/files/zskgke326/files/2021-08/UNDP%20Funding%20Compendium%202020%20.pdf

Villarino, E. (2011, September 6). Top USAID private sector partners, A primer. *Devex.* Accessed May 20, 2022, from https://www.devex.com/news/top-usaid-private-sector-partners-a-primer-75832

Wickstead, M. (2015). *Aid and development: A brief introduction.* Oxford University Press.

Yanguas, P. (2018, March 8). *Opinion: It is time for the aid community to abandon its siege mentality.* Devex.com. Accessed May 25, 2022, from https://www.devex.com/news/opinion-it-is-time-for-the-aid-community-to-abandon-its-siege-mentality-92264

CHAPTER 2

The Imperative to Spend

Among those who are familiar with the development industry, the obsession with donors spending, spending fast, and spending ever more can be seen as a constant. It is something that seems to overshadow all else, and for this reason it wins pride of place or starting point in our attempt to analyze the beast.

The need by donor agencies to shuffle money out the door sometimes approaches the ridiculous, with more money chasing earlier funds where there have been questionable or no positive results, and where stubborn recipient governments continue their egregious ways. Or additional spending is focused in new areas and down new paths that donors tread with enthusiastic self-importance. And this cascade of large grants and even larger loans has been around and growing steadily for decades, in spite of endless talk about the need for efficiency, effectiveness, country ownership, and measurable results. In fact, as Dambisa Moyo (2009, 54–55) put it, moving the money has come "almost to the absurd point where the donor has a greater need for giving the aid than the recipient has for taking it."

This spending phenomenon, sometimes dubbed MMS or "Money Moving Syndrome,"[1] while very widespread and 'resilient' over decades, remains treated, if at all, largely anecdotally in the ever-expanding

[1] For uses of this term, see, for example, Easterly (2003, 18–19). Also, see the dissertation (Monkam, 2008).

D. Sims, *Development Delusions and Contradictions*,
https://doi.org/10.1007/978-3-031-17770-5_2

development literature, restricted to being mentioned in passing and rarely analyzed or tackled head-on. Perhaps it is just too obvious.

Moving the money can be seen in tendencies for donors to brag about the amounts of money being committed and in their very frequent announcements of even more money in the pipeline. All donors enjoy announcing how much money has been spent or is programed for disbursement, and it seems such gleeful pronouncements, in and of themselves, justify their existences. As one very experienced German observer said in 2006, there are dozens of international donors and development banks, "… all of which justify their existence by spending money. Elaborate and complex procedures have been established by means of which the flow of this money is planned, managed, controlled and audited. But—above all—it has to flow!" (Knapp, 2006, 41). In the rest of this chapter we look at the phenomenon to show that, not only is moving the money pervasive and pernicious, but also that there are very fundamental reasons why donors are so obsessed with it and why such an obsession seems to continue to trump all else.

Deploring the Spending Obsession, and Then Moving on to Spend Even More

The imperative to spend is a donor behavior that has been softly criticized in the many decades of Development. In other words, it seems the phenomenon is a bedrock of donor agencies that never changes, despite scattered concerns that raise the issue and bon mots that deplore it.

In the 1970s, Judith Tendler, a perceptive aid observer, was already flagging how the organizational environments of donor agencies put a premium on moving the money and thus converting any sense of mission away from economic development and toward simple commitment of resources, and she added that the same imperative was just as great in the World Bank as in American foreign assistance. She argued that an explanation lies in the standards by which development agencies judge own their performance (i.e., the quantitative estimates of development assistance needs and expenditures in dollar terms) and how the agencies are judged by the outside world.[2] She was prescient in this analysis.

[2] Tendler (1975), especially Chapter VII, The Organizational Economy of Large Projects, and in particular "Moving Money" 88–89.

For example, in 1988, it was pointed out that American foreign assistance managers were mainly rewarded for spending aid quickly and generating more spending opportunities, and that such spending helped gain access to and leverage over local leaders. "… the Agency for International Development … rewards its managers more for spending appropriated funds quickly than for pursuing sensible development policies in poor nations and the State Department treats increased aid spending as an opportunity to buy more access for the U.S. ambassador to the local rulers and leaders" (Edmund, 1988).

Academics in the late 1980s had already identified this compulsion to spend as the driving force of donors that seemed to trump all else. The well-read Aid and Power (Mosley et al., 1991) looked in detail at the effects of the World Bank's imperative to disburse and how it reduces the credibility of any conditionality imposed on borrowers, keeps the Bank from enacting anything like sanctions against recipients who do not implement these conditions, and thus allows nonperformers to keep acquiring loans.

Such warnings about the power of MMS to undercut the ability of donors to impose their will have had little effect. For example, donors' spending obsessions were given some attention in 1992 with the publication of what is commonly known as *The Walpenhans Report*.[3] It confirmed that a "culture of loan approval" at the World Bank had caused a relentless decline in the performance of Bank operations (World Bank, 1992, 12).

In 1999 there was a very embarrassing internal report by the World Bank's Operations Evaluation Department about the need to spend above all else and its link to pervasive corruption in Indonesia. It showed the inability of Bank to "to root out the culture of loan approval" in Indonesia and pointed to the "culture of approval and perverse Bank career incentives that punished staff who contradicted the party line."[4] But getting tough about easy lending in Indonesia would prejudice Bank country operations, and another Bank report said precisely this, arguing that such action would do serious damage to the Bank–Government relationship (Rich, 2002, 51).

[3] World Bank (1992), Report of the Portfolio Management Task Force, 1 July 1992, Operations Evaluation Department, named after the lead author, Willi Wapenhans, a World Bank vice president at the time.

[4] Rich (2002, 49), quoting the *Indonesia Country Assistance Note* of 4 February 1999. This report would have remained internal except that it was leaked to the press.

That Moving the Money resulted in perverse incentives was also the conclusion of an internal Swedish International Development Agency ST, probably the most extensive done on the subject. The study was the first attempt to collect data on the behavior of staff members and other agents involved in the delivery of aid. The authors found that the Agency was not at all immune to the incentives to 'move the money,' and that SIDA officers felt a strong pressure to disburse money, especially at the end of the budget year. The report offers good explanations for this: Sweden's bold commitment to increase aid allocations to reach one percent of GNP, on the one hand, and the fear that uncommitted resources would be considered unnecessary and not re-budgeted in subsequent years, on the other (Monkam, 2008, 403).

In 2006 the then World Bank president, Paul Wolfowitz, seemed to be trying to change this internal culture of the Bank. Wrong (2009, 263) describes Wolfowitz's new approach: "The era when career success was measured by the number of projects was over. Managers would in future be rewarded 'as much for saying no to a bad loan as for getting a good one out the door.'" This approach was part of the President's much ballyhooed fight against corruption in developing countries that, parenthetically, achieved little other than the establishment of yet more control mechanisms and anticorruption safeguards within the Bank to ensure that its own operations were as squeaky-clean as possible, such as beefing-up the Bank's Department of Institutional Integrity. And of attempts to change the internal imperative to spend culture, nothing more was heard. In fact, even the Bank's own hagiographic record of Wolfowitz' time as president totally ignored this initiative (World Bank, n.d.).

Recognizing that perhaps something was amiss, the OECD (2009) published one of its 'better aid' monographs aimed at the whole 'development community.' It boldly states "Most agencies face continued pressure to deliver, i.e. to get a project, programme or lending operation prepared, agreed with government and approved internally within the agreed timeframe, then to disburse money quickly and show early results." However, the report's recommendations on how to deal with this sound like pure dissimulation. It suggests "applying a Managing for Development Results (MfDR) system that can help highlight the development results to be achieved. Incoming ministers introducing new priorities should translate these into outcome and impact targets rather than spending targets" (OECD, 2009, 21).

In 2011, a World Bank research paper promoting more selectivity in project identification bemoaned the incentive structure found in all multilateral development banks as an obstacle to a more 'results-oriented' approach development lending (Limodio, 2011). The paper argued that 'fast lending' tended to be more valued than an emphasis on project screening or on a concentration on a country's pro-growth sectors. It recommended that the World Bank promotes internal reforms to align incentives toward more selectivity and more analytic scrutiny of proposed projects, things that one would think had already have been accepted as key to developing successful projects.

Well, after a decade nothing about these 'internal reforms' seems to have materialized. Instead, the odd references to the pernicious spending culture continued to pop up from time to time, with, again, no apparent impact or follow-up. A good example can be found in a folksy address delivered by the World Bank President at the London School of Economics in 2017 (as in, "Mick Jagger went to the LSE? How cool is that!"), entitled "Rethinking Development Finance" (World Bank, 2017). Jim Yong Kim proclaimed: "For too long, our first thought was, how can we get the loan or grant out the door? But that's often not what's best for poor people and poor countries, and it's not what's best for the world." His solution? "… everyone in the development community should be an honest broker who helps find win-win outcomes—where owners of capital get reasonable return, and developing countries maximize sustainable investments." In other words, the Bank needed to shift from being "a lender to an investor," using its capital, knowledge, and technical expertise to leverage or 'crowd in' private sector investments on 'de-risked' commercial terms. As is endlessly pointed out, private investment flows from the West to the Rest totally eclipse all types of development aid, and moreover in today's world there are trillions upon trillions of dollars sitting in more advanced countries barely able to find positive returns. It would seem a great win–win where some of these funds attracted to finance development projects in the Rest and, at the same time, earn respectable returns on investments. In this way the billions of dollars controlled by the Bank could leverage trillions more. Sound familiar? It should, since such promotion and leveraging of the private sector has been canon in the development business for ages (Chap. 20).

In the same speech Kim hastened to add that he is not advocating simplistic privatization of state assets and more business-friendly regulatory environment. Still, his examples of great success at leveraging private capital sound like the kinds of big-ticket investments that both the private sector and the Bank love to undertake, such as private finance for a new airport terminal in Amman or for power investments in Baghdad. It seems a bit naïve to assume that private capital would somehow also want to invest in public health services, slum upgrading, village schools, or—as he suggests—a road building project in Tanzania. For such mundane projects, it is practically impossible to devise an attractive and low-risk return for an investor, and, in any event, it requires the kind of competent government management that is very scarce in these countries.

As if this were not enough, Kim again attacked the entrenched incentives to spend at the Bank in February 2018, deploring, for example, how the pay of World Bank economists is tied to how many loans they churn out and how 'bureaucratic machinations' confound any reform in the Bank (Thomas, 2018, 7–8). Well, so far the Bank's new role as a middleman for investments by sovereign wealth funds, private equity firms, pension funds, and insurance companies (not to mention foreign direct investment) has remained miniscule. But during Kim's intensive explorations of potential partnerships between the Bank and large Western investors, he himself obviously learned a lot about the private equity ecosystem and made some serious personal connections along the way, since in January 2019 he abruptly resigned as Bank president to join Global Infrastructure Partners, a huge private-equity firm based in New York.

Sourcing the Money

How did this imperative to spend come about, and why is it so entrenched? The answer lies in how aid money is generated, how it flows, and how both aid institutions and their staff are motivated to spend these flows. To understand this, a slightly closer look at the funding process is in order:

All development funding is determined by factors that are external to the donor institutions and to the structures of the industry itself. It is first found in the eternal game of politics in the West, where aid competes with a host of other calls on national budgets, where pledges and 'replenishments' of multinational organizations are politically set, where geopolitical and commercial concerns often dominate, and where catering to the taxpayer (either pulling at their heart strings or trying to equate aid with national interests) usually trump.

In other words, taxpayers count. If the average taxpayer were to simply say, don't give more aid, then there would be a horrible problem with keeping the moneys flowing. But don't worry, studies have shown that there is, over time, a remarkably consistent positive public opinion about aid. Yes, in each Western country there are ups and downs in attitudes towards foreign aid, but these are relatively short and opinions tend to revert to the norm quite quickly. This has been borne out by a number of studies, most authoritatively by the Aid Attitude Tracker 2013–2018, which looked at public opinion about aid in France, the United Kingdom, Germany, and the USA.[5] What this also shows is that disasters and humanitarian assistance have an outside influence on what citizens think and how they react. What seems to work best is promotional material with positive spin (not dwelling overly on misery) and win–win material (aid is good for them and good for us too).

This would seem to indicate that donor agencies need not overly worry about general public opinion and the reactions of taxpayers. But, being forever focused on where the money is going to come from, these agencies certainly do, and obsessively.[6] This obsession can be found in many aspects of donor behavior—as we point out at several points in subsequent chapters—and it would seem to suggest that, ultimately, there is a lot of institutional insecurity in the donor world.

Such insecurity is to be found in the cardinal rule of 'spend it or lose it.' If funding earmarked for a country's international development budget is not spent or at least committed within a certain budget cycle, it becomes hard to justify asking for the same or greater largesse the next time around. Woe be to the agency that leaves funds hanging around or, even worse, has projects and programs on its books that are embarrassingly stillborn failures. This imperative to spend what has already been allocated (or at least penciled in) certainly focusses donor behavior and puts immense pressure on management to Move the Money.

In any event, at some point a donor agency's five-year budget horizon will be penciled in, and the race is on to spend or at least 'commit' what are quite considerable chunks of money to countries and to sectoral programs, with the knowledge that yet more will come in the following years.

[5] According to one of the study's authors, 'What we can see from these trends is that attitudes simply are not as elastic as we imagined.' On the one hand scandals may well produce a spike of opposition (e.g., Haiti 2016 or migrant influxes in Germany), but support quickly reverts back to the norm (Birmingham University, n.d.). The study was amply funded by the Gates Foundation.

[6] The UK's DfID even set up a special unit to counter negative public opinion about its aid programs in 2017.

Furthermore, there is in most donor budgets a constant, and embarrassing, overhang of unallocated and unspent funds, or in other words, money pretty much still up for grabs. And yet more will be up for grabs in the next budget cycle.

Decisions on how to manage these allocated funds are made at stratospheric levels of donor management and are embedded in horizon plans, annual budgets, aid allocation formulae, regional plans, country programs, certain sectors, and contributions to special global funds. Outside voices from academia and think tanks might have some influence—but donors prefer to rely on their own policy and feedback mechanisms to influence funding streams. Thus, internal policy papers, sectoral reviews, and workshop events surrounding the flow of funds are very much part of being inside a particular donor's bubble.

Since the introduction of Country Development Frameworks (CDFs), Poverty Reduction Strategy Papers (PRSPs), and the like by various donors, there are ostensibly processes in place whereby recipient governments are engaged with the donor to come up with three- to five-year broad-brush formulae all can agree on, but these themselves are often irrelevant or simply pro forma. And in theory, a donor's own monitoring and evaluation efforts are supposed to feed into the debate, but, as we shall see in Chap. 7, at best such evaluations and assessments offer muted criticisms, suggesting better ways to spend the same amount of money within the same type of program, and never simply saying that this project/program is a disaster—a 'worst-practice'—that should be terminated and any remaining allocations shifted elsewhere.

These allocation formulae and feedback loops from evaluations and learning-through-doing, not to mention the supposed dialogues with partners, are supposed to inform the scene for further allocations and temper the eyes-shut stampede to spend. But they don't, and only those that justify more spending in more ways seem to have any influence. Most donors have set up internal systems to review and discuss projects and programs in the pipeline that give a veneer that all is logical, and the World Bank, for example, has for some time instituted in-house peer reviews of loan projects at various stages of preparation (and sometimes even peer reviews of policy papers and concept notes), and presumably these are meant partly to ensure that there was no headlong rush to move towards implementation. But these mechanisms have themselves become rather pro forma events, in which colleagues outside the project-under-preparation can show off their knowledge, even though few have the time to dig into the voluminous amount of background information that might just inform their comments.

Attempts to Suspend or Stop the Money Flows: Never Just Say No

There are only very rare examples where a donor's aid program to a particular country is suspended in its entirety or that a particular ongoing project or sectoral support is stopped, and in almost all cases this is not because the aid program or some part of it is a colossal waste or dysfunctional disaster, but because of geopolitical issues, or human rights issues, or simply outrageous and rampant corruption.

Such suspensions of an aid program or some part of it frequently makes the news, but rarely are these measures long-lasting. The examples of Malawi (2013), Tanzania (2016 and 2018), and Mozambique (2016) show that egregious violations of human rights and gross corruption on the part of recipient governments can lead to temporary aid program suspensions by particular donors (but rarely all donors). One could go on and on citing examples of 'moralistic' suspensions of aid financing to the Rest—Mali in 2012, in Rwanda in 2013, in Indonesia in 2015, in Lebanon in 2020, and in the more distant past in Kenya, in Pakistan, in Uganda, in Afghanistan, in Nicaragua, and in other countries, often several times. But in almost all cases these tended to be partial suspensions, the donors maintained a dialogue, and, after a certain period, fences are mended, spats were smoothed over, and the march of development funds resumes.

In fact, compared to the avalanches of development assistance and the volumes of money involved, aid suspensions are miniscule. The World Bank's record of sanctions and suspensions of loan projects worldwide is instructive: Its Sanctions Evaluation and Suspension Office keeps track of cases, and an analysis between 2007 and 2012 found fraud or corruption in 157 contracts worth $245 million. Since the World Bank's lending volume was on the order of about $40 billion a year, this implies that only about one-fourth of one percent of loan volumes over the period involved some form of corruption. The same is true for other donors, and only the tiniest slices of their development expenditures ever are subject to anything like suspensions (Kenny, 2017, 1).

Get the picture? Turning off the aid spigot is simply not part of the game, unless there are outrageous (and potentially embarrassing) moral or human rights reasons, and even then, such suspensions are usually tempered and temporary. After all, as Paul Collier famously said about those in the development industry, "People get promoted by disbursing money, not withholding it" (Collier, 2007, 109).

If donors are reluctant to suspend funding for moral reasons, what about cancelations or suspensions for purely technical failures? It seems that pulling the plug on a project that is obviously off the rails is something donors practically never do. It may not be meeting the agreed objectives, is woefully off the implementation timetable, is technically dubious, or has serious negative policy repercussions, but these reasons seem never to account for much. Instead, once a project is under serious preparation, and even more so once it is approved and implementation mechanisms grind into play, there is a steamroller momentum that pushes it on. A search through the development literature almost never comes up with examples of simply saying no, enough is enough, based on the merits of the intervention itself. Some examples small examples exist, but one has to go way back to the 1980s to find a serious example. This was the Arun III 'run of the river' hydropower project in Nepal in the early 1990s. The project was on a scale "unprecedented in the country's history," was hugely expensive (costing more than the country's annual budget), would condemn Nepal to paying off the loan for decades, and in addition had several environmental, technical, and social problems. This project was conceived by the World Bank and, although multiple criticisms of the project were loudly expressed over a period of three years, "the Bank's senior management persisted in stonewalling on Arun III, such that it risked becoming the Dien Bien Phu of infrastructure projects" (Rich, 2002, 29). It wasn't until James Wolfensohn became president of the Bank in 1995 that the project was cancelled through his personal intervention.

What Happens When an Aid Budget Is Increased Dramatically?

When a donor country decides to dramatically increase its budget to a particular country for overall for political or other reasons, the Imperative to Spend goes into a kind of overdrive, usually with serious negative consequences.

This was definitely the case when, due to the Camp David peace accords in 1977–1979, the small USAID mission to Egypt was suddenly tasked with expanding its program to Egypt to a whopping one billion dollars in *grant* aid a year in what became, for more than a decade, the largest economic assistance program in the world. The scramble to identify projects and to process them required USAID to build up an extensive bureaucracy sitting in Cairo plus an army of American contractors, subcontractors, and consultants. There had been some isolated successes in this program, but, overall, such a rush of money simply allowed the Egyptian government to avoid difficult reforms, continue business as usual, and at the same time enjoy lots of new American-financed projects (Sullivan, 1996). The stubbornness on the part of Egypt was made even easier since over the same period other donors also began poor money into Egypt.[7]

There are other examples of the less-sightly underside when a donor country decides to dramatically increase its total development assistance budget. Such was the case of the British government that, in 2004, declared its intention to raise its aid budget to represent 0.7 percent of GDP, a purely arbitrary level that only a handful of northern European countries had ever managed to reach. By 2013 the goal was achieved and self-congratulations abounded. But there has been much criticism that meeting this budget goal yielded waste, missed opportunities, and was dubious value for money.

Over the years there have been many other examples of donors scrambling to spend suddenly expanded budgets and newly earmarked funds in particular countries and in particular sectors. But what this shows is that, however well managed, these brave attempts run up against the molasses of control and bureaucracy that the donors themselves have imposed (Chap. 4), and, at the same time, make a mockery of their own commitments to aid effectiveness, to learning processes, and evidence-based impact. Even worse, the sudden appearance of donor largess allows the recipient 'partner' to sidestep or otherwise dissimulate the grand policy reforms and conditionalities that are the whole ostensible reason for program aid. In fact, one of the few lessons that recipient governments have

[7] International organizations had been no stranger to Egypt's development scene, having poured millions into development projects in Egypt. For example, between the 1970s and 1990s Egypt received around USD 1.5–2.5 billion per year in economic aid and credits, and in the 1980s, around 80% of Egypt's public investment came from external funding (Dorman, 2007).

learned from working with donors is that they can count on the Imperative to Spend to work in their favor, especially when there is a leap in the amounts of money available.

Spending Aid Allocations on Time

Once funds are in the hands of donor agencies and have been programmed into indicative budgets, there is a scramble to make sure the money is spent, and yet spent on time, or at least as quickly as humanly possible. All niceties about the need for real buy-in by the recipient government and its implementing ministry or agency and for well-designed interventions based on robust on-the-ground investigations, integrated capacity building, community participation, recipient administrative reform, etc. take very much a back seat. Inevitably, stipulations of conditionality are relaxed, redefined, or completely ignored. Even after pulling out all the stops, donor bureaucracies and dithering recipient governments make it well-nigh impossible to get to an agreement signed anywhere near the optimistic timetables set in donor concept papers, aide memoires, and back-to-base reports (Chap. 7). Among other things, this highlights an important factor: those donor cadres in charge disbursement are horribly over extended (sometimes in charge of several projects in several countries), always super busy, with full agendas that include lots of hardly relevant trips to attend conferences, pro forma diplomatic meetings, and retreats. No wonder they have little time, even if they have the inclination, to see that projects are well designed, funds are effectively used, and that even the simplest 'conditions' are respected. Time is of the essence, and the money clock is ticking.

Donors have come to rely on consultants to keep their heads above the ever-increasing workloads surrounding the flows of funds. In fact, reliance on consultants by donor organizations is at an all-time high in the business, and not just for technical work. More and more they are hired for pure management tasks to do with organizing sub-contracts, developing schedules, hiring local consultants, tracking how funds are spent, and ensuring a project is peppered with the requisite workshops and other 'ownership' events. Often consultants are hired simply to oversee or coordinate the work of *other* consultants. But reliance on outsourcing has two downsides: first, it means additional work to bring consultants on board and to monitor their performance, and, second, it results in another layer that further distances the donor manager from a project's reality.

Motivations to Move the Money

It is the regional representatives, country managers, sector heads, and other senior management of donor agencies that are desperate to spend the money, since successful budget disbursement is the main metric by which these bosses are judged by their bosses, and them in turn by their bosses. If a boss can leverage even more money to flow into his bailiwick, for example, from another program or even from another donor, he/she gets extra points in the all-important career ladder. Here we touch on the main reason the Imperative to Spend is so pervasive and so immune to attempts at curtailing it or even to recognize it as a problem. After all, there have been, as far as is known, exactly zero examples of donor agencies consciously trying to lower the tempo of money flows or even to recognize that moving the money is itself a problem.

For someone to gain promotion in a donor institution, it is well known that one needs to have a record of good management, which in turn means having a growing budget and spending it vaguely on time with no embarrassments. For the project officer or middle-level manager: advancement (mainly within the organization, but also in case he/she wants to change ship) is directly linked to the ability to successfully spend the money earmarked. In multinational development banks it is the big loans or even the large technical assistance packages someone has been able to generate in the past that represent his or her 'portfolio,' and it is upon this that one is evaluated and promoted or hired by some other donor. This same iron link between spending and advancement operates in virtually all bilateral donor agencies. And in the UN system, always starved for funds, one gets ahead not only by capturing some of the small core budget, but more importantly, by finding another donor to contribute to a program or, as they say, a 'co-funder' or some form of 'blended finance' mechanism. In fact, top managers within many UN agencies actually spend most of their time in 'fundraising' of one sort or another.

Certainly, a proven record of moving the money is a donor staffer's best way for advancement. But these days in the development world cushy permanent contracts are becoming rarer, and fear of losing one's job has become more acute, especially as winds of frugality and rationalized management periodically sweep these organizations. The result is that mid-level managers are ever aware that their futures are on the line, and that when their performance is measured, their ability to spend will trump all other qualities.

As far as is known, no donor staffer has ever been awarded for just saying no and for simply pulling the plug on some fiasco-in-the-making, and it is likely that she or he will be politely encouraged to take early retirement or shuffled off into some obscure administrative or research position. And no one gets bonus points for having shot down a dubious project concept, for rescuing a budget from duplicated and useless disbursement, or simply for saying a blank no to funding requests from a government ministry or agency in a partner country.

This Money Moving incentive system is never seriously questioned by donors themselves, and, as we have seen, it is only criticized in passing even by observers and academics. As far as can be ascertained, only one researcher (Monkam, 2012) has ever looked in any detail at this money-moving syndrome.[8] It seems to be an accepted part of the game, and one could say that there is silent recognition that any reform away from the wholesale rush to spend could have extreme consequences. This fear is particularly acute with bilateral donors and their domestic cheerleaders, who have to battle each budget cycle to at least maintain previous aid allocations, if not increase them.

More generally, it could be said that donor agencies simply want to keep the ball rolling. Nigela Wrong (2009, 189), writing about donor largess to Kibaki's Kenya in the 2000s, summed the situation quite well: "In every enterprise there is a powerful urge—particularly pronounced in those of a methodical, paper-pushing nature—to Keep the Show on the Road. Habit creates its own compulsion, supposedly temporary projects develop a momentum and logic of their own, and the larger the sums of money and the staff number involved, the harder it is to admit a thing has run its course. The inclination to Carry On Carrying On means donors shrink from walking away, no matter how disappointing the results of their intervention."

Motivation to spend is also found downstream throughout the aid delivery system, including the armies of consultants, service contractors, and INGOs that are hired by donors. Those who run these operations also want to keep the ball rolling—to finish up projects with no embarrassments attached, to get fully paid, and, especially, to pave the way for future work contracts. It is not at all in the interests of consulting firms or INGOs simply to say that a certain project is a complete mess and should be axed,

[8] This article was expanded from her PhD dissertation (Monkam, 2008).

or even that an approach makes little sense development-wise. Were this the case, a considerable stream of future work could be jeopardized. It is better to keep one's head down.

The Imperative to Spend Permeates All Facets of the Industry

As we have already pointed out, it is unknown for a development agency or any of its divisions or country offices to have ever been rewarded for not spending an allocated budget or for saving funds for something more useful in the future. To suggest that perhaps the flow of particular funds should be questioned is antithetical to the donor, which is along the lines: 'I spend therefore I exist.' And the development industry is hardly a normal, corporate one, where success of a manager (or a unit or division) is ultimately measured by sales and profits or market share, by prowess at mergers or acquisitions, or simply by keeping costs down. No, it is an industry that is in the business of spending funds that have already been earmarked, and the bottom line is, simply, the ability to spend them and spend them at least vaguely on time. Whole structures have been built up to pretend that there are other ways to gauge performance—by looking at outcomes, measuring results, worrying about effectiveness and value for money, evaluating impact, etc. But, as we shall see in subsequent chapters, these are very much hollow artifacts that convey only a semblance of dynamic change.

The donor's obsession for spending money also permeates how it deals with governments in the Rest. Virtually all aid funds flow with strings attached (even, e.g., simple budget support deposited in a country's treasury), and it is these strings—called conditionality in the business—that cannot be assured unless the threat of stopping transfers or withholding future moneys are real (Swedlund, 2017).[9] The chapters in Part II of this book well illustrate this conundrum.

One facet of the Imperative to Spend by a donor agency and its individual departments is the need to constantly seek out new ways to move the money. As is well known in corporate management studies, organizations that expand and proliferate their activities also create more positions

[9] Swedlund, Haley, "Can foreign aid donors credibly threaten to suspend aid? Evidence from a cross-national survey of donor officials," *Review of International Political Economy*, 2017, Vol. 24, No. 3, 454–496, https://doi.org/10.1080/09692290.2017.1302490

at the upper reaches of management, thus creating more opportunities for career growth. And the more budget and more staff under a manager's control the more power she or he has, both objectively and in terms of self-worth. How to pursue this power? In the corporate world, this can be called Product Development, and it is very much a fundamental trait of donor agencies, which we take up in the next chapter.

References

Birmingham University. (n.d.). *Development aid: How do you convince the public that progress is possible?* Accessed May 28, 2022, from https://www.birmingham.ac.uk/research/quest/towards-a-better-society/Attitudes-towards-aid.aspx

Collier, P. (2007). *The bottom billion: Why the poorest countries are failing and what can be done about it.* Oxford University Press.

Dorman, W. J. (2007). *The politics of neglect: The Egyptian state in Cairo 1974-1998.* PhD thesis, SOAS. Accessed May 29, 2022, from https://eprints.soas.ac.uk/155/1/Dorman_Politics_of_Neglect.pdf

Easterly, W. (2003). Can foreign aid buy growth? *Journal of Economic Perspectives, 17*(3), 23–48.

Edmund, F. (1988, June 1). *Rethinking US foreign aid.* The Heritage Foundation, archival material. Accessed May 28, 2022, from https://www.heritage.org/node/21798/print-display

Kenny, C. (2017, January 23). *How much aid is really lost to corruption?* Center for Global Development. Accessed May 28, 2022, from https://www.cgdev.org/blog/how-much-aid-really-lost-corruption

Knapp, E. (2006). Budget lines, donor procedures, and receiver dynamics. *Trialog 88, 1.*

Limodio, N. (2011). *The success of infrastructure projects in low-income countries and the role of selectivity, Policy Research Working Paper No 5694.* World Bank. Accessed May 28, 2022, from https://elibrary.worldbank.org/doi/abs/10.1596/1813-9450-5694

Monkam, N. F. (2008). *The Money-Moving Syndrome and the effectiveness of foreign aid.* PhD thesis, Georgia State University. Accessed May 27, 2022, from https://scholarworks.gsu.edu/econ_diss/52/

Monkam, N. F. (2012). International donor agencies' incentive structures and foreign aid effectiveness. *Journal of Institutional Economics, 8*(3), 399–427.

Mosley, P., Harrigan, J., & Toye, J. (1991). *Aid and power: The World Bank and policy-based lending* (Vol. 1, 1st ed.). Routledge.

Moyo, D. (2009). *Dead aid: Why aid is not working and how there is a better way for Africa.* Penguin.

OECD (2009). *Improving Incentives in Donor Agencies: Good Practice and Self-Assessment Tool.* https://www.oecd-ilibrary.org/development/improving-incentives-in-donor-agencies-first-edition_9789264059788-en

Rich, B. (2002). The World Bank under James Wolfensohn. In J. Pincus & J. Winters (Eds.), *Reinventing the World Bank.* Cornell University Press.

Sullivan, D. (1996). *American aid to Egypt 1975-96: Peace without development.* Middle East Policy Council, Vol. IV(Winter), 4. Accessed May 20, 2022, from http://www.mepc.org/american-aid-egypt-1975-96-peace-without-development

Swedlund, H. (2017). Can foreign aid donors credibly threaten to suspend aid? Evidence from a cross-national survey of donor officials. *Review of International Political Economy, 24*(3), 454–496. https://doi.org/10.1080/09692290.2017.1302490

Tendler, J. (1975). *Inside foreign aid.* John Hopkins University Press.

Thomas, L. (2018, February 10–11). *A nervous World Bank embraces Wall Street.* New York Times International Edition.

World Bank. (1992, July 1). *Report of the portfolio management task force.* Operations Evaluation Department.

World Bank. (2017, April 11). *Speech by World Bank Group President Jim Yong Kim: Rethinking development finance. Speech as prepared for delivery.* Accessed May 28, 2022, from http://www.worldbank.org/en/news/speech/2017/04/11/speech-by-world-bank-group-president-jim-yong-kim-rethinking-development-finance

World Bank. (n.d.). *World Bank archives: Paul Dundes Wolfowitz.* Accessed May 28, 2022, from http://www.worldbank.org/en/about/archives/history/past-presidents/paul-dundes-wolfowitz

Wrong, M. (2009). *It's our turn to eat: The story of a Kenyan Whistleblower.* The Fourth Estate.

CHAPTER 3

Product Development

For someone familiar with the development business say forty years ago when things were relatively simple, she or he would be amazed these days at the diversity, complexity, and sheer variety of ways donors are involved in countries of the Rest. It seems that there is almost no area of human endeavor that the development industry does not touch, cannot reach, or cannot fold into the rubric of development. Such proliferation is a corollary of, and is intimately linked to, the development industry's Imperative to Spend, and it is a process that creates new paths and pastures for justifying both the disbursement of aid budgets and the clamor for more funding. This has become one cause of donor fragmentation and confusion in countries of the Rest, and it further clogs up the already chaotic overload on donor operations. We like to call this endless searching for new ways to spend money Product Development, since the phrase—much used in the corporate world—well describes the phenomenon, and it is a phrase also used by the contractors and INGOs that hope to capture some of the largess floating around.

A Bit of History

Back in the 1960s and 1970s, it was usually naively assumed that interventions were to be finite and that there would be an eventual donor exit, with the target (government institution, rural community, or whatever) able to not only benefit but continue on their own afterward. These were

D. Sims, *Development Delusions and Contradictions*,
https://doi.org/10.1007/978-3-031-17770-5_3

sometimes euphemistically called exit strategies, but 'exiting' rarely happened, and instead, while a specific project would eventually close, other related projects or programs would spring up. Also, in the past a donor would tend to concentrate on a few big-ticket sectors—such as rural development; agricultural productivity; big infrastructure such as highways, canals, dams, power stations and the like; primary education and building schools; basic health; certain industrial sectors; etc. in a handful of countries. They may have tacked on some other dimensions, studies, or spin-offs, but the main concentrations or core competencies were rather clear. No more.

Even in the 1980s and, especially, in the 1990s there was an acceleration in the diversity in the types of development projects, their scope and sizes, their elaborateness and complexities, and the various ways they could be reformatted and reimagined into different situations and countries. There was also an explosion in studies and investigations associated with major development themes, which not only provided a more comprehensive, intellectual veneer to a development approach, but also widened the knowledge base, allowing donors to seek out more possible opportunities and venues for development work. And, of course, with the end of the Cold War and the exigencies of structural adjustment, anything that could complement downsized government came to be promoted. This meant a huge new space for all sorts of private sector support, and it multiplied the kinds of investments from IFIs. But at the same time, it was discovered that civil society and NGOs could and should step in, and over the period there was an explosion of social programs with 'participatory' attributes, more emphasis on the vulnerable and marginalized, and gender began to claim its own space as a development pillar.

In effect, what could be called the constant proliferation of themes and modalities became an intrinsic trait of the development industry. And today there are bewildering and almost endless portfolios of projects, programs, advisory services, governance support, budget support, capacity building, debt swaps, sectoral strategies and more, scattered across well over a hundred countries. Add to this donor-sponsored research and studies, donor-financed international events and publications about practically anything vaguely related to social and environmental development issues, and also data-intensive approaches to anything analytical. To confuse things even more, there are also constantly evolving sets of 'cross-cutting' themes that stretch across almost anything that could be construed to fall under the rubric of development. And, increasingly, much of what donors do or sponsor have little to do with straightforward development per se, but also penetrates practically the whole gamut of human endeavors, such as social justice, rule of law, peace and stability, migrants, and refugees. Others involve saving the planet, protecting cultural artifacts, developing civil society, promoting human rights, resolving conflicts and promoting peace, protecting bio-diversity, helping street children, and imposing gender equality, just to name a few.

Today Donor Backyards Are Everywhere

No more do donor agencies have a particular concentration in a few countries or regions. As one study remarked about international donors: "To them, and to the politicians who control the purse strings, plastering the world with flags is a sign of success" (The Economist, 2016). Certainly, such planting of flags is the geographic side of a bilateral donor's proliferation or product development. Go to any donor website and a map or list will proudly show its global reach. Thus in 2016 Germany had, for example, a permanent 'development cooperation' presence in 30 African, 21 Asian, and 8 Latin American countries. In 2017 Britain's DfID[1] had ongoing programs in 32 developing countries, plus regional programs in Africa, Asia, and the Caribbean, and this does not include development activities in additional countries that are handled through British embassies, the Foreign Office, and the British Council. Even small donor countries can have a surprising geographic reach, as is the case of Swiss Development Cooperation, which lists development offices in 27 countries (including North Korea!), not counting seven sub-regional groupings of countries. Some small donors have a tendency to make relatively big splashes in small countries, not because they want to generate real partnerships over decades but because, otherwise, they won't have the clout to access important ministers or enjoy a certain importance in the eyes of their country partners.

By definition multilateral development institutions and IFIs have enormous geographic playgrounds. The mother of all such donors is the World Bank Group. It works in over 140 countries and, in addition, has a bewildering number of regional programs, each of which spans several countries. Its various activities are divided into six regions, three income

[1] In 2020 DfID lost its independence and was merged into the Foreign and Commonwealth Office.

categories (low, lower-middle, and upper-middle), and various special categories. Another behemoth donor organization is the United Nations Development Programme (UNDP), which currently has permanent offices in a total of 140 countries, operating in each of these under bewildering arrangements with some of the over 40 UN specialized agencies, not to mention with other donors. And there are also the regional banks who by definition are limited to specific continents, but these also show that their activities and representation are spread throughout as many countries in their continents as possible. (Thus, you have, e.g., the ADB in 49 countries and 5 sub-regions, the AfDB in 54 countries, and the IDB in 26 countries.) And it should be added that the reach of donors is not confined to capital cities of the Rest, and their projects can be found in numerous provincial towns and in rural settings.

The wide geographic reach of donors has resulted in multiple donors crowding into particular developing countries, especially those that have both the ability and desire to keep accepting more grants and loans, resulting in a concentrated donor presence in certain countries, with an almost mind-numbing list of who's who in the development business. With some laborious digging, it is possible to construct such lists, although only rarely can anything like a comprehensive inventory of current or donor projects be found in one place.

One such compendium of aid projects can be found in annual reports of Jordan's Ministry of Planning, where project agreements are listed. For 2019 the aid agreements signed—valued in total at $ 3.66 billion—showed an impressive complexity.[2] In total there were 67 agreements (which translates to a rhythm of more than 1.3 agreements signed every week, not counting holidays), most of which were for grant projects (53). The usual major donors were well represented—EBRD, UNICEF, WHO, EU, EIB, UNDP, IOM, AFD, GIZ, USAID, FAO, KfW, GEF, and the World Bank—plus Japan, Switzerland, Holland, Denmark, and South Korea, plus Arab donors Saudi Arabia, Kuwait, and the UAE. Grant project values ranged widely, from a tiny $31,000 (for transport of water and wastewater materials in Al Zarqa' from EBRD) to a huge $445 million (budget support from USAID), with grants averaging in the $1 to 3 million range. Loan

[2] Of this total, the composition of loans versus grants was about half and half, and the total includes $712 million in grants that Jordan received to help its government and communities cope with the 1.2 million Syrian refugees. See Jordan Ministry of Planning, https://www.mop.gov.jo/ebv4.0/root_storage/ar/eb_list_page/foreign_assistance_arabic_2019.pdf

agreement values were much larger, with the smallest at $ 17.5 million for budget support from AFD and the largest at $ 950 million from the World Bank for its second employment and growth policy loan.[3]

These new development activities launched in a single year are impressive for a tiny country such as Jordan, with a total population, including refugees, of under 10 million in 2018. Imagine all the administrative work, reports, meetings, and missions—on the part of both donor agencies and their consultants on the one side, and recipient bureaucracies on the other—that lie behind each of these project or program agreements. And just think of all the earlier, conceptual efforts and maneuvers that lie behind these. And all of these projects are multi-year, meaning that for each monitoring, reporting, and other administrative tasks will be running for many subsequent years. Finally, remember that this is only a snap shot of one year's agreements, and Jordan will be signing up for as many or more donor activities in subsequent years.

This short foray into one country doesn't adequately reflect the complexity and depth of development activities either in a single country or a single region. There are many associated activities that are under the radar of host countries, and many of these relate to research and studies on a wide range of development themes and policies. Almost all donors sponsor such activities in one way or another, and Western universities and think tanks are also frequently involved in such country and regional studies, yet almost none of this requires anything like host country approval or collaboration.

Some Call It Fragmentation

The phenomenon of proliferation of donors into practically everything and everywhere—sometimes called 'fragmentation' in the development literature—has been recognized in various international forums as something that seriously reduces the effectiveness of aid. For example, the 2008 Accra Agenda for Action states: "The effectiveness of aid is reduced when there are too many duplicating initiatives, especially at country and sector levels" (OECD, 2008, 17). Two years later the World Bank and IMF's 2010 Global Monitoring Report was more specific and more critical (Easterly & Williamson, 2012, 24)

[3] According to the same report cited above, virtually every one of the 17 SDGs was being addressed, with 28 of the 54 grant projects aimed at two or more SDGs.

> Reducing fragmentation and strengthening aid coordination is essential to enhance aid effectiveness. When aid comes in too many small slices from too many donors, transaction costs go up and recipient countries have difficulty managing their own development agenda. In 2006, 38 recipient countries each received assistance from 25 or more DAC and multilateral donors. In 24 of these countries, 15 or more donors collectively provided less than 10 percent of that country's total aid. The number of aid agencies has also grown enormously, with about 225 bilateral and 242 multilateral agencies funding more than 35,000 activities each year. A recent OECD survey revealed that in 2007 there were 15,229 donor missions to 54 countries—more than 800 to Vietnam alone.

Another factor, closely related to fragmentation, is the lack of coordination between donors, something that should logically be in place to reduce this 'fragmentation' and to give recipient countries simplified and straightforward development choices and options. Yet as was shown in Aldasoro (2009), there is a wide and persistent gap between the rhetoric of political declarations and the donors' actual aid allocation behavior, at least during the period of the study (1995–2006). Few donors are specialized on a limited set of recipients and/or aid sectors, and coordination has remained elusive. In fact, donors are often in direct competition with each other in their search for new fields and paths in which to expand their portfolios.

This donor competition is something that recipient governments have come to understand very well. Donors are desperate to get recipients to sign up for projects and programs, all rhetoric about ensuring good development outcomes aside. One could say there is a kind of Prisoner's Dilemma operating: If a donor doesn't agree to an arrangement, then some other donor with less 'scruples' or 'conditionality' will gobble it up. If trumped, the first donor could lose entry points in a whole sector and carefully crafted friendships, allowing someone else to gain ascendency in a recipient ministry where it has been top-dog for a long time. Thus, donor agencies often find themselves in direct competition. We've all heard about China—the new development boy on the block—and the howls by other donors that it doesn't play fair and undercuts the policies (and conditionality) of the more established donors, but such competitive tensions exist right through the donor community and have for decades and decades.

Project Pipelines: Donor Plates Are Heaped Full, but There Is Always Room for More

A look at any donor's literature these days will show the extremely wide range of subjects and themes that are part of their development agendas. It is as if one were partaking of an extremely elaborate and showy Scandinavian *smorgasbord* or Arab *mezza*, with more and more tiny plates being added as one tucks in.

Take as an example Swiss Development Cooperation, a relatively small donor, which in 2016 spent a total of about $3.7 billion for development activities, with significant funds going to 56 countries[4] (Swiss Development Cooperation, n.d.). According to their website the main themes were articulated as follows: agriculture and food security; basic education and vocational training; disaster risk reduction, emergency relief, reconstruction, and protection; climate change and the environment; migration; private sector development and financial services; water; state and economic reforms; gender and women's rights; health; engagement in fragile contexts and prevention of violent conflicts; and advocacy and good governance. These themes of Swiss Development Cooperation seem to reflect as much Western interests (climate change, migration) and Western values (gender equality, democratization, transparency) as they aim to support economic development or explicit inequality reduction in their 'partner' countries. Moreover, each of these themes is wide enough to drive a truck through! Practically everything under the sun is there—except aid in fields that Switzerland has a comparative strength (such as precision manufacturing or any other form of manufacturing for that matter). It seems the main goal is to cover all bases and make sure any concerned Swiss taxpayer will find something of interest (and make sure Swiss companies can find fertile fields in which to play).

One remarkable trait is the number of quite small activities a donor maintains in some countries. These may be pilot projects or technical assistance or training efforts, or simply a desire for a donor to have a hand in something in as many countries as possible. The suspicion is that such small aid packages are partly driven by the need by Western governments for political representation and potential commercial links, rather than anything developmental. It is no wonder that, according to AidData,

[4] These 56 countries each received Swiss development assistance of over CHF 2 million. There were several more countries listed as having received smaller amounts.

globally, the average size of donor projects plummeted—from being worth $5.3 million in 2000 to $1.9 million in 2013 (The Economist, 2016). For example, in Mozambique in 2015 there were 27 substantial donors engaged in the field of health alone, not counting private givers, and this included bilateral donors such as Belgium, France, Italy, Japan, and Sweden, each of which supplied less than $1 million (The Economist, 2016)

The trend among donors has been towards ever more proliferation, with the spreading of their budgets into as many fields as is possible. For example, Easterly (2012, 39) pointed out that in 1999 "New Zealand concentrated 32 percent of its aid to post-secondary education; however, of the past nine years, New Zealand has fragmented its aid among more sectors with no sector receiving more than 12 percent in 2008, and most much less." The same study concluded that, overall, the trend is for yet more diversification by donors scattered into ever more thematic areas and sectors. Possible reasons could have included the rise of specialized international NGOs and their lobbying for more diverse social programs, the added emphasis on democracy and governance following the Cold War, the rising need for post-conflict reconstruction and 'fixing failed states,' and the increasing emphasis on environment and gender. They conclude "there was a perfect storm that led to sector fragmentation since the mid-1990s to be at historically unprecedented levels" (Easterly & Williamson, 2012, 39).[5]

The specialized UN agencies, most of which were set up to tackle a particular development subject and to concentrate on these as core competencies, have taken product development and diversification very much to heart. In this pursuit, some try to expand their sectoral reach, even if it means poaching another's territory and imaginative convolutions are sometimes made to penetrate and claim a slice of other pastures. For example, the WHO issued new guidelines in November 2018 highlighting that better homes invariably lead to better standards of health and overall well-being. The guidelines state: "Improved housing conditions can save lives, reduce disease, increase the quality of life, reduce poverty, and help mitigate climate change." (Developmentaid, 2018). This was stating the dumbed-down obvious, but it opened the way for WHO to enter the field of housing: "Housing is, therefore, a major entry point" for "public health programmes and primary prevention." The traditional field

[5] Ibid., 39.

of housing is already quite crowded with multilateral banks, bilaterals, and NGOs, not to mention that another UN agency, UN-Habitat, considers itself the king of global housing policy.[6]

This proliferation by donors into anything and everything received a tremendous boost with the declaration of the Sustainable Development Goals in 2015, since this remarkable compendium of 17 goals and 169 targets allows a donor to move transversally into ever more sectors and themes and, at the same time, link them together and underscore just how comprehensive and relevant a new initiative can be. The suspicion is that part of the reason for the SDG idea was precisely to create the widest possible reference system to help donors penetrate more themes, develop more products, and set up more 'integrated' frameworks and 'comprehensive' development strategies.

Mechanisms for Heaping on Ever More Products

How do donors come up with new products and new fields to penetrate? Some ideas are simply cooked up at rarified donor management or political levels, often relating to commercial interests or a prominent politician's pet hobby horse. But there are quite a number of more systematized ways that Product Development is carried out by donors, and here we look at the five most prominent of these:

Sectoral Identification Missions

Launching product identification missions, usually in a certain sector and in one or group of countries, has been an industry stalwart for decades. Every year a donor agency will undertake scores of special missions and studies paid out of technical assistance funds to identify possibilities. These may be in stages, with a first very short reconnaissance mission by donor staff and perhaps a consultant in tow, with meetings both with an array of national and local government officials, their own people on the ground, and perhaps local consultants and academics and NGOs. If fruitful, there might be a proper follow study contracted out to specialized consultants who would develop a final report that: (1) looks at the current state of play

[6] This venture of the WHO into the urban/housing field parallels WHO's Healthy Cities Programme, which started in the 1980s and has since spread globally, the main activities of which seem to be limited to regional conferences and talk-shops.

in the sector; (2) identifies basic development issues, especially classic 'justifiers' relating to fighting poverty, improving basic education and health, stimulating economic growth, creating jobs, or protecting the environment or adapting to climate change; (3) analyses what are the government policies and programs and to what extent do they miss development priorities; (4) restates what are the donor's specific overarching objectives, usually as contained in country development strategies; (5) sketches out the components of a possible project or two; (6) makes at least ballpark cost estimates; and finally (7) identifies what other donors are currently doing or intend to do in the sector being studied. This last item is particularly important, since it may show areas where few donors currently tread, or where there just might be chances for co-funding or, in the case of UN specialized agencies, where a new project might be carved out with some other donor picking up most of the tab. These reports will go back to HQ and be mulled over, perhaps discarded or put on the back burner, perhaps combined with other feelers, and perhaps put into the donor's pipeline of tentative projects.

Best Practices and 'Modeles Voyageurs'

The development industry has for at least 25 years been enamored with 'best practices'—particular policies or interventions that can be considered sterling examples of how things should be done, at least in the eyes of some. This leads to the question: how to propagate these practices and extend them to more situations and more countries? Presumably the underlying logic is that these are such hot ideas and such resounding successes that they will easily overcome the ever-present stumbling block of totally different contexts. These may be 'innovative' forms of financing (such as results-based finance), technical solutions (such as e-business), or social inclusion (such as community-driven development). All donors engage in promoting their best (or good) practices, and the World Bank is particularly fond of highlighting them—it peppers its technical reports, already full of recommendations, with boxes highlighting experiences and success stories from other developing countries, no matter how tenuous or irrelevant these may be to the context at hand.

Best practices that are perceived to be easily applicable across various developing countries have been called by 'modeles voyageurs' in Francophone countries. A good analysis of this was presented in a 2019 paper, which evokes many types of successful models: cash transfers in

Brazil, performance payments for health services in Rwanda, or types of micro-credit in Bangladesh (De Sardan, 2019). Promoting such 'transferable ideas' have become all the rage, but any hope of their success of course depends upon the particular context in which they are applied rather than anything intrinsic to the concept itself. But the fiction must be maintained that these are easy, miraculous solutions and that a bit of social engineering will make them successful almost anywhere. In all cases it is assumed that there are efficient *agences voyagers* that can bend or adapt them to the particular context. It also helps if the intervention can be classified under one—or better yet—several of the SDGs. But in most cases the reaction on the ground is adoption of the façade and not the content. And the worst effect is, yet again, the loss of any home-grown initiatives in the societies that are dependent on these transfers.[7]

Embedding Product Development in Donor Operations

Within projects up and running in a particular country, it is normal for donors to ask for the identification of further opportunities, especially if these have been articulated or at least hinted at in the governing terms of references that guide such work. These may appear in mid-term reviews or in terminal evaluations, or at some other point. In effect, the refrain is always tacked on: Explore more! Find more ways to penetrate! The fact that such ongoing projects usually are themselves multifaceted—with many tangential sub-components as vocational training, IT development, civil society strengthening, e-business, etc.—and this means that each offers potential gateways into other arenas or initiatives that themselves can be applied to other economic sectors.

Related to this, another way to generate more paths for new interventions is to push for multisectoral projects, where limits are blurred, where there is more space for piggybacking and for new concoctions, and where 'Christmas-tree' projects find fertile ground. It is true that many of the challenges facing poor countries cannot be conveniently addressed by purely mono-sectoral approaches, particularly in the case for those aimed at lagging regions or burgeoning cities. But to see that everything will suddenly click under the synergies of myriad interventions across several sectors and themes is not only naïve and confusing, it (again) shows the

[7] These ideas are further elaborated in a workshop on *modeles voyageurs* sponsored by CNRS in 2018 (CNRS, 2018).

all-powerful hubris of the donor who believes its own rhetoric about its ability to be an agent of change. Yet spinning out new ideas and cutting-edge approaches is something donors love to promote, and these have been institutionalized in various ways. There is, for example, an extensive blog run by AFD called Ideas for Development (ID4D) and the even more extensive hub run by USAID called Global Development Lab (GlobDevLab), both of which have some good ideas gleaned from across the development landscape but exhibit a disconcerting enthusiasm for anything that is trendy and high tech.[8]

Additional Financing and 'Phase Endless'

A relatively easy way for a donor to spend is simply to develop another phase of an existing project or expand work in a country's specific sector and somehow call it breaking new ground. Project formulation can mostly be cut and pasted from the antecedent, and—most importantly—the recipient ministry/agency is familiar and comfortable with the interventions and usually has strong interests in agreeing to the new phase. Examples of such 'phase endless' maneuvers are legion. For example, there was the Bhaktapur project (Nepal) where GTZ managed to keep a historic village rehabilitation project going for at least two decades, or, more recently, KfW's school building program in the Palestine Territories, which in 2020 was on its *ninth* phase. And, there is the World Bank's second policy loan of a whopping $500 million for social housing in Egypt, even though the results of the first loan are less than edifying (Stalinist housing blocks in the middle of desert wastelands that stand mostly empty). The key in all of these extra phases and extra funds is the simple bureaucratic convenience of repeating more of the same.

Failed Attempts to Rationalize, Specialize, and Concentrate

Every so often a huge private corporation will decide to pare back its reach, divest itself of some divisions and their products, and concentrate on its core businesses, where it has comparative advantages and market depth. Does this happen in the development industry, under concern for

[8] ID4D can be found at http://ideas4development.org/ and GlobDevLab at https://www.usaid.gov/GlobalDevLab/

efficiency and effectiveness (two OECD-DAC goals)? Some attempts have been made, as we catalogue in the following paragraphs, but it is rare these efforts ever lead to anything permanent, faced with the powerful entropy of Product Development.

Concentrating on Core Competencies?

Rationalization has been attempted by donors from time to time. For example, a highly respected diplomat and development industry stalwart (formerly chairman of the OECD's DAC, and since May 2016 executive director of UNEP) remembers, when he was minister of Norway's international development from 2005 to 2012, of trying to persuade his own country to focus its development efforts on what it really knows about—such as managing an oil boom—rather than on things it had absolutely no comparative advantage, like tropical agriculture. He did not succeed (The Economist, 2016).

Another good example concerns German development cooperation. The Federal Ministry for Economic Cooperation and Development (BMZ) began to recognize around the year 2000 that it had such a bloated portfolio of diverse projects in many countries, and that some tightening up and rationalization was in order. First, the many existing projects of the Ministry's affiliates GTZ and KfW were decreed to need to fall into program frameworks in each country. And then, in 2002, orders went out that in each country German development cooperation would need to be rationalized and shrunk to only two or three focal or priority areas. Thus, in Egypt, after another couple of years of internal discussion and maneuvering by the 29 country project leaders and their colleagues back in Eschborn and Frankfort, it was decided that these would need to be folded into three priority areas of cooperation: renewable energy and energy efficiency, sustainable economic development, and management of water resources. Although such themes were very wide in scope, this move produced howls of consternation and not a little bad feeling among some German managers whose projects could not easily be made to fit into such themes. But what was the result? By 2016 these three priority areas remained on the books, but other activities were preserved or tacked on, including women's empowerment, developing informal urban settlements, human rights, and public administration reform. Furthermore, within each of the priority areas, the number of programs and initiatives had expanded to areas that could only, with greatest imagination, be considered to address the theme they come under. For example, under 'water resources,' funding to Egypt came to include providing access to drinking water, improving health through proper sanitation, improving efficiency in the agricultural use of water, promoting the financial viability of the water sector, and decentralizing and building up local water user communities. And solid waste management, a pet German project in Egypt in the previous decade, was tacked on to the water theme by conveniently dropping the word 'solid.'

It is interesting that, by 2017, German development cooperation had been reformulated yet again, at least in Africa, to fit into three 'pillars' of a German Marshall Plan with Africa: (1) economic activity, trade, and employment, (2) peace and security, and (3) democracy and the rule of law. Not only are these pillars extremely wide in themselves, but floating somewhat detached from these are four 'foundations'—food and agriculture, protection of natural resources, energy and infrastructure, and health/education/social protection (BMZ, 2017).

Other supposed reformist slimming and rationalization exercises have been tried by other main donors periodically—such as USAID, Dutch Development Cooperation, and even the World Bank—with words like 'pillars,' 'themes,' 'practice areas,' or even 'spearheads' heavily used. But these, much as is the case with German development cooperation, seem to be little more than public relations exercises combined with thematic gymnastics.

Concentrating on Certain Countries?

There are many examples of bilateral donors trying to become more selective in the number or countries they work in, but usually with much resistance and, after a certain period of time, excluded countries somehow finding their way back into the fold. Here are a couple of examples: In 2004–2005 Dutch Aid considered itself to be spread too thin over 36 countries, but in spite of efforts to concentrate on fewer countries, soon found itself, either through official aid or other types of Dutch government programs, to be active in over 100 countries (De Haan, 2009, 57). Likewise, in the 2000s DfID decided to limit the number of countries where they are active and terminated its long involvement in Egypt, presumably because the country was no longer poor enough. However, by 2019 British aid to Egypt had crawled back, and there were 17 active UK assistance activities in Egypt under various guises, such as action against corruption (GBP 39 million), the conflict, stability, and security fund (GBP 9 million), and supporting Egypt's reform agenda (GBP 13 million), according to UK Aid's 'development tracker.'[9]

One would have thought that concentrating on certain countries—where there are enough competencies for at least some development efforts to work and a consistent policy environment that puts a premium on economic sobriety—would be a logical approach.[10] But, as we point out in the Introduction, development cooperation serves many purposes—prime among them Western corporate and donor country political interests. And at the same time there is always pressure from within the development industry and NGOs to fund countries most in need (especially desperately poor, fragile and conflict-ridden states), no matter how badly their governments perform and how difficult it is to operate in-county. In other words, it seems that pairing down a donor's portfolio of countries rarely works, and the 'putting out more flags' syndrome' seems to trump all, no matter how thinly spread and ineffective this makes a donor's efforts.

Co-funding and Piggybacking?

One supposed antidote to donor activities that are fragmented and constantly proliferating is to consolidate various donor moneys into one co-funding program under one management umbrella. Sometimes known as piggy-backing or common baskets or pooled funds, such an approach can be a useful way to de-clutter the donor scene. Of course, such consolidation depends on what sectors one is talking about and whether there is a one donor who is the lead decision-maker (Gehring et al., 2017). There are many such examples, such as pooled donor funds for school building in Palestine, or joint financing of water and wastewater projects in Delta governorates of Egypt. In the case of large capital investment projects, pooled funds mean no single donor can overly micromanage or look into

[9] See https://devtracker.dfid.gov.uk/countries/EG/projects Accessed 29 May 2022.

[10] This idea of going only with countries that have what could be called good government or good governance was an underlying concept of the American government's Millennium Challenge Corporation, founded in 2004. As the MCC website states: "For a country to be selected as eligible for an MCC assistance program, it must demonstrate a commitment to just and democratic governance, investments in its people and economic freedom as measured by different policy indicators." Well, the countries selected so far seem to be less than perfect in governance, but that is another story (Millennium Challenge Corporation, n.d.).

all the specifics of what it funds, leaving implementation more in the hands of the executing authority or hired consultants. This can be good or bad, and it very much depends on how well this authority functions.

However, such co-funding exercises can also lead to more proliferation when what is being funded is in itself exploratory. A good example is a climate resilience scoping exercise in several Asian cities, with moneys coming from a $130 million trust fund jointly financed by DFID, USAID, the Rockefeller Foundation, and Swiss Development Cooperation and being executed by the Asian Development Bank. The resulting pipeline of projects not only helped spread the moneys around, but it also gave each of these donors a fast track to develop yet more of its own interventions in what had become a very hot subject.[11]

These days there is talk about having more consolidated, multi-donor combined sectoral funds, somewhat like huge single-disease funds promoted by the Bill and Melinda Gates Foundation. But although the advantages (less duplication, reduced transaction costs) would seem clear, these have remained little more than ideas, probably because bilateral agencies are loath to give up their control (and perceived national interests). For example, why hasn't the World Bank's IDA become such a consolidation vehicle for the poorest countries after some 50 years of operation? After all, the Bank's goals and sectoral approaches are very similar to those espoused by practically all donor agencies. The answer is obvious—bilateral agencies (and their many managers) simply can't handle loss of control and, in addition, want to preserve their own bureaucratic turfs.

Summing Up: Product Development Is a Donor's Core Competency

It is clear that 'fragmentation' and proliferation continue unabated in the development industry, producing ever-more new pastures to graze in and new ways to fix things in the Rest, despite all admonishments to the

[11] According to the ADB tender, some consultant has to zoom around to several countries over one year, discussing with governments and donors how to scale up urban climate change work, build up a pipeline of projects, "identify resilience opportunities in proposed loan projects," and "explore UCCRTF support in other sectors like health, education, transport and private sector." See https://www.developmentaid.org/#!/tenders/view/317849/ta-8913-reg-promoting-urban-climate-change-resilience-in-selected-asian-cities-developing-integrated posted 25 April 2017.

contrary from the OECD, academics, and others. What drives it is the need to find new ways to keep the flows of money going and the need by donors to be seen as confidently in control of at least some chunk of the Development World. And, as we have seen, the mechanisms of Product Development have been woven into the very heart of the business.

It seems that today neither bilateral nor multilateral donor agencies have anything like core competencies or specialized areas of strength. It seems that each *must* have as wide a reach as possible. In this sense donor behavior is very corporate, mimicking huge multinationals who have expanded or bought their way into a bewildering array of businesses, with no common links other than the values and ideologies of corporate management itself. Evidently there is nothing to keep a donor from expanding into other disciplines or areas, and it seems that this has become a holy grail for top management in donor agencies, especially for 'hot' items that have become fashionable like governance, resilience, climate change, and anything that can be a vessel for yet more multisectoral approaches.

The only constraints that donors face to developing more products are (1) getting partner countries and/or ministries to sign up and (2) to ensure that funding continues to be plentiful. The huge technical side of the development business—for which there are no lack of experts and expertise to tap—is mostly a necessary sideshow. The main competency of donors is to keep the momentum of new projects and programs rolling, and for this they need Project Development. And this imperative to develop more and more products received a wonderful boost with the establishment of Agenda 2030. This helps explain why the SDG artifact is so popular with virtually all donors, and why practically everyone who is part of the development world has to appear to love them.

References

Aldasoro, I., Nunnenkamp, P., & Thiele, R. (2009, April). *Less aid proliferation and more donor coordination? The wide gap between words and deeds, Kiel Working Papers No 1516*. Kiel Institute for the World Economy.

BMZ. (2017, January). *Africa and Europe: A new partnership for development and peace*. Accessed May 29, 2022, from http://www.bmz.de/en/publications/type_of_publication/information_flyer/information_brochures/Materialie270_africa_marshallplan.pdf

CNRS. (2018). *Production et diffusion de mécanismes miracles dans l'industrie du développement: Les modèles voyageurs confrontés aux contextes*. REAF 2018.

Accessed May 29, 2022, from http://etudes-africaines.cnrs.fr/atelier/production-et-diffusion-de-mecanismes-miracles-dans-lindustrie-du-developpement-les-modeles-voyageurs-confrontes-aux-contextes/

De Haan, A. (2009). *How the aid industry works: An introduction to international development*. Lynne Rienner Publishers.

De Sardan, J. (2019, September 26). *Industrie du développement: les mésaventures des modèles voyageurs*. AOC Media. Accessed May 29, 2022, from https://aoc.media/analyse/2019/09/25/industrie-du-developpement-les-mesaventures-des-modeles-voyageurs/?loggedin=true

Developmentaid. (2018, November 28). *News stream*. Accessed May 29, 2022, from https://www.developmentaid.org/#!/news-stream/post/34686/better-housing-means-better-health-and-well-being-stress-new-who-guidelines?utm_source=Newsletter&utm_medium=Email&utm_campaign=NewsDigest

Easterly, W., & Williamson, C. R. (2012, May 14) "*Rhetoric versus reality: The best and worst of aid agency practices" draft without figures*. Accessed May 29, 2022, from https://ssrn.com/abstract=2058330

Gehring, K., Michaelowa, K., Dreher, A., & Spörri, F. (2017). Aid fragmentation and effectiveness: What do we really know? *World Development, 99*(C), 320–334.

Millennium Challenge Corporation. (n.d.). *Who we select*. Accessed May 29, 2022, from https://www.mcc.gov/who-we-fund

OECD. (2008). *Accra high level forum on aid effectiveness*. OECD.

Swiss Development Cooperation. (n.d.). Accessed November 2018, from https://www.eda.admin.ch/deza/en/home/activities-projects/activities.html

The Economist. (2016, June 11). *Foreign aid: Misplaced charity*. Accessed May 29, 2022, from https://www.economist.com/international/2016/06/11/misplaced-charity

CHAPTER 4

Control, Compliance, and More Control

The donor obsessions with Moving the Money (Chap. 2) and finding new products to develop (Chap. 3) are, however, seriously compromised by another, countervailing obsession—that of control. This has created what could be called a 'counter-bureaucracy,' a set of control, communications, and compliance systems that have been built up to sanitize donors' ponderous delivery mechanisms to Move the Money and to make sure that only proper, unassailable outcomes result (Natsios, 2010, 2–3).

Everyone who has ever dealt with development work is very much aware of the huge and at times absurd amount of bureaucratic control that pervades development structures. Donor funds come straight from national budgets in the case of bilateral donors, or indirectly from member government allocations and replenishments to international agencies (such as the World Bank and the UN system). So it is obvious that accountability for these funds and the images projected of their outcomes must be carefully controlled and crafted. After all, the development industry's existential angst is that taxpayers and their parliamentary representatives in the West will go sour on aid and force dramatic budget cuts, and over the decades there has been no lack of anti-aid types who have railed against supporting free-rider nations and corrupt dictators (Carbonnier, 2010).

Faced with this reality, over the decades foreign aid accountability and control has been one of the constants, and as donor expenditures have extended to more and more countries and sectors and to penetrate more areas with more complex programs and projects, the task of control has

D. Sims, *Development Delusions and Contradictions*,
https://doi.org/10.1007/978-3-031-17770-5_4

become ever more burdensome. Every time there is even a whiff of a scandal or an embarrassing event, the system doubles down. And for good reason, since in the history of development aid there have been some monumental examples of pilfering, funding black holes, and staff transgressions.

But combatting straightforward bribes, kickbacks, budget embezzlement, and other fiddles are only a small part of the control game that donors feel they need to play, and this chapter briefly charts a range of ways that donors keep a very tight ship. These include being exposed to only the smallest, most manageable sets of risks surrounding interventions; designing projects with no-mud-sticks-on-us safeguards; producing financial agreements, contracts, procurement documents, and covenants that are made to absolve them from any embarrassments and to sanitize donor outputs and evaluations; appearing transparent while ensuring that operation details remain as un-transparent as possible; and constructing public relations and communications strategies to guarantee that the media and the public (and even other donors and other governments) only see the bright side of things. Plus, donors set up internal systems to ensure that their service providers (contractors and consultants and INGOs) are completely in compliance with their ever more complicated rules and regulations.

Before proceeding, it needs to be pointed out that this hyper need for control may sound logical, seen from the donor's point of view. But this all-pervasive control has serious negative effects on donor operations themselves, something well known by all who practice the trade. These controls and risk-aversions act as sticky molasses that gum up the flow of funds, not to mention that they work against new ideas and innovative paradigms in project design and disbursement. And it certainly makes the lofty goals of recipient partnership and 'ownership' almost impossible to achieve. It even restricts any supposed strategic shifts in development thinking to hollow cerebral exercises that rarely get beyond the stage of strategy papers.

These control systems and structures that permeate the development industry, their tremendous costs, and their counterproductive results are rarely criticized. But in 2010 Andrew Natsios, the former head of USAID, made considerable waves by stating that: "USAID is now spending as much money on oversight and control as on implementation of the aid program itself. What is more, the staff time needed to comply with all of these paperwork requirements has crowded out any remaining available time for the actual implementation of programs in the field offices. A point can be reached when compliance becomes counterproductive. I believe we are well past that point" (Natsios, 2010, 5). Although he was talking mostly about USAID, his criticism also included other mainstream donors, and he made the point that such control led to a preference for low-risk, easily measurable kinds of service delivery (especially in health) instead of more 'transformative' development work such as building more effective institutions and encouraging policy reform. It is over ten years since these observations were made, but they remain completely valid and, looking at more recent donor behavior, have become even more pertinent.

Donors Avoiding Corruption, or 'No Mud Sticks on Us'

The biggest bugaboo in donor activities is any whiff of corruption—mainly in contract tendering and awards, subcontracting, financial reporting, and procurement—that could stick on a particular donor. Since corrupt practices, especially bribes and kickbacks and patronage are the order of the day in many countries of the Rest (Chap. 13), and since a sizable portion of any aid ends up in or passes through country governments, fighting any corruption surrounding development funding is a never-ending preoccupation with donors.

Avoiding corruption has always been part of donor operations, but if any boost was needed, they came with Wolfensohn's famous speech in 1996 signaling the World Bank's determination to fight the "cancer of corruption." This opened the floodgates for explicit anticorruption policies and measures and elevated zero tolerance to new heights. For example, the World Bank has since adopted a wide number of control systems and procedures, and in 2001 the Integrity Vice Presidency was created as an independent unit. This unit now also carries out internal audits and risk assessments of upcoming projects and programs to identify weak points in design that might be exploited in implementation. The World Bank also has an Ethics and Business Conduct Department that promotes the development and application of the highest ethical standards by staff members in the performance of their duties. Another example is BMZ's Anticorruption and Integrity Programme, which was formed in 2004 and includes GIZ's Anti-Corruption Works, a support program that identifies corruption risks in sectoral programs. Another is DfID, who is required to carry out individual country corruption assessment reports.

Such means of fighting corruption can be found in virtually every donor organization, but the result is an atmosphere of caution and serious cases of risk-aversion. Brian Levy, writing in 2014, pointed out "the natural response to the anticorruption crusade was extreme aversion to risk. This reached its absurdist limit in an investment project in India that incorporated into its design the recruitment of close to 300 internal financial auditors to monitor how the money would be spent" (Levy, 2014, 206).

What should be clear is that the squeaky-clean imperative is applied almost exclusively to the donor realm, creating islands of probity in seas awash with hanky-panky. But outside these bubbles, the attitude is, 'Please, I just don't want to know about it!'[1] This is not to say that the development industry does not give policy advice to combat more general corruption in the Rest, and since the late 1990s there have been numerous initiatives (and even more dialogue) launched under the rubric of better governance. But these are simply a tiny part of donor agency's huge portfolios of technical assistance and advisory efforts, and they can hardly be compared to donor efforts to keep their own operations beyond reproach.

Of course, someone working in the development business, especially close up on the disbursement side—especially in contracting, tendering, competitive bidding, no objections, or funding release, knows that a huge amount of fiddling goes on that remains below the radar, no matter how much oversight and how many safeguards are in place (Chap. 5). And when such malfeasance does come to light, donors are usually reluctant to investigate potential corruption under their watch unless it is unavoidable.

Designing Projects with Zero-Embarrassment Safeguards

In response to a series of extremely embarrassing infrastructure projects that were executed in the 1980s, the World Bank began installing a system of safeguards to be integrated in all project preparation and implementation processes, something that would ensure that in the future such

[1] The squeaky-clean imperative sometimes simply means keeping one's head down. In the 1980s USAID commissioned an expensive Sinai development strategy. By chance it was noticed that several newly purchased project vehicles still had stickers showing they came from another USAID project. Evidently USAID financed the purchase of these vehicles twice! What was the reaction of the Chief of Party? "Jesus, just don't mention it, and let's get someone in to sanitize the vehicles."

projects would neither have negative environmental impacts nor awful repercussions on the affected populations. Thus were born two safeguard systems, social and environmental. These have been institutionalized and formalized within the Bank for all projects, without exception, and have been imitated, more or less, by all donors whose project portfolios include large infrastructure or investment components.

The World Bank specifies that it is "the Borrower's responsibilities for assessing, managing and monitoring environmental and social risks and impacts associated with each stage of a project supported by the Bank, … in order to achieve environmental and social outcomes consistent with the Environmental and Social Standards" (World Bank, 2018). These are spelled out in no less than thirteen detailed 'operational policies' and various other directives, and they include such subjects as environmental assessments, environmental action plans, natural habitats, water resource management, pest management, indigenous peoples, physical cultural resources, involuntary settlement, compulsory land acquisition, and forests.

The World Bank (and other donors, including USAID) carefully screen their projects for potential negative environmental and social impacts, and this can trigger expensive investigations. Task team leaders and managers, anxious to keep project preparation on track, very frequently modify or simply drop what might be risky sub-components because of the difficulties of gaining the whole range of needed approvals, plus the onerous monitoring required during project implementation. Likewise, projects that require involuntary resettlement or compulsory land purchase, such as slum upgrading, industrial expansion, and flood barriers (very topical these days due to rising sea levels) are very likely to be dropped or limited in scale to only the smallest and least problematic scope.

A flavor of the almost obsessive detail of these strictures can be seen in the 76-page "Environmental and Social Framework" prepared for the World Bank-financed Sri Lanka Local Development Support Project (Ministry of Provincial Councils and Local Governments and Sports, 2018).[2] It not only lays down regulatory requirements and safeguard policies, it delves into the mechanics of managing these during project design

[2] This report, although technically authored by a Sri Lankan Ministry, is the direct work of World Bank staff and consultants and is expanded, with considerable cut and paste, from an earlier 2010 environmental and social management framework.

and execution by contractors, including subproject ranking, screening, impact assessment and mitigation, capacity building, and grievance redress mechanisms, and it also spells out the composition of the teams from the PIU and local administration who will carry out safeguard categorization and screening and which officials will sign off on them.

Some form of safeguard systems may be necessary, but as written up and applied by the World Bank and other donor agencies they certainly have the potential to complicate and bureaucratize project efforts, set up more pro forma window-dressing and box-checking, and at the same time thoroughly confuse recipient governments and agencies. Furthermore, this is another example of donors creating their own islands of excellence, probity, and blamelessness. What about the loan borrower's behavior on non-donor financed projects? Who cares! The idea is sometimes advanced that eventually these safeguard concepts will rub off onto borrowers and be applied generally, a kind of non-mandatory demonstration-by-doing. But it appears this is rarely the case (World Bank, 2018).

The safeguarding approach is also to be found in recent attempts to eliminate sexual exploitation in development projects. In response to embarrassing news coming out of INGO and UN agency operations, and with considerable angst generated by the global #MeToo movement, in 2018 DfID set up a Safeguarding Unit and proceeded to churn out very detailed procedures and guidelines, including zero tolerance for sexual exploitation, abuse, and harassment. Such abuse has unfortunately been part of the development industry for decades, but suddenly it was perceived as a serious public relations debacle that could threaten funding. Global conferences on the issue were organized and 'due diligence' mechanisms came into vogue. A DfID report dripping with self-righteousness claimed: "At the Safeguarding Summit on 5 March 2018, the Secretary of State (SoS) announced that DfID would, with (sic) put in place new, enhanced and specific standards for UK Charities and NGOs. The standards cover partner policies and processes on safeguarding, whistleblowing, human resources, risk management, codes of conduct and governance" (DfID, 2018, 2). This sounds like a sensible if tardy move, but it is another example of donors trying to appear to be squeaky-clean after scandals that, until threatened with negative press, they simply had hoped would fade away.

Control Through Financing Agreements, Contracts, Covenants, and Oversight Arrangements

Financing agreements between donors and recipient governments, the bedrock of most development funding, are usually blessedly brief, simply stating overall funding, goals, milestones, and disbursement schedules. But their ambiguity (a necessary requirement to get an agreement signed) is more than made up by the avalanche of contractual stipulations, covenants, and other legalize that follow, all of which are imposed by the donor. These texts, which are always voluminous (e.g., 35 pages for a simple two-month individual consultant contract) are full of qualifiers that craftily absolve donors from any financial or legal responsibility and with more bureaucracy, more layers, and of course more control. And preparing these texts require more small armies, in this case composed of lawyers and accountants.

Obsession with control enters big time after a project begins to be implemented and funds begin to flow. Payments are dependent on massive reporting and documentation, including time sheets, inspection reports, no-objection certificates, etc. How much time does a donor official or his contractor/consultant spend on making sure there are receipts for expenditures, that they are justified, not over some arbitrary limit, and correctly coded? Arcane rules and expenditure ceilings, some coming from previous fits of donor cost-cutting campaigns, must be followed. And the irony is that waste, fiddles, and sheer malfeasance are hardly curtailed. As long as the reporting is correctly filled out, coded, and submitted on time, a clever contractor can still easily pad paid days, per diems, and expenses. And these control systems make the local or international expert, supposedly key to a project activity, become an integer who often spends as much time making sure the paperwork is correct than in applying his or her 'expertise.'

Beyond this, many are the ways that an obsession for control and apparent blamelessness leads to ridiculous outcomes. For example, there are rigid conflict-of-interest stipulations that bar someone who has worked on preparing a particular project (in scoping a project or in preparing the terms of reference) from being included in a subsequent tender. Well, it is frequently this person who is by far the best one for a study, evaluation, or other assignment, precisely because s/he knows the scene and the usually convoluted background to a program.

Another example is the near-universal prohibition against 'topping-up' salaries in donor activities (Transparency International, n.d.). This had been a widespread practice in the past, where a donor or his contractor, desperate to engage key local officials or functionaries on a project or even to participate in workshops, would offer some small monetary rewards for their efforts, thus helping to ensure a local buy-in to a project or at least its smooth running. For most donors this practice has become a strict no-no, and the fiction must be maintained that government counterparts and their staff are motivated and act strictly with the best intentions. Worse, these local officials are expected to devote considerable extra time and effort on project operations (and attend endless workshops and roundtables) without reward, even if their monthly salaries are only a pittance, often less than the daily subsistence allowance enjoyed by their foreign partners (Chap. 17). The same distortion is found in capacity building activities, where the person chosen to be part of in-country training sessions is assumed to gleefully drop everything for weeks at a time, without any material gain. Or that, to satisfy the donor penchant for ostensible local participation 'at all phases of a project,' the affected citizens are expected to joyfully spend their own time to be part of some participation jamboree without any compensation, even though they are the poor people who are actually the object of the whole exercise.

There are imaginative ways around some of these impositions and a certain flexibility or logic is sometimes actually allowed in procurement. Some donors are better at it than others. But in all aid organizations, especially in procurement and payment processing, the bureaucratic personality is prominent, someone who sees his or her position to be that of a gate keeper and who measures his worth in being difficult if not downright obstructive. It leads to a not infrequent attitude among consultants that bureaucratic control is actually the main activity and *raison d'être* of a particular donor.

To be fair, there is a quandary that is not easily resolved in procurement, especially for technical assistance services. Ostensibly the aim is to hire the best individual or firm for a particular job, but the system has been abused by long-standing cozy relationships between donor agencies and contractors and frequently reinforced by buddy-buddy systems, revolving doors, or simply professional solidarity. Thus, over the last two decades more and more procurement rules and safeguards have been introduced by donor agencies to curtail such favoritism, and the result is an almost impenetrable thicket of bureaucratic steps and formulaic structures.

Managing Risks in a Risk-Avoidance World

Another aspect of control is risk management, which has become another fashion amongst donors, yet again something adopted from the corporate world. The trend started in the 1990s when many donors, especially IFIs, for example, set up risk management units, tasked with looking at risk mitigation for their loans and other interventions in the Rest, on the assumption that the 'risk' was that projects might fall off the design path. Today every donor project document includes a section on risk identification and assessment and how it might be mitigated. Thus, you have risks along the line of "the recipient does not carry out the recommended reforms or improve governance prescriptions" and the rating is low/medium/high. This is supposed to help identify ways to mitigate this risk and allows, if scores are awful enough, for the donor to kill the project. But this almost never happens, and instead some additional technical assistance is usually tacked on to 'mitigate' whatever risk has been identified.

Such a risk aversion and its results can be seen in the Value for Money (VfM) agenda, a circa 2010 development fad much ballyhooed by DfID and taken up by others, that at first glance sound entirely reasonable. It called for accountability of public funds, assurance that these funds are used for their stated purposes, and that all is conducted transparently to avoid corruption and waste. But as Paul Yanguas wrote in the Banality of Certainty blog, "The VfM agenda and its proponents, however well meaning, are forcing foreign aid agencies to choose between irrelevance and subterfuge. Either practitioners will look after their career prospects first and design the kind of low-risk projects that politicians like to talk about but rarely lead to sustainable development, or they will obfuscate the very real politics of development in order to comply with the twin demands of accounting and transparency."[3]

Donors and Fake Transparency

Great pronouncements are made on a regular basis about the importance of transparency in all aspects of the development business. Ever since corruption became a hot issue in development circles in the 1990s,

[3] (Yanguas, 2018) The quote is from "The banality of certainty (book excerpt)," 21 February 2018, https://pabloyanguas.com/the-banality-of-certainty-book-excerpt/ Accessed 1 June 2022.

continuous and oh-so-proper campaigns have been launched to boost accountability and transparency both in aid-recipient countries and within donor structures. The Paris Declaration in 2005 on Aid Effectiveness and the Accra Agenda for Action in 2008 set out accountability and transparency as important goals, stating: "We will make aid more transparent. Developing countries will facilitate parliamentary oversight by implementing greater transparency in public financial management, including public disclosure of revenues, budgets, expenditures, procurement and audits. Donors will publicly disclose regular, detailed and timely information on volume, allocation and, when available, results of development expenditure to enable more accurate budget, accounting and audit by developing countries" (OECD, n.d., 20). These commitments, at least in official reports, reviews, assessments, and indicators, have been revisited in multiple high-level forums on Aid Effectiveness. Going by what these reviews say, both donors and recipients have greatly improved their transparency and accountability, and in fact this has been one of the few bragging points about increased aid effectiveness over the 2005 to 2018 period.

Donors have certainly made public some aspects of their aid moneys and expenditure systems more accessible to the public and country legislatures, especially considering that, since they are repeatedly asking for more transparency among their country partners, they need to seem to be practicing what they preach. But this is a carefully controlled transparency, mainly achieved by publishing bald facts about moneys being spent, even in minute detail. For example, DfID listed every single expenditure item made over a year—mainly airfares—and has posted the monthly salaries of their staff. The same can be said for the World Bank, who posts not only salaries but also the value of perks and retirement benefits. Other donors have made similar disclosures.

But this is trivial stuff that hardly constitutes real information on funding flows, end expenditures, disbursement targets, and conditionalities met/unmet, let alone serious evaluations of project impact or effectiveness or, heaven forbid, frank disclosure of failed projects and wayward funds. Such information may exist in bits and pieces somewhere in the public domain, but it is very hard if not impossible to find. And inquisitive journalists or researchers who try to dig into the operations of donors and look into their internal reports will inevitably be referred straight to the donor's communications department or press office where any requests will be politely stonewalled. This lack of overall transparency remains a constant among donors, and bureaucratic desires to avoid making public anything and everything still dominates.

'External Communications' as Control

Another way donor agencies exercise control over what goes out—and what outsiders see when they look in—can be found in their formidable public relations and communications machines. These are the donor's main organs tasked at presenting a controlled image to the outside world and to influence, shape, and even control how media reports on their work, and they represent carefully crafted antidotes to any inconvenient news about failure or other negative press.

All donors have these entities. They are most frequently called 'external relations' or 'communications' departments these days, and donors have carefully nurtured their evolution and expanded their footprints. In the earlier stages of the Development Era, there were more modest affairs usually called simply public relations or media departments with straightforward roles—that of composing and distributing press releases, preparing speeches for top management, and keeping in good stead with major Western news organizations. But over the decades they evolved and expanded into organizations that have taken on new functions, new names, and new profiles that increasingly exhibit corporate traits and vocabularies. Today, their mission statements and job descriptions are full of phrases like "mitigate reputational risks," "develop and implement coherent communication strategies," "create the business case for investment in process and enhancements," "maintain relationships with critical internal and/or external constituencies to foster strategic partnerships," and, especially, "identify potential risks to (the donor's) reputation."[4] And these entities and their chiefs are now also likely to be very close to the top echelons of donor structures, both organizationally and personally, and to have quite substantial budgets (IBRD/IDA, 2016, Table 3–6).[5]

The World Bank's own external relations machine is a good example. Its Office of External Relations, already a formidable entity, was upgraded in 2013 to come under a new and broader External and Corporate Relations Vice Presidency (ECR). The ECR also manages the WBG's corporate identity and branding, is responsible for the WBG's corporate

[4] There phrases are taken from a World Bank job description for an international affairs officer at its Berlin office, http://gesinesjobtipps.de/world-bank-group-international-affairs-officer-16-7/, Accessed 7 March 2018.

[5] For example, in FY2016 the budget for the World Bank's External and Corporate Relations was $57 million, compared to, for example, $35 million for Evaluations.

online and social media presence, and produces content for a wide variety of platforms, including print, broadcast, and web.

Other donors also have considerable communications and public relations capacities and most have been putting increasing emphasis on these. USAID calls its entity the Bureau for Legislative and Public Affairs, which serves as USAID's central point of contact with Congress, the media, and interested stakeholders from the international development community. The UK's DfID had a Communications Division with 39 specialist communications posts, and in addition it had a number of 'embedded communicators' spread across the organization. And it ratcheted up its communications capacities to combat negative press coverage, particularly from Britain's infamous daily tabloids, by forming what was called a rebuttal unit. Then there is the United Nations Communications Group, which since 2002 has become the common communications platform of the United Nations system. It provides leadership in communications for UN country communications teams, identifying new and creative ways to show how UN programs are delivering results and are promoting a coherent image of the United Nations. Yet each of the 20-odd UN specialized agencies *also* maintains their own public relations units, such as Media Centres (UN-Habitat), Offices of Corporate Communications (FAO), or Divisions of Communication (UNICEF). All these specialized agencies are proud to mention that their communications directors have long experience in the world of communications and a close familiarity with corporate communications.

Not to be outdone, international development NGOs devote huge efforts in external communications—proportionately probably even more than donor agencies—for the simple reason that they are constantly in need of serious fundraising. This fact is brought out in an interesting 2013 study on INGOs on how "power relations, tensions, and position-taking shape the arguments and choices made by NGOs in their efforts to produce material on suffering and development"(Orgad, 2013, 1). There is an ambivalence that "is manifested vividly in the structural relations between the fundraising and marketing departments, and the communications, campaigns, and advocacy departments, and their conflicts over how to visualize the NGO cause" (Orgad, 2013, 6).

The history of the evolution of donor communications bodies shows how their remits are constantly being expanded and how they increasingly capture top management space. A good example of this can be found in World Bank archives about how the World Bank's modest Public Relations

Department of the 1960s evolved over the years into its External and Corporate Relations Vice Presidency in 2013 (World Bank Group Archives Holdings, n.d.). This archive makes for instructive reading, to show not only how frequently the titles, bosses, and names of the Bank's communications and public relations entity have been changed, but also how often top communications management has been replaced and how often lines of reporting have also been shuffled up to top management.

Control Through Public Relations Firms

Although most control of the images of donors and their worth are carried out within their own increasingly sophisticated communications and external relations departments, some donors have taken to hiring outside public relations firms to sanitize imagery and at the same time filter communications with journalists and other outsiders. Such a practice has become quite common in some UN agencies, where expensive PR firms are hired to carefully manage material for release and to be the frontline vis-à-vis outsiders (Crossette, 2021). As one observer put it: "Why would any agency of the UN want to hire high-priced PR firms to speak for them? ... Don't they have enough trust in their own missions to tell the public what is going on within their organizations?" (Crossette, 2021).[6]

Control, Communications, and 'Promoting Ourselves to Ourselves'

When it comes to public relations and communications, donors consistently rely on those who are professionals at precisely that, and who are equally at ease in promoting corporate interests as they are in getting out favorable information about international development, as if there was no difference between the two. Those who work in donor communications departments represent a world that is built upon shared professional interests and is pretty much enclosed upon itself. Thus, it is illuminating as well as entertaining to read a 2019 autobiography by a communications specialist who spent almost 20 years at various posts within UNDP. This book lays bare some of the mundane traits of trying to construct banal and squeaky-clean profiles of how UNDP operates in various countries and

[6] The quote is from Stephen Schlesinger, author of "Act of Creation: The Founding of the United Nations."

how it projects its innovative credentials (Hart, 2018). Her critical take on the development industry and the increasingly important role that communications (aka propaganda) play in it are refreshing: "For me, the innovation lexicon stifled any kind of free thinking (…). So many meetings, conferences, reports and reporting mechanisms, either demanded by donors or internally generated to justify our existence. Too much of the communications work now involved promoting ourselves to ourselves through self-congratulatory Tweets, Facebook posts and web stories" (Hart, 2018, 166).

Criticism Is Not Welcome

A certain amount of subdued criticism is allowed within the development world, especially in obscure lessons-learned texts that show how, although successful, a project or initiative has some faults and that we-can-do-better-next-time-around. But anyone within the industry who publishes sharp critiques of how donors actually operate and the less than edifying results will not be welcome. Such was the case of William Easterly, senior economist at the World Bank, who had been writing serious papers that pointed to some of the Bank's many foibles and who, in 2002, was summarily dismissed. In this case, the Bank pretended he had simply contravened its unauthorized disclosure rules, but everyone knew that it was his critical writing that put him out the door (Rowland, 2003).

Some individual critics from inside the industry can go, as Easterly did, into academia and continue to publish. But for those who are still in need of a job—even as a consultant—criticizing donor agencies is a great way to work one's way out of a career.

Quite a number of former and/or retired donor professionals end up in academia, and although then free to write what they want, this niche for analyzing the dysfunctions of the development world is a small and poorly funded one, restricted to narrow audiences partly dominated by left-leaning thinkers who deplore globalization and neoliberal 'hegemony' over poor countries. Others who end up in professorial positions stick to the techno-objectivity of their development specializations, perhaps putting a slightly sharper edge to their writing, but very cognizant that their audiences are either students who themselves see the industry as a career path or those who are part of the development show and who are convinced that a little reform can nudge the ship back onto correct paths.

There are a handful of watchdog institutions that are devoted to uncovering the foibles of donors, such as the Bank Information System and the Bretton Woods Project. But these are not well funded, and, in addition, they are outsider entities and are precluded from uncovering much of what is wrong with donor policies and behavior. As soon as a donor realizes that a researcher is part of this watchdog world, alarm bells ring and any queries, however benign, are shunted off to the donor's public relations or communications department where they are, predictably, stonewalled.

Evaluation as Another Means of Control

For decades virtually all Western donors have devoted substantial efforts to monitor, review, and evaluate projects, programs, and even strategies. They have enshrined this both in their own structures and in their repetitive commissioning of post-project evaluations. To many, it is these carefully crafted evaluations that are the most prominent outside face of what an aid agency or multinational investment bank does, and we take a good look at this mini-world of evaluations (Chap. 7), where we show that donor evaluations exhibit heavy doses of what is called 'positive bias' in their reporting or in avoiding contentious issues and embarrassing projects. At the same time, these evaluations perform an important form of control over what the outside world sees.

Controlling Show Time

An inescapable feature of development projects is field visits by Very Important Persons, something as old as the industry itself and an endless subject of amusing anecdotes and silly 'clashes of civilizations.' Visits by donor headquarters staff, ambassadors, host country ministers and permanent secretaries, development 'influencers,' and—what is really key—donor country parliamentarians, are arranged by donors on a regular basis. This is control at its most important, that of projecting a carefully crafted image of success to those who really matter. For smaller visits it is the donor's country offices that arrange them, but larger operations—especially if the media is expected—are in the hands of donor public relations personnel. These latter can be real circuses, where visits are carefully choreographed, and where 'beneficiaries' are called on to play star roles along with local politicians, local administrative staff, and project employees.

Everyone involved with a project has to make an effort pull during show time, and even managers and specialized experts are required to help with staged events, speeches, and the like. Such operations are mostly colossal wastes of time and money as well as organizational nightmares (transport, security, refreshments, and media). It is a kind of lets-all-pull-together since, just maybe, these shows will lead to a project extension or to greater funding, and perhaps the chance that those managing the show will gain personal recognition in the wider donor world. And one function of controlling show time is to ensure that the wrong things are not seen by outsiders. Keeping tabs on inquisitive journalists and official visitors and steering them away from anything that might have a whiff of failure are considered as important as presenting glowing success.

Summing Up: Irrelevance Is the Cost of Running a Tight Ship

Donors like to control information on all aspects of their development work, and this control can easily be called obsessive. As we have explained, from the donor agency's point of view this control is perceived as an important part of how to burnish its image and manage risk, but control can seriously slow down, gum up, compromise, and devalue a donor's real development work. The result is a kind of plodding, banal business-as-usual control. We have seen this in efforts to make sure that there is no whiff of corruption or fiddling that might attach to donor operations (no mud sticks on us), in constructing elaborate project safeguard systems to ensure there is no embarrassing social or environmental fallout, in putting in place a bewildering array of formalistic agreements, covenants, and oversight mechanisms of control, in sanitizing all and every donor output, in using evaluations as another tool for control, and in tightly orchestrating VIP visits. And it should be added that sharp criticisms of the development industry from within are not tolerated and can easily lead to ending one's career in development.

The cumulative effect of the obsession with control is counterproductive even to the professed objectives of development agencies. It does not have any positive impact on how recipient countries manage their own development affairs, it makes a joke of recipient ownership, it makes it nearly impossible to be nimble, proactive, and supportive of innovation, and it gums up project delivery systems to the extent that any goodwill is dissipated long before project results are measured. And it certainly doesn't lead to more effective organizations that can operate in what is inherently a risk-filled world.

References

Carbonnier, G. (2010). Official development assistance once more under fire from critics. *Revue internationale de politique de developpement, 1*, 137–142. Accessed June 1, 2022, from https://journals.openedition.org/poldev/141

Crossette, B. (2021, July 14). *Public relations industry grabs a foothold in the UN. Pass Blue.* Accessed June 1, 2022, from https://www.passblue.com/2021/07/14/the-public-relations-industry-grabs-a-foothold-in-the-un/

DfID. (2018, June). *Enhanced due diligence: Safeguarding for external partners.* Better Delivery Department. Accessed from https://www.ukaiddirect.org/wp-content/uploads/2018/07/Enhanced-Due-Diligence-Guide-for-external-partners-June-2018.pdf

Hart, C. (2018). *From Hollywood to Holy Wars: Hounding celebs, dodging bullets, raising a family abroad.* Jalan Publications.

IBRD/IDA. (2016, September 22). *FY2017 World Bank budget.* Accessed June 1, 2022, from http://documents.worldbank.org/curated/en/542111474665164660/pdf/108487-BR-PUBLIC-FY17-WB-Budget-for-Public-Disclosure.pdf

Levy, B. (2014). *Working with the grain: Integrating governance and growth in development strategies.* Oxford University Press.

Ministry of Provincial Councils and Local Governments and Sports. (2018, September). *Environmental and social management framework, North East Local Services Improvement Project.* Accessed June 1, 2022, from http://documents.worldbank.org/curated/en/512251520434465049/pdf/SFG4113-REVISED-EA-P163305-PUBLIC-Disclosed-9-25-2018.pdf

Natsios, A. (2010, July). *The clash of the counter-bureaucracy and development.* Center for Global Development Essay. Accessed from https://www.cgdev.org/publication/clash-counter-bureaucracy-and-development

OECD. (n.d.). *The Paris declaration for aid effectiveness and the Accra Agenda for Action 2005-2008.* Accessed June 1, 2022, from https://www.oecd.org/dac/effectiveness/34428351.pdf

Orgad, S. (2013). *Visualizers of solidarity: Organizational politics in humanitarian and international development NGOs (Visual Communications 2013), LSE Research Online (abstract).* Accessed June 1, 2022, from https://core.ac.uk/download/pdf/16379029.pdf

Rowland, B. (2003). Dissenting economists. *SAIS Review, 23*(1).

Transparency International. (n.d.). *Anti-corruption Resource Center website, Salary top ups and their impact on corruption*. Accessed June 1, 2022, from https://www.u4.no/publications/salary-top-ups-and-their-impact-on-corruption.pdf

World Bank. (2018). *Environmental and social standards*. Accessed June 1, 2022, from https://www.worldbank.org/en/projects-operations/environmental-and-social-framework

World Bank Group Archives Holdings. (n.d.). *External Relations Vice Presidency and reporting units (history)*. Accessed June 1, 2022, from https://archivesholdings.worldbank.org/office-of-external-relations

Yanguas, P. (2018). *Why we lie about aid*. Zed Books.

CHAPTER 5

Procurement

Those comfortably—if somewhat stressfully—employed as donor technical and management staff only account for a small fraction of those who populate the development business. Many, many more people are hired by agencies for time-bound advisory, management, design, and consulting services under a raft of procurement mechanisms. Also, flowing through these mechanisms are the acquisition of goods and a host construction, logistics, training, and various mundane business services. Collectively, all of this procurement represents a complicated and multi-layered bureaucratic world of its own, one that can be estimated to process at least 70 percent of all ODA. It is a world that defines much of what donors are able to do and not to do. But little is ever written about this side of the development business, since it is too banal for most academics, and even donors themselves—normally so ready to reflect-to-death about their noble interventions in the Rest—seem to have largely ignored the subject.

More and more it seems that donors do little by themselves. The span of activities that needs to be 'procured' or outsourced runs the whole gamut of the project or program cycles, from conception all the way through to terminal evaluation. The repeated outsourcing of tasks to consulting firms, specialized service providers, and INGOs is colossal. And these in turn seek out and subcontract both individuals, local NGOs, and other firms. Without all of this procurement and sub-procurement, donor activities in the development world would grind to a halt.

D. Sims, *Development Delusions and Contradictions*,
https://doi.org/10.1007/978-3-031-17770-5_5

Foreign aid procurement in all its aspects represents a little-known world of bureaucratic rules, regulations, and oversight that is supposed to generate competitive markets for needed services, and it is a world that needs to be understood. To do this we first look at procurement itself, the 'markets' that it has institutionalized and its growth, proliferation, and bureaucratization over the decades. Then we look at the 'terms of reference,' the bedrock document from which practically all development work flows. Then we take zoom into the hallowed submarket for experts and expertise, the need for which has been a touchstone of international development for decades. As part of this, consultants, consulting firms, and other service providers are given attention, since it is these animals that have come to be indispensable features of the development landscape. Altogether, this chapter allows the reader to comprehend that the various procurement structures and the people who populate and react to them are important factors in the increasing confusions, contradictions, and even dumbing-down of the development industry.

Development Procurement and Its Global Markets

The procurement of expertise, management, and other services for development work used to be relatively straightforward. Donors would send out a limited Request for Proposals (RFPs) or directly invite firms or individuals to bid for time-bound assignments. Sometimes the recipient agency (or borrower) would themselves carry out tendering, especially for engineering and infrastructure works. Although from the early years all development agencies had procurement regulations in place, a firm was often likely to know about an upcoming bid before formal announcements were made, and professional networks and reputation played a big part in this.

But no more. Development procurement has increased many-fold in size, value, and complexity, and more and more rigid structures and processes have been put in place. Both bilateral and multilateral donors have thick procurement bibles, procurement departments, procurement experts, evaluation committees, award committees, and detailed procurement plans, and they even sponsor procurement training programs and conferences. Plus, the same rules and procedures are imposed on any procurement that partner countries carry out as part of donor loans and grants.

The European Commission has probably outshone all other donors in its rule-bound approach. The EU's procurement bible is called

"Procurement and Grants for European Union External Actions—A Practical Guide" and is known in the business simply as PRAG (European Commission, 2019). It is a huge, formidable, confusing, and frequently updated compendium that governs service contracts, supply contracts, works contracts, and grants, usually for work carried out under the Directorate General for International Cooperation and Development or the Directorate General for Neighborhood and Enlargement Negotiations.[1] Its 2019 edition runs to 210 pages and has 194 separate annexes (mostly model contracts and forms), and since 1996 it has gone through 11 versions. It is anything but 'practical,' and understanding its contents alone makes someone a senior expert! Just mentioning the word PRAG to contractor (both those in the tendering process and those implementing an award) is likely to produce cold sweats if not anxiety attacks.

Although most donors do allow single source contracting, there are so many caveats attached and such rigid procedures to follow that such direct awards are rarely used, no matter how well justified. And neither used is the direct hire of individual experts, although for very short-term assignments some donors (e.g., the World Bank) are mercifully relaxed. Going straight to the individual or firm obviously best for a particular job would save much time and money and reduce the delays, discontinuity, and procedural traffic jams that competitive procurement requires, but this is now almost unheard of. The fear by donor staff of being accused of even a whiff of favoritism through buddy-buddy networks or other improper channels is so strong it can be paralyzing.

It doesn't help that large engineering and management consulting firms in the West, the main beneficiaries of this world of procurement, form important lobbies both within their own countries and internationally, and they are very ready to object to anything they perceive as not fair or above board in a donor's procurement processes. This certainly adds to the fear of any step that might be construed as less than 100 percent by the book, and it keeps donor procurement departments very much on their toes, mainly to make sure they are shielded from any complaints or accusations of favoritism, even those that are spurious.

The main procurement modality for international development is International Competitive Bidding (ICB)—something stipulated by all

[1] For some reason the PRAG does not apply to humanitarian aid and social projection, which comes under another directorate general.

IFIs and also by most bilateral donors—for tenders over a certain value.[2] This opens up bidding from any prequalified company from almost any country, and this is supposed to guarantee the maximum number of bidders and thus the greatest degree of competition, lowest prices, and least amount of opaqueness. Below this threshold, National Competitive Bidding (NCB) applies to much smaller domestic markets. This arrangement sounds logical and, as something that has been in place for decades, is now accepted without fuss. But there are occasional voices from the Rest (in this case Nicaragua) that have pointed out that such a system is eternally pitched in favor of big international (read mostly Western) firms, and the practice "... severely limits the possibilities for developing countries to use government procurement as an instrument of their economic and social development policy, fostering and promoting their own businesses and sectors or regions considered key for national development" (Vogl, 2011, 3). More than this, each donor has their own routines and specifics when it comes to procurement. These may be similar in intent, but each donor insists on its own details, and as a result a recipient government and its many potential recipient ministries and agencies will need to puzzle over the intricacies of several systems.

If the donor itself is the procurer, it uses its own specialized offices and directly deals with bidders. But just as often donors put procurement in the hands of the recipient country and the executing agency that has been designated for a particular project. This is particularly true of IFI loans, the logic being: 'It's their money, isn't it?' But when one looks at the procurement guidelines and pro forma application and disbursement requirements set out by these IFIs, it becomes clear that a borrower must conform to their detailed rules and procedures at every step of the way. The aim is always noble, as, for example, is stated by Germany's development bank: "KfW shall ensure that the funds provided are spent as economically as possible. It will ensure that the contracts are awarded on the basis of fair and transparent competition that offers equal opportunities to all participating bidders. This is designed to identify the most suitable bidder according to performance and price" (KfW Groupe, 2016, 3). But the rules and conditions imposed to guarantee these fine objectives are necessarily complicated and, although efforts are made from time to time to streamline procedures and align them with those of other donors, there is

[2] For example, the threshold in 2020 was between $3 and $40 million for ADB sub-project packages.

an intrinsic bureaucratic and procedural burden that bedevils such procurement and makes a joke out of anything like real 'ownership' on the recipient side.[3]

It is the usual donor agencies that are the major users of procurement systems. A breakdown of procurement announcements by the number of tenders is given by DevelopmentAid for the first quarter of 2020, and this shows that a whopping 14,282 tenders were published by a total of 122 development agencies, the top ten of which were: (Developmentaid, 2019)[4]

World Bank	3285 tenders
UNDP	1928 tenders
ADB	1270 tenders
Non-profits (NGOs and charities)	809 tenders
European Commission	651 tenders
FAO	648 tenders
AfDB	506 tenders
UNICEF	431 tenders
GIZ	372 tenders
US Department of Agriculture	300 tenders

This data only relates to three months of 2020, it may not cover all development tenders, and there may be some double counting. But it gives a general idea of how voluminous tendering is in the development business and how 'the usual suspects' dominate the international tendering process. The load on donors is truly impressive; for example, from this data it can be inferred that the World Bank must deal with new tenders at a rate of 52 per business day! The same source also gives an idea of the main development sectors to which these tenders relate. The top ten are: (Developmentaid, 2019)

Civil engineering	2221 tenders
Information and communication technology	1533 tenders

[3]For example, in 2015 the World Bank, recognizing that the older system had serious shortcomings, issued a new Procurement Framework which was aimed at better project procurement. But these changes were mostly cosmetic. For a critique of the new system and how it remains very complex, see Borson (2017).

[4]Developmentaid (2019), "TOP-10 sectors targeted by international development donors in early 2020," 24 June 2020, https://www.developmentaid.org/#!/news-stream/post/68133/top-10-sectors-targeted-by-international-development-donors-in-early-2020 Accessed 2 June 2022.

Industry, commerce, and services	1122 tenders
Water and sanitation	1010 tenders
Environment and natural resource management	905 tenders
Training	880 tenders
Health	799 tenders
Agriculture	722 tenders
Media and communications	693 tenders
Monitoring and evaluation	668 tenders

This gives a hint of the huge variety of subjects that are the targets of procurement activities, but it also shows that traditional infrastructure projects still dominate the business. If civil engineering and water and sanitation were combined, these would represent a total of 23 percent of all development tenders, and these are on average very much larger in value than those in other sectors.

The Procurement Process for Firms

For almost all procurement for services from firms, the process is similar and can be said to follow five steps, at least for traditional international development work. *First step* is the preparation of the tender by the donor or the recipient government's executing agency, usually with the aid of consultants, and usually quite a lengthy process. The single most important element will be preparing the terms of reference (ToR) or scope of work, and most tenders will state the number person days or months of specific expertise required or will give an indicative total budget allocated for the project. *Second step* is the Expression of Interest (EOI) that is published directly by the donor or national implementing agency, and the EOI is a kind prequalification. *Third step* is the sending out of Requests for Proposals (RFPs) or Requests for Appointments (RFAs) to a shortlist of four to ten prequalified bidders, based on the EOIs received. These are usually very detailed documents and will include the essential ToR and the required expertise and qualifications of experts. Considerable supporting documentation will be required, including detailed CVs and lists of references. And carefully spelled out will also be the requirements for submitting the proposal, including the all-important deadline. And separate financial and technical proposals must be prepared. In other words, there is a huge amount of work for the firms bidding, and all of this must be done within a very short month or two. *Fourth step* is the review of the technical and financial proposals and the evaluation of bids by the donor/client, with the technical proposal normally being opened first. A technical evaluation committee assigns points, and the financial proposal is similarly given points. In theory most tenders have bid assessment systems that put more weight on the technical quality rather than the price, but the mechanical scoring of technical requirements means that total technical scores do not vary much between one bid and another, and thus price is still extremely important, even decisive. *Fifth step* is negotiating contracts, to which the highest scoring firm or consortium is invited, and this in itself can be a long-drawn out and contentious process, sometimes taking over a year or more. (It is rare for the bidder to withdraw from negotiations, being hungry for the work, but this does happen from time to time and then the process of negotiation is repeated for the next ranking bid, causing yet more delays.) An overriding issue, especially when a national executing agency that is in control, is price, and the total duration of the assignment, the expert day rates, the total days, and various miscellaneous costs are commonly whittled down. Other bones of contention are the quality of the experts (particularly the team leader or project director), requirements for reporting and deliverables, etc. The actual contract upon which signatures are put can be quite lengthy (including the terms of reference), thus contractually obligating the bidder to myriad stipulations that can be pulled out if and when project client–contractor relations go sour. In the end, most of these contracts are hard to follow and open to varying interpretations by the various parties.

This is a simplified description of the tendering process and obviously there are many variations. Contracts can be deemed lump sum (also known as global price contracts), or they can be 'remeasurable' or 'cost-plus' contracts, with many variations depending on the nature of the work. Also, some donors have increasingly used 'indefinite quantity contracts' (IQCs) and 'framework agreements,' with the idea that there be pre-tendering for a consortium of companies that, once selected, can quickly be called on for specific projects and assignments when they come up, without requiring preliminary screenings each time. This sounds logical, but the end result has been (1) that large, 'body shop' companies who can quickly supply CVs and other paperwork dominate, (2) that smaller, more specialized firms are excluded unless they hook up as subcontractors to a large company, and (3) that firms need to maneuver and negotiate within a consortium, often competing for expert CVs as a valued commodity.

No matter what tendering/contracting systems and their variations are used, to be successful a consulting company or contractor must devote a considerable portion—often more than half of its staff and management efforts—to proceed through the various procurement steps. More and more these efforts require hiring people who *only* track announcements, negotiate consortium, and put together teams of experts.

The Procurement of Individuals

Recruiting an individual consultant for a time-bound assignment is usually much more straightforward than the process to engage firms. The donor or procurement agency will simply post an announcement in one of the development business clearing houses (described below). This market for development expertise is a sub-world in its own right, with literally thousands of announcements appearing every month. Institutions looking for individuals can be broken down into a number of main types: (1) donors looking to fill staff positions (usually entry level); (2) donors looking for administrators and consultant experts (usually short/medium term); (3) consulting firms or INGOs looking for candidates to put forward on upcoming bids (only rarely do consulting firms advertise for slots in projects they have won or are already implementing); (4) consulting firms and INGOs seeking to fill permanent staff positions, with a heavy preponderance looking for young staffers to work in proposal writing and other 'process' jobs.

Which donors post the most individual job offerings? According to Devex, there were on average 6500 job openings posted every month in 2019. The top recruiter was UNDP, with 8% of the total, followed by UNICEF, ADB, the World Bank, WHO, UN-Women, and WFP (Smith, 2022). For all job postings by donors, the overwhelming majority—some 60–70 percent—were for short-term assignments. For UNDP, the majority of announced jobs fell under institutional development or project management categories, not technical opportunities or positions. This emphasis on what could be called 'process' positions rather than technical expertise could be seen with most other donor postings, even for 'sectoral' agencies such as UNICEF and WHO.

Although these mostly short-term contract and consultant job offerings by donors themselves may seem a colossal number, they are totally eclipsed by the hundreds of thousands of postings coming from private players, mostly consulting firms and INGOs, that appear on the various clearing house sites. Some of these will be firms seeking permanent hires, but by far most of these postings are hardly real jobs and are more like fishing expeditions. Virtually all firms and INGOs undertake these fishing expeditions extensively, casting their nets as wide as possible to line up a team for bids whose members might at least look at least plausible on paper, but who certainly don't know each other, probably don't fit together, and possibly are grossly incompetent.

Development Clearing Houses

How do supply and demand come together in development procurement? Almost all donors have their own websites that announce upcoming projects or other work opportunities, but to get out to the widest possible audiences most donors rely on the phenomenon of worldwide clearing house, such as the UN's Development Business (UNDB or 'devbus' for short). Today IFIs, individual donors and their potential contractors and even INGOs post over 10,000 alerts for projects per year on UNDB, and the platform is much used by thousands of consulting firms and service providers throughout the world seeking procurement notices, early alerts, market insights, and previously awarded contracts.[5] Individuals looking for assignments may also use UNDB, but they much prefer other (and cheaper) clearing house platforms. The biggest of these is Devex, whose main function is the posting of individual job opportunities from donors, private firms, and INGOs, but it also offers considerable business intelligence, development news, and sectoral analyses. There are also two competitors—DevelopmentAid and Devnetjobs—that offer similar services.

Do Procurement Systems Work?

Each donor will say that their procurement operates under market principles and transparent competitive mechanisms to arrive at the best people, goods, and services for the particular job at hand, and at the lowest prices. Certainly, in terms of the huge volume of procurement tenders and job offerings, the system certainly hums along at an impressive rate. But do procurement systems really operate as donors pretend?

[5] UNDB is said to handle 16,000 tenders annually and boasts having 73,545 procurement processes on file (UN Development Business, n.d.).

It may be that procurement for the straightforward supply of goods and civil construction services works reasonably well, but when it comes to almost everything else, the procurement system's rigidities, the complexity and ambiguity of the work demanded, the misunderstandings between the various players, plus the bureaucratic requirements at every step, means that at best the system is hit-and-miss. The randomness of results is partly due to the sheer volume that procurement systems process—the thousands upon thousands of tenders that are launched by donors every year, not to mention the many more thousands of short-term studies and other technical assistance activities—and that each must be processed at great speed. This system overload of 'manufactured competition' *requires* that refuge is taken in the rigid and box-checking aspects of bureaucratic structures and routines. In effect, the result is more like random mediocracy.

This unhappy state of affairs has to do with many things as we shall see in the rest of this chapter—the abiding faith in the terms of reference, the mis-conceptualization and myths of what constitutes expertise, the necessarily counterproductive behavior of consulting firms, and, hiding in plain sight, the very strange nature of the development product itself. But the procurement processes themselves add considerably to the mess, especially in their need for by-the-book haste rather than anything approaching quality.

After all, what is the hurry? Donors themselves may spend several years getting their complicated and often dreamy projects or programs conceived, designed, and fully agreed with the recipient country. But once the RFP is out, the donor's clock begins to run, as if somehow the particular intervention is somehow a crucial game changer. The contractor/consultant is under the gun and must scurry to line up a team, prepare the strategy and methodology, and negotiate the pricing of each input, usually within a month or so.[6] And, in spite of all the thousands of bidders out in the 'marketplace,' due to this time pressure it is not uncommon for an RFP to result in not a single qualified bid, meaning the whole process must be started again.

[6] Often shortlisted consulting firms are invited to comment on ToRs in their proposals, but what bidder wants to alienate the donor by frankly criticizing its ToR, as bad as they may be? For juicy projects, the donor may even offer an explanatory session where all those shortlisted are invited to attend and pose questions, but these are mainly for show.

Haste to get to contract signing is also often encouraged by a certain naïve faith on all sides that—although the contract may clearly be overly complicated or even riddled with contradictions—such weaknesses can be overcome by goodwill and common adherence to overarching project goals. But during implementation, such good faith frequently evaporates into cascading misunderstandings, disputes, held-up payments, and even recourse to legal action. As has been heard many times by neutral observers, many of the contracts under which both sides operate are so bad that both parties were crazy to have ever signed them.

Fear is also a factor. The rigidities of the RFP process and the by-the-book requirements for everything associated with bidding are in part due to the donor's fear that someone will complain officially about some aspect of the tendering process. This someone will most likely be sour-grapes consulting firms who make noisy complaints, something procurement people dread. This fear could be called a spinoff from the donor obsession with control (Chap. 4), and it certainly colors the process of procurement with excessive caution.

What makes the whole process so depressing is that the systems of procurement require the same efforts again and again and again. Sure, in a specific tender tremendous and laudable efforts may be made by a whole cluster of people—managers and staff sitting in the procurement offices, company managers and their technical staff, and donors who shepherd the process along—to overcome obstacles, confusions, and misunderstandings and eventually get to contract signing. But then the whole struggle must be started again for the next tender and the next project. It is as if the same struggles are set to repeat themselves endlessly.

Terms of Reference and Wishful Thinking

All consulting firms, development contractors, and service INGOs respond to terms of reference (ToRs) in their proposals and, more importantly, use these documents as their guiding reference in subsequent work. ToRs themselves ultimately derive from project documents. A single project or program may require several separate ToRs, from simple ones that guide short-term individual experts to those that frame the complex work of large consultant teams over the whole life of a project. ToRs are long-standing and essential fixtures in development, and they are default mechanisms that are both overused and abused. Amazingly, in a business that analyses everything to death, very little is ever written—whether analytical or critical—about this peculiar artifact, other than tiresome how-to-write-instructions that emanate from the copious coaching literature.

A Bit of History

ToRs have been around for a long time. In the 1970s they had already become common, and in this period of comparative innocence they were quite short documents that simply stated the aims, tasks, and products of a project or intervention (with the humdrum details of obligations and reporting and payments left for the actual negotiation between donor and successful bidder), and simple three- or four-page ToRs, even for large team efforts, were common.[7] This was a time when the donor agencies did at least some of their own work themselves. This was also a time when donor staff overseeing a project were more accessible (either in country or through missions), and problems that arose could be addressed through face-to-face meetings or phone calls.

But over the subsequent decades, as the development business itself became more multisectoral, more ambitious, and more complex, the Terms of Reference, *for lack of any better vehicle*, progressively became the document of choice into which more and more complicated aspirations and requirements came to be crammed, and these days a ToR for a multi-year team assignment can run to well over 150 pages, and even a simple individual assignment of a total of 20 person days can easily exceed thirty pages. There seems to be an irrepressible desire to add to the ToR, both for mundane micromanagement details and also for more grand policy and strategy concerns. And it seems that ToRs have sometimes become platforms for a donor's self-aggrandizement, with pages devoted to past donor work in the field and/or region, seminal documents produced, and strategic developmental strategies linked to higher objectives.

In parallel with the rise of the use (and the length) of the ToR has been, at least since the 1990s, a curtailment of new staff hiring by almost all donors. Thus there has been a shrinkage of donor in-house capacities, while the funds they disburse have grown substantially, as have the range, scope, and complexity of international development instruments. The

[7] For example, a simple three-page ToR was prepared by UNDP in 1977 for a two-year effort to produce master plans for the five main cities in North Yemen, based on a request from the World Bank who, at the time, needed such plans to guide the network planning for the first Yemen urban water and wastewater project.

result has been the inevitable explosion of the need for outside services, and as a consequence the ToR has had to serve more and more as the prime vehicle for ordering and structuring this outsourcing.

Who Produces Terms of Reference?

For key Terms of Reference, donor mid-level managers may oversee the main elements that go into the ToR, but since they are usually far too busy, they will rely on the designated project team leader or task manager, who, in turn, is likely to assign the actual writing to a short-term consultant, with lots of back and forth. Many others from inside the donor organization (from other regional offices or other departments) are likely to be invited to review or comment, and drafts are commonly shuffled back and forth. This means that there are more layers and steps, and more opportunities for spurious add-ons.

Some donors (e.g., the EC, DfID, and UNDP) will ensure that the ToR (and/or project document) will include the project logical framework (logframe), whose main purpose, other than to generate unnecessary work and thoroughly confuse everyone, is to project the ***appearance*** of rational order, coherent design, and logical sequencing that is intimately linked to measurable results and outcomes (See also Chap. 6).

Finalized ToRs almost always form part of the RFP, are the base document in discussions about a project, and in most cases are addended to the eventual contract between the donor or executing agency and the consultant firm/consortium, making it a gigantic minefield for disputes, especially when things go wrong during implementation and daggers are out. It well behooves the consultant team leader or project manager to have read the ToR over and over—even to memorize segments—to make sure all concerns and aspects are covered.

In most situations, the partner government and/or their in-country executing agencies will rarely have anything to do with preparing the ToR, even though it is a crucial document with which the partner government or agency will have to live with for the life of the project and even beyond. At best, near final drafts will be sent to the client for comment as a form of protocol. Money matters, especially the budget breakdown for the different components and sub-components, will be of interest, but these will already have been scrutinized in detail by the client during the preparation of the project document or memorandum of understanding (MoU), and in any event budget lines are almost never included in the ToRs.

It Comes Down to Wishful Thinking

The Terms of Reference are a wonderful mechanism for whoever writes them (or whoever contracts out their writing) to have their say, to have their own impact, and, often, to put in everything plus the kitchen sink. The ToR allows a space in which the concept and logic of a project/intervention can be put into a clean, cohesive text. It can project a seamless, logical approach, somehow unencumbered by the all too well-known pitfalls of donor interventions. Of course, such problems may be alluded to as 'risks,' but these can be assuaged by yet more added text, such as a subcomponent for training and capacity building, or community participation, or for monitoring of inclusiveness and gender sensitivity. In other words, the ToR can be a space in which probable stumbling blocks are elegantly sidestepped. They represent a kind of wishful thinking that somehow, by putting it all in a coherent reference document, 'development impact' can be magically realized on down the line.

Some ToRs actually are tight and well written, do not expand the tasks and actions to encompass too much extraneous fluff, and limit what can be reasonably achieved. These more modest ToRs are influenced by a realization that the partner ministry or executing agency can only accomplish so much and that the weaknesses of the procurement system will probably yield up mediocre consultants and useless 'change agents.' But the pressure is always around—either from the sector/practice managers or others ensconced in donor silos—to add their own spin.

Expertise

The international procurement of expertise, a practice that has long been enshrined in donor work, is one that assumes there are experts in a particular field who, because of their technical education and accumulated experience, can operate more or less interchangeably in any number of countries or situations. It also assumes that these experts can quickly be mobilized and deployed, can easily function in unfamiliar environments, and can teamwork seamlessly with other experts.

The Myth of Neutral, Technical Expertise

There is a well-maintained myth, something that goes back as far as the Development Industry itself, which assumes that expertise is purely technical and neutral, that it can be easily absorbed, that it is transferable into any location. Sure, this expertise may have to adapt to 'local conditions,' but such adaptation is considered *itself* to be an expertise that can easily be applied anywhere. In other words, this myth allows a sidestepping of messy local realities and dynamics and the ever-present political and economic dimensions within which Development is pursued. Senior (and not so senior) professionals, whether agronomists, economists, architects, engineers, accountants, statisticians, doctors, educationalists, and sociologists (and yes, even anthropologists) will be considered well-grounded in their professions and will have experience in at least a handful of developing countries. There are also more specifically development theme types, such as community development experts, rural development experts, capacity development experts, public administration experts, monitoring and evaluation experts, and gender mainstreaming experts. And since around the year 2000 whole new sets have appeared whose expertise more or less follows dominant development paradigms. There are climate-change experts, SME experts, resilience experts, microfinance experts, etc. There are also those whose expertise is more or less managerial, able to steer projects, programs, and policies, able to manage budgets, and able to run large teams and ensure that 'deliverables' are delivered. In fact, there is a trend in the development industry that creates more and more of a need for what could be 'process' positions, with titles such as Donor Relations Officer, Partnership Manager, Product Development Specialist, Senior Resilience and Sustainability Advisor, or Chief Impact Officer.

Very rare does an RFP express a priority for international experts with extensive knowledge of and deep experience in a particular country. And even rarer is a command of the local language stipulated. Yes, in the job descriptions there may be a nod for in-country experience and/or a particular language skill, but these prerequisites are at best only 'preferable.' This devaluating of anything approaching deep in-country understanding is very widespread, although one would have thought that such is exactly what most development projects would most need.

The CV and Opaque Mediocracy Triumphant

The main document used in marketing for expertise is the curriculum vitae (CV), an easily manipulated summary of a person's qualifications, experiences, and abilities. It is one that perforce must be written up, changed, and sent around and around in order to feed the industry's vast hunger for thousands upon the thousands of specific short-term expert opportunities that are posted every month. And this is all done in desperate haste by the literally thousands of firms bidding for development contracts, not to mention individuals themselves.

The general format of the CV, as used in Development, starts with a one-page lead with the basics: name and personal details, education and degrees, proficiency in languages, professional association membership, and a paragraph summarizing the person's skills. After this are listed in reverse order (newest job first) all paid assignments. For each of these, the position title, employer, client, and source of funding will be mentioned, along with a short description of duties. CV drafts are usually first written laboriously by candidates themselves. But since almost all donors have their own CV templates or formats (and many have limits to how many pages they can run) multiple versions are necessary.

Key to developing the CV is the very common practice of manipulating or 'massaging' the CV to fit the demands of assignments. Since the donor usually requires expertise as something narrowly defined, the idea is to give them what they want. Many, especially those with a sizable list of past assignments, will develop several versions as part of this massaging. An expert might create a CV that gives emphasis, for example, to experience in gender issues, or to climate change and disasters-resilience, to social development and poverty reduction, to primary health systems, or to statistical and data wizardry. Tailoring a CV to a particular project's ToR has become almost essential, at least for the key experts in a bid. This usually simply involves making sure that important buzzwords gleaned from the ToR are larded into the text of the CV, the more the better. Such a strategy of regurgitating banal jargon has become so common that one suspects that word count algorithms are used by bid evaluators.

The practice of manipulating or 'massaging' CVs has other well-known objectives. First, it is important that a person appears to have been always busy over the years, and expanding the actual dates of an assignment helps fill out any embarrassing gaps. And there is nothing to prevent one from claiming to have undertaken certain project tasks and produced certain project reports that in fact were collective efforts that the person himself had little or nothing to do with. Nor is there anything preventing someone from claiming a high project management role or seminal impact on client performance.

The CV—however imperfect an instrument—has become such an important document in the development industry that all sorts of external help are available to produce better and more effective CVs. Thus, we can find throughout the web the services of professional CV writers, of those who offer CV coaching services, of those who can offer specialized CV templates, of those who run CV writing webinars, and of those who can provide career counseling cum CV preparation. For CVs pitched at international development recruiters, Devex is the industry leader.

It should be added that there is also the practice of outright falsification of information on the CV—such as claiming university degrees that were never obtained, claiming language fluency where there is only the vaguest grasp of even 'kitchen' vocabulary, manufacturing completely ghost assignments, or pretending to have had key project roles when in fact inputs were more or less clerical. And on and on. Of course, donors and the firms that chase donor work are fully aware of these tricks, and many donors insist that a reference with email contact is named for important assignments so that checks can be made. Even so, the sheer administrative weight of CV processing and bid preparation, plus the normally very short deadlines for bids, means that rarely are these checks applied in practice. In fact, *the desperate haste required* means that, whether choosing a particular individual or the team proposed by a consulting firm, the donor must make do and accept the second or third best. And the supply of expertise for a particular position over a particular short period is not at all infinite—few consultants are so desperate as to fly off somewhere the following week. The result, for all to see, are teams of experts that are second best or, worse, that are totally clueless about the assignment at hand.

In other words, the CV is a very imperfect vehicle, even assuming somehow pure falsehoods can be avoided. In fact, many in the development business (and even outside it) are of the opinion that CVs are almost useless—that someone who sounds good on paper may in fact be a disastrous non-performer who spends more time justifying his importance than in actually completing his tasks. And, since there is never anything like a post-project assessment of consultants, there is no organized accountability and any bad apple can easily be slotted into future bids.

Stables of Experts

Rosters of experts are maintained by all consulting, engineering, and management firms active in the business. In simpler days the idea was that, as soon as a bidding opportunity appeared, the expertise called for could quickly be matched with one or more CVs in the company's roster, and thus a consultant team could be built up almost overnight. This team would be an amalgam of some company staff specialists and more outside 'associates' known to the firm. But the reality these days is that—faced with the industry's constant and instant need for consultants—assembling a team has in many cases come to dominate all else. Many are the companies who have no professional core and operate as pure recruiting posts whose real 'expertise' is in preparing proposals, attaching CVs that look plausible, slavishly meeting the donor's terms of reference, and little else.

Even large, well-known firms need to maintain these rosters. For these, sometimes there might be the right staffer for the right assignment, and the firm definitely prefers this, as then he/she would be fee-earning. But what firm can afford to keep a large staff of professionals that just might meet the very diverse and changing requirements in the weekly cascade of RFPs? The whole operation becomes hit-or-miss, and the logic of 'rostering' becomes a necessity, with more and more efforts concentrated on setting up and expanding CV data bases, sifting through them, and spending lots of time constructing plausible teams for bids. And this kind of work requires more and more minions who, since no one wants to be burdened with a large labor bill, tend to be young, cheap, and very short on anything like a grasp of international development.

Experts at Being Experts

Crucial in any development project or program is familiarity with development processes and regulations, how they work, and what really matters to donors. More and more this is the 'expertise' that counts, and technical excellence often takes a back seat.

Most donor agencies have long recognized that one of the crucial requirements of key experts on a particular project is a strong familiarity with their own bureaucratic systems, and almost all job descriptions will include one or more phrases along the line of "prior experience of the candidate with donor x's projects and programs is strongly advised." Thus, EU experience leads to more EU experience, USAID experience leads to more USAID experience, and so on. Without at least one team member with a sound background in the intricacies of how these donors operate and how they process their paperwork, a project is likely to have a very bumpy ride, one that neither the contractor or donor wants.

In any sizable development project, it is the team leader (aka chief of party) who pulls the whole effort together and ensures that deliverables get delivered. This expert was until recently considered absolutely crucial by both donors and consulting firms, and he/she would typically be a strong professional in the field in question but would also have report preparation and basic management skills. In other words, he/she was both substance and process. But more and more the team leader on the ground is being made subservient to what is called the project director or project manager back at the consulting firm's headquarters. It is this person back home who negotiates with and makes representations to the donor and client and also hires the team and replaces members when necessary. In other words, it is another case where firms realize that the importance of 'process' eclipses that of anything like substance.

Local Knowledge and Local Expertise?

The need for at least some local knowledge is almost always indicated in donor ToRs. This local or 'national' expert will almost always be head or be part of an existing local consulting firm, or will be an academic who holds some post—the higher the better—in a national university. There might also be retired freelance engineers or government officials. All will hold decrees (usually more than one). Some of these national experts can be very good, but many are simply awful, especially if they are academics and have simply been teaching what are considered Western high-tech mysteries to their students for decades. This is not the place to go into the unfortunate dynamics of higher education in the Rest, but with a few exceptions the role of a professor is precisely this explaining of Western techno subjects. Thus things 'local'—especially those that embody traditional economies and skills—are devalued and, when studied, are forced into some modernist paradigm or theory, the more obtuse and technical the better. Luckily, the endless rise of those in the Rest who pursue graduate degrees in the West includes some in the social sciences, and not all of these end up back home wallowing in the professor-as-God paradigm. In fact, there are many who set up collaboratives and consultancies that are equal to anything an international firm can offer, but it is very rare that their excellence is recognized in the business.

In all this, the international expert who also has extensive country experience and knows the language is a very odd fish, although there are dozens of examples scattered around the Third World. And although one would have thought that such animals would be in great demand, the opposite is usually true. An outsider having too much local knowledge is actually feared by those in most host governments, and it is preferable that the incoming expert be ignorant of local realities and can be easily steered around. No, it is much more comfortable to have the typical international expert parachuted in with zero local comprehension. Getting out and trying to find out what is going on just doesn't fit in with the normal behavior of these preferred international experts, and when they do get out the field trips are usually carefully staged by their local partners.

And the local or national experts? Yes, they—at least the good ones—should be given much more space and power than the second-string positions they classically occupy in project teams. But the development industry has not found ways to weed out local experts who are hardly competent and tend to blather nonsense. One would have thought that strong and independent local expertise ecosystems would by now have evolved. But no, it seems that donors prefer to maintain the traditional pairing of international with national expertise in which the 'international' is always on top.

Expertise Within Donor Organizations Themselves

Technical expertise is of course valued and nurtured by donors for their own professional staff. But for every true technical specialist with considerable sectoral experience there will be more staffers who are valued for their competencies in administration, processing, and management, whatever their professional qualifications.

A practice manager or department head in a particular agency may have had some real experience in the Rest and in his/her specialty, and some may keep up with the literature and even publish blogs or author the odd knowledge piece. But these are rare, and most donor managers only have a superficial grounding in the subject and/or country at hand. The experience that counts is bureaucratic and managerial, and one is more likely to encounter donor staffers with no or very little background in developing countries *accept as* administrators and managers. Any field work experience they might have had probably dates back to when they were preparing their doctoral theses.

Of course, there will be technical people inside the donor structure who will have a say in project formulation or operation. But more likely than not, their experience is in being project or program officers and in pushing loans or grant projects into and through the pipelines. This teaches them a lot about donor agency bureaucracy and office politics but shields them from most of the rough and tumble. And even when they do go into 'the field,' they keep their donor baggage with them, always looking over their shoulders to see how things they do play out back at headquarters. As one middle-ranked World Bank staffer said, when queried as to why some large budget line was shifted for no good reason to a project that was an obvious sinkhole, he simply answered, 'It's politics.' He didn't mean high level considerations of sectoral policies or development strategies, but simply that some very ambitious manager outmaneuvered his peers and was able to capture more funding for his pet scheme and thus advance in the eyes of his managers.

Donor staff who have solid technical backgrounds, such as agronomists, engineers, or various social scientists, will often complain—at least anecdotally over a few beers—that their expertise is devalued or simply never called on, and that they have become glorified paper-pushers and event impresarios whose normal day involves dealing with emails from HQ, budget reviews, management meetings, hosting visitors, etc. These complaints could be heard even back in the 1980s, especially in large donor missions in especially favored countries, but these days it has become so common everywhere that few country field staff expect any other treatment.

Consulting and Contracting Firms

Consulting firms, contractors, and other service providers pursue work through donor procurement structures, and it is they—in their hundreds if not thousands—have always been a key part of the global development industry. They have grown and expanded in step with the industry itself over more than six decades, coming to perform more and more of the functions that donors themselves were too busy to handle.

A Little History

In the early years most development consulting companies of any size were engineering consulting firms (echoing the industry's early emphasis on basic infrastructure), virtually all of which were located in Western countries and almost all of which already had well-established practices back home. Small, more specialized outfits that concentrated on overseas development began to appear in the 1970s—again exclusively in the West—offering advisory services in various aspects of health, economic development, accounting and management, agronomy and agricultural development, architecture and urban planning, etc., and both they and the larger engineering firms were very attuned to the needs of bilateral donor agencies and the increasing number of MDBs. It was no coincidence that these companies tended to cluster around Western cities where most potential clients were headquartered, with Washington DC and New York having the most allure, plus of course Paris, London, Frankfort/Eschborn, and Tokyo. After the EU became a big development spender in the late 1980s, Brussels became a virtual hive for consulting firms.

In this earlier period, international NGOs and other civil society organizations such as Oxfam, Care, World Vision, and the International Red Cross had only limited roles in overseas development, with their core activities being restricted to their home countries. As they started to expand overseas, their work usually centered at first on responding to disasters, conflicts, and famines. Their funding had originally been mostly through private donations, and they only began to be seen as for-pay service providers to mainstream development agencies in the 1980s, most notably by the World Bank and soon thereafter by USAID.[8] Thus, increasingly the boundaries between for-profits and charitable/non-profits became blurred, with both pursuing the development bonanza in what has been called global 'vendorism.'[9]

In the 1980s and 1990s there was considerable expansion of the competencies of consulting firms and also considerable restructuring and mergers. Markets had become greater, more geographically spread out, and more complex, and by the Millennium the process of larger firms progressively swallowing up smaller, specialized practices was in full swing. These smaller specialized firms—those that had a core cohesion, an exclusively development orientation, and dedicated management—increasingly found it hard to prosper or even survive. They simply could not afford to devote the resources and effort required to meet the increasingly

[8] INGOs began to be seen as important vehicles in the Rest during structural adjustment. For example, it is reported that, from 1973 to 1988, NGOs were involved in about 15 World Bank projects a year, but by 1990 that number had jumped to 89 (Hall-Jones, 2006).

[9] This is a term used by Vijay Nagaraj (2015, 599) to describe the for-profit side of the business, although it could equally be used to apply to INGOs, other non-profits, and even some cash-starved UN agencies.

complicated demands of the donors' procurement regimes, and scrambling for bits of work became harder and harder, having to bid for more and more tenders and to spend scarce resources on hiring 'product development' and marketing troops. The result has been that these smaller firms, even those with good reputations and internal esprit de corps, have almost all disappeared, either having withered away or, more likely, having been bought out by larger firms, with the original owners laughing all the way to the bank and the abandoned troops more than a little peaked.

At roughly the same time, new players began to claim their share of the ever-increasing aid bonanza. The global management-accounting firms (also known as 'strategy consulting' companies) such as PwC, KPMG, and Booze Allen—anchored in the business of advising large corporations—saw new opportunities in international development and quickly set up subsidiaries or arms that catered to both donor agencies and governments in developing countries. Another new entrant into the field was the Western university that began to offer development advisory services to donors in direct competition with consulting firms. Increasingly cash-strapped universities also began to encourage faculty members to take on international consulting gigs, and some of the same universities began to build up departments in development studies, often taught by the same professors that hired themselves out as consultants. Other strange new entrants began to pop up, including in Germany GTZ IS (now GIZ IS) a pure consulting arm of the well-known donor GTZ, that was set up specifically to compete in the wider world of donor tenders. More recently, even the venerable British Council has joined the game, and it now offers consultancy advice to donors (and multinational corporations) on topics such as civil society, education, justice and conflict resolution, skills development, and, of course, English for development.

As a result of these historical trends, today there are a confusingly large variety of various for-profit and non-profit entities who populate what could be called the arena of international development contracting. No one knows even roughly how many consulting firms and contractors active in the international development market, but there are a lot. And most, especially the well-established and successful, continue to be headquartered in the West.

Strategies for Penetration and Expansion in the Development Business

Strategies for firms operating in the world of development are many, but the key is to build up capacities to react to and even anticipate donor desires and donor faddism. This means throwing lots of people and resources towards 'vendorism,' in other words always seeking out opportunities, lining up consultants that fit the RFPs, self-promoting to death, and preparing as many bids as possible, even if chances of winning tenders are slim. The result is an inexorable march towards bigger, more complex, and more process-oriented companies.

In addition to simply growing big and being acutely market oriented, there are also special strategies that many firms pursue to capture ever more of the development dollar. One is for large civil engineering contractors to carve out separate international development units. This is well illustrated by the Arup Group, headquartered in London, with a huge global workforce of over 16,000 staff located in 96 offices, mainly constructing buildings and infrastructure for corporate and government clients. Arup created a separate, supposedly non-profit unit (Arup International Development) that can tap into the larger parent network for contacts, expertise, and representation.[10] A similar strategy has been used to specialize in the kind of 'process' services donors are currently enthralled with. A good example is the Australian engineering firm Coffey (Australia), itself now a division of the huge Tetra Tech, which established an international development arm offering fund and grant management, gender and social inclusion, organizational development and training, project design, project management, monitoring and evaluation, and scaling up.[11]

These are only some of the ways that companies approach the international development market, and someone needs to do an exhaustive analysis of these convoluted setups, corporate maneuvers, and marketing strategies. Company websites offer only the thinnest of details of their

[10] https://www.arup.com/expertise/services/planning/international-development Accessed 3 June 2022.

[11] https://www.tetratechcoffey.com/about-us/ Accessed 3 June 2022. The parent company in California, Tetra Tech with 20,000 employees and 250 offices around the world, confusingly also has another international development subsidiary called MSI that 'helps communities, nongovernmental organizations, and governments solve some of the world's most pressing development challenges around the world.'

strategies and are consistently self-laudatory, with words like 'innovative,' 'dedicated,' 'committed,' and 'globally present' laced into their texts.

Bigger Is Definitely Better

Looking at the landscape today, it is firm size and weight that really counts in the markets for development expertise. Only by growing big can a firm devote the resources needed to pursue every and all opportunities.

Bigness is most visible in those who pursue contracts from USAID, the world's largest bilateral donor (and by some measures the largest donor, full stop). In 2019, its top ten tender awardees captured contracts valued at USD 6.14 billion, almost 40 percent of total awards. And, when looking at these awards, health dominated, and especially international technical, operational, and support services for health. This is particularly the case for Chemonics who led the top 2018 awardees list with a $ 2.51 billion in contracts (Developmentaid, 2019).[12] Other top USAID contractors in 2018 were very familiar in the business: DAI Global, FHI360, Abt Associates, Catholic Relief Services, RTI International, Johns Hopkins Corporation, ARD Inc., Palladium International, and Creative Associates, each of which captured awards from USAID valued at over $200 million. All of these firms (except for Palladium, a global company with headquarters in the UK) were American, which illustrates the continued use by bilateral aid agencies of their own country service providers, something that was supposed to have shrunk after the OECD's much heralded Aid Effectiveness to reduce the practice of both formally and informally tied aid. And it seems that USAID is continuing to prefer the largest possible service contracts, since in 2022 it aimed to create a 'suite' of nine contracts amounting to $17 billion over ten years just for health projects, with one of these contracts being the 'control tower' just to coordinate all the others (Ainsworth, 2022).

These days such large US firms employ thousands. For example, Chemonics claims to have a workforce of 5000, 1200 of whom are based in the Washington DC area. Catholic Relief Services (CRS—also among the 2018 top ten USAID contractors with $440 million of new business) also claims to have 5000 employees worldwide. RTI, another top ten

[12] This is partly due to Chemonics having been awarded, in 2016, the logistics contract for the five-year Global Health Supply Chain Procurement Supply project, valued at $ 9.5 billion, probably the largest single development contract ever.

USAID contractor, claims to have 6000 worldwide, although only about one-third of its business comes from USAID.

The same trend of large projects awarded to large firms can be seen in the UK by looking at DfID's top ten private implementors in 2017 (Wolf, 2018). The top five private firms, each of which earned over GBP 55 million in 2017 from DfID, were PricewaterhouseCooper (UK), DAI (USA but with a branch in the UK), Adam Smith International (UK), Palladium (Australia), and KPMG (Holland). Others in the top ten included Crown Agents Bank Ltd., IMC Worldwide Ltd., Oxford Policy Management, Crown Agents, and AECOM, all of which except AECOM were UK-based.

IFIs also award most contracts to large, well-established firms with global reach, but the mix is different because they tend to concentrate on big infrastructure works. The World Bank averaged about $10 billion annually for procurement contracts in the 2016–2019 period; for civil works contracts, which made up about 70 percent of the total, its biggest awardees were engineering firms most of which were based in either China or India, with Turkey taking up a distant third. (Most work they undertook was for large transport and civil works contracts in their own or nearby countries.) In terms of more 'advisory' consulting services, in 2017 the World Bank gave out hundreds of awards that in total were valued at some $1.5 billion, and these also showed the dominance of globalized Western firms (Coralde & Tamonan, 2019).

The ADB also showed award patterns similar to that of the World Bank, although with a regional twist as would be expected (Rovira & Alcega, 2018). In 2017 the top five civil works contractors (in terms of value of contracts) were Kec International (India), Siemens (Germany), Larsen and Toubro (India), the Uzbekistan Ministry of Finance, and Simplex (India). The largest 'advisory' consulting service awards went exclusively to Western firms (with a total value of $205 million).

Overall, specialization by consulting firms and contractors in particular development issues or sectors tends to become submerged by a 'we can do anything' marketing philosophy. Are there still development consulting firms that pride themselves in specializing? Yes, at least in global health, with examples found in the US firms FHI360 and John Snow. But global health is a mammoth sector in its own right, and both of these companies are big enough to devote considerable resources towards pursuing every and all tenders of interest. And yes, it could be said that large engineering consulting firms still specialize in their strengths, but even these will offer services and expertise in practically any development subject.

Consulting Firms in the Rest: Still Weak Players

As shown above, successful international development consulting firms and service providers have been and remain overwhelmingly Western. However, there has been what could be called a slow rise of the Third World firm. These entities had been around for decades, but they tended to be specific to their home country, acting as the essential if subordinate local partner in bids by a large Western companies or international consortia. These roles still exist, of course. But since the 2000s there have been more and more developing country firms—especially those based in India and the subcontinent and East European firms for EU work—who are cheaper and thrive on having much smaller overheads. Yet rare are the cases where such firms have built up their international businesses to become major or even average players. BRAC Global, whose core work started in Bangladesh in community development, poverty alleviation, and microfinance but now boasts subsidiaries in many countries, is one impressive example that is an exception to the rule. Internationally successful design and engineering firms such as Dar Al Hadassah and Khatib al-Alami are also exceptions, as are some Chinese firms (Engineering News Record, 2019).

Revolving Doors and Alignment of Interests

As has been detailed by Vijay Nagaraj, there is a close alignment of interests through the porous nature of the boundary between consulting firms and contractors, on the one hand, and their counterparts in donor establishments on the other. The largest firms can and do hire staff from governments and development agencies, universities, research centers, and even international and national NGOs. "These experts are, in a sense, the building blocks of an ever-expanding circuitry of knowledge and influence" (Nagaraj, 2015, 602). Consulting firms in the USA are, in particular, staffed heavily with former USAID officials. And the situation is hardly different in the UK and other European countries. This mechanism of 'revolving doors' is critical for expanding spheres of influence and it helps generate a pool of almost interchangeable individuals. And it underscores what Jim Ferguson said back in 1994 that "undifferentiated 'development' expertise ... free-floating and untied to any specific context ... is so easily generalized, and so easily inserted into any given situation" (Nagaraj,

2015, 603). Faced with this dominant paradigm, one can pretty much forget about anything like locally generated knowledge, fitting the context, or even endogenous development.

References

Ainsworth, D. (2022, January 24). *What we know so far about USAID's $17B NextGen contracts.* Accessed June 3, 2022, from https://www.devex.com/news/what-we-know-so-far-about-usaid-s-17b-nextgen-contracts-102481?mkt_tok=Njg1LUtCTC03NjUAAAGCMBh7e9N0rueohGp-163KL9XsO4xqLZ0Y2vkspaUCVvEG6kTDrxp7z1JJg9qI_RUnnBge9aYvJBvcGU9Y6GaenhUlSY2YbhwIbpAVmz9Rd9k6xU0&utm_content=cta&utm_source=nl_newswire&utm_term=article_pro

Borson, F. (2017). Reforms under the World Bank procurement and the policy implications for developing countries. *European Procurement & Public Private Partnership Law Review, 2.* Accessed June 2, 2022, from https://www.jstor.org/stable/26695442?seq=1

Coralde, J., & Tamonan, M. (2019, April 24). Interactive: Exploring the trends in World Bank procurement. *Devex.* Accessed June 3, 2022, from https://www.devex.com/news/interactive-exploring-the-trends-in-world-bank-procurement-96984

Developmentaid. (2019, September 3). *Top 10 USAID Awardees.* Accessed June 3, 2022, from https://www.developmentaid.org/#!/news-stream/post/48501/top-10-usaid-awardees

Engineering News Record. (2019, July). *Top 225 international design firms.* Accessed June 3, 2022, from https://www.enr.com/toplists/2019-Top-225-International-Design-Firms-1

European Commission. (2019). *Procurement and GRANTS for European Union external actions – A practical guide. Version of 15 July 2019.* Accessed June 2, 2019, from https://ufmsecretariat.org/wp-content/uploads/2012/09/ePrag-en-2019.0.pdf

Hall-Jones, P. (2006, May). *The rise and rise of NGOs, global policy forum.* Accessed June 3, 2022, from https://archive.globalpolicy.org/component/content/article/176-general/31937.html

KfW Groupe. (2016). *Guidelines for the assignment of Consultants in Financial Cooperation with partner countries, version of August 2016.*

Nagaraj, V. K. (2015). Beltway Bandits' and 'Poverty Barons': For-profit international development contracting and the military-development assemblage. *Development and Change, 46*(4), 585–617.

Rovira, A., & Alcega, R. (2018, March 23). *Who were ADB's top 2017 contractors for goods and works?* Accessed June 3, 2022, from https://www.devex.com/news/who-were-adb-s-top-2017-contractors-for-goods-and-works-92374

Smith, E. (2022, February 20). Top 10 global development employers. *Devex.* Accessed June 3, 2022, from https://www.devex.com/news/top-10-global-development-employers-96556

UN Development Business. (n.d.). Accessed April 3, 2020, from https://devbusiness.un.org/

Vogl, A. J. A. (2011, April). Procurement, tied aid and the use of country systems in Nicaragua. *Eurodad.*

Wolf, M. (2018, February 23). Top 2017 DfID private sector implementors. *Devex.* Accessed June 3, 2022, from https://www.devex.com/news/top-2017-dfid-private-sector-implementers-92148

CHAPTER 6

Numbers, Indicators, and Technical Objectivity

There are a range of ways in which development policies and operations have become very beholden to numbers, indicators, and 'evidence-based' results as sufficient measures of success and as justifications of what donors do. These have become so pervasive that they could be said to constitute "an obsessive measurement disorder," as a former USAID administrator put it (Natsios, 2010). Natsios went on to state: "… those development programs that are most precisely and easily measured are the least transformational, and those programs that are the most transformational are the least measured" (Natsios, 2010, 3). Well, such pearls of wisdom, even from a USAID administrator, seem to have had absolutely no impact.

The faith in quantitative approaches to describe both the challenges facing developing countries and the array of available solutions is part of this numeric obsession, as is the need for donors to project an aura of objective, techno-determinism in what they analyze and a predictable, linear progression in the programs and projects they carry out. This technological-determinism has also extended to a whole sub-industry of score cards that rank and track how developing countries and their initiatives are performing. This has left little room for locally generated development policy and economic common sense, let alone country ownership of the numbers and indicators that are purported to describe social and economic characteristics in these countries. And it has conveniently kept discussions on development carefully corralled into technical pastures and

D. Sims, *Development Delusions and Contradictions*,
https://doi.org/10.1007/978-3-031-17770-5_6

far away from anything that could be considered political or otherwise contentious.

The fact that solid, quantifiable information on economic and social matters remains in very short supply in most of the Third World has not put a brake on this enthusiasm for numbers; instead, it has only stimulated a redoubling of interpretive analytics and impressive quantitative gymnastics by donors. And although there has been some improvement in the statistical knowledge of developing economies and societies in the last couple of decades, these statistics and the numbers generated from them remain for the most part dubious.

A Bit of History

This obsession with numbers and techno-fixes has been going on for as long as the Development Era itself. It could be said to have started with President Truman who, in his inaugural address in 1949, launched his famous Point Four policy: "I believe that we should make available to peace-loving peoples the benefits of our store of technical knowledge in order to help them realize their aspirations for a better life" (Truman, 1949). This call for technical missionaries set the tone, and, as they say, no one ever looked back. Although there were early doubts about country statistics and national accounts, by the 1970s macroeconomic analysis and annual estimates of GDP (or GNI) became common, and thus GDP per capita become the main metric of a country's economic progress and the reference point for ever increasingly sophisticated analysis economic trends, the huge statistical problems of measuring informal activities in national accounts not-withstanding. Moreover, by the early 1980s project feasibility studies came to be much promoted by donors, and these relied on social cost–benefit analysis and economic rates of return to assess overall impact of proposed projects.[1] (Never mind that the data required by the models had to be massaged or created out of clean air.) By the early 1990s logical framework analysis had gained popularity across much of the donor landscape as a conceptual tool for organizing projects and programs, using rigid matrices that related non-quantifiable goals and objectives to inputs, outputs, results/outcomes, and verifiable indicators, all of which were to be monitored and evaluated systematically. In 1990 the UN

[1] A good example of these complicated project assessment techniques can be found in a widely read primer produced by the UN (UNIDO, 1978).

introduced the Human Development Index (and expanded it in 2010), but this and other more subtle ways of ranking countries never supplanted the industry standard of GDP per capita, which around the same time was made ever more popular by the introduction of the concept purchasing power parity, something that allowed for direct cross-country comparisons of national income and a myriad of other markers. Over roughly the same period analysis of poverty indicators and household income increased in use and sophistication, relying on representative surveys of household income and expenditures. And in parallel the production of a whole range of country-level social and economic indicators—and the annual ranking of countries by these indicators—became a virtual sub-industry, allowing ever more means to envision how countries were improving and how they stack up to each other. In the 2000s randomized control trials became a popular 'rigorously scientific' way to assess how poverty alleviation and social support measures were working, at least in specific micro situations. The same period saw the rise of the use of techniques of measuring evidence and results of development interventions, with the appearance of tools and quantitative methodologies such as RBM (results-based management), VfM (value for money), and PMS (performance measurement systems) becoming quite popular, at least with some donor agencies. This movement was given a boost by the OECD-DAC adopting 'results' as one of the five pillars in the 2005 Paris Declaration on Aid Effectiveness.

The Nature of the 'Technical Game' in Development

Numbers, indicators, and other forms of quantification of development processes and outcomes give a comforting aura of certainty, authority, and precision, and the practice of 'metrology' has exploded worldwide since the 1980s (Rottenburg & Merry, 2015). And as was pointed out in even as early as 2002 by Richard Rottenburg, the development industry has taken this obsession with quantification to a high level of 'technical games' which makes it difficult to be efficient and effective in transferring its technical fixes on the one hand, and on the other makes it almost impossible for recipient governments and societies to construct their own internal positions as to what constitutes development (Rottenburg, 2009).

Poor Statistics in the Rest

Every developing country maintains government statistical offices, even the poorest. These were usually set up soon after independence (and often existed in some form under colonial rule) and have been running for decades, almost always with some kind of support from donor agencies, with technical cooperation from UN's Statistics Division being prominent, as well as advice from the IMF on national accounts.[2] These national offices produce a country's crucial annual national accounts, and from this most economic performance statistics, including gross national product. These also produce demographic data and national censuses, trade and production numbers, commodity prices and inflation numbers, household consumption data (the main source for estimating and tracing poverty levels), labor force data, education and health data, etc. These days many national statistical offices also operate geographical information systems. Statistics generated by these offices are used by donor agencies in their own assessments of national and sectoral economic performance, upon which they base their analyses and designs of assistance programs.

How good are these statistical offices and how reliable are their data? This obviously depends on the country, since there are wide variations, and some middle-income countries enjoy solid reputations for their statistical work. But most who work in developing countries, especially poorer ones, would agree that the data coming out of these offices are often inaccurate, incomplete, tardy, and even consciously manipulated. It is well known that statistical offices suffer from gross underfunding and understaffing and that governments will sometimes put pressure to ensure that a positive spin is put on crucial numbers (especially for poverty levels and economic growth). It is thus surprising (not to mention a bit suspicious) that there is very little in the development literature about the recurring problems from which these offices suffer. In fact, looking exhaustively through the literature, only one book by Morten Jervin seems to have taken up the subject in any detail (Jervin, 2013). Jervin looks at eight African countries and his conclusion is that the numbers are extremely bad: "The arbitrariness of the quantification processes produces observations with very large errors and levels of uncertainty. This numbers game

[2] The Division's 2020 brochure is proud to show that its most important work is to support the development of indicators for the SDG Global Database (United Nations, 2020). Topics of particular concern to the Division include energy, migration, and gender, all of which are just happen to be mostly Western issues.

has taken on a dangerously misleading air of accuracy, and the resulting numbers are used to make crucial decisions that allocate scarce resources" (Jervin, 2013, xi). Do these conclusions for some African countries have relevance to other countries in the Rest? There is no way of knowing since it seems the subject of the quality of statistics is more or less taboo—at least among donors—but there is plenty of anecdotal information to suggest that bad statistics are common, if not so acute, throughout the developing world.

Donors and INGOs extensively use the outputs of these national statistical offices. In fact, they are in most cases the main consumers of this national information, so if it is inaccurate or simply made-up, what does this say for the huge compendium of statistics used and processed by donors in their endless pursuit of 'evidence-based' policies and interventions?

Macro Numbers and the God GDP

No numbers are looked at more than estimates of a country's Gross National Product (or Gross National Income, which is roughly the same), since they are direct indicators of country's economic growth and, as GDP per capita, are proxies for well-being of its population. So, the news was more than a tiny item when Ghana announced in 2010 that its GDP estimates had been revised upward by over 60 percent, propelling the country clear out of the category of 'least-developed' nation. And similar jumps in GDP occurred with Kenya and Nigeria in 2014, as well as periodically with other nations. So, what is going on? As one African development expert said about Ghana's massive upward recalculation of GDP, "Boy, we really don't know anything!" (Jerven & Duncan, 2014, 14).

GDP is an aggregate of the estimated added value of everything produced by a country in a particular year, and it depends on national accounts, which are maintained and revised by national statistical offices and involve a massive number of assumptions, estimations, weightings, and projections of prices across hundreds of sectors and subsectors in an economy. Plus, GDP should include estimates of products and prices found in a country's informal economy, something that is inherently difficult. Thus, these 'guestimates' of GDP, especially in poorer countries, should not be treated as anything enshrined in stone but rather as a number that comes from a complicated process in which a range of arbitrary and even controversial assumptions must be made. And most years only selected production and price figures are used as a proxy for change in whole chunks of the economy, with more revisions of the base year of price calculation (called rebasing) occurring only every decade or two. For many poor countries, the official results are simply pro forma projection exercises from previous periods.

The GDP as an approximation of national economic growth or well-being is criticized by many in the West, since it does not record unpaid work and does not incorporate negative externalities such as environmental deterioration. But in developing countries no one quibbles about such niceties, and nationally produced GDP figures are usually taken as articles of faith by economists and businessmen, with estimates published every fiscal quarter. Moreover, GDP estimates are used as the main reference point for a slew of other indicators of economic health. This is especially true for major negative indices—such as annual budget deficits, balance of payments deficits, new foreign loans, and aggregate sovereign debt—all of which are normally expressed as a percentage of GDP. So, there is every reason for a country to inflate GDP figures, especially since by doing so such embarrassing national indicators can be made to appear to be shrinking as expressed GDP percentages, when in fact in nominal terms they are usually rising inexorably.

So, are GDP figures massaged, and is GDP growth seriously inflated? This is hard to tell for individual countries, since questioning GDP figures is apparently not something donor agencies like to do. Sometimes the IMF will suggest (politely and low key) that they are somewhat out of line. But for sure the temptation of manipulating GDP estimates exists, and, for example, China is said to have been overestimating its GDP growth by almost a third for years (Long, 2019).

A rare critique about how GDP figures and related social and economic data can be manipulated in developing countries appeared in 2022 concerning Egypt (Roll & Batsi, 2022).[3] The article showed how data from the country's statistical agencies have been massaged to present a rosy picture of economic and social progress, and how this data has, almost without exception, been wholeheartedly accepted by the IMF, the WHO, and other international agencies. In particular, the uncritical inclusion of

[3] Roll, Stephan, and Salima Batsi (2022) "More than Window Dressing: On the Credibility of Public Statistics from Al Sisi's Egypt," Orient XXI Magazine, 27 January 2022, https://orientxxi.info/magazine/more-than-window-dressing-on-the-credibility-of-public-statistics-from-al-sisi,5330. Accessed 5 June 2022.

official Egyptian statistics in the IMF's country reports is seen as self-serving, since Egypt is now the second-largest debtor of the IMF, and justifying more and more lending requires a healthy economic picture of Egypt, particularly concerning the country's solvency.

Dense Data and Cross-Country Score Cards

More and more, massive amounts of data are perceived as important for analyzing development issues and to advance the work of the development industry, and such data density has become very prominent in the new Millennium. One need only to look at the World Development Indicators (maintained by the World Bank); Development Gateway and its spinoff OpenGov Hub (also set up by the World Bank); AidData (maintained at William and Mary University); Our World in Data (associated with Oxford University); or any number of UN, IMF, and OECD statistical sites to uncover truly massive amounts of data on various development issues that can be accessed and displayed in a bewildering number of ways. And although the reliability and comparability of the data presented are sometimes inconsistent or even dubious (and although data weaknesses are usually qualified in metadata explanations, these are buried away and rarely read), the numbers presented tend to impart an almost religious certainty. These sets of data are sometimes useful and the themes they illuminate can be insightful. But it seems that the overriding goal is to impart a sense of abstract scientific certainty on whatever subject is taken up and, at the same time, to provide a field day for number-crunching econometricians.

More than this, extensive data sets are often used for cross-country comparisons, something that allows the construction of score cards of how a country is performing over time compared to others—by sector, development topic, region, or any other theme one chooses. This elevates the whole discourse on development to one of aggregate relational metrics which, although it may be useful to drive home a point (as in, "country x had the second lowest percentage of school age children attending classes in Africa"), it doesn't even begin to probe into the complicated country-specifics of a topic or issue, something that one would have thought was the main reason for statistics—to help governments in the Rest to understand their economies and societies.

The introduction of the concept of Purchasing Power Parity (PPPa) greatly accelerated these inter-country data comparisons. PPPa, even though there are numerous problems in definition, methodology, and baselines, has allowed facile cross-country comparisons of a range of consumption and poverty indices, since it seems to overcome the thorny problems of currency conversions and allows a standardization of values in terms of dollars, based on baskets of household goods. These metrics (e.g., country per capita poverty lines of US$ 1.90, 3.20, or 5.50 per day) have come to dominate most of the discussion of how well the fight against poverty is going.

As if these were not enough, various periodic surveys and indices of country performance on a wide number of themes have become a big business, adding greatly to the infatuation for cross-country comparisons. These usually rely on rather subjective questionnaires aimed at local observers and businessmen. Numeric values (1 to 10 or 1 to 100) are assigned to specific sub-thematic topics, and these are then weighted and combined into overall indices. Their use in comparing one country to another is beset by many methodological problems, but they are considered useful, especially in establishing country trends and standings.

The mother of all such indices is the World Bank's annual Doing Business survey. It purports to measure how easy or difficult it is for a private company to function, and it is applied to 190 countries. Subthemes include starting a business, dealing with construction permits, registering property, getting credit, paying taxes, trading across borders, enforcing contracts, and resolving insolvency, and these are aggregated to a country's ease of doing business numerical score that can be ranked with other countries. Since these scores can influence an international firm's decision about where to invest, there is keen interest, and in 2020 embarrassing manipulations were uncovered whereby certain nations (mentioned were China, Azerbaijan, and Saudi Arabia) tried to influence the 2018 and 2019 indicators and thus improve their overall rankings. In subsequent investigations it was found that China, in particular, had tried to gain higher scores with offers of high-stakes capital replenishments to the World Bank, and that some very high-up Bank managers were involved (Igoe, 2021). The Doing Business rankings had been criticized for years for painting a pro-private sector and sanitized picture of business reality, but it took a scandal to put their future use in doubt.[4]

[4]A very negative view of the Doing Business Index was given by Joseph Stiglitz: "The numbers were always squishy, with small changes in the data having potentially large effects on the rankings" (Stiglitz, 2021).

Similar country indices and rankings have been established for a remarkable number of issues. Thus, we have country indices for corruption, for governance, for financial development, for democracy, and many, many others. It is as if having the world awash with these cross-country comparisons provides a certain aura of measurable determinism about global development.

Project-Level Numbers and Mechanistic Games

Every year donors launch literally thousands of time-bound projects and initiatives throughout the developing world. Each is carefully planned and prepared in terms of inputs, staging, funding allocations, tasks, phases, and outputs, and, more and more, the outcomes are to be expressed in terms that are measurable and verifiable. All of this lends a comforting sense of rigid linear determinism. Things at the project level used to be simpler, as noted by Robert Chambers, writing in 2017: "Over the past two decades there has, then, been an insidious creep to lock in the dynamics of the development sector into ever more mechanistic, rigid, formulaic, and dysfunctional procedures imperiously required by funders" (Chambers, 2017, Loc 2384).

This creep can be seen in many ways. Project documents and terms of reference are themselves constructed by donor agencies in deterministic, linear steps and finite timelines, as if messy details and inevitable delays can be conjured away. This can also be seen in the proposals written by contractors who present comforting and detailed schedules and elaborate input–output diagrams for their workplans. Moreover, knowledge of a topic or sector—something that forms the crucial basis for the design of project interventions—are also seen as deterministic and quantifiable inputs for analysis, even though, as pointed out by Chambers nothing could be further from the truth. As he says, there are normally untold errors and myths, blind spots and biases, and mechanistic methodologies that put into question the whole 'scientific' bases for knowledge about development (Chambers, 2017, Chaps. 1–3).

But such messiness about development projects cannot be allowed. Donors *must* present what appear to be logical conceptualizing and planning, sequencing and managing of inputs and tasks, and measurable results. There have been various techniques that have been used for these purposes in development projects, such as ZOPP and SWOT analyses. But the system that has gone the furthest to satisfy this need for objective linearity is logical framework analysis, a methodology that began to be used by donors and INGOs to plan and track development projects in the 1990s. The logical framework itself is a matrix that has (1) a vertical logic as a hierarchy of objectives, activities, and outputs which contribute to outcomes and (2) a horizontal logic showing how progress against each objective can be assessed (measurable indicators and means of verification) and the external factors (assumptions and risks). Logical framework analysis is the use of these matrices in the design and monitoring of projects, and these matrices can be large—easily extending over many pages. For most of those working in a project or its evaluation, the whole logframe process is perplexing, extremely time-consuming, and of doubtful benefit, but these analyses are something that the donor requires (or is assumed to require). As one analyst summed it up: "Logframes produce confusion rather than clarity and generate assessment processes unrelated to real project issues ... Logframes can function to sideline the politics and messiness of development itself, reinforcing (and generating) mechanistic views of the development process in which inputs automatically lead to the specified outputs" (Bornstein, 2003, 398).

Besides these problems, the logframe approach has become yet another mechanism that keeps the conceptualization and evaluation of interventions firmly in the hands of those who think up, manage, and execute these efforts—mainly Western donors and the consultants they hire—leaving the recipient partner or implementing agency or local community conveniently outside the carefully built-up conversation. Luckily, some donor agencies are becoming less enamored with the logframe technique, but after twenty-five years of use, it has momentum and staying power. Also, logframe analysis is an important tool in results-based management systems, and these are popular donor practices that show no signs of fading away.

Objectifying the Poor and Sidestepping Inequality

Numbers and measurement have long been crucial to both the analysis and understanding of the incidence, scope, and intensity of poverty in the Rest, and quantifiable knowledge of the poor dominates much of the development world's numerical landscape, particularly since reducing/eliminating poverty became the Goal One of the Sustainable Development Goals, with no less than 7 targets and 14 indicators.

Practically all of these statistics on poverty derive from large sample household income, expenditure, or consumption surveys carried out periodically by national statistical offices (and then filtered or otherwise standardized by the World Bank or others). These surveys have sample frames that are linked to census data, they have been standard fare in most developing countries since the 1970s, and they are the backbone of estimates of household or individual income/consumption distributions and also of understandings of consumption patterns and their changes, household assets, household savings, and demand for housing and other major investments and how they vary. Thus, there is a wealth of information coming from these surveys, and they are laudable efforts of often underfunded national statistical offices. In particular, national poverty lines (usually based on assumptions of minimum nutritional requirements) are established based on these surveys.

Of course, these surveys are not perfect, and it is well known that they can miss and thus underrepresent the poorest families, especially those in slums and remote rural areas. In addition, not all households in the sample will respond to all questions or even agree to participate, and this is particularly true of well-off households. Even so, the data coming from these surveys are used across the board by donors in their compilations of indicators of country well-being and poverty, including the calculations of the Gini Coefficient, the standard statistical measure of a society's overall inequality. The resulting picture of inequality, as processed by donor agencies, has given a rather comforting impression that gross inequality is not so bad in most developing countries, certainly no worse than what is found in many advanced countries. For example, Egypt's Gini Coefficient is reported to be quite low, implying a remarkable level of equality that has only recently been questioned (Achcar, 2020).

Only starting in the 2000s were attempts made to use other data to give a more illuminating and realistic view on a country's economic inequality that incorporated data on the incomes of the better off sections of a country's population that had been mostly missed by income data derived from household surveys. In 2011 this became the World Inequality Database (Picketty, 2013). At first his research was focused on long-term trends in income distribution in the West, mainly due to the availability of relevant data. These findings were shocking, particularly in tracking the long term, steady, and outrageous rise of the richest one and tenth percent of society and the shrinking share of national income captured by the lowest 50 percentile.[5]

By 2015 Picketty and company had begun to look at India, China, and other developing countries. The concentration of income and assets among the highest percentiles of income distribution was found to be remarkably high, much as had been found to be the case in the West. For example, in 2015 it was estimated that in both India and Brazil the top 10 percent of households took in at least 55 percent of national revenue, whereas in China the same portion was 'only' 42 percent. Regional estimates by Picketty showed that the Middle East was the most unequal area of the world with just over 60 percent of revenue captured by the richest ten percent, and sub-Saharan Africa was not far behind at about 55 percent (Picketty, 2013, 79).

It is hard to understand why mainstream donors had, for years and years, ignored these embarrassing but hiding-in-plain-sight indications of large (and increasing) capture of national income by the very rich. Instead, they seemed to have had an exclusive focus on the lower end of the curve. Sure, this focus might help influence pro-poor policy, but it is also a way of deflecting interest from the outrageously unequal income and wealth distributions in the Rest and the ways governments pamper the rich. It is as if the donors have accepted that the comfortably off are not to be touched, even though they often consume fifty percent of national output (and hold an even higher percentage of a country's assets or wealth). It should have been obvious that a developing country would never be able to get ahead and mobilize the necessary resources as long as those on top could continue to game the system (e.g., by avoiding taxes and preserving their privileges).

Summing Up

It is certainly true that the development industry has, especially over the last 25 years or so, become increasingly dominated—some would say obsessed—with the quantification and numerical measurement of everything. Results- and evidence-based assessment and evaluation systems, as

[5] Picketty and company were able to advance the state of the art by looking at a number of data sources in addition to 'representative' household surveys. These included data from country national accounts, fiscal data on individual taxes, fiscal data on asset holdings and on inheritance, and reporting on huge personal fortunes.

well as methods of performance-based project metrics, have become the main way most development projects are conceived, implemented, and assessed by donors. This has created a rarefied world of special codes, language, skill-sets, and artifacts that conveniently sidesteps the messiness, political dynamics, and power relations found in most development sectors and denigrate locally generated solutions, common-sense social policies, and thus anything approaching transformative change.[6] And at the same time this extreme focus on evidence and results guarantees Western conceptualizations and expertise will continue to dominate how development projects and programs are defined and managed. This quantitative, techno-linear obsession allows the whole development game to remain firmly positioned as something that only requires more and more funds to be disbursed under a false scientism, with the comfortable feeling that such progress can be measured and that donors are getting 'value for money.'

To conclude, a bit of perspective should be added. It was only in 1932 that the system of national accounts was first introduced (in the United States by Simon Kuznets), and it was John Maynard Keynes who, during the Second World War, first called for the use of the concept of the gross national product, mainly as a means to better mobilize economies to prosecute the war effort. This begs the question: How did the world's rich Western nations manage to get where they were by the mid-twentieth century without *any* of these massive data-rich macro conceptions or *any* of these wonderful systems of measurement?

References

Achcar, G. (2020). On the Arab inequality puzzle: The case of Egypt. *Development and Change, 51*(3), 746–770.

Bornstein, L. (2003). Management standards and development practice in the South Africa aid chain. *Public Administration and Development, 23*, 393–404.

Chambers, R. (2017). *Can we know better? Reflections on development.* Practical Action Publishing.

Eyben, R., Guijt, I., Roche, C., & Shutt, C. (Eds.). (2015). *The politics of evidence and results in international development: Playing the game to change the rules?* Practical Action Publishing.

[6]An anthology produced in 2015 analyzes in detail the 'evidence and results' agenda in development management and program design. It is particularly illuminating to see how this agenda and its score-card mentality fits into donor management priorities (Eyben et al., 2015).

Igoe, M. (2021, September 17). *Devex Newswire: World Bank's doing business scandal*. Accessed June 5, 2022, from https://www.devex.com/news/devex-newswire-the-world-bank-s-doing-business-scandal-101633

Jerven, M., & Duncan, M. E. (2014). Revising GDP estimates in Sub-Saharan Africa: Lessons from Ghana. *The African Statistical Journal, 15*. Accessed June 4, 2022, from https://www.afdb.org/fileadmin/uploads/afdb/Documents/Publications/ASJ15%20Section1%20Eng.pdf

Jervin, M. (2013). *Poor numbers: How we are misled by African development statistics and what to do about it*. Cornell University Press.

Long, S. (2019, March 7). China 'exaggerated' GDP data by 2 percentage points for at least nine years, new study says. *South China Morning Post*. Accessed June 5, 2022, from https://www.scmp.com/economy/china-economy/article/2189052/china-exaggerated-gdp-data-2-percentage-points-least-nine

Natsios, A. (2010, July 1). *The clash of the counter-bureaucracy and development*. Center for Global Development.

Picketty, T. (2013) *Capital in the twenty-first century* (*Le Capital au XXIe siècle)*.

Roll, S., & Batsi, S. (2022, January 27). More than window dressing: On the credibility of public statistics from Al Sisi's Egypt. *Orient XXI Magazine*. Accessed June 5, 2022, from https://orientxxi.info/magazine/more-than-window-dressing-on-the-credibility-of-public-statistics-from-al-sisi,5330

Rottenburg, R. (2009). *Far-fetched facts: A parable of development aid*. MIT Press. (Translated from the German: Rottenburg, *Rottengur Weit hergeholte fakten*. Eine Parabel des Entwicklungshlfe, Lucius & Lucius, 2002).

Rottenburg, R., & Merry, S. E. (2015). A world of indicators: The making of government knowledge through quantification. In R. Rottenburg, S. E. Merry, S.-J. Park, & J. Mugler (Eds.), *A world of indicators: The making of government knowledge through quantification*. Cambridge University Press.

Stiglitz, J. (2021, September 27). A coup attempt at the IMF. *Project Syndicate*. Accessed June 5, 2022, from https://www.project-syndicate.org/commentary/coup-attempt-against-imf-managing-director-georgieva-by-joseph-e-stiglitz-2021-09

Truman, H. (1949). *Inaugural address of Harry S. Truman. The Avalon Project*. Yale University. Accessed June 4, 2022, from https://avalon.law.yale.edu/20th_century/truman.asp

UNIDO. (1978). *Guide to practical project appraisal: Social benefit-cost analysis in developing countries*. United Nations.

United Nations. (2020). *Statistics division in brief*. Accessed June 4, 2020, from https://unstats.un.org/home/documents/brochures/2020-UNSD-Brochure.pdf

CHAPTER 7

Chronic Ills of the Industry

In this chapter we look at some of the more common and enduring problems of the development business that don't easily fit into the themes of other chapters. These can be considered chronic symptoms, and each is so well-known and evidently intractable that it suffices to simply give a short treatment that includes answering why they are so problematic and intransigent. We take up the following seven subjects:

- Dubious evaluations and lessons never learned
- Poor operations and maintenance of donor-funded investments
- Institutional amnesia and reinventing the wheel
- Systemic delays
- Lost good work and planned ignorance
- Language barriers
- Donor elitism and privileged bubbles

Dubious Evaluations and Lessons Never Learned

Evaluations and their close cousin monitoring have been around almost as long as development itself. Scandinavians, the Dutch, and the Germans were the first to evaluate their aid projects systematically (starting in the late 1960s), and in 1983 the DAC Expert Group on Aid Evaluation was formed, which in 2003 was renamed the DAC Network on Development

D. Sims, *Development Delusions and Contradictions*, https://doi.org/10.1007/978-3-031-17770-5_7

Evaluation. Development evaluations are anchored in the idea that, through reasoned assessments of ongoing and completed projects, there will be both technical and managerial lessons to learn that can subsequently be integrated into donor project/program cycles and departmental strategies, also known as all-important feedback loops. This has been a bedrock of donor philosophy to which virtually every donor agency ascribes, and this is reflected in both organizational structures and in the ways by which projects are understood.

Over the decades donor evaluations have become quite a sub-industry in its own right. There are special units or departments within donor structures, there are those who are considered experts specialized in evaluation, there is considerable donor and academic reporting and discussion on the issues, and there is a large and growing literature on evaluation in the form of guidelines, manuals, and policy pieces. There are even consulting firms that claim specialized expertise in evaluating development projects, and at least a dozen academic journals take up aspects of the subject.

How successful has this large evaluation sub-industry been? Does it deliver independent, actionable, and hard-hitting conclusions that are absorbed by donors and recipient governments, and does it lead to better, more effective assistance on down the line? Unfortunately, most street level practitioners look at evaluations as merely pro forma exercises that impart little more than positive gloss on what donors accomplish, rarely make substantial criticisms, and never, ever, call a disastrous failure a disastrous failure. One main conclusion of a 2020 paper in *World Development* confirmed this pessimistic view, repeatedly saying that evidence shows that evaluations of development projects are very often 'positively biased,' and that there are a host of other problems (Clements, 2020). Even the OECD-DAC noted in 2010 that there were many 'challenges' (read serious shortcomings) in donor evaluation efforts—especially in coordinating with other donors, in communicating findings and engaging with recipient countries, in integrating findings into donors' own programs or country strategies, and in better formulating of lessons learned (OECD, 2010).[1]

Simply by adding the word 'independent' to a donor's evaluation department (as have the World Band and the ADB, among others) does not guarantee that conclusions will not necessarily tow the donor agency's party line. And by requiring that 'lessons learned' become major sections

[1] This report reviewed evaluation activities of 23 bilateral aid donors and seven multilateral development banks.

of evaluations reports does not guarantee anything is learned by the donor or a wider audience. In fact, the constraints surrounding evaluations and the ways evaluation efforts are practiced make the situation even worse than it first appears. These constraints and weaknesses and that beset the evaluation sub-industry can be briefly listed:

Donors do not rely on outside, independent evaluations to assess any aspect of their work. Virtually every Western bilateral and multilateral donor plus the European Commission and every UN agency maintain and staff their own full-fledged departments tasked with carrying out all evaluations of projects, programs, or sectoral/policy support. And there is no such thing as an independent professional evaluation association, independent joint evaluation teams, or an independent evaluation fund, although such animals have been proposed from time to time (Jacquet, 2006, 177; Clements, 2020, 2; Birdsall, 2008, 529). Thus, although donor evaluation departments may have competent people, hire good consultants, and have gloriously principled mission statements, by no stretch of the imagination can they be considered free and independent.

Evaluation units only carry out evaluations on a very small portion of their projects, rarely more than 15 percent. Evidently the costs are too high to do more. So, the donor is free to pick and choose, and the tendency is not to choose embarrassing projects. Furthermore, there is a trend in the business to move away from single project evaluations, with emphasis being given more to program or even whole sector evaluations that further minimize the extraction of anything concrete.

Almost all evaluations are based on five standard principles or criteria: relevance, effectiveness, efficiency, sustainability, and impact (sometimes with minor variations and additions, such as 'coherence' and especially 'sustainability). These extremely subjective criteria have come into general use since the OECD Development Assistance Committee propounded them in 1991 (OECD-DAC, 1991, 5).[2] The suspicion is that donors have warmly adopted such subjective criteria because it has given them enormous leeway for interpretation, manipulation, and spin, allowing them to be "applied in an analytically vacuous manner" (Clements, 2020, 7).

[2] There is also the OECD publication Evaluating Development Co-Operation: Summary of Key Norms and Standards and the Evaluation Quality Standards and its glossary of key terms used in evaluation. Not to be outdone, there is also the UN Evaluation Group that produces its own guidelines and other literature.

Evaluations are supposed to assess project 'impact,' but this can be a very slippery concept, partly because it is by nature ill-defined and because "the lifetime of a project's impacts is almost always longer than the project's lifetime, and it is not unusual for impacts to extend 20 or 30 years past the project's closing" (Clements, 2020, 3).

Donor evaluation processes almost never include the active participation of the implementing partner. An evaluator on mission may carry out interviews with local project staff or concerned government officials, but it is rare that these people will be involved in write-ups. In spite of noble talk about country ownership, it seems that involvement of the recipient in any substantial parts of an evaluation is simply not part of the game.

Donor evaluation departments only recommend ways to improve the approaches and management of the specific donor's operations. Sometimes an evaluation might lightly offer suggestions about the need for better technical management and policy changes on the part of the partner agency, but these are mostly throwaway lines. And, except for throwaway references to the need for more intra-donor coordination and 'coherence,' evaluations *never* assess and criticize other donors individually or collectively.

It must be added that in most classic project evaluations the lead is carried out by individuals whose specialization and experiences are in evaluation itself, and very rare is the animal who is both expert in evaluations *and* in the sector or field that pertains. Evaluation departments seem to prefer to utilize these 'pure' evaluators for missions, and the suspicion is that donors are more comfortable with them because of their clubby familiarity and the fact that their future employability is likely to hinge on producing assessments that rock no boats.

There are even situations where high-up donor bosses, after looking at a draft evaluation report that can be construed as overly critical—no matter how well-reasoned and professional—is simply never released, disappearing into an administrative void. This is something that is relatively easy since few are aware that an evaluation has been commissioned and even fewer anticipate the results.

In summary, even though it could be said that donors have developed a whole evaluation sub-industry with its own codes, vocabulary, methodologies rules, and even textbooks,[3] it seems to be one that is most effective

[3] For an example of a textbook, there is a 588-page World Bank volume on conducting evaluations (Morra Imas, 2009).

at simply Carrying On Carrying On and not making waves. There are people within the evaluation subsector who are committed and competent, but it is the system under which they work that has taken the meaning out of 'independent' evaluation.

Poor Operations and Maintenance (O&M) of Donor Investments

Routine and preventive maintenance and periodic rehabilitation are particularly important for key networks like roads, irrigation systems, water, and sanitation and also for facilities like schools, health centers, and associated services—all of which are funded by donors. Yet the results, after a project is completed and the managers, consultants, and technicians have gone home, are frankly embarrassing. For example, extensive donor-financed road programs in Tanzania added thousands of kilometers to the national network to the tune of $20 billion over 20 years, but for "lack of maintenance, roads often deteriorated faster than they could be built…" (Easterly, 2002, 10). Elaborate donor-funded wastewater treatment plants in Egypt have only been kept running by simplifying and re-engineering the original high-tech control systems. Schools in Palestine have been left to deteriorate to the point that a new rehabilitation contract can be justified (and paid for) by the donor. And the list goes on and on and on.

These embarrassments derive from the long-established policy that, with few exceptions, donors simply do not fund O&M to keep their past investments running well, considering these to be recurrent rather than capital expenditures that should be the exclusive responsibility of recipient governments. Instead, donors have attached various covenants to financial agreements that require recipient governments to allocate sufficient O&M funds, but host governments have shown a remarkably consistent reluctance to allocate the necessary funds in annual budgets. It begs the question of why, despite much donor-preaching about proper care of capital investments, the situation continues? Is it simply the principle that recipients must be taught to take seriously their responsibilities? If so, such teaching/preaching has had precious little effect.

It is not as if donor agencies have let the O&M problem lie. Over the years more and more technical assistance projects have been devised to instruct recipients on better infrastructure management and, specifically, on how concerned ministries can develop cost-efficient maintenance capacities. Also promoted by donors are performance-based O&M contracts and the building up of maintenance-dedicated departments. In the last few years, the concept of donors funding some maintenance costs as part of an infrastructure reform package has even been tried out.

Some of these donor efforts at improving operations and maintenance have had positive results, and some infrastructure agencies in developing countries are now at least somewhat on top of the maintenance issue. But the O&M dilemma continues in myriad ways in most countries, and lots of donor advice and encouragement simply will not have much effect without at the same time imposing serious sectoral conditionality, such as the strong threat of withdrawing future support.

Reinventing the Wheel and Institutional Amnesia

The phrase 're-inventing the wheel' is unfortunately often heard in development industry circles, mainly because donors have been repeating the same mistakes, duplicating the same efforts, and studying the same things over and over again. Donor personnel are often ignorant of their agencies' past track record in a particular country or sector. Policy reports and strategy papers may have made a small splash when issued, but they quickly recede into oblivion, usually without having been read closely by anyone except the consultants hired to review them. In other words, there is a serious kind of amnesia, something that has been deplored for decades. For example, a World Bank portfolio review in 1997 concluded: "The lessons from past experience are well known, yet they are generally ignored in the design of new operations. This synthesis concludes that institutional amnesia is the corollary of institutional optimism" (World Bank, 1997, 15).

The reasons for this institutional amnesia relate to the interlocking ways development work is organized, justified, and reproduced. Although there are perfectly straightforward means for an institution to have a competent and reasonably accessible system for the archiving and retrieval of information, and although most donor agencies have some such systems in place, somehow there is a disconnect. Part of the reason is simply the immense volume of reports, documents, analyses, policy frameworks, directives, and memoranda that clutter up a donor's landscape, thus making their sifting and ranking and their absorption increasingly difficult. Another reason is the fact that donor managers and technical staff are always overworked (with operational duties, communications, events, and extraneous tasks, not to mention all-important office politics), and they can never seem to find the time to sit back and focus on substantive issues. They may be able to use an intern for simple information retrieval or hire a consultant for targeted investigations or for synthesizing issues, but there is still the problem of the donor manager him or herself being able to absorb and synthesize the information that is generated. It doesn't help that there is the compulsion to make summaries and summaries of summaries, to the extent that what might get read at the higher realms of donor management is two pages of sanitized platitudes with almost all content stripped out.

To make things worse, for the most part recipient governments and their ministries and agencies are terrible at keeping track of their past donor encounters and the copious documentation generated. Few decision makers in partner government agencies actually read what is produced, not even executive summaries and power points.

Another factor contributing to amnesia is a tendency among donors of describing current aid programs as new and innovative, implying that there is little need for digging into and learning from the past. Words such as 'bold new program' or 'fundamental reform' have been repeated for decades, and this devalues any feedback loops from the past that may exist. Thus, efforts at understanding even the recent past, including what lessons might have been learned in a particular country or sector or project or modality, are normally discounted.

Ironically, donors usually only remember their past experiences when a policy or initiative becomes a scandal. It is a kind of reverse amnesia, where what might just be a sound approach is dumped because of a public relations disaster. A perfect example of this was USAID's Helwan New Communities Project in the 1980s, where huge cost overruns were leaked to the press, and a cover article appeared in Forbes Magazine and questions about white elephants were raised in Congressional hearings (Senate Hearings, 1994, 122). This certainly captured USAID decision makers' attention! Not only was the project quickly wound down and eventually aborted, but until today USAID refuses to revisit the subject of affordable and suitable housing in Egypt.

The reasons for institutional amnesia go beyond these weaknesses in information retrieval and institutional memory. Much if not most of the blame can be laid on donor agencies' diktat to periodically reassign personnel and to shift them from country to country and project to project, particularly the practice of limiting an assignment for international staff in a country to two or a maximum of four years. Presumably this rotating is justified as giving professional personnel wide exposure to different contexts, and it has been very widely practiced for decades by all—UN agencies, multilaterals, bilaterals, even INGOs, but it plays havoc with aspects of policy and operations continuity. Whether for a large project loan or a smaller TA grant, the supervising donor project officer or in-country task team leader is absolutely key. But, usually without any forewarning, these key persons, with all their accumulated knowledge of the country and sector and all their relations built up with national counterparts and managers, are reassigned, and everyone must go through myriad adjustments to accommodate the replacements and bring them up to speed.

Why is this damaging staff rotation so common throughout the industry? Here we are in the shadowy area of a donor's corporate culture and human resource policies. Donors talk about nurturing teamwork, broadening managerial competencies, and furthering analytical skills by exposing staff to different contexts, but what is well known but almost never put into words are two concerns: First, there is a fear that international staff who stay too long in a country (or that continue over many years to manage the same project through missions from headquarters) might just succumb to temptations of favoritism or corruption. Second, donors do not want their international staff to become too enamored with the particular country or too comfortable working with issues that are country-specific, since staff just might begin to identify with the country rather than the institution they work for. One would have thought, with all the talk about ownership and the need to 'deliver results for clients,' that keeping someone in a country for as long as possible would be a definite plus, but evidently this is not so. The loss of continuity with each new manager or team leader can be devastating to a donor program and its country owner.

Frequently, these job rotations are accompanied by promotions, and it seems that for donor management this is a way to keep staff oriented to (and even obsessed with) the donor's own corporate culture and management hierarchies. Perhaps it also relates to some management principle of keeping staff on their toes, where the real skill is being able to 'manage' anything, no matter what is the substantive subject or context. If this is the case, it may buy loyalty, but at the expense of anything like a buildup of institutional memory, let alone the delivery of results.

Systemic Delays

A running complaint within the development industry is the extremely frequent and long delays experienced at virtually all stages of the rollout of projects and programs. Even though delays have profound negative effects everything donors do, the delay problem has been around so long that it no longer commands much attention in the we-can-make-aid-better arena.

The kinds of delays are many. Delays can be common in reaching financing agreements with governments, in the long process of project and subproject identification, in the social and other surveys required in setting up the project, in the allocation donor funds to partner agencies, in the cumbersome approvals and no objections required for each step, and in governments meeting their own obligations tied to development projects (for insurance, taxes, customs waivers, etc.). The same can be said for the disbursement of project funds by the executing agencies and their PMUs for capital works, for the hiring of key management personnel, and of course in the process of selection and mobilization of both individual consultants and consulting firms. It is almost never the case that negotiations on contracts or their addendums can be concluded on time, and tales are legion of it taking one or even two years to conclude signing. It doesn't help that a country's program or project steering committee may hardly ever meet.

As a result, it is very common for large loan projects from, say, the ADB or the World Bank, to be stretched way beyond the schedules that were originally penciled in. Project preparation that was to be completed in one year will take two or three, a six-month mobilization period will end up extending over 12 or 18 months, and project implementation that was supposed to run for five years will take seven or even more (Independent Evaluation Department, 2009, 7). Even the official closure of a project can take months and even years after moneys have been spent. Since most projects are broken into phases, getting to the next phase inevitably requires more approvals and more agreements, and these are rarely trouble free.

These delays wreak havoc upon the whole development business. Delays can be very costly, not to mention the fact that they can cause damage to a donor's reputation. Gaining trust with local communities and with partner agencies can be completely compromised, and time-consuming application processes can discourage local civil society organizations. Due to delays, both implementing agencies and consulting firms have to let good people go and then scurry to replace them when funds finally become available. Furthermore, the whole rationale for an intervention may have vanished by the time a donor project rolls ponderously into operation. And since the ultimate justification for most projects is the economic and social benefits (better health, better water and sanitation, better, more efficient transportation, etc.), these, even if they all materialize, will accrue over many more years (and usually bunched at the end) than had been presumed in the cost–benefit analyses and calculations of internal rates of return.

And what about the demonstration effect? Many aid initiatives are justified on their pilot nature and on serving as models to 'go to scale.' How can a project that is ridden with delays and whose 'results' dribble out in fits and starts become a demonstration of how to solve whatever pressing development issue is at hand? And what about carefully nurtured and innovative reform programs and their local champions whose momentum, even survival, can be compromised by funding and programming delays?

So why are delays so ubiquitous? It seems to be a perfect storm of three factors—the uneasy fit and interface between two or more stubbornly bureaucratic systems, the donor obsession for complete control of projects and their moneys, and the recipient government's indifference and lack of any follow-up. If this is the case, then why not simply recognize that everything takes longer than expected and program this fact into the original project timelines? This leads to another factor—consistent overoptimism, especially by donors. Top managers and departmental bosses always want to Move the Money in a hurry, and those under them feel beholden to plan for the rapid sequencing of actions and events to quickly arrive at project approval, project implementation, and disbursement of funds. After all, in the donor world it seems that speed is associated with managerial competence and those who can rush things are more likely to curry favor.

So, it seems that delays in the business will just go on, over and over, causing both endless frustration and unnecessary reputational damage, further shrinking the chances that development efforts will be effective and lead to anything like sustainable policy, program, or sector improvements.

Lost Good Work and Lost Opportunities

Projects commissioned by donors often entail much good on-the-ground analytical work, identify possible solutions, and generate useful recommendations. But frequently such work never sees the light of day, either because issues are too complex, or because what is said doesn't fit with program assumptions or underlying ideologies, or worse, that evidence is uncovered that show the original donor assumptions and the policies they adopted are simply wrong. Still-born ideas and shelved draft proposals often represent the best that copious technical assistance funding has to show, but practically no one pays attention to them, and they give the industry's frequent call for 'innovation' an ironic, bitter taste. Worse, the development opportunities they identify are lost.

Part of the problem is the lack of access by outsiders to the donor's basic work and the internal documents that reflect this work. Draft studies, consultant proposals, concept notes, field work conclusions, snap surveys, and summaries of discussions with local communities or local engineers are often where the real ideas are to be found. They may only point out that there is not enough understanding about the issue at hand, or that donor approaches are un-implementable, or both. They may have been written by consultants or by teams of researchers whose work has been deftly put aside because it simply couldn't fit into overarching project frameworks. But the development industry, especially donors, is loath to consider making these documents available to other development practitioners, let alone academics or the general public.

The best of this work frequently simply dies in some project summary or in a vague reference to a study that cannot be accessed. Mainly this is because it might embarrass either government or the donor or both. Or it may be simply that it is too fine grained, too equivocal, and cannot be reduced to simplistic conclusions. Or that the work proposes solutions that do not require huge capital expenditures and/or imply breaking down contracts into smaller lots that can be tendered to local firms or even local NGOs and communities. Such kinds of approaches can't be made to fit into carefully edited packages of project components and sub-components that are a priori linked to measurable indicators. In other words, such practical approaches are likely to be messy, and it is smooth sailing projects and techno-linear frameworks are what the industry wants.

For all anyone knows, there are hundreds if not thousands of such examples of such good development ideas that are lost forever, simply because they are suppressed, ignored, or don't fit the paradigms. So much for 'innovation.'

Language Barriers

English has always been the dominant language in the world of development, and this dominance continues to increase. Also, the development concepts, jargon, and fashions that increasingly drive the business are almost always invented, expressed, exchanged, and reinvented solely in English. Yes, there are still exceptions to the rule, especially for Spanish in Latin American countries and for French in West and North Africa and also to a lesser extent Russian in Central Asia and Arabic in the Middle East. But even those from such countries—and the French, Belgium, Swiss, and Spanish donor agencies that deal with them—have found it necessary to use English extensively so as not to become sidelined in all-important meta-development discussions. Also, the historical weight of English in India and other countries of the South Asia as well as in former British colonies throughout Asia and Africa gives even more importance to English as the medium of development discourses.

One may say, what is the problem with English dominance? English has pretty much become the global language of commerce, science, and diplomacy, and one could say the development industry is only going with the trend (Mikanowski, 2018). Yes, but the whole idea of development is that less developed countries can, albeit with some little help from their 'international partners,' pursue their own paths and engage with their citizens in national development efforts, grounded in locally generated thinking, debate, discourse, and alliances. Such a nod to endogenous development and self-expression has become the stock of a huge tranche of development theorizing and preaching generated by donors, especially that which talks about transparency, accountability, participation, and, especially, 'ownership' of development processes.

Donors and the various pilot fish of the development industry have made token efforts to accommodate the bilingual if not trilingual nature of their work by engaging interpreters to accompany donor missions and funding translations of at least some of their documentary output. Non-English language skills are sought out—at least on paper—in donor recruitment systems, and some bilateral donors will even pay for language instruction for their staff. Yet much of this is simply per forma. Translations are often of very poor quality, and translated documents rarely appear alongside English versions, coming weeks if not months after the English version has been digested. And the most important documentation related to projects (such as terms of reference, requests for proposals, policy think pieces, etc.) is most likely not translated at all.

In effect, the 'language barrier' remains substantial, and there are quite insidious side effects. For example, there are very competent technical people in various recipient organizations who, because their command of English is imperfect, never gain the recognition and responsibility they should have, remaining little more than worker ants for their (sometimes clueless) superiors who have a good command of English jargon. Plus, these people will never acquire wider understandings of development challenges in their fields since, with rare exceptions, the copious material they need to read and absorb are not to be found in their own language.

Furthermore, the ever-present need for those who can 'talk development' in all its fashionable shades of meaning has created a whole class of what could be called 'development compradors' who insert themselves into the higher intersections between foreigners and locals—in meetings, correspondence, and even interpreting what is happening on the ground. Some of these may actually contribute to interchanges and understanding, but more often they themselves are technically incompetent and rely on their language and jargon skills to appear to be indispensable. And these development compradors are much beloved by parachuting donor staff and their consultants, since they can generate a false aura of the meeting of like minds.

Finally, it needs to be pointed out that in most Third World countries those competent in English are most likely the products of private and expensive international schools whose medium is English or French. These people almost all come from privileged families and are steeped in elitist mindsets and Western values. Those who then pursue development careers carry world views that, if not totally disparaging of their lower-class compatriots, tend to view them in paternalistic terms. And over decades the repeated reproduction of these elitist cadres has solidified this cultural divide. The crushing majority of those who must perforce rely on public education in the Rest remain in circuits that are only marginal to a country's development space, except for aging government officials or military officers or political party stalwarts whose high positions are purely due to seniority or connections. Sure, some information technology, engineering, and science types coming from public school streams can still enter and excel, but for most of those who achieve insertion into the main narratives of development, coming from the small upper classes is a given.

Privileged Bubbles and Donor Elitism

A certain elitism has long characterized how donors operate when their people attend conferences, go on missions, or locate somewhere. Not only are donor staff well-paid, have good job security, and have very cushy benefits, but when travelling they enjoy very comfortable daily allowances, stay in the best hotels, have cars and drivers laid on, and travel first or business class. And for donor staff posted to a country, extremely nice housing (far beyond what they could hope to have back home) is offered along with attractive education allowances for the kids, help with vehicles, domestic staff, and so on. Donor organizations enjoy all the benefits that accrue to diplomats, including customs and tax exceptions, easy visas, etc., and their health and safety have always been carefully looked after. And these days security has become an obsession, leading to absurd measures that do little except reinforce the familiar bunkered-down mentality.

The same can be said for the consultants and contractors that donors heavily rely on. They are well paid (even after the firms that provide them extract their substantial overheads), and they normally enjoy hefty per diems, stay in the best hotels, and often fly business class. However, they do not have anything like the other perks that donor staff enjoy, and few have anything like job security.

Altogether, not only do all these privileges insulate donor staff and their consultants from the realities of the countries they are in, they also easily generate 'us-versus-them' mindsets. And, as we discuss in Chap. 17, such privileges generate considerable rancor and frustration among local counterparts in government and the local professionals who are supposed to be enthusiastic 'partners' in development projects.

Of course, over the years there have been many who have complained about this privileged elitism and the irony of fighting poverty from glitzy bubbles. Foremost among them is Graham Hancock, who castigated the aid industry as an extravagant sinkhole for arrogant free riders (Hancock, 1991).[4] It is telling that most of those working in donor agencies have

[4] Graham Hancock, Graham (1991) *Lords of Poverty: The power, prestige, and corruption of the international aid business,* New York. Atlantic Monthly Press.

never even heard of *Lords of Poverty*, which underscores an impressive ignorance of people in the business about criticisms of themselves. Somehow the irony of discussing extreme poverty, vast underemployment, abysmal health systems, or exploding slums in a Hilton Hotel conference room, with overloaded buffet tables in the adjoining ballroom, just doesn't sink in.

Other critiques of donor elitism and the attendant insulation from reality have been written, mainly academic pieces and observations from those positioned more on the humanitarian side of development. These include pieces by Rosalind Eyben, Lisa Smiri, Astrid Jamar, Uma Kothari, David Mosse, etc., who not only point out the obvious but analyze the ability of such elitism to cloud any comprehension of Third World realities.[5]

What is amazing about the phenomenon is that, despite such criticism over the years, privileged bubbles just sail on and on. The justification, should anyone ever ask, is that it is not only development types who enjoy all these perks and advantages, but something that is also well established in the world of diplomacy and among global corporations. And donors will argue that such perks are needed to recruit the kind of staff they send abroad. This may be so, but it all has the whiff of something more than a bit self-serving.

References

Birdsall, N. (2008). Seven deadly sins: Reflections on donor failings. In W. Easterly (Ed.), *Reinventing foreign aid* (p. 2008). MIT Press.

Clements, P. (2020). Improving learning and accountability in foreign aid. *World Development, 125*, 104670. https://doi.org/10.1016/j.worlddev.2019.104670

Easterly, W. (2002). The cartel of good intentions: The problem of bureaucracy in foreign aid. *Journal of Policy Reform, 3*(4), 223–250. https://doi.org/10.1080/1384128032000096823

Hancock, G. (1991). *Lords of Poverty* (originally published 1989). London: Mandarin Paperbacks.

Independent Evaluation Department. (2009, August). *Viet Nam: Sector assistance program evaluation on urban services and water supply and sanitation sector. Reference Number: SAP: VIE 2009-27*. Asian Development Bank.

Jacquet, P. (2006, September). Evaluations and aid effectiveness. In N. Birdsall (Ed.), *Rescuing the World Bank*. Center for Global Development.

[5] Good examples of this genre of criticism: Smirl (2015) and Jamar (2017).

Jamar, A. (2017, March 3). *Breakfast in Aidland: Quotidian relations and structural contradictions*. Allegra Lab. Accessed June 5, 2022, from https://allegralaboratory.net/breakfast-in-aidland-quotidian-relations-and-structural-contradictions/
Mikanowski, J. (2018, July 27). Behemoth, bully, thief: How the English language is taking over the planet. *The Guardian*. Accessed June 5, 2022, from https://www.theguardian.com/news/2018/jul/27/english-language-global-dominance
Morra Imas, L. G., & Rist, R. C. (2009). *The road to results: Designing and conducting effective development evaluations*. World Bank. Accessed June 5, 2022, from https://openknowledge.worldbank.org/handle/10986/2699
OECD. (2010). *Better aid: Evaluation in development agencies, OECD DAC Network on Development Evaluation* (p. 2010). OECD.
OECD-DAC. (1991). *Principals of evaluation for development assistance*. Accessed June 5, 2022, from https://www.oecd.org/dac/evaluation/2755284.pdf
Senate Hearings before the Committee on Appropriations. Subcommittee on Foreign Operations, Export Financing, and Related Programs. (1994) *Foreign operations, export financing, and related program appropriations, fiscal year 1994.*
Smirl, L. (2015). *Spaces of aid. How cars, compounds, and hotels shape humanitarianism*. Zed Books.
World Bank. (1997). Reviews of sector portfolios and lending instruments: A synthesis. World Bank Quality Assurance Group, Portfolio Improvement Program 22 April, 1997 (draft internal report). In J. Pincus, & J. Winters (Eds.), *Reinventing the World Bank*. Cornell University Press, 2002, 247.

CHAPTER 8

Acts of Congregation

It was William Easterly who, in 2002, came up with the term "easily observable outcomes" to describe a recurring penchant among donors to spend considerable resources and to devote significant amounts of time in the production of events and texts. Addressing the issue of donor bureaucracies, Easterly says: "Similar to the tendency to redefine output as money disbursed is a tendency by the aid community to stress low-return observable outputs like international meetings of statesmen, glossy reports for the public, and the proliferation of framework and strategy papers" (Easterly, 2002, 223). These are the easy outputs, those that do not require tough negotiations, conditionality, or arm-twisting with governments on the receiving end of donor largess, nor do they require complicated procurement or monitoring and evaluation or measurement of donor-funded outputs and impacts. These considerable hassles, long part of mainstream donor assistance to developing countries, are conveniently absent from these easily observable outcomes.

In this chapter we look at events or 'acts of congregation' as a phenomenon of the development industry, one that seems to be ever popular, even in the Covid Era. In the next chapter we take up the phenomenon of texts that are churned out by the development industry, most of which are never read except by the unlucky few whose job it is to read them. Both of these phenomena contain a set of important functions, in that they enable industry actors to feel good about themselves and to confirm their presence on the national and international development stage. In addition,

D. Sims, *Development Delusions and Contradictions*,
https://doi.org/10.1007/978-3-031-17770-5_8

these phenomena are potent weapons in justifying their otherwise questionable existences. And, to repeat, they can be funded and executed without any of the contentious and drawn-out maneuvering that is unavoidable with mainline development aid going to recipient countries.

The Cascade of Development Conferences and Confabs

Few realize just how much conferencing goes on in the development business. A look at Development Aid's announcement of 'major events' for August and September 2018 shows that in just two months a total of twenty-one summits, international forums, and global conferences are listed (Developmentaid, 2018). This works out to a rhythm of 126 per year or one mega event every three days. Looking at this listing in some detail, we find that all were multiday events with lots of key speakers and hundreds if not thousands of attendees. About half of these events were in the West and the other half sprinkled around the Rest, either in major cities where five-star hotels are in ample supply or in remote, swanky resorts (the better to capture the attendees undivided attention). The main sponsors include the usual multilateral donors plus the World Economic Forum, UN agencies, and some others. No bilateral donors are sponsors in this two-month sample, but they are very well represented as speakers or panel discussants, as are global company CEOs. Half of these meetings had something to do with the environment, especially with climate, air quality, sustainability, resilience, oceans, forests, and energy.

And this is just a tip of the event iceberg. Over the same period there are untold hundreds if not thousands of smaller regional and country seminars, technical workshops, symposiums, roundtables, panels, and colloquia, sometimes open to anyone, more often not. Many of these events are linked to or are outcomes of ongoing development programs and projects, but more are stand-alone events that deal with various development topics and themes, the trendier the better. For example, the World Bank's Events website lists a total of twenty-two seminars, forums, and panels that were scheduled over the same August to September 2018 period (World Bank, 2018).

This parade of development events has been going on for some time. The first serious development event probably goes way back to the Bretton Woods Conference in 1944, a 20-day closed gathering of 730 delegates where it was decided to set up the World Bank and IMF. In the 1960s and 1970s global conferences, often UN led, increasingly became important dates in the schedules of development industry players, and the idea came in vogue that no expense should be spared in making these events appear important and successful. Graham Hancock describes in entertaining detail the extravagant joint annual meeting of the Board of Governors of the World Bank and the IMF held in Washington DC way back in September 1986 (Hancock, 1991, 38–40). He records the circus of 10,000 attendees at the exclusive Sheraton-Washington, how VIPs normally scattered over the four corners of the world get together replete with "staggering displays of dominance and ostentation … blended with empty and meaningless rhetoric about the predicament of the poor," with "gas guzzling limousines" in such prominence that journalists started describing the traffic as 'limo-lock.'

In the 1990s and on into the new century, development events continued to expand in number and scope. For example, Easterly mentions that over two years in the mid-1990s the World Bank's IDA alone chaired ninety formal meetings and provided substantial input to thirty-eight others chaired by other donors (Easterly, 2002, 228). But such references to development events are purely anecdotal, since as far as is known no one tries to track how many events, large or small, are spun out by the development industry over a given time period and what they cost. It is in no one's interest to do so, and with the odd exception, nothing is more dead and forgotten than a conference that is over, conference papers, press kits, and other artifacts not-withstanding.

Conference Mechanics

Conferences take considerable effort to organize and setup, with the sponsor defining the theme, constructing a first list of VIP attendees and speakers, and securing a budget. Some development agencies have in-house conference services but most rely on specialized management firms. Depending on complexity, the lead-time for a conference can take anywhere from a couple of months to a year or more. Choosing a date that does not conflict with possible competing development events (or which falls during major holidays) is a crucial first step, as is choosing the host city and conference center and/or hotel(s). Given that the presence of important government officials and prominent personalities can be crucial for a conference, securing their attendance early on is imperative. In fact, this often is the first task, feeling out whether ministers, general secretaries, and prominent speakers with name recognition are likely to attend. The burden for most of this advance planning falls on the sponsoring agency staff, including the always time-pressed top managers, even should a conference services firm be outsourced (Who else is going to contact and invite a sitting minister, if not the organizer's head?). A frequent complaint from donor technical staff is that such in-house conference preparation is so time-consuming that their normal project, program, or policy work inevitably suffers, sometimes horribly.

One particularly onerous task in preparing for an international conference is the travel arrangements—visas, flights, hotels, per diems, etc.—for those invited to attend. These are relatively straightforward for those coming from Western countries, but for people coming from the Rest, especially if they are government prima donnas, lots of time and diplomatic back-and-forth are spent ensuring their attendance. The absurd visa requirements, the authorizations for business/first-class air tickets, per diems, and stop-offs, these can drive even the most seasoned administrator to despair.

Most conferences are normally based around plenary sessions, with one at the beginning that features the head of the sponsoring organization plus at least one host country minister or other powerful government or UN official. What follows are various panels, forums, side events, and breakouts organized according to sub-themes.[1] Such thematic structuring of the event gives the semblance that the subject is carefully considered, but the short time allocated for individual sub-themes and the rather hit-or-miss collection of speakers that populate sub-events means that it is rare that anything is covered logically. In any event, there must be at least one wrap-up plenary session, where in theory conclusions are reached and, perhaps, uplifting declarations are signed. Unfortunately, rarely can anything meaningful be extracted from the activities that have taken place, and the result is that the wrap-up simply regurgitates the conference goals and aims.

In almost all cases simultaneous translation and services are a must. So is printing a conference schedule, posters, nametags, and glossy

[1] Recently 'speed dating' panels have become popular, where the members of a panel are given just a couple minutes to introduce themselves and their topics, leading on to a more open and flexible Q&A format that follows, supposedly aimed at avoiding the deadly effect of long-winded speakers and spurious topics.

information packets. Microsoft's PowerPoint has become the default means of illustrating a speech or lecture, and to some the PowerPoint itself as medium is the whole message, usually crammed with too many words and terrible graphics, to the extent that it has been referred to as 'PowerPoint poison.'

An outside observer might be puzzled by the almost inevitable choice of large glitzy five-star hotels as the venue for a conference on development, particularly if the theme is centered on social safety nets, slum upgrading, microfinance, smallholder farming, community empowerment, etc. After all, the people about which one is discussing at great length wouldn't even be allowed into the premises, unless part of a carefully crafted show organized by one of the participating NGOs. But as development events become larger and more complex, the conference services these hotels offer become the overriding factor. Humbler yet practical venues rarely exist. And who wants to ruffle the feathers of the VIPs that are inevitably invited? The irony of this situation sometimes comes up in casual small-talk, usually between conference attendees who are milling around yet another sumptuous buffet lunch table.

Conference Costs

The costs associated with a conference can be very large, but obviously this depends on its size, length, and complexity. First is the cost of renting the venue(s) and accompanying services such as interpreters, meals, drinks, and special entertainment sessions, and these can be quite steep for five-star hotels or for dedicated conference centers. Second, there are the costs of conference services, plus printing of material and advertising and promoting the event. Third are costs associated with important invitees and speakers, mainly airfares, hotel accommodation, meals, and/or daily allowances. Fourth is the remuneration that needs to be paid to speakers and experts and to those writing conference papers, and these costs may be substantial for big-name personalities or little or nothing for the less prominent. Finally, there are a host of miscellaneous costs for the conference itself and for preparations, including communications, ground transport, special posters and branding, conference hostesses, etc.

How much do conferences in the development business cost? One will never find estimates of the all-in costs of a mega event or even make a breakdown of direct expenses, since the sums involved are just too embarrassing. In an article published in 2017, *The Guardian* undertook its own analysis and came up with total costs of $200 million for the super-mega 4th World Water Forum in Mexico, with its 20,000 attendees, and at least $12 million for the smaller World Water Week in Stockholm, with 3000 attending (Kircherr & Biswas, 2017). These amounts may seem large, but they are probably manageable, given the very deep pockets of many donors, institutes, sponsors, and other conveners.

Who pays for all this? In very rare cases the sponsor pays the whole bill, but usually the actual costs to which the sponsor itself is exposed can be dramatically reduced, and this perhaps explains why 'acts of congregation' are so popular. First, many attendees either pay their own way (independent consultants and specialists) or are paid by their employers (consulting firms, donor agencies, universities, institutes, etc.), thus reducing expenditures. Second, the host country or city itself might be persuaded to provide the venue and organize special events, and third, sometimes large companies or big donors will agree by paying sponsors.

Who Attends?

Obviously, who attends a particular conference depends on its subject, but one could generalize and say there are certain kinds of people who are invited and actually show up.

There is inevitably a ranking of people by their importance, and one sees this in seating arrangements in the plenary session hall and, more importantly, in the luncheon and dinner tables. In the top rank of attendees are (1) the chiefs—executive directors, presidents, sector heads, etc.—of the sponsoring organization(s) who, in almost all cases, must make opening and/or concluding remarks, (2) ministers of the host country or the mayor of the host city and, one hopes, even the prime minister, and (3) keynote speakers, usually academics or authors or CEOs, the more famous the better. Few if any of these top-rankers will actually spend much time at the conference, and they are more likely to leave abruptly after the opening speeches. In other words, it seems as if the pointlessness of the conference is already confirmed by the absence from its most important moments by the very decision makers for which the messages are targeted.

Following the top rank, there are those who have been assigned to head sessions and otherwise contribute. They will be staffers from donor agencies, perhaps university professors, and often professional animators—those called communications specialists or knowledge experts or well-known influencers. Then there are those from development institutions or big INGOs—usually staffers—who are sent either to show the flag or to network.

Following this are those who usually pay their way, such as businessmen and consulting firm representatives with an eye for contacts and opportunities. If the conference talks about investment opportunities, expect serious attendance from development industry CEOs, especially if the conference takes up the subject of real estate, infrastructure, or climate action where lots of potential projects might be discussed.

It is common for sponsoring agencies to make an effort for at least some 'real people' to attend their conferences. These may be lower, technical staff of developing country governments, but here language often becomes a barrier. Or, they may be activists and others from advocacy NGOs, and these can perform two important functions: They may provide a splash of 'character' to the otherwise dreary and predictable lineup of attendees (especially if they show up in indigenous dress). More importantly, the presence of these activists can impart a certain legitimacy and reality to otherwise abstract proceedings, coming from what some consider to be the 'front lines.'

The Attractiveness of Events

Why are acts of congregation, especially splashy global events, so popular in the development business, given the costs, hassles, and pointlessness? For the institution that is sponsoring/chairing/convening the show, events are clearly perceived as a kind of affirmation of importance and relevance of the sponsor. And for the host country, especially a developing nation, it is seen as a way to promote a country's attractions and show its ability to support conference mechanics, not to mention providing a direct boost to inward tourism expenditures.

For the individual attendee, the most popular reason, frequently mentioned, is simply the ability to network with others. One can meet up with old colleagues, establish new contacts, show one's face to those who are powerful, and perhaps even have a way to influence donor budgets. This is particularly important if one is an independent consultant or representative of a consulting/contracting firm, since attendance at a conference is a tried-and-true means of marketing one's services, sometimes well-worth shouldering the costs of the trip, fees, and accommodation. Even academics might pay their own way to sniff out possible research funding. It is no coincidence that 'successful' conferences have numerous lunches, coffee breaks, and other opportunities for milling around and striking up conversations.

But this only explains part of the attraction. For those representing donor agencies, international NGOs, civil society organizations, universities and research institutes, or even global businesses, attending a conference is perceived as a way to 'show the flag,' expanding an organization's profile and demonstrating its interest in whatever is the development topic being discussed. However badly organized, boring, or pointless an event, this promotion is probably the main driver for most institutional attendees.

Criticisms of the Phenomenon

As far as we can tell, almost never have the pointlessness, waste of time, and extravagance of these development sector events been criticized in the mainstream development literature (and especially not by donors themselves, not even for the purposes of simple cost-cutting), but they are very common in off-record grumblings and anecdotes, and they are making their appearance more and more in the blogosphere. Take, for example, Duncan Green, who wrote an amusing piece on 'conference rage,' where he states "my mood in conferences usually swings between boredom, despair and rage. The turgid/self-aggrandizing keynotes and coma-inducing panels, followed by people (usually men) asking 'questions' that are really comments, usually not on topic." He makes a very good point by then asking: "Conferences frequently discuss evidence and results. So where are the evidence and results for the efficacy of conferences?" (Green, 2016). In an earlier blog about an OECD World Forum in Delhi, Green comments on the mind-numbing atmosphere: "A few 'keynote speakers', bleary with jetlag, stumble through their papers. … Dry-as-dust panels of disconnected presentations—chairing is feeble in keeping to time and/or panels are over-stuffed with speakers, so there is never enough time for questions or interaction between the speakers" (Green, 2012).

In 2009 a whole anthology was published entitled *Impacts of Megaconferences on the Water Sector*, in which an evaluation concluded that "except for the UN Water Conference, held in Argentina in 1977, the impacts of the subsequent mega conferences have been at best marginal in terms of knowledge generation and synthesis, poverty alleviation, and/or environmental conservation" (Biswas, 2009, 21). There are undoubtedly similar works that offer serious critiques of the world of conferences, but these are not easy to find, they seem to have absolutely no visibility in the sea of literature churned out by the development industry, and they obviously have had no impact on reining in the event phenomenon.

A story of similar 'diminishing returns' relates to the UN super-mega conference—the International Conference on Population and Development—that took place in Cairo for the first time in 1994. With 20,000 attendees, this was *the* development conference of the 1990s, and for the first time it put front and center women's reproductive health and shifted the focus from top-down population control towards the empowerment of women as individuals. Well, twenty-five years on, another huge Population and Development conference took place in Nairobi, and it was depressingly clear that almost none of the commitments set out in the Cairo declaration have been met. But even though the tone of the Nairobi conference was reported to be enthusiastic, "in quintessential UN and international development culture, attendees are celebrating announcements as if they were achievements" (Merelli, 2019).

Summing Up

As we have seen, the development world has always had a penchant for a wide variety of conferences, symposiums, and other acts of congregation, including various kinds of recurring talk shops. These mechanisms are extremely pronounced and promoted and, though some have value, it can be said that the large costs and efforts devoted to conference-making mostly aim at purposes that have little or nothing to do with ostensible development goals. Rather, they simply help justify the existence of both the sponsoring donor agency and participating development players, and it gives them all-important visibility and weight. The fact that such events dissimulate, confuse, and clog up the more humdrum business of development seems to bother no one.

The event obsession is something that is pernicious and almost completely unnecessary for the development business, yet it seems to simply grow and grow, as if it had a logic of its own. Could not it be curtailed? Perhaps what is needed is (1) a requirement that there is a comprehensive estimate of all costs associated with every event—direct, indirect, and in-kind—and that these be published and (2) another requirement that the long run impact of expensive conferences be assessed and evaluated against real actions and serious policy shifts on down the line as a result of a particular event. But who is going to enforce such requirements?

It is hard to tell what lasting effect the impact of Covid-19 will have on the development industry's penchant for conferences and other events. After more than two years of the pandemic, development players have shown a remarkable ability to adapt to the situation, taking virtual modalities to ever higher levels. It has proven easy to launch online events and to entice impressive numbers of 'attendees' simply with a couple of clicks (Chap. 12). And these attendees do not even have to make an appearance (press mute and no video), so no longer can one see that most of the audience is either dozing or thumbing through their smart phones. Of course, person-to-person networking—the main attraction for physical conferences events—suffers greatly, but there are virtual ways to eventually hook up. And donors and other funders will be saving lots of money that would otherwise be spent on attendee travel, accommodation, etc. So, one can imagine that virtual formats will have staying power after the pandemic, probably running in parallel with physical events and generating yet more and more irrelevant discussion and self-promotion.

References

Biswas, A. (2009). Impacts of megaconferences on global water development and management. In C. Tortajada & A. Biswas (Eds.), *Impacts of megaconferences on the water sector* (p. 2009). Springer.

Developmentaid. (2018). *List of major upcoming events in development sector in October – November 2018*. Accessed June 5, 2020, from https://www.developmentaid.org/#!/news-stream/post/29122/the-list-of-major-upcoming-events-in-development-sector-in-october-november-2018

Easterly, W. (2002). The cartel of good intentions: The problem of bureaucracy in foreign aid. *Journal of Policy Reform, 3*(4). https://doi.org/10.1080/1384128032000096823

Green, D. (2012, October 23). *Why are international conferences so bad, and what can be done about it?* Accessed June 6, 2022, from https://oxfamapps.org/fp2p/why-are-international-conferences-so-bad-and-what-can-be-done-about-it/

Green, D. (2016, June 1). Conference rage and why we need a war on panels. *FP2P*. Accessed June 6, 2022, from https://oxfamapps.org/fp2p/conference-rage-and-why-we-need-a-war-on-panels/

Hancock, G. (1991). *Lords of poverty (originally published 1989)*. Mandarin Paperbacks.

Kircherr, J., & Biswas, A. (2017, August 30). Expensive academic conferences give us old ideas and no new faces. *The Guardian*. Accessed June 6, 2022, from

https://www.theguardian.com/higher-education-network/2017/aug/30/expensive-academic-conferences-give-us-old-ideas-and-no-new-faces
Merelli, A. (2019, November 14). The case against holding any more women's rights conferences. *Quartz Magazine*. Accessed June 6, 2022, from https://qz.com/1747082/the-case-against-holding-any-more-womens-rights-conferences/amp/
World Bank. (2018). *All events*. Accessed June 20, 2018, from https://www.worldbank.org/en/events/all?lang_exact=English&pastevents=on

CHAPTER 9

Texts and Documents

All industries in the West produce documents—corporate annual reports, analyses of marketing dynamics, industry trade publications, how-to manuals, and the like—as do government ministries and departments. But the development industry—and in particular donor agencies and apex champions (such as OECD-DAC, UN bodies, and the World Bank)—has taken the imperative to produce texts to stratospheric levels. Strategy reports, pamphlets, web-pages, international declarations, policy frameworks, and global treatises abound, not to mention the donor's bread and butter outputs: sector reviews, program documents, project documents, implementation reports, evaluations, etc. Together these represent a virtual avalanche of the printed (or digital) word that seems to be growing in ever more profusion.

Most of these artifacts—especially those intended for general distribution—are professionally edited, glossy, diplomatic, and non-contentious, representing considerable efforts by donor agencies and those they commission to write, edit, and polish them. No one knows in total just how much text is being produced and by whom, but most in the development business simply accept this as being a long-standing and essential part of what donors do. That these products are rarely read by anyone (except sometimes by those in the business who are paid to do so) and that the huge volume itself swamps any clarity on issues has been pointed out by outside observers and even by donor personnel themselves, but nothing seems to change, and the avalanche continues unabated.

D. Sims, *Development Delusions and Contradictions*,
https://doi.org/10.1007/978-3-031-17770-5_9

What is going on? These documents could be called 'easily observable outcomes,' as are conferences and other events, as discussed in the preceding chapter. Donor agencies only require sufficient funds, a stable of writers, and a slick publishing department. The process is internal to the agency itself, except of course for the actual writing of these texts, which is almost inevitably outsourced. Unlike with the donors' main business of disbursing grants and loans, there is no need for long and often contentious maneuvers with recipient governments to launch and execute projects and programs.

Could it be that there is a felt need for donors to justify their existences simply by churning out reams of (carefully sanitized) text? Are there reasons for this that help to understand donor behavior? Might this just be a symptom of a donor's own insecurity? Here we briefly look at the phenomenon and its dimensions to answer these questions.

A Bewildering Range of Donor Documents

Trying to analyze the flows and characteristics of documents coming out of the development world is a daunting task, simply because of the sheer volume and enormous range of types and formats. Here we run through the main types of texts that donor agencies produce. (And, remember, beyond these donor products is another whole world of literature *about* foreign assistance.)

First, there are key 'corporate' documents that are produced for those who control the purse strings of donor agencies. These documents mainly take the form of annual reports, which for bilateral agencies are aimed at their parliamentary funders and for international financial institutions at their boards of directors or trustees. They project carefully crafted corporate images that show how much they are engaged in the development field (especially fashionable topics), how much they are in control of strategic objectives and plans, and how much they are responsibly tracking and managing funds and accounts. A good example of this is DFID's thick annual report (DfID, 2019), which runs to 196 pages.

Second, there are donor strategy papers of various types, mainly strategies that an agency has formulated for particular countries or regions or sectors. These can be produced as stand-alone pieces or as periodical updates, but the importance is not so much to direct and guide an agency's work or those of its government partners in developing countries. Rather, the aim is to impart an aura of being thoughtful and on top of things. The number of these strategy reports is impressive. A review by Devex counted 205 country strategy papers produced by 25 donors over 2019–2020, with Bhutan for some reason being the object of the largest number of country strategies, followed by Haiti. Overall, the highest quantities were generated by the UN system (26 percent of the total, mainly from WFP, UNDP, UN-Habitat, UNHCR, and UNICEF). Following this, greatest production was by the United States' CDC, then the ADB, then IFAD, then the World Bank (Stibi, 2020).

Third, there are issue-specific reports that are also favored by donors. The issues involved are either classic development topics or sometimes cross-cutting issues, such as gender, poverty, climate, etc. especially those that are regional or international in scope. Perhaps the prime example of such 'issues' approach is the World Bank's annual World Development Report (WDR), which is much read and can be considered the Bank's flagship publication. The WDR is a rare example of good writing and useful data analysis that also allows in some refreshing, even critical insights into donor policies. But most issue-specific reports produced by or for donor agencies remain shallow, sanitized, and uncritical.

Fourth, donors like to show they carry on important investigations and research efforts. Almost all donor agencies produce analyses and research papers that take up anything and everything that just might be relevant to developing countries. The World Bank is second to none when it comes to this 'knowledge' embodied in texts. The Bank churns out Policy Research Papers at the astounding rate of roughly 30 to 40 per month (World Bank, n.d.). Even more weighty are the Bank's Policy Research Reports—produced at a rate of one or two per year—on empirical and conceptual dimensions of global issues. In addition, there are Research Policy Briefs and Blogs at 5 to 9 per year, two plus monthly periodicals—the World Bank Research Observer and the World Bank Economic Review.

Fifth, there is a whole subsector of documents relating specifically to donors' operational projects and programs. In terms of volume, these probably exceed any other type of donor documentation (For example, the ADB is pushing out documents at the rate of roughly 120 per month, most of which are directly related to ongoing projects.) (ADB, n.d.). These most technical texts describe projects and their progress, and they also address project topics such as social monitoring, procurement plans, safeguarding due diligence, proactive integrity, project administration, etc. There is also a whole host of technical documents that must be produced in the run-up to the approval document. All of these are mostly internal documents and very rarely is general distribution authorized.

Sixth, once a project or program is operational, there will be the need for donor-generated assessments and reviews and, especially after its completion, project evaluations. The evaluation is another unique genre of document, as has been discussed in Chap. 7 above.

Seventh, especially after the 2005 Paris Declaration on Aid Effectiveness, a considerable volume of documents has been and continues to be produced relating to problems of effective development assistance. These look at such themes as country ownership, alignment, transparency, accountability, and harmonization of development initiatives, mostly generated by the OECD. A good example is the OECD's "Making Development Co-operation More Effective—2016 Progress Report," which runs to 170 pages (OECD, 2016). And there are many more self-referential texts that are about the development industry itself in one way or other. Often these are commissioned by development-related institutes and foundations such as Brookings, ODI, and CGD, but the mainstay of production remains the OECD.

Eighth, there is the 'how to' genre. These are guidelines, toolkits, operational manuals, handbooks, etc. There are of two types: those aimed at instructing staffers or donor agencies (and their consultants), and those aimed at a more general global or country readership. The first type are guidelines on how a donor staffer should do his or her job, such as operations manuals that contain the policies, directives, procedures, and other instructions to staff that apply to donor operations. These manuals and directives are written to ensure that everyone is on the same page when it comes to conforming to Bank corporate policy and bureaucratic processes.

The second type of the 'how to' genre are manuals/toolkits that presume to make practically any development intervention deceptively simple, reduced to dumbed down step-by-step instructions. Examples of this sub-genre are legion, especially these days. UN-Habitat, a global leader in nonsense texts, has a City Resilience Action Planning Tool as well as a Results-based Management Handbook. USAID also loves the tool-kit approach, offering Improvement Methods Toolkits, an Evaluation Toolkit, a Monitoring Toolkit, a host of Collaborating, Learning, and Adapting toolkits, and a number of Community Contribution toolkits. And GIZ is no slouch, having produced an Adaptation Monitoring and Evaluation Toolbox, a Sustainable Industrial Areas Toolbox, a Practical Chemical Management Toolbox, a Toolbox on Solar-Powered Irrigation Systems, and an 'instrument' called Climate Proofing for Development.

Ninth, there are donor agency websites. These contain what are perhaps the blandest of all development texts. They describe in easy and sanitized language their overarching goals, strategies, and visions. They also post their projects, core competences and services, programs and initiatives, events, and their main countries of operation. Sometimes these websites lead with 'latest news,' which is just a way to headline their work and its importance—as if everyone is breathlessly waiting for such 'breaking' news. Also, it is common for them to list the number of projects and countries and beneficiaries or other simple numerics. And glossy graphics and pictures are obligatory.

Tenth, there are project-specific websites that run for the length of a donor project, are very much involved with visibility and raising awareness of the issues at hand. They make huge efforts to convince site visitors that what they do is important, widely followed, and even newsworthy. But once project funding ends, these websites abruptly cease to exist.

Eleventh, there are project-related reporting documents. Whether for a small technical assistance or training project, or for a huge multi-subproject infrastructure loan (and everything in between), such bureaucratic reporting is carefully respected, or else no one gets paid and projects cannot continue to flow. Inception reports, interim reports, draft final reports, final reports, progress reports (monthly or quarterly), aide memoires, back-to-office reviews, annexes, and minutes of meetings, plus much, much more. These can represent a tsunami of texts that flow back to donor headquarters from each of the virtually thousands of development projects that are underway at any one time. These are quaintly called 'deliverables,' and pity the poor box-checking office troll or his boss who must read them. Also, pity the project manager or consultant team leader who must make sure they get produced, an effort that can take up between a quarter to a third of his or her time. With this reporting Sword of Damocles hanging overhead, no wonder more important tasks are perforce shuffled into the background. *These deliverables are bureaucratically the ultimate result of a project or program* and are treated as such by donors.

Guiding Principles in the Preparation of Development Documents

A review of the immense outpouring of texts and other mediatic communications from donor agencies can illuminate some basic principles which seem to apply, although these are rarely articulated. These are pervasive throughout the donor world, no matter which agency one is talking about or whatever the sectoral or geographic reach:

Being Seen as an Important Player with Overarching Goals

There is a need for ostensibly well-crafted goals, objectives, plans, etc. to appear to be on top of things, to show that a donor agency is omnipotent, and to demonstrate that, by the sheer volume of documentary output, these agencies communicating throughout the development world. In the same vein, there is the need to show that the donor is well aware of (and thoroughly engaged in) any new development subject or paradigm.

This imperative has been imbedded with donors for decades, but it reached new heights with the publication of the UN Sustainable Development Goals in 2015. It was almost as if the SDGs (17 main goals and 169 sub-goals or targets) were created specifically for development agencies and institutions to be able to prove their concern for everything and anything developmental simply by referring to these goals, usually without any detail or elaboration. The fact that these goals are bland and crafted not to offend anyone made them perfect vehicles. As William Easterly pointed out, these SDGs could also stand for Senseless, Dreamy, and Garbled (Easterly, 2015, 322–324), and having these overarching and wishy-washy goals, and repeatedly referring to them, seems to be exactly what was called for. And as far as is known no major player in the development industry dares to criticize these SDGs. Ever!

Up-Beat Stories Are de rigor

Glowing success stories are one of the bedrocks of development texts. These may be unabashed propaganda about projects, especially those found on donor websites, but the imperative for mentioning up-beat narratives even extends to a kind of general development optimism.

The Standard Template: An Awful Situation, but We Have the Solution

If there is a template for development texts, it seems most often to follow the storyline, "Oh how bad it is (poverty, pollution, unemployment, poor health, bad education, congested cities, water scarcity, degraded slums, flooded countryside, capacity-challenged government, and on and on), but, oh, how there is now a commitment/groundswell/opportunity to act in transformative ways, and oh, how donor agency X is uniquely situated to build a framework to address the challenges." This is quite a template, and one that has been used over decades. And it is remarkable in how many documents it will fit—in Terms of Reference, concept papers, project descriptions, program strategies, and other basic documents.

Lacing Your Text with Lots of Technical Filler Lends an Appearance of Credibility

Even the most innocuous analytical reports need to impart an aura of technical determinism, and this is achieved by inserting lots of tables and charts and infographics. Some of these might be informative, but most are simply page fillers for the benefit of those who casually flip through a report. These artifacts imbedded in texts impart a comforting sense that whatever is being discussed is grounded in and backed by lots of hard numbers and impressive statistical displays.

Such obligatory use of images, charts, diagrams, and tables is mainly meant to enliven crushingly boring texts. Even if the subject doesn't lend itself to imagery, for example, on governance, training, management, etc., at least there must be lots of photos of meetings and field trips (with project personnel standing next to flip charts in front of captivated audiences). Another way to enliven texts is to insert lots of arrow diagrams to show process and cause/effect, a kind of visualization of how all the actions and concepts under discussion fit together seamlessly. Most of these diagrams are so simplistic and tautological that they should never have been included, but they perform the important functions of both page-filler <u>and</u> as superficial evidence of well-thought-out conceptualizations.

Development Texts Must End with Recommendations, Preferably Lots of Them

It is a cannon of policy papers and sectoral documents that there must be a set of recommendations and actions to address the issues at hand. Modesty must be thrown out the window, and simply saying that the subject is complicated and needs more data collection or focused analysis is not sufficient. No, recommendations for action aimed at the whole range of 'stakeholders,' usually presented in tabular formats, are the order of the day. Having a long list of recommendations in a document obscures and devalues any useful, straightforward conclusions that it just might have. But the need for these lists of what needs to be done trumps anything like cohesion or clarity, and one can only suppose that they are necessary to confirm the donor's infallible knack for problem-solving.

Beware of Circling Critics and Making Sure Not to Offend Anyone, Ever

Way back in 1975, the underlying fear of texts and the written word in the world of development had already been identified by Judith Tendler: "Because of [the USA's Agency for International Development] vulnerability to outside attack, this power of the written word was to some extent based on the fear of it" (Tendler, 1975, 50). Thus even almost 50 years ago it was recognized this that there were Western critics (in parliaments, in the press, and in other sections of government) who were waiting to pounce on anything that might just provide material for scandal or negative press. And as textual production generated by development agencies proliferated in quantity and scope over the decades, this fear only became more acute.

As if this were not enough, there is another kind of fear of the written word, in this case the stark fear of offending the sensibilities of 'partners' in recipient governments. Fear of offending these people has become so pervasive that it is well-neigh impossible to make salient points about a weakness or failing in the host country. No project manager or departmental head will want a document produced on his watch to contain anything that could be construed as criticizing a government's actions or inaction, even though, time and again, these are precisely what is wrong with a situation or subsector. Donors feel they need to preserve impeccable relations with their 'clients' in order to proceed with their projects and programs and, more importantly, get those in the pipeline agreed on with minimum hassle. If sanitizing texts to the point of near meaninglessness will help, why not?

Any 'Virtuous Circle' Remains in the Literature

Some documentation coming out of the development industry–especially that which is sector- or country-specific and technical—can be relevant, to the point, and at least somewhat critical. These texts, however rare, could be considered to represent evolving discourses or 'virtuous circles' about important development issues and the political dimensions they expose. But such documentation rarely leads to policy breakouts or logical conclusions beyond the confines of the technical literature they inhabit. It is the fear of disagreeing with donor management, of antagonizing and embarrassing partners, and of exposing deep disconnects between conclusions and action that keeps these virtuous discourses safely 'on the shelf' in the comfortable realms of technical discourse.

Jargon, Buzzwords, and Other Development Babble

No matter what the genre of texts, they all contain a lexicon of jargon and buzzwords. These fuzzy concepts, value-laden terminology, and obfuscating word craft are an important feature of development documents. The use and misuse of this jargon, plus the facility by which trendy new terms are coined and wholeheartedly adopted, have been a common complaint of many who work in development. They tell a lot about how the industry defines itself, how it is constantly in search either of new paradigms, new approaches, or new silver bullets, and how the ineffectiveness of donor interventions can be obfuscated by adherence to the hottest new buzzwords.

But you may say, every industry has its own codewords and specialized vocabulary. Yes, but language does matter for development. As pointed out by Andrea Cornwall in 2007, development's buzzwords are not just passwords to funding and influence, and they are more than specialist jargon that is characteristic of any profession (Cornwall, 2007, 471). These words may have some intrinsic meaning, but unfortunately any meaning has been devalued and diluted by cavalier usage. This conveniently allows the writer to mean many things (or more likely nothing) every time they are used.

It is understandable why such catchwords and phrases are so often used in the development texts. First, the author may be badly informed and unsure of what she is talking about, thus she throws these words in to show he has at least some scattered grasp of the subject. Second, the aim is to hit core development themes to gain legitimacy, since in most cases the same buzzwords are being used in the meta texts she must conform or respond to.

This is not to say that these terms are universally tossed about in a slipshod, cavalier way. Some use the terms more or less rigorously (especially academics and those ensconced in donor research departments), but even they may slip into hard to define jargon. Examples include:

> *Stakeholders*, sometimes 'key stakeholders,' or 'multi-stakeholders,' is a conveniently amorphous way to refer to almost everyone involved in a project or policy.
>
> The same could be said for *community*, as in 'community of practice' or 'development community' or that overworked phrase 'community participation.' Closely related to 'community participation' is the misuse of the word 'empowerment' in situations where, no matter what the donor or allied NGOs might cook up, communities are not going to gain any power that lasts longer than the funding stream that helped set them up in the first place.
>
> Then there are *partners* and *partnerships*, words that have been so widely used as to completely debased. OECD's DAC has even declared that now developing countries are called 'country partners' and donor agencies are to be called 'international partners.'
>
> *Action*, as in *action plans*, are frequently used as part of the cascade of recommendations found in many development texts, and they usually mean more research, more discussions, more results matrices, and other 'easily observable outcomes. They rarely have anything to do with what could be considered on-the-ground actions.
>
> In addition, there are operant phrases that imply a certain scientific rigor or thoroughness. Such is the case of *evidence-based* conclusions, as if the development business has somehow been transformed into a detective story! Such phrases as 'knowledge management,' 'drilling-down,' 'rigorous approaches,' and 'robust analysis' impart the same sense of rigor.

Another buzzword cluster includes *replicability*, *mainstreaming* and *going to scale*. These are often evoked to show that a small donor project is a well-crafted pilot which will lead to great success, will demonstrate its more universal application, and, once other donors cough up co-financing, it can truly 'go to scale.'

Finally, *sustainability* or *sustainable development* must be what has become the mother of all buzzwords in the development industry. Its pedigree derives from concerns in the 1980s and 1990s about the ecological limits to headlong global economic growth, but it has been progressively extended to practically all endeavors aimed at the developing world and consequently any residual concrete meaning has almost totally evaporated.

One could go on and on talking about semantics and the trendiness of jargon and buzzwords in the development industry. After all, it is a huge subject. But we can end this discussion by simply recommending an excellent anthology on just this subject, unambiguously called Deconstructing Development Discourse: Buzzwords and Fuzzwords (Cornwall & Eade, 2010). The preface and introductory chapter by the editors are particularly worth reading, and other chapters of interest include uses and misuses of such words as *capacity building*, *country ownership*, *best practices*, and *good governance*. There is even a chapter on the various meanings of the meta-word *development*. It would be interesting to know what the authors think of the super-charged jargon of the SDGs, which appeared some five years after the book was published.

WHO PRODUCES ALL THIS TEXTUAL STUFF?

In the distant past most documents produced by donor agencies were prepared internally by their own technical staff, dipping into their stable of consultants/academics when necessary, and perhaps polished up and archived by a publications department. Professional writers might occasionally have been commissioned to write up important pamphlets, articles, or speeches. Well, these days donor document production capacities have exploded. Any vice president, sector manager, department head, communications boss, or country office director will have some budget to hire writers or web designers or to commission document production, and there is often a perception that one's worth and reputation within a donor organization depends on having been the driving force behind some prominent publications. And further on down the donor pyramid, staffers and team managers see direct visibility and possible advancement by conceiving and commissioning reports.

The main bulk of texts—usually technical reports that look at economic sectors or subsectors and suggest strategies, policies, and programs—are mostly written by consultants, especially those who have gained a reputation in their particular field for being able to pull together a lot of information and end up with a cohesive final product. Rare is the donor manager or task director who has the time to write, and such tasks are best left to someone working to a contract with deadlines whose output can be closely controlled. No one is going to win a literature prize for these efforts, but even pulling together a passable chunk of expository prose from reams of raw data, disparate conversations, and disjointed texts is no small feat.

Summing Up

Documents could be called the main artifacts of the development industry, something that is left behind, long after a project is signed off, an initiative is buried, or a conference is wrapped up. Never mind that most of the vast quantities of these documents are never read. Documents are easily observable outcomes that don't cost that much and, more importantly, are totally under the control of the donor. By submerging the reader in countless self-referential documents peppered with all-important jargon the message is clear: We produce, therefore we exist, therefore we are masters of almost any development topic you can imagine, and therefore we are worthy of (yet more) funding.

References

ADB. (n.d.). *Projects and tenders.* Accessed June 8, 2022, from https://www.adb.org/projects/documents?page=6

Cornwall, A. (2007). Buzzwords and fuzzwords: Deconstructing development discourse. *Development in Practice, 17,* 4–5.

Cornwall, A., & Eade, D. (Eds.). (2010). *Deconstructing development discourse: Buzzwords and fuzzwords.* Practical Action Publishing in association with Oxfam UK.

DfID. (2019, July 11). *Annual Report and Accounts 2018-19.* Accessed June 7, 2022, from https://assets.publishing.service.gov.uk/government/uploads/system/uploads/attachment_data/file/815787/ARA-2019.pdf

Easterly, W. (2015, September 28). The SDGs should stand for senseless, dreamy, garbled. *Foreign Policy*. Accessed June 8, 2022, from https://foreignpolicy.com/2015/09/28/the-sdgs-are-utopian-and-worthless-mdgs-development-rise-of-the-rest/

OECD. (2016). *Making development cooperation more effective*. Accessed June 8, 2022, from https://www.oecd.org/dac/effectiveness/making-development-co-operation-more-effective-9789264266261-en.htm

Stibi, E. (2020, February 21). What do strategies from 2019 tell us about donors' priorities? *Devex News*. Accessed June 7, 2022, from https://www.devex.com/news/what-do-strategies-from-2019-tell-us-about-donors-priorities-96490?access_key=yJwc9EoWCVShSlMBht6ycu4Kw4cFFpyy&utm_source=newsletter&utm_medium=newswire&utm_campaign=forpro&utm_content=text&mkt_tok=eyJpIjoiTVRBMk1UTmhaVFl6TkRZeSIsInQiOiJ3dGhwWUkrT1VtS0JqNFdoNHJJQ2dqXC80dkxVdVd6TkpFYTNqZXlcL09KUGRNQ2dVbnIxbmJ2SDFyaUtidWJiNW5Uc3MzdDlZaWZXYmdDMHFRNzR0SFdqRGtHdmcxOUZaVDJiZGpXUmVyUFJvTWd0dmM2NUExRkVRWHZIKzJxeExxpIn0%3D

Tendler, J. (1975). *Inside foreign aid*. Johns Hopkins University Press.

World Bank Group. (n.d.). *Research publications*. Accessed June 8, 2022, from https://www.worldbank.org/en/research/brief/publications

CHAPTER 10

Herd Instinct

Faddism is one dimension of the development industry's need to appear to be on the vanguard of development thinking. Soldiers in the trenches know well this penchant for fashions sweeping down from donor heights, and they may roll their eyes and point out the absurdly of faddish approaches that wash through the system. But like it or not, the troops must ride with these trends, at the least by sprinkling faddish concepts throughout whatever texts need to be written. Ignoring these fads and refusing to insert them into a program or project rationale will *not* help score points, capture more work, or advance careers.

Often fads are heralded as emerging and transformative ways one 'does development.' These can rapidly become enshrined in donor bureaucracies, in the methodologies they adopt and policies they promote, and in a plethora of knowledge activities and projects they support. For particularly robust development fads, it seems that practically everyone in the industry feels the need to join up.

This penchant for fads and fashions has sometimes been criticized as being pernicious, and they were identified as such by the respected aid observers Mosley, Harrigan, and Toye back in 1995, when they concluded: "The besetting sin of development policy throughout its life has been vulnerability to fashion" (Mosley et al., 1995, 308). Looking at the phenomenon today, it seems they have become ever more an essential part of the development business, something that just becomes more and more common.

D. Sims, *Development Delusions and Contradictions*,
https://doi.org/10.1007/978-3-031-17770-5_10

In this chapter we chart the remarkable affinity of the development world for fads and fashions. Since the phenomenon is so vast and so imbedded in industry behavior, we cannot claim to cover this particular development behavior in detail, but we try to set out why fads are so appealing, so readily taken up and diffused, so durable, and so rarely criticized. To add some detail, at the end of this chapter we look at two rather recent fashions that have preoccupied donor agencies and which well demonstrate donor herd instincts: *resilience and political economy analysis.*

The Rollout of Different Development Fashions Over 50 Years

Throughout its history the development industry has been susceptible to fads, and starting even in the 1960s the first hint that classic approaches—aid as providing investment capital and technology transfers—weren't working. A list of fads and fashions can be constructed by the decade that they appeared on the development scene (we may have missed some). Note that the number of these fashions have tended to increase by decade, especially in the 2000–2020 period:

1970s

Basic needs
Integrated rural development
Massive infrastructure
Rapid industrialization

1980s

Participatory rural appraisal
Logical framework analysis
Community participation/participatory development
Microfinance and SME support

1990s

Gender mainstreaming
One-stop shops
Impact evaluation and impact indicators
Good governance

2000s

Knowledge hubs
Cash transfers
Public–private partnerships
General budget support (and policy lending)
Mitigating climate change
Ownership
Accountability
Stakeholder analysis
Tool boxes and toolkits

2010s

Political economy analysis
Evidence-based evaluation
Resilience
Financial inclusion
Blended finance
Payment by results (PBR)
Localization
Locally led development
Green finance
Green transition

Characteristics of Fads and Fashions

What defines a fad or fashion in development? It can be described as some idea or concept (usually encapsulated in a single word or short phrase) that comes along, gains exposure, and then with amazing rapidity is taken up and internalized by most if not all donor agencies and other key players. *It is definitely a case of herd instinct.*

There are different kinds of fads. Some fads are built around specific aid techniques, such as conditional and unconditional cash transfers to the poor (which one would have thought was an obvious way to deliver assistance to the poor, but which seems only to have been discovered around

2000 and is still not widely practiced).[1] A similar faddish technique is e-government and one-stop shops as a way of streamlining business permitting and public services. Yet another is logical frame analysis, a way of organizing and rationalizing project design. These may in themselves have useful roles in specific tasks, but they can hardly be described as transformative mechanisms. Other fads have had more comprehensive scope and have been accompanied by claims of fundamentally changing the way to do development in a certain sector, such as integrated rural development (all the rage in the 1970s) or microfinance (having risen in the 1980s and still going strong). And there are fads which unabashedly claim to impact practically the whole gamut of development thinking or claim to be a better means of aid delivery, such as 'basic needs' or 'participatory development' or, as we shall see below, 'resilience.' Finally, some fads are little more than the widespread use of buzzwords (Chap. 9) that can be attached to almost any development theme.

What Drives the Penchant for Fads?

It seems that donors (and most others in the industry) simply want to appear part of the game, to feel that somehow if they don't join in, they will be seen as yesterday's players. If donor programs were actually successful and could be measured as such, why would it matter if they were part of the latest fad? But in a sense, this is what donors are really about: to show they are with the trends, to confirm their membership in the club, and to inoculate them against charges of irrelevance. At the same time, development institutions have a need to appear to be dynamic and changing, and often fads become institutionalized in development institutions as new practices or activities. Teams, units, and panels are set up to promote the application of certain fads, and these become solidified as little bureaucratic niches with trendy names, and the wider development organization can breathe easy and carry on as normal.

[1] For example, the World Food Programme only began experimenting with cash transfers in 2009, and it only began to use cash transfers to Syrian refuges in 2017 (Shana, 2017).

Faddism Has Some Serious Negative Effects

First, there is the sheer waste in terms of money and time that fads consume. Millions upon millions of dollars are allocated by donors and other development players toward funding conferences, policy papers, and glitzy wed sites that extol a particular donor's buy-in to a fad or fashion. But donors have lots of money to play with, especially when it comes to polishing their images. Compared to the sums that a donor lends or grants to developing countries, budgets for these fads and fashions are miniscule.

Second, fads and fashions can bestow confusion within donor structures and make a mockery of attempts to adhere to 'coherent' policy frameworks. This is especially true since fads are usually construed as add-ons onto existing development paradigms or as cross-cutting concepts. Also, it is rare that a fashion can be precisely defined.

Third, if donors become confused, what about recipient countries? National officials and professionals in the Rest have seen how donors are sensitive to new fashions and certainly notice how donors and their consultants are quick to elaborate on faddish concepts. But with weak capacities, very thin budgets, and oppressive top-down bureaucracies, recipient partners cannot do much more than try to show they are on board by parroting the concept from time to time.

'Innovation' as a Marker of Faddism as Well as a Fad Itself

Often the development industry's compulsion for faddish approaches derives from the concept of 'innovation,' something that implies that there is always a dynamic process of invention and progress imbedded in what goes on inside donor institutions. Especially, since around 2008, the word has come to be used throughout the industry to describe a wide range of endeavors, such as novel business or organizational models, new operational or production processes, or new products and services. And in much of the literature there seems to be a calculated close relation between 'innovation' for development and science and technology more generally. This is reassuring, since it implies legitimacy derived from the astounding amount of technical innovation that has come out of Western universities and corporate R&D departments in the last few decades. This can be seen in reports and papers generated around the idea of innovation, a good example of which is a pamphlet prepared by the OECD's Directorate for

Science, Technology, and Industry entitled "Innovation for Development," in which it announces it has developed an "Inclusive Innovation Policy Toolkit." It also refers to a bewildering array of other reports and initiatives, including an OECD/World Bank publication "Innovation and Growth: Chasing a Moving Frontier" and many others (OECD, 2012).

Could 'innovation' itself be considered a fashion, especially after say 2010? It certainly meets the criterion of being at the same time uplifting, cross-cutting, and vague, and a scan of development reports and pronouncements would lead one to believe so. For example, at a G-20 meeting, Bill Gates pronounced: "innovation fundamentally shifts the trajectory of development" (Sharma, 2011). Some donors have even inserted innovation into their structures. In 2014 UNDP set up an Innovation Facility and has an annual report (*Spark, Scale, Sustain*) on innovation and the SDGs. In the same year USAID launched an 'innovation hub' called the United States Global Development Lab, with such guiding principles as being open and inclusive, evidence based, catalytic, and agile. And starting in 2015 the World Bank set up a number of 'Innovation Labs' dealing with such topics as big data, social enterprises, and block chain. In 2018, a little behind the trend, the European Commission set up an EU Innovation Fund, in this case mainly for low-carbon technologies. Finally, in 2020, AFD announced the establishment of a Fund for Innovation in Development, headed by Nobel laureate Esther Duflo, with blessings from no less than Emmanuel Macron. This last initiative awards grants that are, according to Duflo, "the equivalent of venture capital for social innovation," and that are described as showing "the need to shift from a disbursement mentality to an impact mentality" (Chadwick, 2020). Heard this before?

So just how far can one take the idea of innovation for development? A rare critical article entitled "Is Innovation Essential for Development Work?" cautions that "innovation is a fashionable term that has entered the development vocabulary in so many ways that it speaks to everything and nothing. It has become a buzzword that may signify a shared connection with up-to-date thinking, but it is often used with no clear meaning." The author concludes, "Genuine innovation is valuable but rare. The ubiquity of vague ideas about innovation in development may ultimately serve to devalue it. Maybe the problem isn't lack of innovation, but too much of it" (Lewis, 2012).

An article written in 2015—entitled "Development innovation: Fad, silo or catalyst?"—was another rare cautionary voice about the avalanche of innovation boosterism. The author warned that there is a risk that development innovation becomes "an institutionalized silo of activity, that there is emphasis 'more on enabling exciting new projects to happen, and less on assessing their added value in a clear-headed way.'" And he adds that the "history of development is one of flawed attempts to cut-and-paste new ideas into contexts with little attention to how well they fit in them" (Ramalingam, 2015).

But like many valiant efforts to criticize undesirable or embarrassing traits of the development industry, these two voices seem to have remained passing complaints that have had, to our knowledge, zero impact. Certainly, looking at all the innovation hype sloshing around the development industry in 2019–2022, it would seem that no one has read them.

It should be added that the fad for innovation in development, and even the few critiques of it, reflects discourses that are emphatically centered upon Western development institutions. It seems that countries in the Rest and what innovation means for them (buy-in, adaptation, or just confusion?) hardly capture any interest.

Resilience: Fad du jour or Fashion of the Century?

'Resilience,' which first appeared in 2009–2011, might just be the mother of all fads, at least in the last quarter century. Its rise, spread, and nimble application in practically everything humanitarian and developmental has been truly phenomenal. And, resilience as a fad has already shown—at least over the more than a decade of its existence so far—its ability to be a very adaptable and durable concept, a fad that could be described as, well, 'resilient.'

The concept of resilience displays most of the prerequisites of fads—it is 'new,' or at least appears to be, it is a concept that can be attached to a large swathe of development endeavors, and it can be adopted and expanded very rapidly into donor structures, in their objectives, strategies, and policy frameworks, and in the discussions of development outriders such as NGOs, think tanks, academics, and even consultants/contractors. Resilience may also have wide appeal because it points to various agendas that need to be defined, programmed, and funded, and it "opens up new academic space for thinking about old problems, drawing upon such diverse fields as ecology, complexity and system theory and econometrics" (Ramalingam, 2015). Almost without exception, the overarching rational for a focus on resilience has been to help the poor and vulnerable who, as is tirelessly repeated, are most hurt by disasters, conflicts, and climate change.

Background to 'Resilience'

How did the term resilience come to be applied wholesale to development discourses? According to one analysis, the concept of resilience, being grounded in engineering and ecology, mainly looked at the ability of a system to respond to change and recover from it (Notice the scientific spin?). Thus, as disasters and climate-induced events seemed to multiply, it was seen that poor communities often bore the brunt of these crises, and there was an almost perfect fit with a 'new' kind of development discourse.

The rise of the 'resilience' fad probably resulted from the confluence of three factors: the increased vulnerability of economies due to the 2008 financial crisis, the 2007–2008 leap in world food prices due to bad harvests, the sky-high price of oil, and, of course, the increasing worries about climate change and natural disasters. The rise in the number of fragile, conflict, and unstable states may also have kicked in, and increasing terrorist attacks may also have had a knock-on effect.

As with almost every endeavor in the development world these days, the question soon arises: How do you measure 'resilience' and construct indicators that can be used to measure vulnerability and as a way of assessing the success of efforts to support resilience? A 2014 article prepared by the ODI came to the conclusion that there were so many resilience concepts that trying to come up with anything like comprehensive indices was methodologically impossible. In fact, the paper makes a telling statement: "the appeal of the same concept to so many disciplines has resulted in the reification of resilience, whereby resilience has come to be seen as a many-sided 'thing', rather than as a way of thinking about many different kinds of problems" (Levine, 2014, 1 and 23). The ODI piece didn't follow through with what should have been the logical conclusion—that is, simply drop trying to measure 'resilience' and minimize usage of the concept as a separate platform or discipline. No, as we will see, the ODI became one of the leaders in resilience thinking.

The Flood of Development Players Hitching onto 'Resilience'

A scan of major donor agencies will show that virtually all of them have incorporated the concept of resilience into their portfolios, either by setting up separate units, re-packaging existing programs to give them a resilience spin, or simply shouting 'resilience' in some form or other from the roof tops. Here we present a brief roll-out of the resilience fad:

The *World Bank* has been an early resilience aficionado. As early as 2012 it produced a serious 108-page think piece called *Resilience, Equity, and Opportunity*, all of which focused on the Bank's social protection and labor strategies in developing countries (World Bank, 2012). And in 2013 the Bank leveraged in climate change, seeing the need "for closer collaboration between the climate resilience and disaster risk management communities through the incorporation of climate and disaster resilience into broader development processes" (World Bank, 2013, abstract). This was followed in 2017 by a huge 201-page publication entitled *Unbreakable: Building the Resilience of the Poor in the Face of Natural Disasters, Climate Change and Development* (Hallegatte et al., 2017).

USAID, not to be outdone, leapt into resilience in a big way following the droughts in the Sahel and Horn of Africa in 2011–2012. It focused at first on disaster mitigation, relief, and preparedness, followed by increasingly more complicated interventions, including in 2015 the establishment of a Resilience Leadership Council and a Center for Resilience headed by a Resilience Coordinator. And the challenge of shocks and stresses of natural disasters was seen as too narrow a focus, and other threats to livelihoods needing resilience included "price volatility, population pressure, conflict and instability, climate change and variability, and idiosyncratic shocks such as a health crisis or the loss of a wage earner" (USAID, 2016a, 5). Wow!

The ADB was an early convert to resilience, starting in 2012 and 2013. Its main efforts have been in making infrastructure (water supply, sanitation, irrigation, flood control, transport and energy) more resilient to 'climate variability,' but it has also added social sectors such as education and health. Since 2013 the ADB has produced dozens of reports on aspects of resilience. And it, like the World Bank, has moved into the urban side of resilience in a big way.

Australian Aid (DFAT) was slow to take up the resilience fad, but it made up for this in 2015 when Australia endorsed the *Sendai Framework for Disaster Risk Reduction 2015–2030* and then developed a series of disaster preparedness, risk reduction, and social protection projects in its Indo-Pacific backyard, all under its 'resilience' label (DFAT, n.d.). Among Australia Aid's many resilience initiatives, in 2014 it joined the OECD in developing a resilience measurement index for societies and communities.

Several UN agencies had already been heavily oriented towards disaster, risk, and relief long before the concept of 'resilience' came along, yet they had to quickly join other donors in hyping the concept as something new and compelling. The UN Office of Disaster Risk Reduction, active since 1999, quickly aligned itself with the resilience concept, as did UNDP, which already had its Bureau for Crisis Prevention and Recovery. Furthermore, the UN's Office for Humanitarian Affairs (OCHA) also entered the fray with a "Resilience Position Paper" in 2012, and in April 2013 the UN system as a whole managed to produce a "United Nations Plan of Action on Disaster Risk Reduction for Resilience."

Resilience as a Fad: Here to Stay?

It would seem, looking from 2022, that resilience as a fad will be with us for some time. It embodies everything that fads and fashions are about in the development industry. And one of its key advantages is the link to the poor and vulnerable and the need to prepare them to 'bounce back.' It is a bit rich that the poor in the Rest are in need of outsiders to tell them how to become resilient, when in fact it is they who in their daily struggles are the most resilient people on earth. And there is a suspicion that the whole concept is one of the development industry's exercises in sidestepping real issues—such as exploitation, marginalization, and gross inequality. Instead, let them eat disaster preparedness!

Political Economy Analysis: Fad *du jour* or Useful Tool?

Political Economy Analysis (PEA) began to appear in development circles around 2003/2005 and, under different guises, came to be progressively taken up by a wide range of donors as a tool of analysis of recipient countries, holding out the promise of better understanding the political and economic power contexts within which donor projects and programs operate and, thus, to allow these projects to be better designed. The reasoning was that the prior, long-standing obsession with highly technical and super non-political approaches to foreign assistance was a main reason why donor interventions and approaches had little traction and disappointing results. Thus, PEA became to be seen by donors as a potential game changer by finally taking up the messy world of politics and power head on and allowing donors to "think and work politically" (TWP) and 'go with the grain.' The rapid take up of PEA among donors and the considerable activities spawned by it certainly qualifies PEA as a fashion in development and a good example of herd instinct.

However, PEA is not—like 'resilience,' for example—a huge fashion that everyone in development has heard of. In fact, it was designed for donor agencies, and it tends mostly to involve country office directors, sector managers, and development strategy types, even though it seems practically all donor staff have been forced to take PEA orientation courses or at least read the PEA manuals and toolkits. Consultants and other service providers in the development industry have rarely even heard about PEA, unless of course they themselves have been hired to write one of the many country- or sector-specific political economy analyses written over more than a decade.

For older experts with extensive experience in low-income countries, hearing about PEA and its faddish importance in getting 'development to work better' is frankly a bit much. Are donors so naïve that they need to structure knowledge of country's political economy? Shouldn't an awareness of the political dynamics of a country and the power structures within the economy be something donor management should know anyway? And if donor staffers have been newly posted to a country, can't they simply take up the subject in conversations with the heads of national NGOs, local academics/consultants, or even long-term expatriates? Or simpler yet, can't they take the time to read up on the country? The answer, as we shall see, is no. It seems that donors needed yet another connect-the-dots analytical way to perceive the political dimension and to formalize and endlessly reproduce it.

What Is Political Economy Analysis?

A generally accepted definition of PEA is the following: "Political economy analysis is about understanding the contexts—national, sectoral and local—in which development happens and the incentives that determine how the relevant actors behave and interact with each other" (ODI, n.d.). Stakeholder analysis features prominently, and the identification and promotion of 'development entrepreneurs' and reform alliances are frequently seen as key to PEA. Virtually all PEA is aimed to inform donor management and staff, allowing them to better understand behavior of recipient governments and the people in them.

The origins of the PEA as concept or tool could be said to originate back in the 1990s as a spin off another of the development industry's fashionable concepts—'governance' or, more pointedly, good governance. This has been defined as the "strong rule of law, capable bureaucracies, low corruption, and accountability of politicians and public officials to citizens" (Levy, 2014, xiii). However, even after several years the concept of 'good governance' continued to have little traction, especially among host governments who bristled at the thought that they were somehow part of the problem. "Rather than becoming a powerful tool for increasing the effectiveness of development practice, the new focus on governance and institutions seemed to be embroiling development practitioners and donor agencies in endless new cycles of conflict—often with countries and governments that, from a more traditional development perspective, seemed to be model performers" (Levy, 2014, 4). Simply put, even cooperative recipient governments were frequently showing their autocratic, patronage-ridden, and corrupt undersides. It didn't help that the good governance prescriptions seemed, taken together, to be little more than advocating that all countries emulate enlightened Western market economies and democratic governments. In effect, the many proponents of good government were becoming frustrated, and the question 'what to do?' became ever more pressing.

History of the PEA Concept

Although the rise of PEA in development is a bit murky, it was probably DfID who started the trend with its Drivers of Change (DoC) program, conceived in 2003. The key question addressed by DoC was how reforms that benefit poor people emerge and endure. DoC studies had been applied to 25 countries by 2009, and although it was recognized as having helped inform DfID country strategies, they did not sufficiently translate analytical findings into operational recommendations. Thus, in the same year DfID revamped its strategy and developed a more explicit PEA approach.

In parallel to DIFD, other donors who were early into the PEA game included SIDA with its 'Power Analysis' and the Netherlands' Ministry of Foreign Affairs with its "Strategic Governance and Corruption Analysis." Predictably, the production of tools, guidelines, and reports concerning

PEA and associated investigations also proliferated, and according to DAC's 2008 sourcebook on 'Donor approaches to governance assessments,' a political economy approach was already used in nine of the seventeen general tools for governance assessment, and four of the thirteen thematic tools (DAC OECD, 2009).

The year 2009 marked the beginning of what could be called the wholesale metastasis of the PEA concept throughout large chunks of the development industry. As we show, this has definitely been a case of herd instinct:

The World Bank moved into the field decisively, starting in 2009 with its widely read "Problem-Driven Governance and Political Economy Analysis: Good Practice Framework" and the mobilizing of mechanisms within the Bank to apply it (Fritz et al., 2009). This 'problem-oriented' framework emphasized that the issues must first be defined before examining the institutional context and uncovering the underlying political economy drivers. This would then allow strategies and operations to be developed that either fit the existing space for change or proactive strategies that expand the space for change itself. (A beloved distinction made by many of the PEA aficionados.) By 2014 the Bank had considerable experience in the methodology (Fritz et al., 2014). Subsequently, it set up its own Political Economy Community as a joint endeavor of various units within the Bank.

In 2012 DfID helped set up, along with Australian aid, the Thinking and Working Politically (TWP) Community of Practice operating out of Birmingham University, where it has conferences and working groups on aspects of PEA, produces toolkits, application guides, and learning material.

USAID, although a bit tardy, seems to have adopted the approach with enthusiasm. The first version of its "Field Guide: USAID Applied Political Economy Analysis" appeared in February 2016 (USAID, 2016b). It explains that the word 'applied' is meant to reflect the commitment to give effective, operational strength to PEA. However, it seems its main preoccupation was in giving USAID's staff and missions abroad a better feel for classic PEA as a means of uncovering 'why' development initiatives don't work, without any specific link to the 'doing' part of the equation. Thus toolkits, orientation courses, and other 'how to' outputs have dominated. USAID has also come up with its own PEA methodology called Collaborating, Learning, and Adapting, which has been taken up across USAID and seems to demand considerable time among staffers.

In the 2011 to 2013 period the European Commission had started applying forms of PEA in at least six countries through its knowledge and capacity for development unit (Capacity4Dev), relying mostly on external consultants. However, in June 2013 the Commission decided to stop all outside PEA work, based on a decision that such work should be part of the core tasks of desk officers and staff in EC delegations across the world. Furthermore, it was found there is an inherent political risk of pulling together detailed information on the political context of countries or sectors (Bossuyt, 2013).

UNDP joined the PEA fad in 2012 with its "Institutional and Context Analysis Guidance Note." This note was aimed at incorporating PEA ideas into UNDP methodology—both at the country level and at the sector or project level (UNDP, 2012). Supposedly, "the Guidance Note has emerged as a direct response to demand from Country Offices" (UNDP, 2012, vi), but it is more likely that UNDP management simply felt it shouldn't be left out of the PEA fashion which, at the time, was sweeping the donor world.

The ADB took up the PEA fashion in 2013, with its own guide, called "Guidance Note: Use of Political Economy Analysis for ADB Operations" (ADB, 2013). In it the ADB was underlining that it already had taken concepts of political economy on board under different guises and that it was in no way a latecomer to the PEA fashion. After 2013 no references to the use or application of political economy analysis in ADB's research or operational activities can be found. It appears that the ADB, like UNDP, has simply used its Guidance Note to proclaim 'been there, done that.'

Applications and Varied Facets of PEA

The application of PEA, at least in terms of studies and 'how-to' materials, has been quite impressive. It seems that, if there is a problem or issue confronting donors in a particular country, it can't hurt to throw some well-reasoned intellectual weight at it in the form of applied political economy. By 2014 there were numerous PEA approaches being used for particular global policies, to particular sectors, to particular countries, and even to particular cities. A partial list would include roads reform in Uganda, decentralization reforms worldwide, disaster risk management, medicine distribution in Malawi, health sector reform in Nepal, water and sanitation in Colombo, locally led development in Nigeria, and mainstreaming gender globally (Governance and Social Development Resource Centre, 2014).

Some countries have been the focus of more political economy analysis than others. Kenya, a donor darling of sorts, is an example. Publicly accessible reports on PEA in Kenya are legion and a partial list would include sectoral PEAs covering low-carbon energy, horticulture, non-communicable diseases, budget processes, and public finances oversight. And this list does not include those PEA analyses that donors have deemed too sensitive for public consumption. This very much shows how Kenya is favored by donors; it has a vibrant democracy, a very active civil society, many articulate players, and, we might add, continues to be astoundingly corrupt.

Conversely, it should be added that other countries have not enjoyed much PEA attention from donors. For example, although there are many academic studies of India's political economy, as far as can be ascertained, donor agencies have avoided including PEA to support their work in India. And Egypt, although a very significant and long-standing consumer of donor largess, has been the object of exactly zero published PEA studies.

As is the case with many fashions in the development world, once a methodology has been well established, it needs to be taught, and PEA is no exception. The ODI in the UK has been running a course for donor staff on applying PEA since 2008, with multiple donor clients. Other training exercises have been undertaken at the Development Leadership Program at the University of Birmingham and other universities and foundations in the West.

Is PEA Working? Criticisms, Constructive, or Otherwise

Even among the many proponents of the various PEA approaches, it seems that some recognize that the 'thinking' part is well covered, but that the 'working' part remains very sparse. Such criticism was expressed in 2013 during a conference in which the general acceptance among donors of PEA approaches was noted, but that the incorporation of 'politics' into the design and practice of development, however, has not been as smooth as this rhetoric might suggest. "The commissioning and use of political economy analyses (PEA) by donor agencies has been widespread for years but has largely failed to gain traction at the operational level" (ODI, 2013). At the conference, the problem of PEA diffusion was laid to questions of donor organizational incentives, dynamics both between and inside donors, the sensitive nature of PEA work and the tenacity of an 'anti-politics', technical mentality at the heart of many development institutions. Such doubts as to the easy application of PEA are also reflected in two widely read books (Carothers & de Gramont, 2013; Levy, 2014).

After 2014, the problems of applying PEA effectively seems to have led to a diminishing of enthusiasm for the concept. In 2015 a critical article entitled "Barriers to Political Analysis in Aid Bureaucracies: From Principle to Practice in DfID and the World Bank," appeared in *World Development* (Yanguas & Hulme, 2015). And in 2018 an insightful book was published that also questioned the application of PEA (Yanguas, 2018).

The Missing Other: The Object of the Whole Exercise

Applying PEA is very much a Western game, with Western institutions using Western funds to form Western teams to produce reports about how Westerners should better understand the dynamics operating in developing countries. Local input to PEA exercises is restricted to hiring individuals for short stints (usually local academics, NGO leaders, or ex-officials) to join PEA reviews. As far as is known, there has never been any aid-recipient government, political party, or civil society involvement. And local stakeholders who are invited to join discussions with donor PEA teams often simply do not show up.[2]

Looking Forward: Does PEA and Its Variants Have Any Future?

As we have seen, some donor agencies have only embraced the PEA fashion in a lukewarm manner and a couple have managed to avoid it altogether. Where PEA and its variants seem to have staying power is in the creation of homes for continued advocacy (within niches of the World Bank and USAID, e.g.) or where funding has allowed quasi-independent bodies to continue the efforts. In these cases, this staying power is usually associated with particular PEA gurus who have championed PEA approaches since the early years and continue to attract funding, either within the agencies themselves or in academia.

But is this fashion going to last? After all, PEA has been around for well over a decade and, as is often pointed out, PEA might help understand why donor-led development doesn't work, but it is decidedly feeble on

[2] A good example was USAID's look at Madagascar fisheries. It resulted in an extensive report about applying PEA. However, the locals who were lined up to join the effort were 'unfortunately unavailable.' (USAID, 2016c).

showing how it could be made to work. Moreover, PEA poses questions about political and economic power, and this kind of probing, were it ever applied to the development industry itself, would raise some seriously embarrassing questions. Thus, the prognosis for a future of PEA in the donor world is bleak, but talk about the concept and its application will probably bumble on with diminishing noise for another decade or so.

References

ADB. (2013, June). *Guidance note: Use of political economy analysis for ADB operations*. ADB Publications. Accessed June 10, 2022, from https://www.adb.org/documents/guidance-note-use-political-economy-analysis-adb-operations

Bossuyt, J. (2013, July 26). *Is there a future for political economic analysis in the European Commission?* European Commission for development policy management. Accessed June 10, 2022, from https://ecdpm.org/talking-points/is-there-a-future-political-economy-analysis-european-commission/

Carothers, T., & de Gramont, D. (2013). *Development aid confronts politics: The almost revolution*. Carnegie Endowment for International Peace.

Chadwick, V. (2020, December 17). Exclusive: France to launch innovation development fund chaired by Esther Duflo. *Devex*. Accessed June 9, 2022, from https://www.devex.com/news/exclusive-france-to-launch-development-innovation-fund-chaired-by-esther-duflo-98806

DAC OECD. (2009, January). *Tools for political economy analysis: A brief guide and signposts to additional resources*. Accessed June 10, 2022, from https://www.alnap.org/help-library/tools-for-political-economy-analysis-a-brief-guide-and-signposts-to-additional

DFAT. (n.d.). *Pacific regional: Climate change and resilience*. Accessed June 9, 2022, from https://dfat.gov.au/geo/pacific/development-assistance/Pages/resilience-pacific-regional.aspx

Fritz, V., Kaiser, K., & Levy, B. (2009). *Problem-driven governance and political economy analysis: Good practice framework*. World Bank.

Fritz, V., Levy, B., & Ort, R. (Eds.). (2014). *Problem-driven political economy analysis: The World Bank's experience*. The World Bank.

Governance and Social Development Resource Centre. (2014, December). *Political economy analysis. Topic guide*. Accessed June 10, 2022, from http://gsdrc.org/topic-guides/political-economy-analysis/

Hallegatte, S., Vogt-Schilb, A., Bangalore, M., & Rozenberg, J. (2017). *Unbreakable: Building the resilience of the poor in the face of natural disasters, climate change and development*. World Bank.

Levine, S. (2014, July). *Assessing resilience: Why quantification misses the point, Working Paper*. ODI Humanitarian Policy Group. Accessed June 10, 2022, from https://cdn.odi.org/media/documents/9049.pdf

Levy, B. (2014). *Working with the grain: Integrating governance and growth in development strategies*. Oxford University Press.

Lewis, D. (2012, July 25). *Is innovation essential for development work?* Guardian Global Development. Accessed June 9, 2022, from https://www.theguardian.com/global-development/poverty-matters/2012/jul/25/innovation-development-funding-capability

Mosley, P., Harrigan, J., & Toye, J. (1995). *Aid and power: The World Bank and policy-based lending* (p. 1). Routledge.

ODI. (2013, May 15). *Politicising or depoliticising aid? The political economy of political economy analysis*. ODI Conference. Accessed from https://odi.org/en/events/politicising-or-depoliticising-aid-the-political-economy-of-political-economy-analysis/

ODI. (n.d.). *Political economy analysis in action*. ODI the Policy Institute. Accessed June 10, 2022, from https://cdn.odi.org/media/documents/12261.pdf

OECD. (2012). *Innovation for development*. Accessed June 9, 2022, from https://www.oecd.org/innovation/inno/50586251.pdf

Ramalingam, B. (2015, March 12). *Development innovation: Fad, silo or catalyst? Development impact and you*. Accessed June 9, 2022, from http://diytoolkit.org/development-innovation-fad-silo-or-catalyst/

Shana, N. (2017, August 10). Jordan's Syrian refugees to get food aid in cash. *Sci Dev Net*. Accessed June 9, 2022, from http://www.scidev.net/global/aid/news/syrian-refugees-food-aid-in-cash.html

Sharma, Y. (2011, November 4). Gates tells G20 innovation is the key to development. *Sci Dev Net*. Accessed June 9, 20200, from http://www.scidev.net/global/networks/news/gates-tells-g20-innovation-is-the-key-to-development.html

UNDP. (2012). *Institutional and context analysis guidance note*. Accessed June 10, 2022, from http://www.undp.org/content/undp/en/home/librarypage/democratic-governance/oslo_governance_centre/Institutional_and_Context_Analysis_Guidance_Note.html

USAID. (2016a, September 9). *Resilience at USAID: 2016 Progress report*. Accessed June 9, 2022, from https://www.usaid.gov/documents/1867/resilience-usaid-2016-progress-report

USAID. (2016b, February). *Draft working document: Field guide: USAID Applied Political Economy Analysis*. Accessed June 10, 2022, from https://www.usaid.gov/sites/default/files/documents/2496/Applied%20PEA%20Field%20Guide%20and%20Framework%20Working%20Document%20041516.pdf

USAID. (2016c, September). *Marine biodiversity and fisheries in Madagascar: A biodiversity and extractives political economy assessment.* Accessed June 10, 2022, from https://pdf.usaid.gov/pdf_docs/PA00M9HQ.pdf

World Bank. (2012). *Resilience, equity, and opportunity.* World Bank. Accessed June 9, 2022, from https://openknowledge.worldbank.org/handle/10986/12648

World Bank. (2013, November). *Building resilience: Integrating climate and disaster risk into development.* Accessed June 9, 2022, from https://openknowledge.worldbank.org/handle/10986/16639

Yanguas, P. (2018). *Why we lie about aid: Development and the messy politics of change.* Zed Books.

Yanguas, P., & Hulme, D. (2015). Barriers to political analysis in aid bureaucracies: From principle to practice in DIFD and the World Bank. *World Development, 74*, 209–219.

CHAPTER 11

Plus Ça Change

In the previous chapter we looked at the donor-wide penchant for taking up fads and fashions, with little logic other than the herd instinct of copying each other and little effect other than widespread confusion. A related theme is the ostensible attempts of donor institutions to reform, to adopt new paradigms and modalities, or to reinvent or remake themselves. These pronouncements of and intentions for change and reform can take many forms, as we enumerate below, but it is certainly telling that these good intentions and lofty pronouncements, not to mention reorganization plans, change strategies, and innovation imperatives, etc. rarely get beyond policy papers, thematic conferences, strategic studies, and administrative reorganizations. In the rare occasions that these intentions actually result in some structural impact, either they are limited to creating more agendas, forums, and initiatives that are little more than talk shops, or they result in cosmetic operational changes that are often left to atrophy over time.

Here is not the place to delve into an understanding of bureaucracies and their strong resistance to change. This has been thrashed out conceptually ever since Weber and Wilson, with most work on having been devoted to corporate bureaucracies and public sector reform in the West.[1]

[1] A good example of the latter focus, including such theories of bureaucracies in developing countries using principle-agent, embeddedness, and developmental state concepts (and their links back to Weber and Wilson) is found in Pepinsky (2017).

D. Sims, *Development Delusions and Contradictions*,
https://doi.org/10.1007/978-3-031-17770-5_11

What is hardly ever covered is anything like sustained analyses of bureaucratic operations and culture within development institutions themselves.[2] Yet both multilateral and bilateral development agencies are huge and solipsistic bureaucracies, which, as argued below, are probably more resistant to change and fundamental reform than other types of institution. But perhaps because of this, these international development institutions seem to have an obsession with producing and reproducing the appearances of change.

The History of Donor Agencies and Their Obsessions with 'Change'

It is worth tracking some of these 'change' obsessions over time, since they show a consistent pattern of donor malaise and thus a need to appear on the cusp of breakthroughs and paradigms shifts—that flounder in the face of bureaucratic inertia, sloth, the obsession with preserving and expanding funding possibilities, and the need to accommodate special interest realities.

This has been going on for a long time. Even back in 2002 William Easterly had already pointed this out (Easterly, 2002). For example, the World Bank, founded in 1946, had its first reorganization in 1952 with at least five more following in the 1990s. US foreign assistance was reorganized five times before USAID was finally created in 1961, and at least six further reorganizations occurred prior to the establishment of the parallel Millennium Challenge Account in 2002. Other bilateral aid agencies as well as multilaterals have had similar reforms and reorganizations in their recent histories.

In 2002 an anthology entitled Reinventing the World Bank, appeared (Pincus & Winters 2002). It was a collection of hard-hitting analyses, mainly by academics (most prominently from SOAS), and its observations are still relevant after twenty years. It looked at various attempts to change, streamline, and reform World Bank operations and policies, especially concentrating on such thorny issues governance, corruption, and environment in developing countries, and at the Bank's place in the wider development world. It catalogued many of the Bank's ostensible reforms,

[2] There are the odd exceptions to ignoring the bureaucratic dimension in the development industry, mainly found in academia. Exceptions include Roger Riddell and of course William Easterly.

its obsession with new goals and new paradigms and the resulting 'mission creep.' And the conclusion? "... it is unrealistic to expect an institution that has grown to unmanageable proportions on the basis of internally driven change to manage its own reform program. The World Bank cannot be reformed and certainly cannot reform itself: it must be reinvented" (Pincus & Winters, 2002, 3). In other words, huge development bureaucracies like the Bank have a kind of internal self-reinforcing logic or 'path dependency' that make them pretty much immune to any long-lasting improvements and can only be changed by extremely strong external forces.

And these various comments were made in 2002. Since then, there have been ever more appearances of reform and change that have buffeted the World Bank as well as other development agencies. For example, in 2014 a wave of administrative reform swept the World Bank, after the then President Jim Kim, helped by scores outside management consultants, deemed a fundamental restructuring necessary, the centerpiece of which was reorganizing the bank's operations and budgeting into 14 'global practices' focused on policy areas—as opposed to the original geographical organization of the Bank into regions—which in turn was based on the almost imperial concept of the Bank firmly in the driver's seat of global knowledge.[3] These practice areas included 'water,' 'governance,' 'poverty and equity,' 'energy and extractives,' 'social protection and labor,' and so on. A wonderful but confusing catch-all practice, 'social, urban, rural, and resilience' was also invented. In any event, this centralized global structure "left a swath of demoralization and semi-destruction behind," according to one former senior manager (Edwards, 2019a). Included in the reform package were redundancies, pay freezes, benefit cuts, demotions, and promotions, which made changes considerably more difficult for staff to swallow.

The consternation was palpable, even in what were normally routine missions. For example, in July 2014 Bank staffers who had gathered in the plush Metropole Hotel in Hanoi for a conference on Vietnam's urban development couldn't talk about anything else but the upcoming restructuring. Conversations revolved around the latest rumors of staffing changes, interpretations what these global practices meant for career paths,

[3] Starting in 1996, then president James Wolfensohn rebranded the Bank by articulating a formal vision of a "Knowledge Bank"—a provider of state-of-the-art expertise on virtually all aspects of development.

and, as always, what all this implied for the re-configuration of the all-important constellation of higher-up bosses in the Bank.

How did all of this radical reform in the World Bank play out? Well, five years later practically all of Kim's restructuring measures were reversed. In 2019 interim president Kristalina Georgieva changed the senior management structure to align staff back under global and regional directors as opposed to practice directors. It came as a watchdog released a report criticizing Kim's reorganization as inhibiting collaboration and causing "inefficiency, fragmentation, and internal competition" (Edwards, 2019b). So all that effort, angst, and reshuffling of Bank people and their carriers over several years came to naught, and more effort, angst, and reshuffling were required to get back to a bit of regional and country focus.

The World Bank is not by any means the only large development bureaucracy that talks up change and reform while basically continuing with business as usual. The list of other agencies that have—over decades—announced their own reinvention and paradigm shifts is long. In 2011 the European Commission came out with a policy communication called "Increasing the impact of EU Development Policy: an Agenda for Change" which talked about sweeping reform that would "equip the EU with high-impact development policy and practice for the coming decade and give it a leading role in setting a comprehensive international development agenda" (European Commission, 2011). Well, it seems this impetus for sweeping reform (which one would have thought should have been in place already) was subsumed in 2019 by a new EU reform agenda called 'Policy Coherence for Sustainable Development' which is very much linked to and justified by the SDGs and Agenda 2030 (European Commission, 2019).

USAID has also been talking about the reform of how it does business for many years, but in 2018 it raised the rhetoric to new levels and established a 'Transformation Task Team' to fundamentally rethink how USAID delivers foreign assistance. It talked about reform of program design and procurement processes for "more effective co-creation, innovative financing and partnerships with a diverse array of actors" and formulated a new Private Sector Engagement Policy to increase USAID's "collaboration with the private sector to catalyze sustainable, enterprise-driven development" (USAID, 2018). For the largest bilateral development agency in the world and a huge bureaucracy constrained over decades by political party interests, such a 'transformation' certainly needs more than just a task force.

USAID also claims to have bought heavily into the recent fad of 'localization,' a sub-fad under the larger theme of 'country ownership' (discussed in Chap. 16), whereby more of a donor's funding goes directly to implementing agencies and NGOs found in recipient countries rather than international service providers. In November 2021, the USAID administrator Samantha Power announced that the agency would increase the amount of funding that goes straight to 'local partners' from just 6 percent to 25 percent (Saldinger, 2021). Just how this will be achieved remains to be seen, but faced with USAID's obsessive need to control and oversee every dollar it spends, it is likely that this worthy initiative will fizzle out. Either it will require more and more complicated layers of oversight as to nullify the whole concept, or the definition of 'local' will continue to be distorted to include funding international organizations registered in-country.

Often bilateral agencies claim to be slimming down and concentrating on a smaller set of countries or a smaller set of sectors or both, based on the idea that they can be more effective that way and have more lasting impact. This is also called 'selectivity' or defragmentation' in the business. But guess what? As discussed in Chap. 3, such exercises never seem to stick, given the imperative for product development expansion and the 'planting flags' that mesmerize donors.

It should be added that certain modes of operation popular with aid agencies have come in for sharp criticism time and again, but without any effect. Such is the case of technical assistance (TA). In 2000 an article appeared enumerating the many well-known problems generated by the massive overuse of form of grant assistance (Arndt, 2000): TA was overly supply driven, it had a poor capacity building track record, it placed excessive emphasis on tangible, measurable outputs, it compromised recipient country ownership, and there were massive distortions in the market for TA. The author also advanced a number of suggestions to make TA more focused and directed more towards institutional reform. Yet two decades nothing seems to have changed, and this was underscored by a review of TA in an Open Society Publication (Cos & Norrington-Davies, 2019). The massive use of TA had even increased as a percentage of total ODA (to 30–35 percent!), and the same (and even more) criticisms of TA practices were listed. For example, TA was being used as a crutch for aid delivery, as being overly supply driven, as a substitute for capacity building, as a practice that insisted on technical solutions for political challenges, as a means of replicating Western institutional models, and as a mechanism for building false capacities (Cos & Norrington-Davies, 2019, 15–24).

Do Donor Agencies Ever Really Change?

Discounting these many loud noises about reform, it is remarkable how little of substance has changed in donors and how they operate. Straightforward, time-bound projects with rigid cycles still account for the bulk of spending (programmable aid), budget support, structural adjustment, and other convenient quick-disbursing mechanisms continue to claim a good chunk of ODA, technical assistance continues to provide a cornucopia of moneys for practically anything a donor needs to study or to justify, the IMF continues its monetary policing under the 1980s rubric of structural adjustment, humanitarian aid continues to be disbursed under modalities that have been around at least a quarter of a century,[4] obsessive and control of operations are ever more dominant, and most organizational reform relates to little more than cosmetic (and confusing) change in appearances. After all, donor bureaucracies have shown extreme 'resilience' to anything that just might fundamentally shake things up.

Financing the Private Sector and 'Billions to Trillions'

One particularly stubborn reform imperative that has been trumpeted over recent decades is what could be called 'billions to trillions.' In 2015, and coincident with the declaration of Agenda 2030 and the SDGs, a call went out from a multitude of big-name donors that the private sector needed to dramatically increase its investments in developing countries, especially the poorest, and especially for infrastructure. The multi-donor document underlined that trillions of dollars were needed for infrastructure in developing countries *every year*, both to meet the needs of growing populations in the Rest, to underpin economic growth, to adapt to climate change, and, of course, meet the Sustainable Development Goals (World Bank, 2015). However, these lofty aspirations ignored the fact that private capital goes to where good returns can be made, risks are acceptable, and

[4] As a recent CDG report on the need for fundamental change in the world of humanitarian assistance stated: (Konyndgk, 2019) "… humanitarian action in the 21st century remains constrained by a 20th-century aid model: siloed, supply driven, and centered on the individual mandates and sectors of major international aid agencies." Many of these problems link back to "entrenched power imbalances" and to humanitarian agencies that are rewarded more for individually "marketing their product" to their donors than for jointly improving it for their beneficiaries.

the local regulatory, tax, and capital repatriation environment is favorable to inward direct investment. Needless to say, such conditions only exist in some developing countries some of the time. It was as if this hard reality—well known in the development industry for many decades—could now be gleefully ignored. A 2019 paper by ODI took a look at the concept and its record and showed that it was more like 'billions to more billions' at best (Attridge & Engen, 2019, 11).

Evidently such questions, asked time and again over years and years, have simply been ignored. In fact, this recent push to leverage more finance to the private sector provokes a strong sense of *déjà vu*, since it has been a very prominent feature in the development business for many decades. The World Bank Group's IFC and MIGA have been in the business of supporting private ventures in developing countries with loans, equity participation, and risk guarantees since 1956, and billions upon billions of dollars have been provided as loans and equity investments to private companies and their projects in developing countries (see also Chap. 18). Over the same period the IFC and MIGA's successes and impacts have also been scrutinized time and again, and it is not a pretty picture. For example, an academic paper back in 2002 catalogued a whole series of dubious actions under a subsection with the title "Corporate welfare or poverty alleviation?" (Rich, 2002, 37–42). Since 2002, the rather embarrassing outcomes of IFC-backed private investments have continued been catalogued by many, pointing out that they are a kind of welfare for corporations, allow them to earn excessive profits, and stretch the whole meaning of helping poor countries (Bretton Woods Project, 2013).

A similar story can be found with the fifteen or so development finance institutions located in the West (and in most cases wholly owned by Western governments) that also lend to private firms. Some were set up as far back as the 1960s,[5] and these bilateral financing institutions have a long record of favoring their own countries' corporations—usually those with global footprints—in their business penetration in developing countries, usually in those countries and sectors that are better off. The chummy relation between these institutions and major corporations has repeated itself over many decades.

[5] Such bilateral institutions were set up by the UK in 1948, Germany in 1962, Denmark in 1967, the Netherlands in 1970, the USA and Belgium in 1971, France in 1977, Switzerland in 1979, Finland in 1980, Spain and Austria in 1988, Norway in 1997, Switzerland again in 2005, Portugal in 2007, and Canada in 2017.

What has changed to justify a new wave of support for private companies post 2015? Is it simply that now there is the overarching excuse of the SDGs to revisit the need to leverage private sector investments for development and to elevate it to a 'billions to trillions' narrative? Reading the industry literature, it would seem so. In any event, there was a tremendous uptick of the theme in 2021, when building-back-better from Covid-19 coincided with COP 26 in Glasgow to generate yet more enthusiasm for finding ways to encourage private investment in developing and emerging economies (Chap. 12).

Climate Change and Green Economies: Old Wine in New Bottles?

What seems to have introduced a whole new imperative for reform into the development business is the need for action over global warming. But, looking at the ways donors have responded to the challenge, it seems that they have merely adapted their standard practices to this new green world and have, at the same time, unleashed carefully crafted narratives to pretend that they are devoting more and more efforts (and moneys) to responding to it.

It must be realized that climate change is no longer what could be considered a 'new' challenge, having been raised to the international level in 1992 at the UN Conference on Environment and Development in Rio de Janeiro and the coming into force of the United Nations Framework Convention on Climate Change (UNFCCC) two years later. In effect, over almost thirty years the discussions, conferences and accompanying angst have certainly cemented climate change as *the* go-to issue for any donor agency that wants to stay relevant. And over the same period a bewildering set of international mechanisms for financing climate adaptation and mitigations in poorer countries have been set up, such as the Global Environment Fund, the Special Climate Change Fund, the Adaption Fund, and the Green Climate Fund. Also thrown into the mix are the Clean Technology Fund and the Strategic Climate Fund (collectively known as the Climate Investment Funds, managed by the World Bank and dependent on individual country financing pledges). In 2009, at the Copenhagen UNFCCC summit on climate, rich countries collectively committed to a goal of jointly mobilizing $100 billion dollars a year by 2020 to address the needs of developing countries. However, as is often the case with such very public funding pledges, what constitutes the sources of this finance was and remains extremely vague. Contributions to these climate funds are supposed to be in addition to what counts as ODA, but such is not always the case, and serious double accounting is common. In any event, only a tiny fraction of this international funding pledge was met by 2020.

Of course, the rush into climate issues is spurred at least partly by Western guilt—for having caused global warming in the first place—and also partly by direct self-interest—since by reducing emissions that cause global warming, and by helping poorer countries down this path, it is Western countries and citizens that will benefit as much as anyone. But there is evidence emerging that all this new world of fighting climate change represents in many ways the same old, unchanging behavior of international cooperation. For this we look the twin imperatives to *mitigate* global warming by reducing carbon and methane release into the atmosphere and to help (mainly poorer) countries *adapt* to meet its negative consequences.

For mitigation, much trumpeted is the accelerating increase of private investment in renewables and new ways to effect carbon capture, including in developing countries. Technological advances have dramatically reduced both the cost of installing wind turbines and solar farms to the point that they are able to compete with electricity generated from fossil fuels. And probably nowhere in the developing world have the introduction of these alternatives been more pronounced than in Egypt, blessed as it is with both abundant sun, excellent wind profiles, and lots of vacant publicly owned desert available for installing these land-hungry systems. Earlier efforts that started in the 1990s concentrated on wind farms in the Red Sea, with KfW and the Danes leading the way with heavily subsidized finance. With considerable pressure from donors, by 2016 the Egyptian government had established attractive feed-in tariff systems, and by 2019 more and more renewable energy projects were being set up, and in particular solar power had become a real boom industry in Egypt. The Benban site for photovoltaic projects is the most shining example (said to be the largest in the world). Completed by the end of 2019, it is composed of 41 separate concessions in the desert near Aswan and which collectively will produce, it is said, more electricity than the Aswan High Dam. It represents a match made in heaven: On the one hand there are 25-year guaranteed revenues based on KWH purchase rates that are very attractive, much higher than what, on average, the Egyptian government was selling its electricity to consumers in 2019, and on the other hand there is huge concessional financing from multilateral banks. This financing is a virtual roll-call of major donor financiers: IFC, EBRD, EIB, AfDB, AIIB, CDC (of the UK), Finnfund, Norfund, the Dutch Development Bank (FMO), Proparco (France), and the Green Climate Fund, as well as a number of Arab banks, all of which extoll these investments to show their climate-friendly policies. But it is private consortiums that really benefit, usually joint ventures of large, specialized foreign firms and Egyptian companies—but no one pretends that the Egyptian firms are more than secondary partners.[6] The foreign firms include Scatec (Norway), EDF (France), Mounting Systems (Germany), ib-Vogt (Germany), GE (USA), Alcazar Energy and Access Energy (Dubai), Enerray (Italy), Acciona Energia (Spain), etc. Many more solar projects are on the way in Egypt, and this increase in renewable energy generation is much welcomed, yet at the same time they represent a bonanza for mainly Western corporations. Sound familiar? And what does Egypt gain? More electricity generation at high cost (the country has a big surplus in power generation) and only the tiniest number of permanent jobs are created from installations that are extremely capital intensive, the components of which are almost all imported.[7]

For adaptation, donors are scrambling to adjust their project portfolios to show they are making every effort to reduce the negative impacts of global warming in poorer countries. Climate-resilient agriculture, flood and sea-rise control, disaster preparedness, weather early warning systems, resilient housing, and other costly projects financed by donors have become much trumpeted as a new way of doing business. But to what extent do these efforts represent fundamental change? It is revealing to look in a little detail at the World Bank Group's own climate financing to unpack the reality. The Bank claimed that in FY2018 32.1 percent of its financing had climate benefits., with a record $15.7 billion coming from the IBRD and IDA (World Bank Group, 2018). Half of this amount was classified as financing for adaptation, with social, agriculture, and water sectors commanding the lions share. But a look at the list of adaptation projects shows that considerable imagination was applied to calculate the share of funding that went to various kinds of adaptation. Take, for

[6] Infinity Solar of Egypt is the sole exception.

[7] At a private investment cost of $2 billion and at best 4000 permanent employees, the investment cost-per-job in Benban will be considerably over $500,000 (Energy Egypt, 2018).

example, a rural connectivity project in Madhya Pradesh that was considered to devote 89% of total financing ($187 million) for climate change adaptation. The aim of the project is to improve a large network of gravel roads, with accessibility and economic benefits going mainly to the rural population, most of which are poor. So where is the climate adaptation? Project documentation clearly shows that this was a classic roads improvement project. Yes, it is expected that the monsoon rains will increase in duration and intensity over the next 35 years, but to ascribe practically all of the benefits of the project to climate adaptation seems to be stretching the point considerably (World Bank, 2017).

Such bending of project purpose can be found in most of the other 250-plus projects listed by the Bank in its "World Bank Climate Finance 2018" (World Bank Group, 2018). These included projects in livestock and fisheries, in community access and urban services, in cashew value chains, sustainable cities, in emergency social stabilization, in irrigated agricultural productivity, in road corridor development, in earthquake housing reconstruction, and in improved watershed management, just to name a few. Almost all of the listed projects represent exactly the same thing that the Bank has been funding for decades. Some of these were solid, useful interventions, but by sprinkling into project documents phrases such as increasing rainfall, rising sea levels, water stress, and ecological threats, and by adding in some technical assistance for studying climate links, then magically the appearance of a fundamental metamorphosis of the Bank's portfolio has been engineered.

The UN System: 'Cacophony into Symphony'

The UN system is, of course, not immune to this change obsession. Over decades UN agencies have been sponsoring what have been considered earth-shaking global paradigms that have quietly disappeared or have had to be resuscitated periodically. It is telling that the UN's website on development reform talks extensively about a totally new arrangement for UN development agencies, one of 'cacophony to symphony.' This is to be based on the emergence of a new generation of country teams, centered on a strategic UN Development Assistance Framework, supported by a new and 'robust' dual management and accountability framework, and led by an impartial, independent, and empowered resident coordinator (United Nations News, 2018). Actually, 'cacophony' is certainly a good way of describing UN country development over decades, with as many as

25 separate UN agencies present in a country running projects and programs that are directly tied to their central offices (in Geneva, Rome, New York, Vienna, Nairobi, Paris, etc.), scrambling and competing for chronically scarce funds (CBS News, 2019) within a bureaucratic culture that emphasizes hide-bound, sinecure-producing little empires whose 'core' funding is usually exhausted by salaries, travel, conferences, and perks. But the idea that this will somehow all change into a 'symphony' by simply setting up more administrative frameworks and hiring an "an impartial, independent and empowered resident coordinator" in each country staggers the imagination. In an interview (United Nations News, 2018) Amina J. Mohammed (UN Deputy Secretary-General) talked about these reforms as the "biggest transformation of the UN development system in history." Matt Wells of UN News asked a simple question: Why does the UN development system need reform? Ms. Mohamed's response was both straightforward and evasive: Reform is imperative because of this amazing new framework agreed in 2015—the SDGs. In other words, somehow the need for reform of one of the most ossified and bureaucratic development systems in existence, whose dysfunctions have been well known for decades, only now needs reform because of the SDGs, which the UN had the main role in creating. Talk about circular reasoning! This little example shows how the SDGs have allowed a quantum leap in rhetoric about change imperatives, as we show in the next section.

The SDGs and Raising the Talk About Change to New Levels

As has been underlined in Chap. 9, the SDGs are an uneven collection of platitudes and wishful thinking that are devoid of any logic except that the goals and sub-goals can easily be agreed by all and can stimulate endless discussion on how to achieve them. As an article in The Guardian puts it, "warm and cuddly" SDGs are simply not going to work, since they raise the rhetoric manyfold without any real accountability. None of the 17 goals are, after all, binding on UN member states or development agencies, and "it seems as if the SDGs simply offer member states a free pass to pat themselves on the back, despite their collective failures" (Sriskandarajah, 2017).

The SDGs should have been politely acknowledged as utopian ideals and then politely filled away as just more fluff. But in a change-obsessed development world they have provided almost infinite space to ramp up the rhetoric of virtuous posturing about development challenges. It is as if everyone was just waiting for the chance to declare not only their wholesale buy-in to the SDGs but to create ever more multi-dimensional and cross-cutting paradigms to fit with them. For example, the OECD has weighed in with a new concept called Policy Coherence for Sustainable Development Framework (2019 was its third iteration). It is "an approach and policy tool that supports the integration of the economic, social, environmental and governance dimensions of sustainable development across all stages of policy making, facilitating integrated approaches to proposed solutions for the SDGs" (OECD, 2019). In another OECD policy report from 2018 it is stated that "to keep the collective promise of achieving SDGs for all, leaving no one behind, and reaching the furthest behind first, business as usual development co-operation will not suffice. Providers need to make new deliberate, systematic and co-ordinated efforts to adapt their narratives, management practices and financing to maximise individual and collective impact" (OECD, 2018, 32). The question is, why are such lofty goals for impact considered 'new' in 2018, when the same issues have been around for decades?

If one were to look at almost any donor agency website and its content posted since 2015, the references to the SDGs as justifications for new policy postures and the need for transformational change will most likely be prominent. But why should this be so? Those who produce this content should be well aware of how dreamy almost all of these Agenda 2030 goals are, and how nonsensical it is to blur development issues by repeatedly evoking the SDGs. Yet it seems that there is something inherent in today's development world that requires that this mask of purported dynamic change be pulled over the whole industry.

Why Such an Obsession with Change and Reform?

It should be clear that the desire for change, reform, and 'doing development differently' is firmly embedded in the DNA of the development world and has been for some time. This is true whether one is talking about donor agencies or the more general industry-wide discourse. But why is this desire for change so strong?

First, there is a lot of funding for 'change' and the bandwagon that goes along with it. As we have seen, donor agencies are very quick to program funding for hot topics that appear to be new (or at least are presented as if they are so). And bilateral, multilateral, and foundation donors evidently can easily find the moneys to support the many conferences, the piles of documents, and the platforms and higher-committees that promote such 'change.' In addition, there is a strong link between the search for new paradigms and new initiatives (the larger and more global especially) and the imperative of all donors to be developing new products and expanding into new fields (Chap. 3).

But there is a lot more going on. It sometimes seems as if this obsession for reform and change is nothing more than the donors' need to confirm their continued relevance no matter what, a kind of convenient smokescreen for entrenched positions. One good paper by Nilima Gulrajani summed it up pretty well: "It is a truth, although not at all universally acknowledged, that an international foreign aid agency in search of higher performance must be in want of some kind of reform. Given the stubborn persistence of disease, poverty, conflict and unemployment, efforts at continual improvement are the modus operandi for most donor organisations struggling to demonstrate their effectiveness and self-worth. As the world continues to perceive the international aid system as having failed to achieve the elimination of poverty—or worse, contributed to the endemic problems of corruption, inflation and aid dependency in developing countries—donor organisational reform has almost become endogenous to the act of aid-giving itself" (Gulrajani, 2015, 154). In other words, seeming to reform can be considered as purely a defense mechanism to ensure a donor agency's relevance and even survival, not to mention something that naturally enhances the career possibilities of those in donor management.

All of this obsession with the appearances of change wouldn't be so bad if it did not overload and clog up donor agency management with additional signals and layers and tasks. And it must be added that such constant noise about change and reform totally confuses countries of the Rest, who have had a hard enough time keeping up with all the previous development paradigms and that have washed ashore.

References

Arndt, C. (2000). Technical cooperation. In F. Tarp (Ed.), *Foreign aid and development: Lessons learnt and directions for the future*. Routledge.

Attridge, S., & Engen, L. (2019, April). *Blended finance in the poorest countries: The need for a better approach*. Overseas Development Institute Report.

Bretton Woods Project. (2013, March 12). *IFC investments 'rarely touch the poor'*. Accessed June 12, 2022, from https://www.brettonwoodsproject.org/2013/02/art-572001/

CBS News. (2019, October 8). *United Nations could run out of money in a few weeks, Secretary General warns*. Accessed June 12, 2022, from https://www.cbsnews.com/news/united-nations-could-run-out-of-money-in-october-secretary-general-antonio-guterres-says-today-2019-10-08/

Cos, M., & Norrington-Davies, G. (2019, January). *Technical assistance: New thinking on an old problem*. Agulhas Applied Knowledge for Open Society Foundations. Accessed June 12, 2022, from https://www.shareweb.ch/site/DDLGN/Documents/OSF-Technical%20Assistance-Jan-2019-Edited.pdf

Easterly, W. (2002). The cartel of good intentions: The problem of bureaucracy in foreign aid. *Journal of Policy Reform, 3*(4), 223–250. https://doi.org/10.1080/1384128032000096823

Edwards, S. (2019a, February 4). As Jim Kim steps down, a tumultuous World Bank presidency comes to an end. *Devex*. Accessed June 12, 2022, from https://www.devex.com/news/as-jim-kim-steps-down-a-tumultuous-world-bank-presidency-comes-to-an-end-94247

Edwards, S. (2019b, April 10). World Bank reforms found ineffective, bank shuffles senior staff. *Devex*. Accessed June 12, 2022, from https://www.devex.com/news/world-bank-reforms-found-ineffective-bank-shuffles-senior-staff-94665?mkt_tok=eyJpIjoiT1RKak9HWmxOV1k0TmpNNCIsInQiOiJXd0VURStVNEgrW1Y3R05cLzFKeXhcL0x3YkNqY1Mzd3BCOVpuU-W9qOGRqSTJqcFdNK2dMZUxcL044XC96SmduTXU4SVBtSUZCa-zJROVg0TGxuTFNoYm1GVURST1drMW5kQmRWZURxa2JMUTgrMjJ-pMWJ5V3pLVzhHTXRnZ1J6UUZVSkgifQ%3D%3D

Energy Egypt. (2018, March 16). *Egypt inaugurates first phase of 1.8 GW Benban solar park*. Accessed June 12, 2022, from https://energyegypt.net/egypt-inaugurates-first-phase-of-1-8-gw-benban-solar-park-in-aswan/

European Commission. (2011). *Communication from the Commission to the European Parliament, the Council, the European Economic and Social Committee and the Committee of the Regions: Increasing the impact of EU development policy: An agenda for change*. Accessed June 12, 2019, from https://eur-lex.europa.eu/legal-content/EN/TXT/?uri=celex%3A52011DC0637

European Commission. (2019). *Policy coherence for sustainable development.* Accessed June 12, 2022, from https://ec.europa.eu/international-partnerships/policy-coherence-development_en

Gulrajani, N. (2015). Dilemmas in donor design: Organisational reform and the future of foreign aid agencies. *Public Administration and Development, 35*(2015), 152–164.

Konyndgk, J. (2019, August 19). *Five takeaways on the future of humanitarian reform.* Center for Global Development, abstract. Accessed June 12, 2022, from https://reliefweb.int/report/world/five-takeaways-future-humanitarian-reform

OECD. (2018). *Development co-operation report 2018: Joining forces to leave no one behind.* OECD. Accessed June 12, 2022, from https://doi.org/10.1787/dcr-2018-en

OECD. (2019). *Policy coherence for sustainable development.* Accessed June 12, 2022, from http://www.oecd.org/publications/policy-coherence-for-sustainable-development-2019-a90f851f-en.htm

Pepinsky, T. B., Pierskalla, J., & Sacks, A. (2017). Bureaucracy and service delivery (June 21, 2016). *Annual Review of Political Science.* Accessed June 12, 2022, from https://doi.org/10.2139/ssrn.2798912

Pincus, J., & Winters, J. A. (Eds.). (2002). *Reinventing the World Bank.* Cornell University Press.

Rich, B. (2002). The World Bank under James Wolfensohn. In J. Pincus & J. A. Winters (Eds.), *Reinventing the World Bank.* Cornell University Press.

Saldinger, A. (2021, November 4). Samantha power lays out her version for USAID. *Devex.* Accessed June 12, 2022, from https://www.devex.com/news/samantha-power-lays-out-her-vision-for-usaid-102003

Sriskandarajah, D. (2017, December 5). Warm and cuddly global goals? The international community must get real. *The Guardian.* Accessed June 12, 2022, from https://www.theguardian.com/working-in-development/2017/dec/05/warm-and-cuddly-global-goals-sdgs-international-community-has-to-get-real

United Nations News. (2018, May 31). *Vital reform of UN development system will end 'cacophony': Deputy UN chief (audio transcript).* Accessed June 12, 2022, from https://news.un.org/en/audio/2018/05/1011091

USAID. (2018, November 29). *Transforming our programs.* Accessed July 2019, from https://www.usaid.gov/what-we-do/transformation-at-usaid/transforming-programs

World Bank. (2015). *"From billions to trillions: transforming development finance. (Prepared jointly by the AfDB, ADB, EBRD, EIB, IDB, IMF and World Bank Group for the 18 April Development Committee meeting).* World Bank. Accessed June 12, 2022, from https://thedocs.worldbank.org/en/doc/622841485963735448-0270022017/original/DC20150002EFinancingforDevelopment.pdf

World Bank. (2017, March 21). *Combined project information documents/integrated safeguards datasheet (PID/ISDS)*. Madhya Pradesh Rural Connectivity Project. Accessed June 12, 2022, from https://ewsdata.rightsindevelopment.org/files/documents/54/WB-P157054_4UeHPRo.pdf

World Bank Group. (2018). *World Bank climate finance 2018*. Accessed June 12, 2022, from http://pubdocs.worldbank.org/en/744511553696049991/World-Bank-2018-CFData.pdf

CHAPTER 12

Responses to Covid-19

The coronavirus pandemic has been quite a game changer in many ways. It has had profound effects on economies around the world and on how international development is perceived, talked about, and reconfigured. As such it presents a chance to look briefly into how the development industry is responding to covid, how the long-standing interest of major players is being reinforced, and how they are positioning themselves for the post-covid future.

Covid-19 and Donor Funding

Due to the economic effects of the pandemic, Western government budgets have come under increasing strain and have racked up never-seen-before deficits. In the political maneuvring to face these budget crises, it is inevitable that some parliamentarians and observers have sought to trim government expenditures, and foreign aid programs would seem to have been an easy target. Has this happened?

The OECD reported that total ODA increased significantly by 4.4% in real terms in the 2020–2021 period to USD 179 billion (OECD, 2022). However, most of this increase was due to expenditures on vaccines and related assistance, and this meant that, overall, foreign aid from DAC countries has remained rather stable in 2020 and 2021. This represents a considerable victory for factions in the West that support continued development funding. For example, some major multilateral donors,

D. Sims, *Development Delusions and Contradictions*,
https://doi.org/10.1007/978-3-031-17770-5_12

particularly the World Bank, have ramped up funding pledges dramatically due to the pandemic, and this will eventually lead to a call on its member countries for a significant capital replenishment (Igoe, 2021a). In fact, so far only the UK has announced dramatic reductions in its overall aid budget: In November 2020 the Conservative government announced the country would reduce its standing target of spending 0.7% of GDP on official development assistance in 2021 to only 0.5% (Igoe, 2021b). Predictably, this led to an outpouring of comments and articles deploring this move and advancing arguments for preserving former aid levels. And, most prominent in these reactions were those that would be most affected, including especially INGOs who have raised their voices against such a move. One NGO activist in Sierra Leone was quoted as saying, a bit dramatically, these cuts were a "gut punch that will crumble life-saving work" (Hodal, 2021).

It is hard to predict what will be the long-term effects on foreign assistance brought about by the global pandemic. It may well be that external factors—especially sharp inflation and dramatically higher interest rates in 2022 and beyond—will herald a significant belt-tightening in Western allocations to foreign aid. In any event, the history of development cooperation shows an impressive ability for the industry and its lobbyists to continue to do what they are best at, which is to Move the Money and to construct new fields to conquer, no matter what the winds of change. This ability is illustrated, as it concerns Covid, in the rest of this Chapter.

Donors Remaining Relevant: Generating Covid Related Projects

Western donor agencies, like everyone else, were caught completely unawares by the coronavirus pandemic and its extremely rapid spread in early 2020. But in almost no time donors could be found to be churning out pronouncements and general advice aimed at their client countries about the virus and its impact on livelihoods and economies. Such actions had become quite widespread as early as April 2020, in spite of the fact that—as it turns out—very little was known about the virus or effective measures to contain its spread. A good example of this is a UNDP press release (UNDP, 2020) that calculated that the UN's Human Development Index for most developing countries would decline in 2020, and that, according to some obscure logic, this meant that all responses to the pandemic should be directly linked to the 17 Sustainable Development Goals. This trumpeting of the SDGs could also be found in many other UN texts about combating the virus pandemic, such as a policy brief in June 2020 which smugly preached that "thoughtful and targeted [Covid-19] actions can place the world on a robust trajectory towards achieving the SDGs" (United Nations, 2020).

Beyond these many pronouncements and sometimes self-serving advice disseminated about the pandemic, donor agencies also began to review their project and program pipelines to show how these could be modified to demonstrate their awareness of the crisis and, underlying this, to avoid disruptions in the business-as-usual rollout of yet more and more activities. A perusal of development project tender announcements on Devex makes this clear (Devex, 2021). For example, in the single month ending on 5 March 2021 there were 6413 tenders and grants posted, of which 1025 or about 15% contained the key word 'covid,' and, of these, roughly a third had 'covid' in the project title. Some of these tenders involved the mundane procurement of Covid-related materials, equipment, and personnel, but many more announced what could be considered existing development projects or programs with, at best, a Covid spin put on them. Thus, we have, for example, a huge EIB loan of 425 million Euros to support small and medium enterprises "amidst the Covid-19 pandemic in Egypt," something the EIB has been funding big time in Egypt for at least a decade (Ahramonline, 2020). Over a single month in 2021 (February–March) multilateral donors announced a bewildering raft of other 'extended' and 'supplemental' loan financing projects, such as:

- Covid-19 Green Response and Recovery Support (worldwide, OECD coordinated)
- Bandesal Sustainable Energy and Covid-19 Response in El Salvador (EIB)
- Potable Water Covid-19 Response in Senegal (EIB)
- Covid-19 Emergency Response Project in Mali (Additional Financing, EIB)
- Nicaragua Covid-19 Education Sector Response (WB)
- Ecuador: Strengthening of Utilities in a post Covid-19 Recovery (WB)
- Emergency Crisis and Covid-19 Response Social Safety Net Project in Lebanon (WB)
- Responding to Covid-19 by Developing Modern and Resilient Agrifood Value Chains in Guatemala (WB)

- Social Protection Project in Mozambique (Third Additional Financing and Covid-19 Response, (WB)
- Additional €2.7 million to Boost the Financing of Micro-Enterprises Amidst Covid-19 in Jordan (EIB)
- €300 million Loan to Support the Energy Sector Amidst the Covid-19 Pandemic in Tunisia (EIB)

In other words, apart from some emergency pandemic funding, it appears that donors are simply reconfiguring or rebranding ongoing activities and initiatives to give them an appearance of coronavirus relevance while keeping their pre-virus operations and emphases safely intact. And, at the same time, they seem mostly to be using existing channels and partner agreements to keep their project pipelines humming.

Jobs in Development: Could There Be a Welcome Change?

Very soon after Covid-19 became a pandemic, gloom and doom began to be felt throughout the development industry's huge and varied job markets. By August 2020 a Devex survey reported that 59% of 'development workers' had lost a job or knew someone who had, up from 37% in April (Smith & Chadwick, 2020). It seems that most losses are related to INGO staff and short-term employee hires, but, based on anecdotal information, it is certain that an even greater gloom could be found among freelancer consultants. In stark contrast, donor staff themselves have been pretty much immune to these trends, and most donors continue to advertise for in-house positions.

The reason for these curtailments is of course the covid-related travel, distancing, and meeting restrictions that made getting on a plane and moving around extremely difficult. No longer could the old practice of parachuting hordes of development types into a certain country be continued. And, needless to say, no longer could the many short-term assignments that are related to conferences, workshops, training, or other events be easily rolled out. Of course, there were zoom, webinar, and other virtual forums, but these could not generate anywhere near the level of exchange, missions, and 'experts on the ground' that was common in the pre-covid period.

Could there be a silver lining to all this? Both donors and large INGOs rely on their national personnel who are present on the ground. As is discussed in Chap. 17 below, these staff are essential to in-country donor operations, but they have been very much undervalued. Likewise, while national consultants and experts are found in abundance in most countries, there is a tendency to see them as junior partners in development teams, with most conceptual and coordination tasks falling on the expatriates. Thus, it seems that during the pandemic donors and INGOs have perforce had to rely more on these in-country professionals.

To what extent is such a shift really taking root? Looking at various job posting sites in 2020, 2021, and 2022, it seems that donors are *not* turning wholeheartedly towards in-country expertise. Most job offerings aimed at locals are lower level 'process' and administrative positions, and, furthermore, there have been many remote (home-based) assignments posted that are aimed mostly at international experts. In other words, international consultants as well as donor staff themselves are continuing to fill the higher management and team leader functions, something that allows donors to steer and maintain oversight over what is going on in-country. This is ironically one of the outfalls of the rise in virtual communications tools. As was pointed out in a posting from an Australian aid worker in the Pacific: "The Covid-19 lockdown has provided some space for nationals of our partner countries to take more leadership, but we have also actively limited that space.... Our capacity to work remotely has meant that generally, we have not relied upon national experts to take the lead and continue our programs. If a disruption the size of Covid-19 does not force us to change our approach, then it is clear the status-quo will be maintained indefinitely unless we choose otherwise" (Hehir & Tupua, 2020). Perhaps there are some examples of real shifts in responsibilities towards local cadres, but overall the control over how development projects are planned, how they are managed, and how they are assessed remain firmly outside the countries and people most concerned.

Virtual Events: A New Mode in the Development Industry?

Donors and others who promote large and splashy events on development topics have very quickly taken to Zoom, Teams, and other virtual platforms in the Covid era. Events have always been a staple in the industry (see Chap. 8), and now it seems that they have been given a new impetus through the convening of ever more conferences, workshops, and discussions on line. These only require a small amount of IT expertise, are easily announced and arranged, and do not entail all the logistical hassles and costs of face-to-face events. And, since the main metric of an event's success is simply audience participation, the medium is a perfect way for the sponsoring institution to project its importance and influence on whatever development arena is at hand.

It seems that, as the pandemic begun to wither away (2022), virtual events are surviving as important, supplementary means for development industry players to show they remain relevant and important. After all, attendance is only a couple of clicks away, and participants need not even attend a whole session (thanks to muted with video off).

Talking Big and Hope Eternal

One marked change that has surfaced in the development world during the pandemic, even after it began to wane, is a ramping up of the 'we can change things' rhetoric. Already a staple of commentary in the business, such inspirational posturing seems to have reached new heights under the pandemic theme of Building Back Better. Thus, we have, for example, the World Bank's Vice President for Latin America and the Caribbean, who after mentioning that "the Covid-19 pandemic has thrown much of the Western Hemisphere into the worst crisis it has experienced in over a century," added in the same breath that "it also offers an unprecedented opportunity to set the region on a more sustainable, prosperous, and equal path" (Welsh, 2012). Well and good, but how the World Bank can help this departure from its normal practices is not mentioned. Instead, it seems that the pandemic conveniently justifies reinforcement of the Bank's long-standing policies and ways of doing business.

The same game change optimism was also in play at the (virtual) WEF in January 2021. Session One was entitled "Grassroots Globalization: Beyond the Pre-COVID Consensus," (which is pretty rich, considering that Davos is the total antithesis of anything grassroots). Various development gurus pondered the question of how could "international organizations and legal/economic frameworks be reformed or complemented to accommodate countries at all levels of development, and to ensure that more people and communities can participate in the global economy and multilateral initiatives on their own terms?" (Project Syndicate, 2021). It was as if the question had never been asked before.

Then there are those who consult and coach on the internal dynamics of development cooperation who also see opportunities for change under Covid-19, as a 2020 Australian blog states: "[T]his is also an opportunity for us to think more broadly about the kinds of organisations that we want to create, and to re-align our values and ways of doing business to enable us to have more impact while taking care of ourselves at the same time" (Wilson, 2020). Much in the same vein, there have also been calls for new ways of interaction in development cooperation and for a post-Covid "smart recovery" approach, "one that does not replicate the unsustainable patterns of the past" (Izmestiew & Klingebiel, 2020). It seems as if practically anything can be improved in the bounce back from Covid-19.

We could list many more examples of this high-sounding and hubristic optimism due to the pandemic. The point is that Covid-19 gives almost limitless additional space for platitudes about how things in the development world must change, must be rethought, and must be restructured. And yet, ironically, these same calls for change reflect nothing more than the standard philosophies that major donors and other development types already preach. This is a great example of the Plus Ça Change phenomenon we saw in the previous chapter.

References

Ahramonline. (2020, December 31). *Banque Misr receives Euro 425 mln from EIB to support Egyptian SMEs amid coronavirus crisis.* Accessed June 13, 2022, from https://english.ahram.org.eg/NewsContent/3/12/397887/Business/Economy/Banque-Misr-receives-%E2%82%AC-mln-from-EIB-to-support-Egy.aspx

Devex. (2021). *Find funding, filtered for Funding Activities.* Accessed March 7, 2021, from https://www.devex.com/funding/r?report=funding_info-137390&query%5B%5D=covid&filter%5Btype%5D%5B%5D=funding_info&filter%5Bstatuses%5D%5B%5D=forecast&filter%5Bstatuses%5D%5B%5D=open&filter%5Bstatuses%5D%5B%5D=closed&filter%5Bupdated_since%5D=2021-02-05T11%3A19%3A23.778Z&sorting%5Border%5D=desc&sorting%5Bfield%5D=_score

Hehir, T., & Tupua, L. (2020, October 12). COVID-19: An opportunity to empower. *Devpolicy Blogs.* Accessed June 13, 2022, from https://devpolicy.org/covid-19-an-opportunity-to-empower-20201012/

Hodal, K. (2021, January 27). UK aid cuts of up to 70% a 'gut punch' to world's poorest, experts say. *The Guardian*. Accessed June 13, 2022, from https://www.theguardian.com/global-development/2021/jan/27/uk-aid-cuts-of-up-to-70-a-gut-punch-to-worlds-poorest-experts-say

Igoe, M. (2021a, April 7). What is the World Bank doing about its shrinking bank account? *Devex Inside Development*. Accessed June 13, 2022, from https://www.devex.com/news/devex-newswire-what-is-the-world-bank-doing-about-its-shrinking-bank-account-99597

Igoe, M. (2021b, January 28). The United Kingdom's plan to reduce aid spending is causing major blowback. *Devex News*. Accessed April 7, 2022, from https://www.devex.com/news/the-uk-s-0-7-blowback-ethiopia-s-aid-prospects-and-google-s-moonshot-miss-this-week-in-development-99012

Izmestiew, A., & Klingebiel, S. (2020, May 1). *International (development) cooperation in a post-COVID-19 world: A new way of interaction or super-accelerator?* Development Policy Centre. Accessed June 13, 2022, from https://devpolicy.org/international-development-cooperation-in-a-post-covid-19-world-a-new-way-of-interaction-or-super-accelerator-20200501-1/

OECD. (2022, April 12). *ODA levels in 2021- Preliminary data*. Accessed June 13, 2022, from https://www.oecd.org/dac/financing-sustainable-development/development-finance-standards/ODA-2021-summary.pdf

Project Syndicate. (2021, January 29). *Grassroots globalization*. Accessed June 13, 2022, from https://events.project-syndicate.org/event/grassroots-globalization

Smith, E., & Chadwick, B. (2020, August 20). Covid job losses accelerate in development sector, survey results say. *Devex*. Accessed June 13, 2022, from https://www.devex.com/news/covid-19-job-losses-accelerate-in-development-sector-survey-results-say-97946

UNDP. (2020, May 20). *COVID-19: Human development on course to decline this year for the first time since 1990*. Accessed June 13, 2022, from https://www.undp.org/press-releases/covid-19-human-development-course-decline-year-first-time-1990

United Nations. (2020, June 22). *SDGs still offer best option to reduce worst impacts of COVID-19 and to recover better*. Accessed June 13, 2022, from https://www.un.org/sustainabledevelopment/blog/2020/06/recovery/

Welsh, T. (2012, February 20). World Bank's Latin America chief sees chance to overcome 'crisis of historical proportions. *Devex*. Accessed June 12, 2022, from https://www.devex.com/news/world-bank-s-latin-america-chief-sees-chance-to-overcome-crisis-of-historical-proportions-99215

Wilson, K. (2020, May 11). *Time to end the hustle culture in international development*. Development Policy Centre. Accessed June 13, 2022, from https://devpolicy.org/time-to-end-the-hustle-culture-in-international-development-20200511-2/

PART II

When the West Meets the Rest

CHAPTER 13

Background: Governments in the Rest

Governments in developing countries receive almost all development assistance or are the official conduits through which it passes. They also either receive or at least have a say in the funds coming from foreign NGOs, foundations, and charities, and they also have at least nominal control over humanitarian relief aid. Thus, it is not simply idle curiosity trying to understand how these governments operate and perform. Western donors have for decades been knuckling their collective brows over the issue, and since at least the 1990s their concern has become almost obsessive.

Trying to generalize about governments in the Rest is difficult, if not impossible, since one is looking at 130 plus developing countries, each with its central, regional, and local levels of government, each with its myriad ministries, agencies, commissions, and authorities, and each with its own presidential, parliamentary, military, or monarchical systems. But with the error definitely on the 'sweeping generalizations' side, this chapter makes an attempt. We feel we are in good company, since the development industry itself is often prone to lump all developing countries together in discussions, analyses, and recommendations.[1]

[1] Sweeping generalizations that lump all countries in the Rest together are common in mainstream development literature and its hubristic recommendations. Just one example is a United Nations University working paper (Repucci, 2012). It lists eight principles for effective reform across all 'developing countries' and identifies six barriers that need to be overcome. The sixth 'barrier' is donors themselves.

D. Sims, *Development Delusions and Contradictions*,
https://doi.org/10.1007/978-3-031-17770-5_13

Bad or poorly run governments are obviously expected to be found in fragile or rogue states and where conflict is endemic. These 20 or 30 nations have, so to speak, an excuse for having awful governments, but such is not the case for the majority of relatively stable and unthreatened poor countries, and it is these 'average' aid-recipient countries worldwide that are of interest here.

With some exceptions that we enumerate below, the generalization of bad government in most of the Third World has held for decades, in spite of considerable interest in civil service reform on the part of donors since the 1970s and 1980s and the introduction in the late 1990s of 'good governance' as the cure-all for a country's development problems. This generalization holds whatever a country's colonial antecedents, no matter whether there has been a strong socialist, monarchical, or free market underpinning, or whether or not there is a semblance of multi-party democracy. And, according to some commentators and indices, awful government in the Rest is getting worse.

Mostly, a Depressing Picture

That governments in the Rest are, with some exceptions at certain times and in some sectors, ineffective and self-serving is a well-recognized perception. Judith Tendler, writing in 1997, summed it up (Tendler, 1997, 1):

> Public officials and their workers pursue their own private interests rather than those of the public good. Governments over-extend themselves in hiring and spending. Clientelism runs rampant, with workers being hired and fired on the basis of kinship and political loyalty rather than merit. Workers are poorly trained and receive little on-the-job training. Badly conceived programs and policies create myriad opportunities for bribery, influence peddling, and other forms of malfeasance. All this adds up to the disappointing inability of many governments to deliver good public services and to cope with persistent problems of corruption, poverty, and macro-economic mismanagement.

Robert Calderisi, a long-serving World Bank staffer, catalogued in his 2006 book a litany of egregious examples of purely self-serving and awful behavior of African rulers, their henchmen, and the top officials of governments they control (Calderisi, 2006). As he tells it, kleptocratic entrenched interests usually triumphed, national budgets went almost exclusively for salaries and perks, subsidies were wasted and precious little if any reached the poor, and oil and mineral revenues were appropriated unabashedly by rulers and their families. It didn't seem to matter whether a country was run by an elected political party, a benevolent dictator, or a series of *coup d'état* generals. Although most of Calderisi's blame aims at recipient governments and their rulers and strongmen, donors do not escape his ire, especially in their bending over backwards to protect the smooth flow of their money pipelines, their country's diplomatic (and often commercial) imperatives, and their need to be very politically correct. And he is talking only about Africa, where it is generally recognized that governments take the cake for being the most rapacious. In other parts of the Rest, some governments are not so bad, as we will see below, but the generalization holds.

A detailed account of how Third World rulers and their cronies have looted their countries' resources can be found in a book by Tom Burgis. Many African and as well as other countries figure prominently, as do huge multinationals and even the International Finance Corporation. Burgis points out that according to Global Financial Integrity, between 2001 and 2010 illicit outflows from the developing world amounted to $5.9 trillion (Burgis, 2015, 168).

Finally, it is worth adding the litany of the unappetizing characteristics of the numerous authoritarian regimes and one-party states found in the Rest culled by an LSE professor who looked at the political economy of aid relationships in 2016 (Brett, 2016, 8):

> ...patron-client relationships, neo-patrimonialism, systemic patronage or cronyism; corruption, state capture, wealthy and/or dominant elites determined to hold on to state power, the politicization of businesses and the phenomenon of 'shadow states' (or polities); personalistic political parties; ... weak, divided, deferential ... or impotent civil society organizations, ... limited or weak political 'demand' for rapid or realistic institutional reform, and minimal or non existent 'political will'; [no] clear and agreed overarching national economic strategy, project or set of socio-economic goals (other than in rhetoric); low levels of 'stateness', and hence, governance, with demoralised and politicised bureaucracies, dubiously independent judiciaries and (sometimes) militaries.

How Did Things Get This Way?

First, unlike in the West, most government structures in the Rest and the enabling legislation that underpins them did not grow and evolve over decades or even centuries. (The one exception is in Latin America, but one could say the colonial hangover from independence in the early nineteenth century effectively condemned these countries to much the same fate.) There was no progressive building up a corpus of rules and practices and legal traditions that both reflected a particular society's outlooks and values and were able to slowly change and mature. Such processes are particularly important for creating a cohesive compendium of civil laws and codes that could accommodate and co-exist with executive legislation being issued by governments.

In most of the Rest there were no such processes. Instead, almost all developing countries have had deep colonial pasts, where both laws and government structures were bequeathed from the outside in the form of colonial administrations and where protecting the privileges and power of colonial administrators was the name of the game. Independence for these former colonies came at the earliest in 1947 and had largely been completed by the mid-1960s. New governments—with rare exceptions—simply adopted what had been in place and quickly populated colonial structures with their tiny educated elites (some of whom had already been groomed for such roles by their colonial masters), with all the perks that were part of the long tradition of colonial privilege. And in many cases, colonial legislation was left intact.[2] This period of post-independence transformation, and the appropriation of colonial symbols and trappings of power by the new leaders and bureaucrats, is amusingly and accurately described by Tarzie Vittachi in *The Brown Sahib* (1962). What a glorious time! New leaders (mainly in Asia) were wined and dined by their ex-colonial masters, cricket and social clubs and gymkhanas were taken over by these new elites, and their children were quickly sent to the same

[2] Even today the basic laws of land and property in many West African countries remain French, usually dating from the 1930s. And in Kenya, for example, the same arbitrary land laws that had been put in place to ease the settlement of white farmers in the 1920s and 1930s were used by Presidents Moi and Kibaki to make it particularly easy to grab huge tracks of land for themselves and their tribal associates. What an irony!

in-country private schools and out-country universities that had serviced previous colonial generations.[3]

By the 1960s and 1970s, 'development' and catching up with the West had become the holy grail of most new governments, sanctified by a burgeoning United Nations system, increasingly funded by sometimes conscience-ridden Western donors, and made politically acceptable by the Non-Aligned Movement and (later) the Group of 77 and the New International Economic Order. This coincided with rapid population growth in most countries and also with rapidly expanding systems of primary, secondary, and higher education. How were these millions of young people to be employed? No one wanted their sons and daughters to become technicians that just might have to work with their hands from time to time. The obvious solution was to exponentially expand the civil service and other public sector institutions. Quickly, more upper-level positions were created and filled through systems of connections and patronage, and these positions promised total job security, a white-collar job with one's own office (and peon), and with housing allowances and other perks. The rush was on.

In attempts to modernize at breakneck speed, budding legal minds were quick to write lots of new legislation and related rules and procedures. These served to build up state bureaucracies and to reflect the nationalist and often socialist flavors of the times. But often their models were laws and systems found in the countries of their former colonial masters, and in all cases new legislation was mainly written cut and paste without thinking out how it could be possibly applied and enforced.

In parallel, those in power had lots of fun establishing new ministries, authorities, public enterprises, permanent commissions, and high-level task forces. They also enjoyed imposing theoretical government control over ever more aspects of society, again without thinking through the implications. And, as described in Vittachi's sequel *Brown Sahib Revisited* (1987), much of the aim of all this was to create space for the perpetuation and expansion of those in power, their buddies, their relatives, and—especially—their children. Even in countries with little or no colonial

[3] Of course, a small number of developing countries were never colonized (such as Thailand, Iran, Nepal, Bhutan, Turkey, and Saudi Arabia), but Great Power influence over them was still pronounced. And there were other countries that had gone the socialist route after colonization (e.g. Cuba, Vietnam), yet it is surprising how quickly these revolutionary movements erected governments and promulgated laws that both guaranteed the exclusive power of the new State and special places for its elites.

history—such as Ethiopia, Iran, and Thailand—the same lock and stock borrowing of legal and administrative frameworks and categories from the West or the Soviet block was very much in vogue, often with the help of advisors sent from these places or various UN agencies.

Up to the 1980s these trajectories of increasingly bloated bureaucracies, of more labyrinthine requirements for citizens to follow, and of predatory mechanisms for enormous insider gain continued. The cold winds of huge foreign debt and the consequent imposition of belt-tightening structural adjustment programs may have had devastating effects on social safety nets, on subsidized goods, on currency stability, and on other shocks, but feeble admonitions by the IMF and other donors aside, the huge bureaucracies in the Rest and their wasteful ways were hardly affected in any serious ways. Of course, neoliberal advice from abroad, especially in the 1990s, talked endlessly about the need to minimize the role of the state and to restrict it to ensuring a business-friendly environment, but this advice had little effect in most countries. Government hiring in some of the most indebted countries was ostensibly put on hold, a few public enterprises were put up for sale, and limited-duration 'contract' hiring was introduced to lighten the enormous wage bills faced by governments. Starting in the 1990s talk about public management and administrative reform exploded, underwritten by donors with copious advice from consultants and academics. Some reform programs during this period were modeled on those found in the West, especially concepts of New Public Management, even though it should have been apparent that these were not easily applied to non-Western systems. And, of course, the fertile fields of training and capacity building aimed at public officials continued to be generously funded by donors.

After 2000, donors ramped up their preaching about fiscal restraint, business-friendly approaches, and smaller government. There were lots more studies and more reform programs, but not much success; some improvements in the management of public finances were noted but there was a continuing disappointment over civil service reform. In 2014 an article in *Public Administration and Development* reviewed donor efforts at supporting public sector reform, and it summarized the situation well (Repucci, 2014):

> Many reasons have been given for why civil service reform has not made greater strides, including the interdependencies and complexity of the system, the conflicting interests of stakeholders combined with the sensitivity

of the changes that must take place, the delayed and sometimes ambiguous nature of results and what caused them, a lack of consensus on what the most important civil service objectives should be, and an absence of a theoretical model to guide practitioners in how to approach and monitor reform. ... *But regardless of the reasons, civil service reforms have been ad hoc at best and misguided at their worst.*

Typical Government Weaknesses and Failings Today

Here we run through the most common weaknesses and stubbornly problematic behaviors found in government systems in most of the Rest. Yes, there are exceptions (see below), but overall it is not a pretty picture:

1. Pyramidal structures and armies of civil servants

   Government power remains very much concentrated at the very top, and this power extends through very large bureaucratic institutions, patronage systems, and elite crony networks that donors rarely seem to understand (or don't want to). Everyone is very deferential to the boss, who will most likely be a man with a huge ego and very worried about any competition from below. And despite lots of donor advice, there is practically no delegation of authority, either within an agency or department or from lofty ministerial heights down to the mainline departments.

   In addition, practically all developing countries have armies of employees that populate these very centralized bureaucracies. These positions, although usually poorly paid, offer perks and advantages and are much sought after, especially because they represent extreme job security, advancement by seniority, and a certain social prestige. These armies of government employees consume hefty portions of the State budget, and they are extremely difficult to whittle down, despite half-hearted efforts at early retirement, redundancy payments, and other mechanisms. In effect they constitute a huge interest group that no one, especially a ruler who craves continued stability, wants to touch. Whether socialist, monarchical, military, or market oriented, poorer countries have used appointment for civil service as a reward for political loyalty and a place to park relatives, as well as a way to soak up the idle and reward those who have sleepwalked through creaky education systems. In many countries, the wait to land a government position can take many years, and this has given rise to specialized models about 'queuing' to describe labor force dynamics.[4]

2. A culture of fear is pervasive

   Dominating these bureaucratic systems is what could be called the big autocrat personality. Power and decisions are almost always concentrated jealously at the ministerial level or above, even when there are good middle-level managers with ostensible authority. As a consequence, access to the boss is everything, and decisions are made (or endorsed) only by the boss or *his* boss. And if endorsed, it is standard practice for it to appear it was the boss's idea in the first place. There may be a formal desire for meritocracy and technical proficiency, but this gets subsumed by these exigencies of vertical power and obeyance. In effect, there is a pervasive fear of the boss's ire or disapproval. One consequence is that information is rarely given out unless it is specifically okayed by the boss. Such information is perceived as power and something to tightly control, which plays havoc with anything like knowledge development or transparency; however, much of these are proclaimed to be pillars of modern institutions. Another consequence is that independent action and experimentation are non-starters.

3. A free press and fair elections are in very short supply

   In terms of accountability to its citizens and feedback from those it should be serving, most governments in the Rest perform very badly. And without this ability to have government behavior scrutinized or to vote out sitting officials, there are no checks—other than demonstrations and rioting—on bad government. There are global indices of liberty and democracy that compare different countries around the world, and the Democracy Index (Economist Intelligence Unit, 2020) showed that, for 167 countries, overwhelmingly better accountability to citizens was found in advanced countries and those with abysmal scores were the exclusive domain of poor countries with 'hybrid' or 'authoritarian' regimes.[5] For example, of the 22 countries classified as 'full democracies' only four—Uruguay, Mauritius, Costa Rica, and Chile—can be considered developing

[4] See, for example, Assaad (1997).

[5] Economist Intelligence Unit (2020) "Democracy Index 2020: In Sickness or in Health" https://www.eiu.com/topic/democracy-index. Accessed 16 June 2022.

countries; conversely, virtually all 54 countries at the bottom of the ranking, deemed 'authoritarian,' were obvious developing countries.

4. Sidestepping dysfunctional governments is a common strategy

   As bureaucracies in developing countries become nearly dysfunctional and stuffed with supernumeraries, some governments have tried to create parallel systems to by-pass blockages and cumbersome routines. Sometimes special categories of 'elite' cadres are introduced, with better training and much better salaries, but these tend to be filled with those enjoying personal connections. The same story holds for new, supposedly independent agencies, commissions, and funds, another common sidestepping ploy. It also holds for the practice of building up coteries of slick and modern 'advisors' in a minister's office who take over most of the cadre functions from traditional line structures (and are even sometimes paid by donor agencies). Unfortunately, the systems they put in place are rarely effective, and at the same time, they create resentment among the majority of employees and often introduce even more opaque and self-serving mechanisms.

5. Military, security, and intelligence apparatuses feature prominently

   If military and security/intelligence agencies are involved in different levels of government, then rigid, self-serving, and insular government structures become even more pronounced. In most developing countries there are rules that shield the military and its enterprises from any scrutiny; budgets are not published, military-owned companies pay no taxes, and vast areas are considered no-go strategic or military zones. Often there is a whole parallel economy under the exclusive control of the military, and an astounding portion of high-level civilian government positions is filled by retired generals. And when the security of the state becomes an overriding preoccupation, more and more police and intelligence personnel poke their noses in practically all aspects of normal life.

   Not all developing country governments and economies suffer from excess penetration by military and security apparatuses, but enough do to make it a common feature of life in the Rest. Two extreme examples can be cited. In both Thailand and Egypt there are no external military threats, but this has not prevented extreme penetration of military involvement in practically everything. Thailand has had "hegemonic military capitalism," also called 'camouflaged khakistocracy' for over 90 years (Beech, 2020, 3). In

Egypt, which has had military-influenced governments since the 1950s, the involvement of the military and security apparatuses in an astounding array of economic activities reached new heights after 2013, as has been thoroughly described by Yezid Sayigh (2019).

6. Feeble government revenues

Having significant and buoyant government revenues, especially if a country pursues a policy of rapid and broad-based economic growth, is crucial. Most tools for development (and governance) depend on being able (1) to provide investments for the crucial infrastructure and human development sectors, (2) to apply tax and other incentives to steer private investments in the right directions, (3) to fund social safety nets so they can buffer the vicissitudes of growth policies, and (4) to ensure government services, especially those businesses need, are efficient and effective. A fifth good reason for robust state revenues is that then a country need not pile up endless debt and, parenthetically, avoid the conditionality and other burdens of foreign aid.

Yet time and again developing countries spend way beyond their means and, at the same time, carefully avoid raising taxes and other unpopular means of increasing revenues. Many governments, even those in the West, are prone to run budget deficits and cover them by borrowing, but the standard practice in most developing countries is so outrageous that it makes a mockery of the phrase 'fiscal probity.'

Donors give copious advice to countries in the Rest about the need for better revenues—better tax collection, better coverage, wider tax bases, etc.—and fiscal restraint has become one of the hardest conditions in any structural adjustment loan or other rescue lending. But in spite of such pressure, it is amazing how, over years and decades, revenues remain pathetic in most developing countries. The main reason is that in such poor countries there is only a thin layer of the economy from which revenues can be extracted, formal businesses and crony capitalists have many ways to avoid or reduce payments, and personal income taxes are simply un-collectable from the majority of citizens. This leaves few tax objects other than regressive sales and VAT taxes, customs duties, service charges, and extractive or other lucky rents. Overshadowing all this is the ease with which one can bribe a tax collector to look the other way.

Reducing expenditures is also difficult for these governments. There are some items that a government can only reduce at their peril, especially employee wage bills, bread and other subsidies, military budgets, and showy infrastructure works. General or even targeted subsidies, once well established, tended to be considered sacred entitlements by the public.

Theoretically, according to the IMF and mainstream macroeconomists, fiscal probity and judicious capital expenditures would eventually lead to what has been called a 'virtuous circle,' where once a country's economy is running well, new economic activities will be able to generate sizable revenues that will alleviate stretched government budgets and allow higher expenditures on a host of needed investments, further stimulating the economy, the kind of self-sustained growth so beloved by Walt Rostow (1960) and others in the 1960s. Yet the track record for most poor nations is not good, particularly on the revenue side of this virtuous circle, as a look at the World Bank's global index of revenues (World Bank, 2020) will show.

Other Failings of Governments in the Rest

The above six failings are only the most prominent. Others should be added, such as: poor statistics and manipulative approaches to information, excessive regulation and lack of support to the private sector (except for politically connected firms), and large and growing compendiums of complicated but rarely enforced laws that are only applied arbitrarily. Another failing is the common practice of governments simply mimicking what governments should do and should look like, a kind of elaborate charade of form over function, or what has been called "looking like a state" (Andrews et al., 2017, Chap. 1). And, of course, there is the problem of bribes, kickbacks, and other corrupt practices in such governments, which deserves its own section.

Corruption? What Corruption?

Academics and journalists have been raising the issue of deeply imbedded graft and corruption in Third World countries for decades. These allusions have even been made by literary greats like Evelyn Waugh and George Orwell in later colonial times, and Gunnar Myrdal devoted a whole chapter to corruption in his classic Asian Drama (Myrdal, 1968). But it was not until World Bank President Wolfensonn gave his famous speech (in 1996) that the donor world even began to use the word 'corruption.' Since then, the development establishment has made many attempts to advise on anti-corruption measures, copious studies have been commissioned on aspects of the subject, and public sector reform and 'capacity building' have gained in popularity.

That corruption is widespread and seemingly endemic in most developing countries is underscored by cross-country indicators. Transparency International has a Corruption Perceptions Index, and its 2019 edition covered 180 countries. Among the 40 'cleanest' countries only seven small developing nations could be found (Uruguay, Bhutan, Chile, Botswana, and three Caribbean statelets). And at the bottom of the list, the 80 'least clean' countries are virtually all in the Rest (Transparency International, 2019). Much of the same skewed ranking can be found in the World Justice Project's Rule of Law Index (2020, 16 and 17) of 128 countries. All of the 20 highest-ranking countries are rich democracies, and all of the 30 lowest countries are classic developing nations. And both of these indices show that, overall, corruption and lack of rule of law have been increasing in most countries over the last 15 years.

Here we run down the main types of corrupt behavior found in the average developing country. Inevitably, we have missed some.

1. *Profitable positions, or the open drawer:* Well known in the 3rd world are endless routines and bureaucratic mazes citizens have to deal with. These systems of procedures and licensing and permissions have served an important purpose for those on the inside—the more nonsensical rules and routines, the more opportunity for certain administrative blockages through which a 'consideration' or bribe was practically the only way to pass. These 'gates' or 'profit centers' or 'open drawers' have come to dominate much of the lower levels of government service and, in addition, the practice has become quite institutionalized, with such profitable 'rent' positions either given to someone through patronage or nepotism, or, just as likely, sold to the highest bidder (see below). And employee bosses take substantial cuts to condone such systems.
2. *Doling out and selling positions:* This practice is related to bureaucratic profit centers described in the preceding paragraph, with the added dimension of a certain value articulated for such positions. This mechanism was wonderfully described in 1989 in an article on recruitment and promotions in public office in India (Wade, 1989).

Wade describes the irrigation department of a South Indian state and surveys how officials are assigned to bureaucratic posts. Wade looked at positions filled by engineers, the most desirable of which were in construction and O&M units where opportunity for rake-offs are many, but the 'sale' of water to farmers was an especially attractive form of steady income. Not only did the appointment to these positions have a known price, this price was based on what the future stream of revenues from bribes and gifts should be. And this stream was well known within the administration, especially with those in the Chief Engineer's office in control of appointments. To secure the appointment, an employee needed to assemble a once off payment and agree to a recurring cut for his immediate superior. This is an example of pernicious systems that are self-reinforcing. The purchaser of the appointment has to amass or borrow a considerable amount of capital that he would be desperate to recoup.

3. *Contractor and supplier kickbacks:* Kickbacks are very lucrative and almost impossible to uncover. Envelopes of cash, false invoicing and other tricks (e.g., phantom goods and even phantom companies) are the preferred route. Another variant is shuffling construction or supply contracts to friends (for present or future favors) through rigged procurement committees and inflated invoices. It should be noted that these practices are also big in global trade, are often used in money laundering, and are not at all restricted to just developing countries. Even donor money flows are easily prey to this, multiple safeguards and procurement regulations not-withstanding.
4. *Embezzlement and pure theft of large chunks of a government's budget:* Disappearing government money has become almost standard media fare across the developing world over the years. Usually, it involves very high up officials and other well-connected types (especially relatives of rulers). The Malaysia 1MDB scandal, which began to come to light in 2018, is a perfect example, involving the pure theft of $4.5 billion from a government development fund, of which some $731 million appeared in the then Prime Minister's bank account (Ellis-Petersen, 2020). Many other top officials and politicians also benefited. Furthermore, it was discovered that the global

financial firm Goldman Sachs was the key intermediary in this theft, and as a result it had to pay a whopping $3.9 billion fine to the Malaysian government (BBC News, 2020). Such outright thefts are sometimes exposed and reported, but for every massive theft scandal that makes the news, there must be many more that remain in the shadows. Robert Chambers notes how such corrupt practices are "universally acknowledged, and a commonplace of gossip, [but] institutions and individuals find themselves constrained to employ strategic ignorance, even actively taking precautions not to know" (Chambers, 2017, loc 1214). And through such 'strategic ignorance' these various systems of corruption have become deep-seated, carefully protected by all involved, and stubbornly resilient to reform efforts. This is perhaps the most pernicious aspect of most Third World governments—that corruption and especially the feeling of entitlement and impunity have become perfect self-perpetuation machines. Worse, this sense of pervasive entitlement has seeped into societies as a whole. There is a widely felt attitude a civil servant and/or elected official is there for one thing: to make as much as possible before retiring or being voted out. In fact, many citizens perceive that the whole structure of a Third World government, and the rules it imposes, are mainly created and maintained to enrich certain connected officials and their family members. This sometimes leads to the depressing attitude that it is the very rich that should be appointed to ministerial and other high posts, on the logic that they need not use their public positions to amass fortunes.

Some Exceptions?

This bleak picture of governments in the Rest should not be overly generalized, and a run through the many developing countries and their thousands upon thousands of government departments and units will certainly come up with islands of at least near-excellence, with some good managers and properly run bureaucracies. In particular, some governments in East Asia have performed as well as those in any Western country. The civil services in Malaysia, India, and Thailand are sometimes admired for their competitive entrance systems and esprit de corps, and Mexico, Turkey, and Chile have been included in the 2017 International Civil Service

Effectiveness Index.[6] In the literature, better bureaucratic performance is associated with greater power and autonomy of government agencies to formulate policies, good career opportunities in the public sector, and good pay for public servants.

But on average, governments in poor countries perform extremely poorly, hardly providing the framework for rapid economic growth and anything like shared prosperity, and this has been the case since at least the 1980s. There is a slight correlation with better governance as one moves up the scale—from lower to lower-middle to upper-middle income countries—but un-transparent, irrelevant, patronage-riven, and predatory governments full of kleptocrats and firmly established cultures of bribes and kickbacks are the rule rather than the exception.

Is the Development State a Panacea?

Much ink has been used to talk about the development(al) state, which usually is ascribed to countries that have experienced rapid economic growth and rising living standards under development-oriented governments.[7] These are strong governments that have captured resource and other rents for investment purposes, strengthened ties with domestic capital, and oriented incentives and state-backed finance to promote export economies. The state has taken an unequivocal lead in stimulating growth, and it has usually done this while ignoring social demands that might just get in the way. The concept was first used to describe an ascendent Japan, and it was soon also applied to the four Asian Tigers (and even, sometimes, Botswana). It has recently been applied to a handful of countries, most notably Rwanda and Ethiopia, steered by unified and strong single-party governments. Other countries that sometimes get mention as developmental or proto-developmental states include Brazil and Argentina in Latin America and Malaysia, Vietnam, Thailand, and Indonesia in Southeast Asia.

Rwanda and Ethiopia have come to be beloved by donors, with serious donor funds financing a range of development initiatives over the years.

[6] This index, new in 2017, only covered 31 countries (Canada ranked highest) (Blavatnik School of Government, 2017).

[7] See for a review of the concept of the developmental state Jewelland Nem Singh and Jesse Salah Ovadia, "The Theory and Practice of Building Developmental States in the Global South," Third World Quarterly, Vol 39, 2018, Issue 6; https://www.tandfonline.com/doi/full/10.1080/01436597.2018.1455143

Many of these have been successful (at least as evaluated by donors themselves), and these two states certainly know how to talk the donor talk. But neither regime is particularly cuddly. Both have drawn stiff criticism for their human rights abuses and their short patience for any opposition at home (or even abroad).

For the advocates/admirers of the development state concept, the reasoning goes that a little authoritarianism can be tolerated as long as there is sustained growth, and that once general prosperity begins to arrive, more democratic and people-centered governments will naturally evolve, as they did in parts of East Asia. Well, for Rwanda and Ethiopia, their current GDPs per capita are so low that 'sustained growth' will need to go on for decades and decades before anything like high living standards can be reached. In 2020 Ethiopia's political stability was seriously challenged, and who knows how long regime stability will last in Rwanda and at what cost to basic freedoms.

Then there is China, which certainly can be considered a development state. It has a strong government led by a unified leadership and backed by one supreme and rigidly organized political party, and it has, as has been endlessly repeated, lifted hundreds of millions out of poverty, brought prosperity to the largest middle class on earth, and is the factory of the world. But if trends since 2013 continue under Xi Jinping, the already super-control government may well become more and more the ideal of the 'surveillance-authoritarian state' with hegemonic tendencies in Asia and beyond.

In effect, it seems that the concept of the development state is pretty vague and one that hardly allows a direct parallel between the successes of the four Asian Tigers in the 1970s and 1980s with those of, say, Ethiopia and Rwanda (and Vietnam?) in the 2010s. As was argued in 2020, "first, the 'developmental state' provides an attractive and malleable imagery and language through which donors can justify—to themselves as well as to the outside—their lack of engagement on democratization and human rights in a profoundly authoritarian state" (Brown & Fisher, 2020, 186–187).

Government Reform Efforts and Donors

Civil service reform and better public management were quite the rage with many donors in the 1990s. But it is interesting that by the 2010s little had been added about the need for reform of civil service management, downsizing (or rather 'rightsizing') government employment, or increasing public sector revenues. Of course, these pearls of wisdom still pop up from time to time in various discourses, but it appears that the wind has been taken out of donor sails, and that, after hammering on ineffectively about bad government and the need for accountability for decades, quieter and more subtle approaches are in order. However, donors remain very engaged in helping in the fight against corruption, Western literature on corruption and the need for government accountability is voluminous, and donors promote and even financially support 'independent' anticorruption commissions in many countries. Also, divesting state assets—in particular public sector enterprises—remains a pillar of policy advice emanating from the West.

One area of public sector reform that donors have spent lot of effort—with very little to show for—is to promote decentralization of government systems. As is well known, in developing countries the centralized, unitary state is the norm, and rigid, top-down control within ministries, specialized authorities, and state enterprises is commonplace.[8] For many years, donors have been promoting more devolution of responsibility towards local authorities, seeing this as a means to soften such strict verticality and a way of being more responsive to its citizens and closer to the problems they face. Well, in almost all cases, this donor advice has been a total failure, and it is apparent that those at the top of rigid structures do not take kindly to such efforts at decentralization.

In these and other facets of public sector reform, donors have limited impact. They can only dance around on the margins, since public service reform is an extremely sensitive subject and one where important special interests are involved. After all, this is where power lies and is exercised, and thus it is extremely jealously guarded, especially from anything that could be construed as foreign meddling. The ways donors react to this standoffishness and how they develop new adaptive paradigms and more modest theoretical approaches were well described in a 2015 article on public sector reform in developing countries (Brinkerhoff & Brinkerhoff, 2015).

[8] Of course, some countries have federal systems, but these are almost always huge (Brazil, Nigeria, and India) and their states or federal districts are, size-wise, countries in their own right. In some countries considerable power (at least fiscal) lies with local government, and in Brazil municipalities have evidenced considerable local control over budgets, which led to the development of 'participatory budgeting,' which became quite a donor fad in the 2000s.

In effect, there is little that donors can do. And their frustration is reflected in frequent recourse to that old standby, the call for political will on the part of un-enthusiastic partners. It is not that the rulers of these countries don't have political will, it is just that such political will is tied up in their own political survival and promotion of their own allies.

Summing Up

This chapter has painted a negative and politically incorrect view of governments in the Third World and how they operate, and it shows how they are structurally constrained from promoting anything like inclusive development. Of course, there are exceptions, and there are large and considerable differences among developing countries themselves. Nevertheless, it is surprising how often one can uncover truly awful governments—no matter in what geographic part of the Third World and no matter whether socialist, monarchist, militarist, parliamentary, or simply authoritarian. It must be added that some of what is enumerated here could be applied almost equally to bureaucratic behavior in some ministries, departments, and agencies in the West, but the difference is partly a matter of degree, and partly it is due to having completely different histories and institutional landscapes.

We hope this chapter has proven illuminating. It is not meant to be simply a bashing of governments and bureaucracies in the Rest. Certainly, there are dedicated and selfless government employees who soldier on in spite of depressing ground conditions as well as some top administrators who try their best to minimize corruption, nepotism, favoritism, cronyism, kleptomania, and rent-seeking. In this chapter the aim has simply been to set the scene for the seven chapters that follow, to give context to the many ways things can go wrong when the donors rush into the Rest.

References

Andrews, M., Pritchett, L., & Woolcock, M. (2017). *Building state capability: Evidence, analysis, action.* Oxford University Press. Accessed June 16, 2022, from https://oxford.universitypressscholarship.com/view/10.1093/acprof:oso/9780198747482.001.0001/acprof-9780198747482-chapter-3?print=pdf

Assaad, R. (1997). The effects of public sector hiring and compensation policies on the Egyptian labor market. *The World Bank Economic Review, 11*(1), 85–118. https://doi.org/10.1093/wber/11.1.85

BBC News. (2020, July 24). *Goldman Sachs settles 1 MDB scandal with Malaysia for $ 3.9 bn.* Accessed June 17, 2022, from https://www.bbc.com/news/business-53529075

Beech, H. (2020, November 3). Talk of yet another Thai coup. *New York Times*, International edition.

Blavatnik School of Government. (2017). *International civil service effectiveness index.* University of Oxford. Accessed June 17, 2022, from https://www.bsg.ox.ac.uk/about/partnerships/international-civil-service-effectiveness-index-2017

Brett, E. A. (2016, April). *Explaining aid (in)effectiveness: The political economy of aid relationships.* Department of International Development, London School of Economics. Accessed June 14, 2022, from https://www.academia.edu/24883781/Explaining_Aid_In_Effectiveness_The_Political_Economy_of_Aid_Relationships?email_work_card=abstract-read-more

Brinkerhoff, D. W., & Brinkerhoff, J. M. (2015). Public sector management reform in developing countries: Perspectives beyond NPM orthodoxy. *Public Administration and Development, 35*, 222–237.

Brown, S., & Fisher, J. (2020). Aid donors, democracy and the developmental state in Ethiopia. *Democratization, 27*(2), 185–203. https://doi.org/10.1080/13510347.2019.1670642

Burgis, T. (2015). *The looting machine: Warlords, oligarchs, corporations, smugglers, and the theft of Africa's wealth.* Public Affairs.

Calderisi, R. (2006). *The trouble with Africa: Why foreign aid isn't working.* St Martin's Griffin.

Chambers, R. (2017). *Can we know better? Reflections on development* (Kindle edition). Practical Action Publishing Ltd

Economist Intelligence Unit. (2020). *Democracy index 2020: In sickness or in health.* Accessed June 16, 2022, from https://www.eiu.com/topic/democracy-index

Ellis-Petersen, H. (2020, July 28). 1 MDB scandal explained: A tale of Malaysia's missing billions. *The Guardian.* Accessed June 17, 2022, from https://www.theguardian.com/world/2018/oct/25/1mdb-scandal-explained-a-tale-of-malaysias-missing-billions

Myrdal, G. (1968). Asian drama: An enquiry into the poverty of nations. *Pantheon.*

Repucci, S. (2012). *Civil service reform: A review.* UNU-WIDER, United Nations University (No. 2012/90). Accessed June 14, 2022, from https://www.wider.unu.edu/publication/civil-service-reform

Repucci, S. (2014). Designing effective civil service reform: Lessons from past experience. *Public Administration and Development, 34*, 207–218.

Rostow, W. (1960). *The states of economic growth: A non-communist manifesto*. Cambridge University Press.
Sayigh, Y. (2019). *Owners of the republic: An anatomy of Egypt's military economy*. Beirut.
Tendler, J. (1997). *Good government in the tropics*. John Hopkins University Press.
Transparency International. (2019). *Corruption Perceptions Index*. Accessed June 16, 2022, from https://www.transparency.org/en/cpi/2019
Vittachi, V. T. (1962). *The Brown Sahib*, Andre Deutch, (earlier edition 1957).
Vittachi, V. T. (1987). *The Brown Sahib (revisited)*. Penguin Books.
Wade, R. (1989). Politics and graft: Recruitment, appointment, and promotions in public office in India. In P. Ward (Ed.), *Corruption, development, and inequality* (pp. 75–109). Routledge.
World Bank. (2020). *Revenue, excluding grants (as % of GDP)*. Accessed June 16, 2022, from https://data.worldbank.org/indicator/GC.REV.XGRT.GD.ZS
World Justice Project. (2020). *Rule of Law Index 2020*. Accessed from https://worldjusticeproject.org/sites/default/files/documents/WJP-ROLI-2020-Online_0.pdf

CHAPTER 14

Donor Overload

As we have seen in Chap. 3, donors are always keen to develop new 'products' and to expand their portfolios in developing countries. The result is a bewildering array of interventions in particular countries and sectors, something that in many cases could be called donor overload. The sheer volume and complexity of stuff that the recipient government and its agencies (and its civil society and professionals) need to deal with can be more than challenging, and most countries in the Rest find themselves in a constant mode of reaction and catch-up, even in what should be their own backyards. Not only do donors pile on their presence in projects and programs that touch almost everything, they further infuse their footprints with scores of missions, scores of studies, scores of events, scores of program and project reviews, scores of focal points and liaison officers, and scores of temporary structures such as PMUs and PIUs. Even more, as we shall see, it is donors and their funding that generates much—sometimes most—of what is known about a country's development prospects and challenges, and even in larger countries this expanding compendium of knowledge about a society or an economy seems steered in certain directions.

Throughout this chapter, we look at the ultimate effects of such donor activities on governments and societies in the Rest, which result in much more than just large doses of confusion and bewilderment. Collectively, they allow these governments and national contractors, consultants, and

D. Sims, *Development Delusions and Contradictions*, https://doi.org/10.1007/978-3-031-17770-5_14

other professionals in the Rest to continue doing what they have always done, which is to act simply as adjuncts to the development scene, with every excuse to avoid anything like real reform or even to take back the ascendency in understanding their own economies and societies.

Clogging Up Recipient Bureaucracies and Confusing Everyone

In 1999 the World Bank President Wolfensohn said (World Bank Group and the International Monetary Fund, 1999):

> At a recent meeting in Stockholm to assess progress on the Comprehensive Development Framework, President Mkapa of Tanzania said: "… Our people must be encouraged and facilitated," he said "to be owners of their development: not just beneficiaries, but doers of development." We must heed this call as we plan our development agendas in the years ahead. But we must go further. We must recognize our own role in helping not hindering those doers of development by better coordinating our own activities. It is shameful that Tanzania must produce 2,400 reports each quarter for its donors. It is shameful that Tanzania must suffer 1,000 missions from donors a year. And Tanzania is by no means alone.

A good point, this recognition that small, struggling countries in the Rest must put up with so much work and so many activities to meet donor requirements. Such a recognition became a mainstream concern, especially following the 2005 Paris conference on aid effectiveness. Usually, it is folded into the concept of 'aid fragmentation,' which talks about the duplication of donor activities and presences in developing countries and the increasing number of smaller and smaller projects on more and more marginal and obscure subjects.

Yet what has been the effect of this dose of mea culpa on the part of donors? As with much in the development industry, little has happened except lots of bons mots, especially given the overwhelming imperative to spend more and more and to spend it in more and more ways. Government 'partners' in the Rest are thus often swamped with what is sometimes called 'development bloat' or 'mission creep,' as can be seen by a number of indicators (Bellemare, 2014):

First, the numbers of donor activities are growing at an impressive rate. Globally, it is calculated that the number of international aid projects jumped from 8000 in 1990 to 83,000 in 2008, whereas the average size of these shrank from USD 12.8 million to USD 2.1 million (in constant 2000 dollars) over the same period (Fengler & Kharas, 2011, 4). This trend towards many more but smaller and more diverse aid projects (largely due to the increased popularity of stand-alone technical assistance projects) has since continued.

Second, each of these many projects and technical assistance carries with it a concomitant large bureaucratic load, and any perusal of upcoming project ToRs or implementation plans will show that the mechanisms required to establish projects and see them through remain many, are complicated and riven with aid-speak, and are onerous on the recipient government and its implementing agencies. Also, there are project-specific requirements that the donor (usually people sitting back at HQ) will insist on: social safeguards, environmental safeguards, procurement plans, results matrices and evaluation frameworks, due diligence, etc. These may mostly be the tasks of donors and their consultant henchmen, but they still need inputs from governments, from their PIUs, and even from hardly ever-convened project steering committees. In the end, for a single project to be up and running smoothly, thousands of pages must be written up and churned out in appraisal documents, memoranda, aide memoires, mission reports, timelines, schedules, etc., requiring at least nominal inputs from recipient partners. Frustration among donors becomes palatable, since it is the recipient government agencies that are 'the chokepoint' for foreign assistance programs and actions.

Third, even before a donor's desirable initiatives can be slotted into country programming, there are virtual blizzards of requirements of time-consuming preconditions and frameworks to make it seem as if a project fits into an integrated and cohesive whole, such as Poverty Reduction Strategy Papers, Country Development Frameworks, Systematic Country Diagnostics, Country Partnership Frameworks, and so on. These 'framework' products are almost always prepared by donors themselves, but they require at least some contributions from country officials and some forms of country approvals.

Fourth, what about those time-consuming missions and reporting requirements, seemingly such a problem for the World Bank's president—and Tanzania—back in 1999? Well, they continue to multiply. By 2010, official donors were sending out more than 30,000 missions annually in total to manage their aid projects. Of these, more than 400 donor missions travelled to Cambodia each year and government officials there reported spending 50 percent of their time meeting with and reporting to donors. In Tajikistan, a recipient of only tiny amounts of foreign aid, there are more than 200 missions a year, with senior government officials spending half their time (on average, two meetings a day) with donors (Fengler & Kharas, 2011, 14–15).

Fifth, government ministries and agencies that execute donor projects normally must set up PMUs, PIUs, or other bodies, and, not only do these place additional demands on other government stakeholders (at both central and local levels), they also generate a lot of missions by donors and their consultants in order to ensure acceptable performance. A 2010 survey to monitor the Paris Declaration on aid effectiveness found 2473 active PIUs in partner developing countries. Since this sample covered countries receiving just over half of ODA, it could be that the total number of these PIUs and PMUs globally was approaching 5000 at the time. Quite impressive (OECD, 2012, 55–56).

It should be added that there is something called Quiet Time, which shows just how much mission bloat has been recognized by all. In 2007 the Kenyan government and their donors agreed on a two-month period every May and June when donors would not schedule meetings or missions, thus giving its government officials breathing space before presenting their budgets to parliament. And such a mission free period was also instituted by Ghana in 2008, ironically coinciding with the global aid effectiveness conference in Accra (Reisen, 2008).

It seems that tiny, aid-dependent countries feel the overload most. In 2008 the miniscule island nation of Tuvalu (pop. 17,500) suffered under an almost surreal deluge of development types. In a typical one-week period there were over 35 researchers, consultants, film makers, donor staffers, trainers, and trust fund advisors, all of which arrived on development aid business. Over the year this flow was equivalent to 10 percent of the island's population (Overton et al., 2019, Chap. 1). Such mission phenomena were just the tip of what has been called the "inverse sovereignty hypothesis" in Pacific island states (and elsewhere), which postulates that all the efforts to improve aid delivery put in motion since the Paris Declaration on Aid Effectiveness actually had a reverse effect—by putting ever more pressure on scarce local management capacities and further reducing what little 'ownership' the government had over its own development policies (Overton et al. 2019, Chap. 1).

Of course, in bigger, more prosperous countries donors tend to be less omnipresent. Yet even in these countries, and even in well-trodden donor paths such as infrastructure projects, donor overload continues to be, well, overloading. Take, for example, a project in Egypt (pop. 100 million) and another in Sri Lanka (pop. 22 million), both countries are considered as lower middle-income countries on upward paths:

In Egypt, the World Bank's Upper Egypt Local Development Project, running from 2017 to 2021, was an ambitious 'locally driven' infrastructure project estimated to cost USD 1 billion (including a "program for results" (PfR) loan from the Bank of $500 million). Goods and services for the project were to be mostly procured through the two governorates of Qena and Sohag, so there was some excuse for heavy Bank support and follow-up. The project was certainly designed for this, with an Implementation Support Plan that called for a total of 66 missions/trips per year by Bank staff from Washington or Cairo to the two governorates, or 5.5 trips on average each month. And this was in addition to the operation of two project Local Implementation Units to be staffed with consultants hired locally as well as by seconded government workers, not to mention a similarly staffed Project Coordination Office in Cairo (World Bank, 2016, Annex 9).

In Sri Lanka the World Bank funded the Metro Colombo Urban Development Project (2012–2021), which had mainly to do with improving the city's long-neglected storm water drainage, roads, and sewerage, costed at USD 321 million, two-thirds of which came from a Bank loan. The project was implemented by the Ministry of Urban Development and Housing in Colombo and through a PIU located within it. The procurement of works aimed at hiring 34 contractors, with the bulk of expenditures going to just 5 international firms. The procurement of consulting firms aimed at 18 companies, of which 10 were to be international, also capturing the large bulk of expenditures (World Bank, 2017, 8–11). Moreover, the number of documents generated by the project were numerous, some 30 documents before loan effectiveness and another 40 (and counting) as of November 2020. No information could be found on the number of missions, but together the technical and administrative load shouldered by the Bank and international consulting and contracting firms was considerable. And it must be stressed that this project was a straightforward donor infrastructure project the likes of which have been passing through the Battaramulla offices of the Ministry for over two decades. Which raises the question: Why should such micromanagement practices and the resulting donor overload still be required? And, even with all this help, why should the overall results indicators throughout the life of the project be reported as 'moderately unsatisfactory,' almost the worse rating that can be given?

These and many other examples show that, more than twenty years after Wolfenshon's complaints about too many missions and too much micromanagement by donors, the situation is very much more of the same, as is often the case in the Development World. And if this were not enough, over the same twenty years donors have been throwing out ever more complicated concepts of new paradigms, new agendas, new financing mechanisms, and lots and lots of new jargon that keep recipients in a state of bewilderment. It is very clear that donors treat recipient government structures in the Rest as free, costless goods, to be cajoled into furnishing whatever the program or project pipelines require, somehow ignoring their own reports about poor governance and sclerotic bureaucracies in these same countries, and somehow assuming that the bureaucrats will somehow drop everything and perform as the donor wishes, over and over, and on time.

It is important to understand that this overload is not just something that can be conveniently classified as benign-sounding 'transaction costs' to be borne by recipient governments. It is much more, and extends into practically every nook and byway of a country's development machinery, from policy deliberations to strategy formulations, through to sectoral projects and programs through implementation phases, and on to evaluations and lessons learned. It puts recipient government policymakers and technical cadres very much on the back foot, unable to come to terms with project requirements before a new set arrives. Often one result of all of this overload is a kind of catatonic miasma, where the recipient doesn't even try to play the 'partner' role seriously. Instead, it simply goes through the minimum motions required, considering them a sort of irksome cost of doing business with donors. Thus, evaluation reports and lessons learned are hardly ever read, let alone acted on, and copious amounts of advice are rarely absorbed. The cumulative effect is to maintain the frame of reference outside of, and largely irrelevant to, what goes on in-country, and this 'outside framing' is constantly reinforced.

Recipient Attempts to Manage the Flood

In a strictly formal sense, there is no lack of protocol systems between donors and the host country, usually through a specialized ministry or department that deals with international cooperation. These units concentrate on maintaining official relations with donors, in forwarding draft cooperation and financing agreements to cabinets or parliaments for formal endorsement, in cataloguing and tracking donor projects, and in assisting donors in their dealings with counterpart ministries and agencies. Usually these relations are organized around 'desks,' where a team deals with a group of donors (e.g., the North American desk, the South European desk, or the Asian desk), and in the case of very important donors (such as the World Bank Group or USAID) they may be a whole desk designated to them. Sometimes this coordination function with donors is handled by stand-alone ministries, but more often 'international cooperation' forms only half or less of a ministry, usually its weakest part. Sometimes, this function is folded into the ministry of foreign affairs. And sometimes, to keep the reins tight, international cooperation units will be situated directly under a prime minister or president.

These international cooperation units or portals do little but carry out formal, diplomatic functions and assist in bureaucratic matters. In fact, most parachuted-in consultants and other development troops don't even know they exist. Most of these international cooperation units compile lists of donor projects that are currently running in the country, but these are rarely exhaustive and, in almost cases, are not easily accessible. Donor project task managers, when they are on mission, may feel the need to meet with their assigned desk officer and keep them informed about comings and goings, but that is about it. As far as is known, there is no effort by these departments to analyze donor project funding nor to see whether there is too much overcrowding and duplication, nor to undertake any other analytical functions. It is telling that, if one wants to gain an overview of international cooperation and development in a particular country, it is best to look to donor documents, usually under the rubric 'donor stakeholders' in a particular country, rather than material from the responsible country unit.

Besides these formalistic structures for international cooperation, probably the only other attempt by recipient countries to manage (some of) donor invasions are 'social funds' or SFDs. These organizations, much supported by donors themselves, came in vogue in the late 1980s and early 1990s to combat the negative social effects of structural adjustment and austerity programs imposed by the IMF. Independent and lean SFDs were set up through which donors were to channel their funds, at least those that dealt with social sectors, and these islands of good management were to be better able to allocate and spend donor moneys and, most importantly, to track these funds and provide better accountability of how they were spent. Some of these SFDs soon became quite powerful, represented a funnel for donor largess, and some carried out remarkably good work.[1] (Yemini and Egyptian social funds come to mind, attracting good people and even building good relations with perpetually neglected provincial administrations.) But they also represented a separate layer of government administration that was not always welcome by line ministries and municipalities, and their own freedom of action sometimes became compromised by arrogant and overbearing donors who shoveled often unwanted technical assistance grants down their throats. Since the 2000s these SFDs have either become less prominent, have withered away, or have metamorphized into other specialized development entities (In Egypt the SFD was rebranded in 2017 as the Micro, Small, and Medium Enterprises Development Agency, but it remains mainly a conduit for donor-funded microfinance and bank credit and social infrastructure work.).

Other than international cooperation portals and holdovers from social development funds, there are no apex structures in recipient governments that make strategic attempts to control and manage the presence and activities of donors. Sure, at cabinet and presidential levels there may be much discussion about good and bad donors and ways to maximize benefits from them, but this is more in the realm high-level foreign relations. As we shall see in subsequent chapters, recipient governments have many ways to extract benefits from donor projects that are up and running and to control or even block their scope of activities, but this is hardly evidence of cohesive development policy.

Another Kind of Overload: Monopolizing Country Knowledge

What is rarely mentioned or acknowledged—even in critical development literature—are the truly massive efforts made by donors to investigate, research, and analyze what goes on in developing countries. There are many reasons for what could be called an obsessive hoovering-up of information about a country and the presentation of this as neutral, objective

[1] For a general description of SFDs during their hay day in the late 1999s, see Bigio (1998). Bigio, Anthony (ed) *Social Funds and Reaching the Poor: Experiences and Future Directions*, Washington DC, the World Bank.

knowledge. These reasons mostly relate to setting the scene for donor projects and other interventions, justifying them in a kind of techno-superior haze, and generating the numbers and indicators that are so important to the donor for project formulation.

Over the decades the importance of 'knowledge' in development has come to be highly regarded in the development industry. In 1987 Hollis Chenery, professor at Harvard and ex-chief economist at the World Bank, concluded an entry for the Palgrave Dictionary on foreign aid with the statement: "Finally, the most enduring aspect of aid is likely to be the discovery and dissemination of knowledge to fit the development needs of poor countries .... Knowledge is a classic case of the economist's 'public good,' and the expansion of this aspect of the international aid system should command wide support" (Moeduch, 2008, 377). Such a glorification of knowledge for development generated by donors reached a high point in 1996 when the then president of the World Bank, James Wolfensohn, declared he was presiding over a 'Knowledge Bank,' and donor agencies, with the Bank in the lead, have all seemed to agree to the importance of knowledge as essential to spur on development. That the audience for such knowledge to fit the development needs of poor countries is largely restricted to those *within the development industry itself* is a fact that is rarely acknowledged, and this form of self-reference has a number of unintended consequences, as is shown in the following paragraphs.

Donor-funded knowledge products are typically in the form of reports, either stand-alone or part of some larger project or policy document. They are very often data-heavy descriptive reviews of a particular economic or social sector, but they can also take the form of feasibility studies, stocktaking analyses, stakeholder reviews, legal and institutional investigations, sector diagnostics, or post-program evaluations. Some of these products may involve primary data collection through representative sample surveys and even random control trials, sometimes in collaboration with national statistical offices, but most are a hodgepodge of statistics, information from informants, perhaps some field and/or opinion surveys, with much culled from previous studies and reports commissioned by other donors. The assembling, analyzing, and writing up this copious knowledge output are usually contracted by donors to a team headed up either by an international consulting firm or an INGO or a university/institute. Local experts will normally play useful although not lead roles in these teams. Contracts may also be made by donors directly with national universities and institutes, although their services are more likely be secured through donor-financed international consultant teams. In all cases, as far as can be determined, the major purpose and output specifications will be defined by the donor.

The subject range of these products is truly impressive. In any one country these will probably include analyses that look at weaknesses and opportunities needed in most if not all of the following: the economy (both macro and micro aspects and specific sectors); business environments and related constraints; standards of living, poverty levels, and disadvantaged sub-populations; labor markets, labor skills, and wages; financial markets, trade liberalization, levels of investments and savings; banking systems and financial intermediaries; educational, vocational, and higher education systems; systems of both preventive and curative health, specific diseases, maternal and child care (and of course family planning); forests, fisheries, and other natural resources; agricultural productivity, crop mixes, irrigation systems, and agrobusiness; manufacturing, industrial concentrations, and exports; tourism and ecotourism, the hospitality industry, and airports; urban problems, transport, ports, and other infrastructure, social and private sector 'affordable' housing; GIS-based resource and rural and urban map making; environment and air pollution; and public administration, government organization, reform, and decentralization. This already impressive number of subjects can be considered mainstream, but in recent decades more focused work on social aspects of society has also been sponsored by donors, such as disadvantaged and ethnic groups, informal labor markets and informal housing, youth and women, microfinance and informal credit, smallholder farmers and their problems, customs and prison reform, environmental protection, and ecological diversity. But even more arcane subjects have been included in donors' shopping carts, including antiquities and archaeology; aspects of culture; police training, civil society, and charitable organizations; and elections, political parties, and democratic representation. Subjects such as disaster response, risk management, climate change, refugees, sexual harassment, and resilience have also been added to the compendia of knowledge about individual countries.

Except in China, India, and a couple other very large developing countries, this production and accumulation of knowledge about a country and its development prospects by donor agencies eclipses anything that could be considered purely home-grown. A simple search on the internet of any of the subjects listed above by country will show that most if not all of the underlying research or investigations derive either directly or indirectly from some donor project, technical assistance intervention, or Western academic field work. Sure, in-country universities and research foundations/institutes may carry out significant work that adds to the whole, but very often this 'native' work uses data and information generated by previous donor-backed research or, just as likely, repeats methodologies and addresses hypotheses generated by Western academe. In fact, much of local production of knowledge, even if completely independent from donors, represents attempts to fit into Western frameworks of knowledge and the narratives that populate them, mainly to gain international credibility.

It is important to reiterate the fact that almost all of this accumulation of knowledge about developing countries is financed by donor agencies or other Western foundations and research institutions under a range of mechanisms. This means all such knowledge (and the advice usually packaged along with it) has no intrinsic price tag or 'market' weight from the point of view of those who are actually supposed to use it. It is a kind of free good, with all the moral hazards this implies. Since it didn't have to be financed by the country partner, its value can be discounted or simply ignored. Even worse, it means that a government and its associated institutions will practically never design, fund, and commission their own studies that they themselves value for the knowledge that can be applied to their countries. Why should they, when there are donors galore eager to fund all sorts of things?

But one may say, such governments do have their own statistical capabilities and do commission their own research and data collection studies. Yes, they all have statistical offices, but while they may do good basic work under very difficult circumstances (Chap. 6), these agencies usually have been supported at some point by donors (especially through either the UN system for demographic work or, for economic and poverty data, with help from the IMF, the OECD, or the World Bank). And yes, these governments will actually spend their own money for certain investigations and advice, but mostly these tend to relate to the hiring of big-name international management/accounting firms who will prepare plans and feasibility studies that justify some prestige megaproject or program.

But one may also say, what's wrong with free knowledge? If it adds to the understanding of a country's development requirements and possibilities, such 'neutral' information should be welcomed. And it is true that some of what donor agencies fund can be valuable in various development sectors, at least that which is rigorous and avoids leaping straight to a cascade of pre-formed recommendations. But rarely is it completely neutral, since the framework within which it is conceived and designed leans heavily towards what donors perceive as important, towards interventions that they might wish to fund, and behind which are often certain globalist agendas. Don't forget, development subjects at the global level are almost completely defined by Western donor agencies or Western academia and it is they who dominate the discussions surrounding them (in spite of rather marginal south-south cooperation), and this global consensus steers what is chosen by donors to apply to individual countries. The irony, as was expressed by Desmond McNeal in 2014, is that such donor control replaces the often-heard obsession for 'evidence-based decision making,' with its opposite, "decision-based evidence making" (McNeal, 2014, 4).

More than this, towards whom is all this accumulation of country knowledge directed, and by whom is it intended to be consumed? Unfortunately, edifying words about partnerships and the build-up of local knowledge aside, most seems aimed at those who determine donor polices and donor project pipelines—in other words donor managers and their inexhaustible supporting cast of Western experts, advisors, consultants, and academics. Thus, the knowledge remains largely framed as external to the country itself and is accumulated outside it. And, as has already been pointed out, the very fact that it is free, is defined by foreign entities, and is perceived as serving these entities means it is devalued in-country. It doesn't help that, with the odd exception, government officials themselves have little or no technical roles in the studies, and that their involvement is limited to procedural matters such as overall approval and security clearances.[2]

Donor Overload and the 'Foreign Fingers' Complex

When one stands back and looks at the ponderous weight of donor activities in a particular country, the myriad projects they fund and micromanage, the government bureaucracies that they insist on overloading with their standard prescriptions, and the extensive chunks of country knowledge that they generate and monopolize, one might pose the question: how do officials, government cadres, and local academics and

[2] And it does not help that few developing countries have anything like well-established cultures of report-writing (or even the reading of reports in international languages), other than skills at churning out PhDs and other academic work to standard formats.

professionals—not to mention normal patriotic citizens—react? Are they simply (and eternally) grateful for the beneficence of all of this Western largess, as many on the donor side presume? Or is there not resentment at this overload, with what appears to be arrogant 'foreign fingers' getting into almost everything?

In-country reactions to donor penetration and the domineering attitudes of various players in the development industry is a dimension that is rarely considered, even though it is certainly 'hiding in plain sight.' As we will see in the following chapters, it certainly makes donor–recipient partnerships and recipient ownership of donor programs much more difficult and contentious than would first appear. And as is taken up in Chap. 18, there are a number of ways that recipient countries have found to fight back against this donor flood, and these reactions can hobble donor interventions and completely nullify their carefully crafted intentions.

References

Bellemare, M. (2014, January 5). Development bloat: How mission creep harms the poor. *Foreign Affairs*. Accessed June 17, 2022, from https://www.foreignaffairs.com/articles/africa/2014-01-05/development-bloat

Bigio, A. (1998). *Social funds and reaching the poor: Experiences and future directions*. The World Bank.

Fengler, W., & Kharas, H. J. (2011, February). Delivering aid differently: Lessons from the field. In W. Fengler, & H. J. Kharas (Eds), *Delivering aid differently: Lessons from the field*. World Bank Premise, 49. Accessed June 17, 2017, from https://openknowledge.worldbank.org/bitstream/handle/10986/10108/595510BRI01PUBLIC10BOX358284B0EP49.pdf?sequence=1&isAllowed=y

McNeal, D. (2014, July). *Knowledge, politics, and development policy: Reflections over four decades*. Bartlett Development Planning Unit, DPU60 Working Paper Series: Reflections No. 167/60.

Moeduch, J. (2008). The knowledge bank. In W. Easterly (Ed.), *Reinventing foreign aid*. MIT Press.

OECD. (2012). *Aid effectiveness 2011: Progress in implementing the Paris Declaration, better aid*. OECD.

Overton, J., Murray, W., Prinsen, G., Ulu, A., & Wrighton, N. (2019). *Aid, ownership and development: The inverse sovereignty effect in the Pacific Islands*. Routledge.

Reisen, H. (2008, August 13). *En route to Accra: The global development finance non-system*. VOX EU – Centre for Economic and Policy Research. Accessed

June 17, 2022, from https://voxeu.org/article/development-aid-duplication-rivalry-and-mission-creep
World Bank. (2016, August 25). *Program appraisal document on a proposed loan .... to the Arab Republic of Egypt for an Upper Egypt Local Development Program-for-Results.* Accessed June 17, 2022, from https://documents1.worldbank.org/curated/en/698361597088470663/pdf/Disclosable-Restructuring-Paper-Upper-Egypt-Local-Development-PforR-P157395.pdf
World Bank. (2017, March 28). *Procurement plan, metro Colombo urban development project (P122735).* Accessed June 17, 2022, from http://documents1.worldbank.org/curated/en/613271567400096973/pdf/Sri-Lanka-SOUTH-ASIA-P122735-Metro-Colombo-Urban-Development-Project-Procurement-Plan.pdf
World Bank Group and the International Monetary Fund. (1999, September 28–30). *Board of Governors Annual Meeting (Press Release 2), Annual Meetings Speech by James D. Wolfensohn, "Coalitions for Change".*

CHAPTER 15

Partnerships?

If one reads standard donor texts of what they do and what they accomplish—either in a certain sector, in a particular country, or overall—one comes away with the impression that solid partnerships between them and recipient governments are the fulcrums for these accomplishments. This idea of partnership has become ever more a catchword in development-speak, leading some to call the post 1980s period the 'partnership era' in international development cooperation (Fraser & Whitfield, 2009). The concept received a further boost after the Aid Effectiveness deliberations and pronouncements of the 2000s that promoted recipient 'ownership.' In 2011, the OECD sanctified this snug relationship by declaring henceforth donors would be called 'external partners' or 'development partners' and recipient or host countries would be called 'partner countries' (OECD, 2012).

These well-crafted pronouncements rest on an assumption that there is immense amount of goodwill and trust between the two sides. But there is a reality that everyone dealing with the launching of projects or programs and in seeing them through know very well, but rarely articulate. Both sides know that these relationships are characterized by hard and often contentious negotiations and maneuvers during conceptualization and formulation and on foot dragging and obfuscation after agreements are signed and projects lumber to their completion. This has been called the 'development dance' by one

D. Sims, *Development Delusions and Contradictions*,
https://doi.org/10.1007/978-3-031-17770-5_15

rare book on the phenomenon, which characterizes it as (Swedlund, 2017, loc 2612–2620):

> … a seemingly never-ending process of bargaining and negotiation between donor agencies and recipient-country governments. It is a dance that both partners willingly join. But it is a dance that leaves neither side particularly satisfied. Time and time again, donor and recipient government officials enter into new arrangements, adopting new aid policies and practices with the hope that this time their hard-fought compromises will be politically sustainable. However, again and again, both parties are left disappointed, as compromises break down and have to be renegotiated.

These contentious dances delay the whole development business, add costs to programs, make any semblance of planning for the future difficult for both sides, and bring in a lot of confusing political posturing. As a former World Bank country director put it, the situation results in constant aid mood swings, where "the 'highs' are high, but the 'lows' are really low." (Swedlund, 2017, loc 169).

A Bit of History

Negotiations between donors and recipients is a story as old as development assistance itself, and a handful of researchers and academics have looked at the phenomenon. Up until structural adjustment loans came into vogue in the 1980s, it could be said that these negotiations were relatively straightforward and at least ostensibly harmonious. Required documentation (terms of references, project documents, financial agreements, etc.) were more or less to the point, and most agreements came out of short donor missions and involved a limited set of decision makers on both sides. But after the contentious 'lost development decade' of the 1980s (Singer, 1989) differences between the two sides grew more acute, and more negotiating techniques (and posturing) became the norm. Over the subsequent decades the playing field became much more confused and cluttered, and both sides have had more external factors to deal with (Whitfield & Fraser, 2010, 350):

> The aid talks of the 1980s involved a mission team from each donor agency flying into a country briefly to bargain head-to-head with national officials. In their place, we now typically find multi-annual, multi-sectoral, multi-donor planning exercises that bring together in-country donor staff, local officials and a class of middle-men (consultants and NGOs) sometimes all paid for by a range of different donors. In some cases, most of a country's

> donors agree to be bound by the outcomes of mega-negotiations, such as those over debt relief packages, and all sign off on the same policy matrix or planning document. The location at which policy is contested shifts under these circumstances among micro-level negotiations over projects and programs, mezzo-level negotiations over sector policy and strategies, and macro-level negotiations over the aid management structure and objectives of the national plan. Thus, contemporary aid relationships make it much harder to identify the positions adopted by either actor 'prior to' the negotiation.

Ironically, the donor establishment's increasing attempts in the twenty-first century to introduce new funding modalities and the donors' penchant for ostensible reform of their own structures and strategies have further complicated donor–recipient negotiations and agreements. These shifting sands have made it less and less possible to form and maintain what little commonality and agreed rules of the game that had been built up, even between countries and donors with decades-long histories of working together. The relentless search for innovation and reform so trumpeted by donors, plus fads and fashions that sweep the industry, have come to plague negotiations and can undermine the adhesion to compromises reached between donors and recipient governments. And the entry of new donors and other development players into the arena have further complicated relationships.

Political and Foreign Policy Preconditions

Both bilateral and multilateral assistance programs cannot begin without what could be called political and foreign policy preconditions. All development assistance funding to a particular country (and its sectoral breakdowns) is determined back at donor headquarters, and these deliberations are usually between three and seven years. These allocation decisions are almost invariably conditioned by prior discussions at stratospheric levels, usually involving heads of state, prime ministers, ministers of finance and planning, and multilateral bank presidents and vice presidents. In other words, the process of setting donor allocation plans is not at all based on technical or feasibility considerations of particular development interventions in particular contexts. Sure, some of those who make allocation decisions may have been influenced by any number of analytical reports and strategic discussions about how well the donor's projects have worked in the past, what are the donor's sectoral strategies and preferred modalities, and what have been past experiences in a particular country. But given how overloaded and isolated top managers are, it is rare they have the time or inclination to carefully absorb all of this, and they are always pressured to quickly pencil in indicative funding levels.

Negotiations and Negotiating Capital

Once a donor has some idea of expected budget allocations to a particular country, discussions begin with the recipient government about the overall aid package and its elements, through formal meetings as well as more informal discussions and stretching over various lengths of time. It is then that the recipient side will begin to marshal what can be called its 'negotiating capital,' of which there are many forms. One prominent form is to play the instability card, hinting that going too far in insisting on cutbacks subsidies and other measures of fiscal probity will provoke widespread discontent, social unrest, and even revolution. And sometimes this trump card works, in these negotiations, at least to soften conditionality. Recipient governments can point to domestic political considerations as another kind negotiating capital, such as finely balanced coalitions, powerful interest groups, a weak electoral mandate, or a less friendly opposition waiting in the wings. Certain recipient governments can also leverage their perceived political or geo-strategic importance to gain favor in negotiations. Loss of export revenues, galloping inflation, civil wars, droughts, and famines—anything that makes the plight of a country's poor worse—can also be brought into the discussions. And, of course, one useful negotiating card, especially, is to imply that the country has other potential sources of foreign assistance under better conditions, either from different donors or from particular regional allies. Finally, a recipient's own development policies can provide negotiating capital, and donors will typically find it hard to challenge a recipient's priorities as long as they are constructed within anything like a coherent policy framework, particularly one that draws strength from wider international discourses.

Negotiating capital frequently takes on strategic or political dimensions that have nothing at all to do with development per se. For example, a stable country in a turbulent region (Ethiopia in the Horn of Africa, or Jordan in the Near East) may be considered to be useful in bargaining visa-vis the United States or the World Bank, whereas a horrific human rights record may represent a definite negative in negotiating capital towards Northern European bilaterals but might not be of particular concern towards other donors. In fact, it is surprising how often mainstream Western donors continue their long-established aid relationships while ignoring (at least some) human rights issues.

There are also ideological dimensions. A country that proclaims neoliberal concepts of small government, a dynamic private sector, and free markets can consider this political capital in some negotiations, as can voicing strong pro-poor concerns or respect for electoral processes and the rule of law. Numerous other issues can be thrown in whenever donors and recipients get together to hammer out a package of new financial assistance. But, overall, these ideological stances have little to do with the merits of particular development interventions.

Obviously, some developing countries—especially in Africa—are much more aid-dependent than others and thus are in more difficult negotiating positions, with less wiggle room when it comes to negotiating financial agreements. An illuminating study by researchers was carried out that compared negotiating strategies of eight African countries (Whitfield, 2009) and their successes at reaching advantageous terms both for projects and for overall aid programs. For many years all of these countries had relied on foreign aid transfers that represented significant percentages of their country GDPs and much of annual government expenditures. By far the most 'successful' recipient was deemed to be Botswana. It had successfully lowered its aid dependency profile since the 1980s, and more importantly it could negotiate with one strong, consistent voice through the Botswana Democratic Party. Also, the government sensibly refused projects where subsequent recurrent costs could not be managed by the country, and it insisted that projects be located in and integrated with ministries. Overall, the country had performed well and donors became accommodating as a result, giving Botswana the categorizations as one of Africa's first 'donor darlings.'

Second of the eight countries in terms of the degree of negotiating control was Ethiopia. The country had remained, since the rise of the ruling EPRDF, extremely aid-dependent, and more recently it had been receiving a huge and increasing share of its state finances from mainstream donors and China. Yet, the Ethiopian government maintained a policy of adopting those policy prescriptions that fit with its own development agenda and rejecting others, and it largely succeeded in controlling the pace and degree of reform efforts.[1]

Rwanda is placed third in the spectrum of the eight countries reviewed. Although Rwanda had to accept heavy donor involvement in social and economic policy-making in order to leverage considerable aid, the Rwandan Patriotic Front Government repeatedly ignored donor opposition to certain practices (such as repeatedly invading the DRC and repeatedly suspending elections) without losing access to external funding. Rwanda set up 'red-lines' across which donor comment, let alone pressure, was not welcomed. How did Rwanda get away with it?' The strategic use of the legacies of the 1994 genocide, plus the wholehearted acceptance of certain development interventions promoted by major donors such as USAID, explains much of this.

The remaining five African countries were at the weak end of the spectrum. Although each adopted standard prescriptions of participatory planning, consensus building, and 'sensible' development policies, each country's weak control of their own development space, and their acquiescence to donors taking the initiative in designing new aid systems and in promoting new policies meant that recipient governments spent most of their time in reactive modes responding to donor demands, rarely introducing their own policy innovations and never having anything like the upper hand in talks.

What can be generalized from this look at eight African countries is that it is political and economic realities—external to the project or program or even sector of interest—that mainly influence the negotiating strategies that were put in play, rather than consideration of whether donor-supported modalities are actually beneficial. These negotiations also seemed to discount the solidness of a recipient's own national policies and development priorities and instead put value on the recipient government being able to present a strong, united front vis-à-vis donors.

Uncertainties After Negotiations: Can Both Sides Keep to Their Promises?

One dimension that often plagues donor–recipient relations is the fact that promises made during negotiations cannot be kept, usually due to external factors and changing circumstances. For example, the recipient may renege

[1] For another view, see Feyissa (2011).

on its promise to raise the primary education budget (and fund weapons purchases instead), or a donor finds that political winds from headquarters force it to shift its commitment from building schools towards combating HIV-Aids. Or a donor may find that cross-the-board cuts to its aid programs have been mandated (after, for example, the financial crisis of 2008) that forces it to back out of some of its new programs. Or a recipient government's president demands that huge investments be made to create a new capital city, requiring the cancellation of its promise to allocate funds to support slum upgrading. The examples of such commitment problems are endless.

These broken promises further complicate already difficult donor–recipient relationships and can cause damage to any partnerships based on trust, however carefully negotiators on both sides have worked in good faith. Both donors and recipient governments can suffer greatly from the unknowns that these inevitable broken promises produce, and these difficulties have driven both parties (and the development industry in general) to explore alternative ways of delivering aid to help limit the problem. This helps to explain the frequent shifting of aid paradigms and what seems to be the cascade of fads and fashions in the industry (Chap. 10).

Project Formulation: Partnerships Fray Long Before Anything Starts

Assuming the overarching political and foreign policy climate is conducive for Donor X to continue and even expand operations in Country Y, the real game starts when the donor looks at its medium-term country allocation and disbursement strategy. There may be calls for new sectors and programs, calls for modifications of existing programs, or simply a repeat of existing initiatives, perhaps expanded geographically or expanded to encompass more categories of what are considered the target population. Of course, the easiest stance is basically to carry on the same development approach and the same sectoral clients as in the past.

In any event, the project or sectoral program concept will probably be discussed briefly with the recipient government's leadership and the technically competent ministry, and there may be a honeymoon period where, conceptually, there is agreement and even enthusiasm about a policy and its attached interventions. This euphoria may even extend into the long-slog preparatory work of project formulation, since during this phase the donor normally controls the work and pace, issues are seen as purely technical, and contentious points are pushed off down the road. Project documents and other lengthy meta-artifacts (and their annexes) need to be written, reviewed, and submitted for approvals at various levels within donor structures, and these are usually produced by donor staff and their consultants. During this preparatory period there may be frequent missions to the country, and sometimes there may even be expert teams established in-country for a year or so (as is the case with the ADB's long-standing practice of Project Preparatory Technical Assistance), but these efforts are mainly technical operations that are little more than exercises to identify and cost subprojects and pad out the technical aspects. Normally there is little or no substantial input from national partners (other than drawing up specific wish lists, going on field trips with the donor team, and okaying ideas as they bubble up). Socio-economic surveys may generate interesting discussions and local NGO staff may contribute useful insights during project formulation, but the ball is definitely in the donor's court.

Once the donor's bosses approve a project, serious efforts begin to reach a signed financial agreement between the host country and the donor. On both sides, those with substantial technical and social understanding of the many facets of a project normally have little decision-making clout, something that is reserved for top managers and isolated high-up bureaucrats who, almost inevitably, are either clueless about substantial issues or have little time to delve into the details. Further complicating the process is the fact that on each side there may not be complete consensus about the mix of project components, with pro and against factions that carry on their own little wars within both the donor and recipient camps. Further complications arise due to the empire-building tendencies of certain managers on both sides. On the recipient side there are often turf battles that rage over who should host a donor program and/or be the implementing agency. Conversely, turf battles between divisions and departments and 'practice areas' within donor structures can totally confuse the recipient side. One might have thought that in development sectors of great need (poverty alleviation, basic health services, smallholder agriculture, slum upgrading, etc.), there would be enough space for everyone to confront the challenges and experiment. But no, different factions on both sides are extremely jealous of their turfs and perceived power, and these will make every effort to preserve or enhance their hegemonies.

Sometimes of course there are particular donors that have a long history and clout in a recipient country, especially say USAID or the World Bank, with whom the recipient government feels comfortable (or at least has, after a number of projects have flown by, an understanding of how the donor thinks). This certainly smooths negotiations and the overall relationship, especially if what is on offer is largely grant financing or relatively painless budget support or policy lending.

For large grant agreements that include serious physical investments, the donor has pretty much full sway. The recipient will probably object to too much attached technical assistance components, too many advisory services, and too many social add-ons, preferring moneys for these be shifted to the physical investment side. But, otherwise, the recipient ministry or agency has little to argue about, except the specific composition of investments, where they will take place, and how project management decisions should, as much as possible, be in local hands. After all, these grant programs are perceived as free flows to the government, and, who is going to look the gift horse in the mouth?

For large sovereign loan projects, the recipient government is in a better position to impose certain conditions, since in theory the money belongs to the recipient. In these situations, additional recipient negotiating strategies may include arguments that repayment of the extra debt burden will be painful for the state budget, and/or that there needs to be additional funding for technology transfers, capacity building, and other goodies. For results-based loan agreements, much time and effort can be spent arguing over which indicators should be used, how these should be measured, and how these are linked to the release of payment tranches, with the recipient often gaining the upper hand.

Overshadowing these processes are two basic attitudes that push for agreement: the recipient's well-founded perception that the donor is keen to conclude a deal and move the money as quickly as possible, and, conversely, the donor's knowledge that the recipient government and/or executing ministry is cash starved and needs an agreement, the sooner the better, to allow funds to begin to flow. Thus, there is on both sides a tendency to compromise and paper-over outstanding, even killer issues, just to reach a financing agreement (and the press coverage and photo-ops that accompany these). In other words, there is all too often the attitude, especially on the part of the recipient, that its own interests can be made to prevail 'down the road' during implementation.

Project Implementation

The execution of signed financial agreements between donors and recipients is almost never smooth sailing, and it is in these implementation phases of development programs and projects where the Development Dance heats up, mainly because so many issues were shuffled under the proverbial rug in proceeding conception and design phases.

No wonder project implementation—usually extending well over five or more years and often repeated in other phases—can be so messy. First, donor personnel responsible for reaching the original agreement will rarely have anything to do with implementation (usually having been transferred out of the sector or region), and likewise the recipient's senior leadership who signed the agreement (usually old apparatchiks and regime loyalists) will not have much if any interest in all of the complicated running of the project itself, leaving such crucial work to designated project directors, who themselves have little power to fine-tune arrangements or to shift budget items and whose technical backup hardly exists. Thus, during implementation, when so much relies on the recipient, there is a tendency for its agencies to back-peddle on onerous conditions and obfuscate and delay parts of the project that are seen as inimical to existing government power structures. In addition, most donor projects call for at least some reform of existing executive agencies, and these implied changes can be unpalatable to long-standing local rent-seeking arrangements. To make the best of a bad situation, it is the donor who must try to make do and push the project to 'measurable' results, thus heaping on more missions, more reviews, more consultations, and more consultants. For a donor to simply pull the plug on a project that is going nowhere is almost unknown (Chap. 3); key donor staff have too much personal interest in seeing a project through, and their bosses don't want black marks to be attached to their departments, something their bosses look closely at when restructuring and personnel moves are contemplated.

Sometimes it seems (at least from the donor's point of view) that the recipient 'partner' is just being ornery. Overly prolonged negotiations with firms or individuals who are crucial for project implementations, especially for the all-important PMUs, can be very common; so too can demands for summary replacement of consultants or team leaders, refusing to pay as per agreement; or simply not staffing the PMU with anything but dead wood. Other foot-dragging can come into play, such as withholding information, pretending scoping studies have already been carried out, or only reluctantly appointing focal points or coordinators who, in many cases, never coordinate (Chap. 18).

In some situations, the national staff of in-country donor agencies can play a very useful role in mitigating the confrontational atmosphere surrounding project implementation. These desk officers can convey the logics of donor interventions and how these can help the country, and they can do this in their own language and using local frames of reference, something that is well-nigh impossible for expatriate donor representatives. And they can circumvent rigid bureaucratic structures by using personal networks. These factors have been identified as a useful means of overcoming intransigent positions on the recipient side in, for example, Tanzania, and in smoothing otherwise confrontational posturing (Sundberg, 2019). Yet, it is hard to see how these mitigating effects can work more generally. After all, as we point out (Chap. 17), national staff of donor agencies have in many ways become quite distant from their fellow compatriots in government, especially with their higher-class status, their language competencies, and their much higher levels of remuneration. To government officials and their cheerleaders, especially those suspicious of foreign intentions, these donor employees can be construed as having greater loyalty to their employers than to their country and thus are perceived as part of 'them' rather than 'us.'

Summing Up

In the preparation and implementation of donor development efforts in a particular country, there are often very drawn-out negotiations, below-the-surface tensions and confrontations, and clever obfuscations. And in some recipient countries, negotiations and their attendant confrontations have become well-nigh permanent features of the donor–recipient landscape. In these cases, there is nothing even remotely like a seamless partnership between donor and host, and there is more likely to be a perpetual bazaar of shifting conditions and alliances. Due to diplomatic niceties, papering-over these confrontations is the rule, and most donor-supported development initiatives thus simply lurch forward towards mediocre finishes.

Furthermore, it seems concrete lessons are never learned about particular aid modalities or frameworks, nor are better ways to configure donor–recipient relationships that actually reflect conditions on the ground. Thus, these confrontational positions are set to repeat themselves for future programs and projects in the pipeline and beyond, and so the Development Dance reproduces itself again and again.

Perhaps things would not be so bad were negotiations restricted to the technical merits and the economic and social feasibility of implementing interventions. But usually this only happens, if at all, on down the line after the particular intervention and its budget and institutional framework have already been decided at strategic levels. It is at these levels where overarching 'negotiating capital' has been thoroughly sloshed about by both sides. Past experiences in prior programs may have a minor influence on what is chosen to be included in a donor's country portfolio, but in most cases it is country-to-country political dynamics and macroeconomic maneuverings that rule the game, and what works and doesn't work, what really has impact and what doesn't, rarely gets fed back into these high-level negotiations. These are, unfortunately, usually carried out by self-important high-ranking negotiators on both sides, for whom details are, well, just details.

References

Feyissa, D. (2011). Aid negotiation: The uneasy "partnership" between EPRDF and the donors. *Journal of Eastern African Studies, 5*(4), 788–817.

Fraser, A., & Whitfield, L. (2009). Understanding contemporary aid relationships. In L. Whitfield (Ed.), *The politics of aid: African strategies for dealing with donors* (pp. 74–107). Oxford University Press.

OECD. (2012, July). *The Busan partnership for development cooperation*. Accessed June 17, 2022, from https://www.oecd.org/dac/effectiveness/Busan%20partnership.pdf

Singer, H. W. (1989). The 1980s: A lost decade—Development in reverse? In H. W. Singer & S. Sharma (Eds.), *Growth and external debt management*. Palgrave Macmillan. https://doi.org/10.1007/978-1-349-10944-9_5

Sundberg, M. (2019). Donors dealing with 'aid effectiveness' inconsistencies: National staff in foreign aid agencies in Tanzania. *Journal of Eastern African Studies, 3*(3), 445–464.

Swedlund, H. J. (2017). *The development dance: How donors and recipients negotiate the delivery of foreign aid* (Kindle edition). Cornell University Press.

Whitfield, L. (Ed.). (2009). *The politics of aid: African strategies for dealing with donors*. Oxford University Press.

Whitfield, L., & Fraser, A. (2010). Negotiating aid: The structural conditions shaping the negotiating strategies of African governments. *International Negotiation, 15*(3), 341–366. https://doi.org/10.1163/157180610X529582

CHAPTER 16

Country Ownership?

The idea of recipient ownership of development programs and policies has been part of the development industry's vocabulary for some time, and as an operational concept it went into overdrive in the early 2000s. Today it permeates practically all discussions on aid modalities, aid effectiveness, and aid evaluations. Yet this noble principle of country ownership—and local implementing agency ownership of development projects—runs directly up against donors' existential need to control how their moneys are spent, and although it sounds nice to give the conceptualization and management of donor programs to the countries who benefit, the reality is much different. In fact, as we shall see, the result is the worst of all worlds, creating a kind of half-way, shifting, and contentious landscape where some local sovereignty is included, but where at the same time the donor redoubles efforts to direct, control, and sanitize all outcomes.

Here we take a short look at the origins of the concept of ownership, then we look at how the ownership concept is applied at four different levels: *First,* at the overarching policy level, where donors are now supposed to support national development policies and plans as articulated by recipient governments; *second*, at the program and project level, where once an agreement is signed, the national government, through the designated implementing agency, is supposed to be in control, with donors simply providing funds, advice, and perhaps coaching and building capacity; *third*, at the procurement and budgeting level, where donors should as far as possible align themselves with host government budgeting and

D. Sims, *Development Delusions and Contradictions*,
https://doi.org/10.1007/978-3-031-17770-5_16

procurement systems rather than insisting on their own; and *fourth*, at the level of communities, where local inhabitants themselves are supposed to be in control and where 'demand driven development' gives local governments and societies the space to be involved with what donors fund.

There is very little agreement of exactly what is meant by country ownership. For example, a review of the literature on country ownership carried out for USAID in 2013 shows that most observers have interpretations that cluster around four different and somewhat opposing themes: (1) power and legitimacy, (2) commitment and responsibility, (3) capacity, or (4) accountability (Watson et al., 2016, 8–11). As we shall see below, this fuzziness of the concept has been both its strength (anyone can buy into whatever aspect they want) and its weaknesses (imprecise generalities, little to measure, and lots of hot air clogging up the atmosphere).

Some History

Token obeisance to recipient 'ownership' in development cooperation strategies, programs, and projects has been around for some time. In the 1980s and early 1990s the World Bank and the IMF lectured repeatedly on how those at the receiving end of structural adjustment programs were supposed to 'own' the belt-tightening and other prescriptive policies that came along with them, since, after all, these were construed to be in their own interests, however painful. Of course, in the fuzzy world of policy texts there is always enough wiggle room that a recipient government could be seen to agree with at least some features of whatever is under discussion. But ownership, when it got down to details, was generally understood by the donors to be local buy-in of whatever policies and programmatic approaches the donor wanted in order to secure the donor grants or concessionary finance. Donors fundamentally saw this as possible and admirable, and for them 'ownership' was ownership of *their* policies and approaches.

Some development agencies—especially the World Bank Group—spent considerable efforts to set up systems through which there could be closer alignment of development policy and programs between the donor and a specific country. In 1999 the former World Bank President James Wolfensohn—always one for sweeping declarations that came to mean little—claimed that "ownership is essential," and that "countries must be in the driver's seat." (Wolfensohn, 2000). By constructing elaborate multi-year Country Development Frameworks for most partner countries, along with Poverty Reduction Strategy Papers, strategies could be constructed that would be country-driven, result-oriented, comprehensive, partnership-oriented, and based on a long-term perspective. The Bank claimed that this would allow for more effective implementation of Bank-supported development strategies, and this 'ownership' became the main country-specific strategy link between the Bank and its partner countries starting in 2000.

The concern for and attention to ownership received a huge boost when the Paris Declaration on Aid Effectiveness was proclaimed in February 2005, under the aegis of the OECD's Development Assistance Committee. The concept of country ownership became a central pillar of this Aid Effectiveness movement, which also included other fundamental principles such as alignment, harmonization, managing for results, and mutual accountability. These Aid Effectiveness reforms were supposed to redress long-standing problems in donor–recipient relationships, and it certainly spawned a huge number of discussions and declarations over several years in which country ownership and alignment was somehow seen as a means to harmonize what were sometimes contentious relations, in spite of its extreme ambiguity as a concept (Keijzer & Klingebiel, 2019). Then, as icing on the cake, in 2015 national ownership was also enshrined in both the 2015 Paris Climate Agreement and the Sustainable Development Goals. So the 'ownership' train has continued to move ahead, at least rhetorically, as a voluminous Swedish policy paper showed (Keijzer et al., 2018).

'Ownership' at Macro Policy Levels

Who owns the space when it comes to setting national or sectoral objectives and development policies in poor countries? It is clear that this space has long been a donor prerogative, especially in least-developed nations. But huge efforts have been made by the 'donor community' over at least three decades—and especially since 2005—to set up the frameworks for better country ownership of development strategies. At the same time recipient governments have tried to stake out more of this policy space and take advantage of the ownership rhetoric.

How have these countries fared? As might be expected, some Southeast Asian countries have had more success than those, say, in the Middle East or Africa. Although the subject has received little attention in the literature, a Japanese institute published an interesting study on the subject (Ohno, 2006). It conceived policy ownership as having a creative element, not just commitments to a development path by taking off-the-shelf prescriptions. Rather, "(t)rue ownership should mean the capacity of a developing country to choose from alternative policy prescriptions even if they are not granted by the international aid community …. When a country decides to rely on external advice or foreign models, policymakers and technocrats must conduct a thorough assessment of alternatives and carefully adapt the policy content and sequencing to the country-specific context at both the design and implementation stages" (Ohno, 2006, 8). The study also underlined the need for a process of internalization, adaptation, and trial and error when recipient governments import external models—rather than having donors set the scope for policy choice and interpretation. "This may sound idealistic, but we consider such a process vital to avoid the risk of financial dependency degenerating into intellectual aid dependency" (Ohno, 2006, 8).

The Japanese study zeroed in on three countries: Thailand, Vietnam, and Cambodia and concludes that only the Thai government has been able to develop a strong capacity for managing donors and steering the development process to achieve its national goals (especially those of export capacity building). Thai leaders also demonstrated pragmatism in adjusting their policies and measures in response to fiscal crises. In other words, the locus of policy content resided with the Thai side rather than with the big donors. "The Thai government was capable of designing and implementing concrete plans for industrial structure transformation and export capacity building measures and fully integrated aid into government policies in such processes" (Ohno, 2006, 13). Sadly, Thailand's self-reliant upward economic trajectory has, since 2005, been seriously compromised by seemingly endless internal political crises.

In contrast to some Southeast Asian countries, most Sub-Saharan African nations have become very dependent on both financial and technical support from donors, and the degree of space for real policy 'ownership' is correspondingly quite low, in spite of numerous cosmetic attempts to promote endogenously prepared policies. This is well illustrated in a study on foreign aid and ownership in Mali and Ghana. The author found that (Brown, 2017, 336):

> … formal ownership is strongly applied, in the sense that both countries have authored and adopted national development plans, rather than having them imposed by international actors, as often used to be the case. However, three deficiencies undermine the substance of the ownership principle: First, each country has multiple plans without sufficient prioritization among them. Second, the plans also lack prioritization within them. Together, the

lack of strategic priorities undermines the very notion of a nationally owned planning process. Third, weaknesses in the actual implementation of the plans suggest that broader ownership exists more in theory than in actual practice.

In both countries there had been support by donors in the preparation of Policy Reduction Strategy Papers and medium-term development strategies, and praise for such policy ownership in both countries had been common. However, as the author points out, three significant problems challenged these positive assessments (Brown, 2017, 345). First, there were multiple plans, and these were not necessarily coherent and muddied the waters of what was actually being owned. Second, such plans did not provide strategic prioritization; that is, if virtually everything was included in an unrealistic wish list, then the content of ownership is hollowed out to the point of meaninglessness. Third, even if the plans were good, follow-up and alignment of day-to-day governance to overarching policies could easily be sidestepped by lack of political will, short-sightedness, clientelist and crony politics, and the business-as-usual turf battles among different ministries and sectors.

In other words, it seems relatively easy to play the policy ownership game, mainly by having recipient governments (1) prepare specific documents and strategy papers, often with financial as well as technical support from donors and (2) agree to engage in lengthy 'partnership' consultations and dialogues at the highest levels possible, again with donor support. In fact, this is what is often pathetically measured as success. For example, the OECD/UNDP effort to track and monitor the Aid Effectiveness agenda (OECD/UNDP, 2016, 18–19) gleefully talks about country ownership of development priorities, but only in the vaguest of ways, and it doesn't even try to measure country ownership.

One criterion for national ownership *should be* that country leaders can tell donors to 'get lost'—in other words, to turn down donor programs and attached financing that does not fit national plans and policies. But this almost never seems to happen, since in most cases there has been a long history of donor–recipient development dialogues (with donor-financed in-house advisors in abundance), and it is much easier to simply tell donors what they want to hear in order to obtain more funds. The rejection of any grant financing is almost unheard of, and even the rejection of loan financing from international development banks is rare and has more to do with country indebtedness levels than any considered weighing of a particular loan's development merits.

In a way, there is a pick and choose game going on. In many countries, it is simply a case of the donors choosing to agree with and support those national policies and strategic initiatives that sound good and that they are comfortable with. At the same time, they can continue ahead within their own niche sectors and ignore obviously counterproductive and dead wrong policy arenas. This allows donors to continue to function without directly confronting pig-headed or grandiose development approaches so common in many developing countries.

Ownership at the Project Level

It is at the project or 'get-things-done' levels where donor funding is supposed to produce results and where success and impact can be measured and improved on. Thus, this is the arena where concepts of government or national ownership of development would seem to be best applied, and over the decades almost all donors have evolved processes that at least nominally given more responsibility and management to host governments in various aspects of project implementation. Key to this is the concept that the designated implementing agency (a ministry or specialized agency) should be in the driver's street, and that the donor is there simply to provide the finance support, technical advice, and needed capacity building. But, measures to 'ownerize' have only been half-hearted, donors continue to have an almost Pavlovian need to stay in tight control, and the result is a confusing playing field of half-measures, overlapping responsibilities, and contradicting lines of command that compromise project implementation, project results, and anything like learning from the experiences. Worse, it seems that such a schizophrenic world is not slowly withering away, but has become instead the unfortunate new normal.

It needs to be repeated that, in the conceptualization and design of a donor-financed project, the recipient government rarely has had much real say (Chap. 15), nor has this changed since talk of 'ownership' came into vogue. Informed national consultants may be used during identification and scoping missions, national in-country donor staff may have inputs, and protocol meetings with government officials may lead to useful discussions. But that is about it, except in rare cases where the government has viable alternate schemes ready to propose. Guidelines for project preparation may emphasize the need for local stakeholder consultation, but such participation is usually little more than box-checking exercises. The all-important Project Document or Project Appraisal Document—the defining references for a donor's project that must be signed off by both sides—will be laboriously prepared by donor staff and their specialist consultants. These documents are prepared to convince top donor management of the worth of the project as part of the donor agency's portfolio. Key recipient decision-makers rarely even read these long-winded documents and their many annexes, and even summaries are barely glanced at.

Perhaps there may be internal memos or guidelines lurking somewhere in donor offices that talk about practical ways to make a project more 'owned' by a recipient country, its implementing agency, or even the project intermediaries and the beneficiaries, but none has been uncovered. Even so, there are strong efforts on the part of some donors, particularly multilateral development banks, who have taken the veneer of ownership about as far as they can at the project level. That is, they have insisted that project management decisions be taken by the government's implementing agency, and that procurement be carried out by the beneficiary implementing agency (PMUs or PIUs)—including the hiring international consultants, financial management, monitoring, evaluation, and social protections. On paper at least. But in reality, practically everything is either determined by or stewarded through by the donor's project leaders and in-house consultant teams. After all, who writes the many terms of reference needed both before the project starts and as it lurches along? Who sets up the PIU or PMU structures and prepares job descriptions? Who shepherds along the criteria, regulations, and routines for safeguards, evaluations, and reviews?

Part of this donor–recipient disconnect is due to the clash of bureaucratic cultures. In most cases detailed reports, analytical studies, long-winded emails, periodic *aide memoires,* and other mainstays of Western bureaucratic life are beloved by the donor but abhorred by most clients. People at higher ministerial and permanent secretary levels rarely deign to read anything except short emails, tailored PowerPoints, and executive summaries, and they simply do not write up anything themselves. Furthermore, any local professional who is fully inculcated with Western reporting culture will most probably not be in government; rather he/she will be working directly for donors or will have found space in academia, the modern private sector, or will have simply left the country for greener pastures. If by some rare chance he/she remains in government, chances are that he will already be so high up as to disdain to do anything perceived as drudge work.

Some of the most difficult situations occur when the power of contracting expertise or project services is handed over by donors to the national executing authority, as is often the case under loan agreements and is even sometimes under grant financing. In simpler times such contracting would be carried out by the donor itself—defining the assignment and output, hiring the expertise, monitoring performance, and signing off for deliverables or services. But enamored by the need for 'ownership,' the donor will now insist that the national implementor is in charge, at least nominally, of such contracting. The scope of work, selection criteria, monitoring, and acceptance of deliverables for such expert services are still most likely carried out by the donor, but the actual contracting and of course payments are now the responsibility of the recipient. This is a half-way recipe for disaster, since the recipient most probably did not see the need for the expertise in the first place and, worse, the close presence of the expert(s) in project affairs may be seen as an unwelcome intrusion on what otherwise could be kept out of the donor's sight.

Alignment of Financial Procedures and Harmonization of Budgets

All donors consider good financial management systems to be extremely important, and budget and procurement alignment between donors and their partner governments are often considered a main objective of harmonizing development assistance, and this 'alignment' constitutes another pillar of the Aid Effectiveness agenda. In terms of budgets, the idea is that the more donors use recipient country budget structures and accounting systems, the easier it is for these countries to monitor such flows. Both donors and recipients pledged in the Paris Declaration for Aid Effectiveness to make greater use of national procurement systems reduce reliance on special donor bidding and tendering, distinguish between capital versus recurrent costs, and discontinue or at least reduce the use of opaque special accounts.

Theoretically, such aims of alignment in procurement and budgeting sound very logical, but the reality is much different. External cooperation has been, and continues to be, channeled through an extensive and varied mosaic of funding arrangements, often carried out under special covenants and often through special units. Under these conditions, the hundreds of development projects underway in a country at any one time, together with the many financial demands and requirements of donors that have been placed upon them, each has its own logics that reflect donor concerns. Removing these arrangements to increase procurement and budgetary 'alignment' is, in most cases, simply not possible if donors are to keep control and be able to justify their actions to their parliamentarians, taxpayers, or boards of trustees (Chap. 4).

It is rare for a developing country to have anything like budgeting and procurement processes that are transparent, understandable, and subject to anything like consistent administrative, parliamentary, and/or judicial oversight. In fact, in many cases, national as well as local budgets are opaque and peculiarly structured around arcane sectors and line items, and even those who specialize in reading these budgets have a hard time understanding them. 'Off-budget' accounts, special funds, and special economic authorities are common, and for power-obsessed top officials the budget under their control—and information about it—is carefully protected and kept from prying eyes. Plus, there are often yawning gaps between prepared budgets versus final budget accounts that appear, if at all, years later. And, as we have seen (Chap. 5), procurement regulations and their administrative arrangements are often confusing, contradictory, and seem to be easily bent to accommodate special interests and powerful groups, especially at the tender award level.

National budgeting practices in most developing countries are hardly edifying, as even the politically correct 2016 progress report for Making Development Cooperation More Effective makes plain. Although the survey round talked in very diplomatic terms, it admits: "The results suggest that most countries still need to make improvements in: making their budgets more comprehensive and credible; linking their budgets effectively to policy priorities; implementing expenditure in a controlled and predictable way; and subjecting budgets to timely and accurate accounting, fiscal reporting and public auditing" (OECD/UNDP, 2016, 61).

Given these realities, what were those who framed this imperative for financial 'alignment' thinking back in 2005 and 2008? Did they actually expect that some 40 donors would align themselves to the financial management systems of over a hundred recipient countries? And did they expect that concrete, useful results indicators could be extracted that would steer both donors and recipients to full blown alignment? If so, they should be totally disappointed. Even according to their own monitoring of the Aid Effectiveness Agenda, in 2019 it was shown that, overall, there was only a tiny increase in donors' use of national financial management and procurement systems (from 49% in 2010 to 53% in 2018), and that in some details there was either no improvement or even a degree of backsliding (OECD/UNDP, 2019, 114–115).

What Are the Results of These Obsessions with 'Ownership' and 'Alignment'

It seems that, with all of the hype about aid effectiveness spun out since the 2000s, some progress of alignment of donor and recipient priorities has occurred as long as one only looks at the high, policy level of development priorities and strategies, but that there has been practically no progress in 'ownership' at the more humdrum program and project levels.

Such is the case if the reader looks at one of the very few studies on progress towards more country ownership. A 2016 study by the Center for Global Development looked at US government practices across 126 countries as seen by country partners, and it provides evidence that US aid agencies were generally perceived as aligning their policies with partner country priorities. However, they were also perceived as continuing with heavy-handed control at program and project levels, mainly by insisting on lots of technical assistance interventions and on the heavy use of project implementation units (Rose et al., 2016). Such is also the case of the follow-on from the Aid Effectiveness conferences of the 2005–2011 period (Paris, Pusan, and Accra, plus Addis Ababa and Nairobi.) After so much hype about ownership, by 2020 things had pretty much reverted to the status quo. Tracking and monitoring aid effectiveness has continued through the secretariat of the Global Partnership for Effective Development Cooperation. However, its monitoring reports talk about country ownership of development priorities only in the vaguest of terms (OECD/UNDP, 2016, 18–20) and only briefly discussed are 'alignment' issues such as donor use of country budgeting and procurement systems. Also, these reports have conveniently sidestepped the more contentious ownership issues at project levels, as well it might, since the concept has largely been found to be confusing and, moreover, has proven to be un-measurable.[1] This decay of the whole Aid Effectiveness initiative was brought out forcefully by an academic article that traced the unraveling of the concept and its 'norms' from 2011, resulting by 2019 in what could be described as a hollow vessel that in no way fundamentally changed the status quo, with donors clinging to their own self-interests and recipient governments simply maximizing financial inflows and defending their own policy space (Brown, 2020).

In other words, the overarching and global Aid Effectiveness jamboree has fallen very flat. Part of the reason is that any potential progress at installing true 'ownership' has been confused and sidetracked by other changes in the donor world post 2008—new players, new financial modalities, and new agendas such as the SDGs, each of which takes up parts of the development arena and demands its own donor–client relations, and ownership at whatever levels just doesn't fit into these paradigms. To further confuse the issue, development cooperation is not anymore just government to government, but has branched out into a multifaceted world that is supposed to engage directly with the local private sector and with elements of civil society. Finally, donor disbursement pressure and risk adversity are becoming more pervasive in a world where bilateral aid budgets are perceived to be under attack, as has been pointed out in a 2018 paper (Keijzer et al., 2018). All of these trends make it more difficult for any kind of progress on the ownership front, even if there were both the paths to make true ownership and self-reliance work, which, as we have seen, are very few.

Demand-Driven Development as Ownership?

Theoretically, it would seem that true country ownership of development should start with a simple premise: that ideas for development interventions and their design should originate in the partner countries themselves, either being conceptualized and proposed by governments units or bubbling forth from community organizations, local NGOs, or municipalities. Donors would simply look at these proposals and fund those that

[1] Instead, it seems the GPEDC has found spurious ways to make itself sound relevant by supporting various global causes—such as financial inclusion (Better than Cash Alliance), local resource mobilization (Tax Inspectors without Borders), formalizing the informal economy (Trade Union Development Cooperation Network), and women and children's health (WHO's Independent Accountability Panel).

pass certain criteria. Well, such a concept is almost never to be found in the real world of development cooperation, and, in the very few cases where it has been tried, the 'demand' side of the equation has been completely leached out.

The problem is that donors cannot just sit back and wait for proposals. They have their own financial pipelines to construct and protect, and it seems they must first define what development issues are to be addressed and towards what interventions should be aimed, and then they must impose covenants, financial monitoring, and other tight forms of control. The concept of demand-driven development has been around at least since 1995, but only a few concrete examples can be found in the literature, and these for the most part represent only tiny elements of ongoing donor-promoted sectoral or thematic projects.[2] And most have been limited to eliciting plans for subprojects from communities or civil society organizations, with considerable hand-holding from donor consultants and other intermediaries. Larger demand-driven setups are very rare, such as the European Commission's South Sinai Regional Development Programme (2005–2010, a program valued at Euro 64 million), where individual grants of up to 2 million Euros were made available to community groups for infrastructure and cultural heritage works (Proman, n.d.). This program became a good example of a common problem in demand-driven projects, where local intermediaries and elites capture most of the funding.

Somewhat related to the concept of demand-driven development, at least in name, are the World Bank's community-driven development programs. These are mainly a means to mobilize poor communities to plan and participate in their own local development activities, and as of January 2020 such programs were active in 90 countries with a total of 327 projects. These projects are supposed to "operate on the principles of transparency, participation, local empowerment, demand-responsiveness, greater downward accountability, and enhanced local capacity," but only by a great stretch of the imagination can they be considered demand-driven. Communities are pre-selected by project staff, and community representation and planning mechanisms are carefully steered by the same people, as are the resulting subprojects (World Bank, 2022).

In other words, it seems that any 'demand-driven' aspects of donor-sponsored interventions are carefully orchestrated within rigid formats

[2] Such was the case of agricultural extension services in Pakistan 2002–2005 (Qamar, 2011).

and frameworks. As far as is known, the wider idea of simply soliciting formal proposals from governments or other national actors for new, large development interventions has almost never been tried. Donors just don't operate this way; they have budgets to spend and programs to run, and their management structures are geared with these imperatives in mind.

Summing Up

It should be clear that at the rarified policy levels, the concept of 'country ownership' has been relatively easily finessed. It is simply a matter of throwing enough effort behind preparing strategy documents and keeping objectives at such levels of generalization that both the donor and recipient sides can both agree. After all, who is going to object to reducing by x the percentage of families living in poverty, or increasing by y the percentage of girls who complete secondary education, or increasing by z percentage the rural families with access to maternal and child health services? In fact, it could be said that the whole idea of grand policy alignment presumes that host governments are already led by people for whom national development is the central objective, whereas in reality public policies are often shaped by short-term considerations and that "these usually dictate a clientelistic mode of political legitimation, not one based on performance in the delivery of the public goods required for economic and social transformation." (Booth, 2011, 4).

On the more mundane, project and program levels, 'ownership' or 'alignment' remain little more than slogans. Donor obsession with control and spending (and the resulting need for micromanagement) generate a kind of schizophrenic situation where there is a veneer of recipient ownership but where processes are anything but 'owned,' being drowned in excesses of technical assistance and micro-control that are seen by the host government as impositions. And the result is frequently the worst of all worlds, with confusion, unnecessary obstruction, and bumbling ahead towards mediocre results. And the game begins again when the next project is designed and implemented. Hardly ever, as far as is known, is there any progression in the framing of projects that would, as they say, 'puts the recipient in the driver's seat.' The operational ideal—when the host government and its executing agencies are in control, using funds over which they have discretion *and* accepting the consequences—of course hardly ever arrives.

References

Booth, D. (2011, August). *Aid effectiveness: bringing country ownership (and politics) back in.* Overseas Development Institute, Working Paper 336.

Brown, S. (2017). Foreign aid and national ownership in Mali and Ghana. *Forum for Development Studies, 44*(3), 335–356. https://doi.org/10.1080/08039410.2017.1344728

Brown, S. (2020). The rise and fall of the aid effectiveness norm. *The European Journal of Development Research.* https://doi.org/10.1057/s41287-020-00272-1 Accessed 18 June 2022.

Keijzer, N., & Klingebiel, S. (2019, January 21). *A new old principle: Ownership for sustainable development cooperation.* Deutsched Insitut fur Entwicklungspolitik (DIE, German Development Institute). Accessed May 8, 2022, from https://www.die-gdi.de/uploads/media/German_Development_Institute_Author_Keijzer_Klingebiel_21.01.2019.pdf

Keijzer, N., Klingebiel, S., Örnemark, C., & Scholtes, F. (2018). *Seeking balanced ownership in changing development cooperation relationships, EBA Rapport 2018:08.* Expert Group for Aid Studies, Sweden, 170. Accessed June 18, 2022, from https://privpapers.ssrn.com/sol3/papers.cfm?abstract_id=3310599

OECD/UNDP. (2016). *Making development cooperation more effective; 2016 Progress report.* Global Partnership for Effective Development Cooperation (GPEDC). Accessed June 18, 2022, from https://doi.org/10.1787/9789264266261-en

OECD/UNDP. (2019). *Making development cooperation for effective: 2019 progress report.* Accessed June 18, 2022, from https://www.undp.org/sites/g/files/zskgke326/files/publications/UNDP-OECD_Making_Development_Co-operation_More%20Effective_2019_Progress_Report.pdf

Ohno, I. (Ed.). (2006). *True ownership and policy autonomy: Managing donors and owning policies (with contributions from Yasutami Shimomura, Kenichi Ohno, and Masashi Nagasu) Tokyo.* National Graduate Institute for Policy Studies.

Proman. (n.d.). *Detailed description of project.* The South Sinai Regional Development Programme. Accessed June 18, 2022, from http://proman.lu/project/south-sinai-regional-development-programme-sector-specific-support-for-grant-recipients-social-service-provision/

Qamar, M. K. (2011). *Introducing demand-driven extension approach in a traditional region: A case study from Pakistan.* FAO.

Rose, S., Kalow, J., Parks, B., & Masaki, T. (2016, December 12). *The use and utility of US government approaches to country ownership: New insights from partner countries.* Center for Global Development. Accessed June 18, 2022, from https://www.cgdev.org/blog/new-look-us-government-approaches-country-ownership

Watson, S., & Xiong, K., & Thomas, J. C. (2016, May). *Country ownership in international development: Toward a working definition, working paper by MEASURE Evaluation.*

Wolfensohn, J. D. (2000, January 21) *A proposal for a comprehensive development framework.* Memo to the Board, Management and Staff of the World Bank Group. Accessed June 18, 2022, from https://openknowledge.worldbank.org/handle/10986/33432

World Bank. (2022, April). *Community driven development.* Accessed June 18, 2022, from https://www.worldbank.org/en/topic/communitydrivendevelopment#1

CHAPTER 17

Pay Scales

Whenever the West and Rest interact in the development business there is an uncomfortable fact, one that permeates practically all activities and one that is the source of much suspicion, jealousy, and tension. This is the obvious but rarely recognized fact that a Western donor official (as well as the Western consultants and contractors he or she hires) will enjoy levels of remuneration and perks that are multiples of those of local hires and many multiples to that of his/her counterpart, the government official or local professional (who is supposed to be an equal development partner). How can one even begin to talk about real 'partnership' or 'ownership' when this is the case? How can one talk about teamwork when members of the same team, performing more or less the same tasks, have pay differentials that are colossal? Moreover, this huge inequality sets in motion a number of distortions that plague many aspects of development work, such as building up cadres of smart, motivated national professionals and managers, improving institutional capacities, transferring knowledge, and much more.

This disturbing fact has been around as long as international cooperation has been in existence, but it is almost never talked about. It is simply part of the landscape. And the differentials are absurd: three to eight times in the case of local versus expat consultants or, in the case of expats versus their government counterparts, between 15 and 40 times.

D. Sims, *Development Delusions and Contradictions*,
https://doi.org/10.1007/978-3-031-17770-5_17

In this chapter we look at these pay differentials and what are the direct and indirect effects upon aid delivery and on the carefully constructed concepts of partnership between donor and recipient.

Salaries and Perks in the Donor World

Donor staff in the development industry are quite well paid. While the highest-ranking donor officials, as public servants, have caps on their salaries and thus these cannot begin to compare with the salaries and various bonuses and stock options of CEOs in Western companies, they certainly enjoy quite comfortable remuneration that is usually higher than those in other Western government agencies, especially when considering the many add-ons.

This is certainly true for bilateral donors, who tend to pay their permanent staff quite well. For example, the UK's Department for International Development (DfID, now FCDO) has a staff remuneration structure that is much higher than the average for British government workers, with the Department's median annual salary at GBP 52,000 in 2016, almost twice the civil service average (Martin, 2016). In Germany, staff at GIZ enjoy even better conditions, with tax free salaries ranging up from 100,000 Euros per annum (2014) for Entwicklungsfachkräfte (development professionals). Some GIZ employees earn more than 160.000 Euros per year. A German Ambassador earns about two-thirds the amount a GIZ manager earns (Schäfers, 2014).

The same comfortable pay scales can be found in international development agencies. The World Bank pays its several thousand strong army of professionals very well, probably the best rates in the business. In 2017 the average annual salary for a younger professional was $118,900 (plus $59,970 for other benefits), and that for a senior professional was $158,200 (plus $83,160 for other benefits) (World Bank Group, 2018). And in the World Bank salaries are free of US income taxes, retirement benefits are very generous, health, disability, and life insurance packages are excellent, and termination payments are outstanding. Bank employees also have opportunities for self-improvement and training, including paid time-off to write professionally. The only downside is that on average 40 percent of a Washington staffer's time is likely to be on mission away somewhere (of course staying at the best hotels, business class air travel, per diems covering meals in the most expensive restaurants, all transportation, etc.) The ADB and other multilateral banks maintain similar pay structures and benefit systems, and in fact they tend to take the World Bank's pay scales as a model. Finally, the United Nations, with a large number of both general and specialized development agencies, also pays well, although not quite so well as, say, the World Bank. Instead, the UN system excels in terms of benefits, emoluments, promotion by seniority, and security of tenure.

High-up expatriates in international service NGOs, who carry out a large portion of the day-to-day development and humanitarian work for donor agencies, are usually paid between a third to two-thirds that of donor staff, but they will have quite substantial benefits, especially if they are assigned to what is considered a hardship post. For example, an INGO evaluation and monitoring expert assigned to South Sudan would expect a base monthly salary of at least USD 7000, plus a huge housing allowance, health insurance, contributions to retirement account, rest and recreation, home leave, danger pay, and post-differential pay (Villarino, 2013).

The armies of Western consultants and experts hired for project work by donors—either directly or through contracting firms—are also quite well paid. For long-term employment (usually professional staff of one of the thousands of Western consulting firms who assemble teams for project bids), monthly salaries for mid-level experts in 2018 ranged from US$ 8000 to 9000, plus the usual retirement and health benefits, and more if one has skills sought by the corporate sector, such as financial analysts. For short-term freelance consultants, usually hired on by consulting firms for specific projects, the day rate for a 50-year-old professional with an advanced degree and considerable experience is $500 to $750, usually more if hired directly by bilateral or multilateral donor agencies. Of course, these day rates include no extras or perks.

There can be wide variations when talking about average remuneration in the large and shifting arena of international jobs and consulting. For example, freelance consultants can be desperate for work and accept low average day rates. And at entry levels it may be a case of oversupply, with an unending stream of recent graduates looking for any toe-hold in the business. For consultant day rates there is also considerable variability. Consulting firms take a big overhead bite and a firm's profitability may well depend on finding cheap individual consultants, leading to the trend of hiring professionals from Eastern Europe and Third World countries, either directly or through sub-contracted firms. For individual consultants some UN agencies can be quite stingy, with the result that they can rarely attract good senior consultants. Conversely, the World Bank and other multinationals, as well as some bilaterals such as DfID and Australian Aid, will gladly pay well for good short-term consultants, with day rates in excess of $1000 and even $1500 becoming more and more common. These day rates may sound quite good—$17,000 to $32,000 per month if you multiply out by the standard 21.75 days per month—but they come with no benefits, no holidays, and of course they are very temporary. Rare is the independent consultant who can cobble together a string of short assignments to end up with an annual income anywhere near that of those in the donor organization who hires him.

Among the perks enjoyed by all Westerners (and some lucky Third Worlders) are per diems or, in the parlance of the UN system, "daily subsistence allowance," (DSA, an acronym that has got to be one of the most absurd in the industry). In the EU, USAID, UN, and other donor systems these per diems while on 'mission' are quite substantial, being pegged to what a Westerner businessman should expect—5 star hotels, expensive restaurants—and are calculated for every city in each host country. For example, the US government (end of 2020) set a post daily rate of $400 for Addis Ababa and $335 for Dhaka. However, with the World Bank and some other donor agencies, hotel expenses are repaid against receipts and only meals, taxis, and communications are supposed to be covered by much smaller per diems.

These high per diems lead to some interesting distortions. It provides a way to greatly supplement a young EU or UN consultant's remuneration on assignment since, if he or she stays at a cheap hotel or with friends, this per diem (tax free by the way) can easily add 50 percent or more to his/her income. It certainly makes being 'in the field' attractive, and calculations of this cash supplement are carefully made by both the receiver and the hiring firm during pay negotiations.

These juicy per diems create a jarring comparison: For example, in 2018 the EU *daily* per diem allowance was Euro 266 for Cairo, equaling on average *three weeks* of the pay received by a donor's Egyptian government counterpart. Such advantageous remuneration systems for donor employees and their service contractors have been in place for decades. Occasionally 'value for money' and cost-cutting campaigns have surfaced, but these tend to look at marginal items such as first-class travel and other obvious elitist benefits, rarely at salary structures and associated rights. And it seems that most cost-cutting campaigns themselves quiet down after a time.

More importantly, any attempt to reign in pay creep or cancel out some of the more obvious featherbedding is countered by the pressure donor staff can bring to the debate. Those at the highest directorship levels were probably donor foot soldiers in their youth, and there is a solidarity that extends both vertically and horizontally through these organizations, and pay and benefits are one issue upon which all can unite. This was underlined in 2014 when GIZ employees assigned overseas threated to strike if they were to be subject to some tiny German taxes (Mkenya Ujermumani Website, 2014). Sometimes it seems that such preoccupations with calculating remuneration and benefits occupy much of a staffer's time.

Donor Local Hires: Relatively Well Paid, but …

In every donor's country office, a sizable portion of the professional staff are nationals. And for every in-country operation funded by donors, whether managed by an international engineering contractor, INGO, or consulting firm, national professionals are crucial. These people perform a wide number of key functions in close sync with their expat co-workers. Among these are arranging and attended meetings with government officials, holding the hands of clueless short-term experts, navigating government bureaucracies, writing proposals and background papers, and crucially, decoding both the language and the cultural signals of the country, without which their expat counterparts would be like fish out of water. And although some are hired for short stints as trainers, event organizers, or translators, most are long-term employees, and—importantly—it is they provide the institutional memory that is otherwise so lacking in donor offices.

How does the remuneration of these essential local professionals compare to those of the expats they work with, and what are the consequences? Good studies of the subject seem impossible to find, but what sparse information exists points to the fact that, while the remuneration of locally hired professionals is multiples of what government professionals earn, this remuneration is only a fraction of what their international colleagues enjoy. On average in less development countries, expatriate aid workers receive four times more than local hires for doing a similar job, and in some African countries the ratio climbs to ten times or more (Carr & McWha-Hermann, 2016). Obviously, these dual salary structures perpetuate dominance and injustice and undermine pride. Local hires also suffer from what could be called a 'concrete ceiling,' beyond which they could not advance to higher positions that are reserved for expatriates.

It seems that recently there has been a small trend that could represent a welcome change in how donors manage their local hires. GIZ Egypt has allowed some of their best local hires to apply for jobs in GIZ offices in other Arab countries, thus allowing them to circumvent the concrete ceiling and gain stature as international experts. It is still very rare. Also, SIDA has recently started to allow younger professionals from some 35 partner countries to apply for its Junior Professional Officer program, something that used to be an introductory career path for young Swedes (SIDA Press Office, 2020). And some World Bank country offices have begun to promote their best local professionals to take on project task management positions within their own countries, with a chance of obtaining 'international status.' Overall, such systems might lead to a small opening up for nationals from the Rest into at least parts of the international expertise high ground, but it will probably never be generalized.

Recipient Government Salaries and the Absurdity of 'Partnership'

If the pay duality *within* donor structures in the Rest causes problems, what about remuneration differentials *between* donors and recipient governments? After all, donors spend almost all their money on projects that are managed through government agencies, and—by their own logic—success depends mainly on the ability of these government agencies to perform as partners.

Overwhelmingly, public officials crucial for development activities in the Rest are paid a pittance, as we shall see below. There are, of course, some exceptions, particularly where the former colonial wage pyramid for higher public officials has somehow been preserved (such as in parts of West Africa). Also, countries of the Rest that enjoy significant resource rents can afford to pay top officials quite attractive salaries (Nigeria, Arab Gulf States, Malaysia, etc.), and there is a rule of thumb that countries that are more advanced economically can pay their professional cadres more than struggling low-income countries. In addition, there are some sectors of government where pay is better than others, especially in the diplomatic services, in special economic authorities, and in petroleum and civil aviation. Conversely, local government pay is likely to be even more abysmal than that of central government.

To understand recipient government remuneration in the Rest, it is important to look at civil service structures. *First*, the salaries of political appointees—such as ministers, governors, state commissioners, etc.—can be considerable, and even better unofficially, although still pathetic when compared to Western norms. The same could be said for various kinds of high-flying advisors to cabinet ministers, an increasingly common phenomenon. Yet these appointees are not part of the civil service and thus come and go, and in any event their importance and aloofness mean that they do not normally deal with donors or their projects consistently. *Second*, those just below the top—permanent secretaries, vice ministers, general directors, and the like—are those with whom donors deal for crucial operational agreements and many other project and program details. They are civil servants, their salaries are set by grade and seniority, and total remuneration is almost always very low, even considering various perks. *Third*, there are mid-level managers/professionals, who may have quite a number of employees directly under them, who may have already benefited from training, study tours, etc., and who have reached where they are mainly through seniority. These might be ostensibly leading project teams on donor-financed projects, and their all-in monthly salaries are normally very low, say in the $250 to $750 range, depending on the country. *Finally*, there are young cadres and entry-level professionals in government, also key for donor-supported projects, whose starting salaries are almost always abysmal and hardly provide a living wage.

Whatever the levels, these managers, officials, and professionals populate very large bureaucracies in systems that, as many studies show, are stubbornly inefficient, non-transparent, and riddled with patronage and favoritism. In addition, there is considerable jealousy at the lower levels towards those at the top, and as a consequence it is extremely hard to raise the pay of key managers or cadres to anywhere near a fraction of international rates without 'raising all boats,' with catastrophic budget consequences, even were there the political will to do so. Most governments in the Rest worry about the immense drain of total wage bills on national budgets, and there is a constant battle led by ministers of finance to keep it under control. Permanent state employees enjoy small pensions and limited other perks, such as access to subsidized goods, health insurance, housing, subsidized holidays, and sometimes specialized training. But overall the atmosphere is one of extreme bureaucracy, formulaic drudgery, fear of the boss, and a pathetic take-home-pay.

It is rare to find a middle-level government official or professional with total remuneration more than the equivalent of $350 a month in low-income or lower middle-income countries, and $500 a month in the lower half of upper-middle income countries. For a senior official it will be hard to find monthly salaries of more than $800 a month in these countries. And starting professional salaries in government service can be truly pathetic, at $150 to $250 per month. Of course, there are exceptions. First, some governments, especially those with well-developed if small meritocratic civil service systems, pay more, such as in India, Thailand, and Asia in general. Conversely, countries with socialist histories are likely to have the worst paid cadres on average and also to have the most bloated public sectors, such as Egypt, Algeria, Vietnam, etc. And with some countries, it is simply difficult to say what total pay is, since base salary grades are only part of remuneration, and various sundry supplements are discretionary and very opaque (as in Indonesia).

In one sense donors are aware of the tiny salaries their partners in government receive, and for years there has been the practice of what is called 'topping-up.' Government managers and technical personnel who are deemed crucial for the success of a particular donor project or program will sometimes be offered relatively generous monthly supplements by the donor, and these can greatly increase both the performance of the official and the time he devotes to the particular donor project. But these days such practices are often forbidden by specific donors (such as GIZ, UN agencies, and JICA) because of their disrupting and distorting nature. According to one of the few survey articles on the subject, negative effects include opportunistic behavior, incentives for and perceptions of corruption, risks of nepotism, the undermining government rewards systems, and draining civil service of vital staff (U4 Anti-corruption Resource Center, 2013). However, there are many other maneuvers used to reward government officials who participate in or work to promote donor projects. These include donor DSAs and supplements that are easily hidden in study tours, travel allowances, work after office hours, etc.

What Are the Consequences of Pay Differentials? What Is the Effect on Partnerships?

How absurd are the pay differentials? Just to summarize: The senior, higher-level government civil servant who deals directly with a donor project officer will have monthly take-home pay that is only 1/10th to 1/40th of that of his direct foreign counterpart. And the same absurd ratio will apply to an official who has a close team relationship with a donor's consultant or contractor as part of a project or study. For the younger bureaucrat or technician, the ratio is even worse, and their remuneration can be below 1/70th of the foreign counterpart salary.

So much for a professional relationship among equals, where team building and partnerships are considered so important. The effects of these huge salary differentials can be devastating to a person's sense of self-worth, let alone the supposed collegial atmosphere within project teams. And don't think, as some donors do, that somehow government cadres are ignorant of these huge differences. Over the years, these poorly paid officials have come to know, through their own informal networks, fairly precisely what are the salaries plus perks of foreign donor officials and (perhaps more rankling) those of their local hires. And this knowledge tends to raise the question, how do I, the government official, get on this gravy train or otherwise benefit? And if I can't, why should I even go through the pretense of selfless cooperation? (Chap. 18).

It is interesting (and instructive) to point out that there is little systematic information about West-Rest pay differentials in the development business, let alone any focus on the subject. This is surprising, given that almost everything else about the Development World is bisected and dissected at great length in donor-sponsored literature. It seems that this is one area best left alone. Donors may sponsor many kinds of support for improved governance, and they will fund exhaustive analyses of public service systems in the Rest and the multiple ills that bloated, inefficient, and corrupt bureaucracies produce, but somehow such interest does not extend to the enormous West–Rest pay gaps and the multiple ills that *they* produce.

Brain Drain and Poaching Talent

Everyone has heard of brain drain and its negative effects on developing countries. It is a big issue (e.g., the exodus of desperately needed doctors and nurses) and has been bemoaned for decades. Yet it is very understandable from the point of those whose income can easily increase by ten or twenty times simply by traveling to a Western country, and it is understandable that these people should make tremendous efforts to achieve such a move. It could be called achieving 'escape velocity,' something that has become a well-honed skill through many pathways.

Some attention has been paid in development literature to the problems of out-migration by those with higher education and skills, which leads to a loss of precisely those who are crucial for the economic and social development of the home country. Of course, this is due to the order-of-magnitude higher earning potential, not to mention the advantages of Western lifestyles and personal rights (Docquier & Rapoport, 2011). These usually relate to the classic, point-to-point migration, but it can also mean back-and-forth existences, with at least one foot rooted in at least one developed country and the freedom to move over international borders. And these various movements to the West have been going on for well over a century—much longer than the development industry—and involve many more diverse mechanisms of escape than the industry itself could ever offer.

The point is that attaining Escape Velocity has been and remains an extremely important (and very understandable) factor in the life decisions of a large chunk of the Third World's youth, and this tends to color everything, including how skills for and careers in the foreign aid industry are developed. There are several ways that the Donor World provides opportunities for those wishing to escape their countries and prosper. One is for a bilateral donor agency (or other Western diplomatic footprints) to offer help and bursaries to promising students in the Rest to pursue university work, and although these students are supposed to eventually return to their own countries, many do not, going on for more post-graduate studies and teaching assistantships, with aspects of their own country usually prominent in the research they pursue and in the seminars they attend. Another well-trodden route is through first working in one's own country for an INGO (or more rarely, a local civil society organization or international consulting firm) and, once learning the ropes of the business, being assigned out of country. As quoted in a report prepared for USAID in

2013, one Filipino pointed out: "When [INGOs] leave the country, they don't leave behind a capacity gap. The capacity was local anyway—the heart of the problem is salary. The tendency for someone who worked for an INGO or a big U.S. contractor is to move out and up—and not come back" (The Capable Partnership Learning Agenda on Local Organization Capacity, 2013, 10). After all, learning intricacies such as constructing logical frameworks and preparing complicated spreadsheets on results indicators are skills that are easily acquired on the job and are in great demand in the development industry abroad.

Less noticed is what could be called the 'internal brain drain,' where those with professional, IT, and/or language skills will be 'poached' out of government positions into higher-paying (and more rewarding?) donor jobs within their own countries. It is these kinds of people that are desperately needed inside government, especially in management and technical positions and particularly such rare birds as economists, finance specialists, geographers, environmentalists, and others with development-oriented specializations. This phenomenon of 'poaching talent away' is an often-heard passing critique of donor operations, although one that, as far as is known, has never been studied in depth. In any event, donors are not the only ones who practice poaching, and there are many other relatively well-paying jobs to pursue that can be found in the local private sector (especially in IT, marketing, banking, airlines, and tourism). Anyway, as we have already shown, in most developing countries educated locals who are hired by in-country donor offices are rarely government employees, except perhaps in the lowest income countries. In other words, it seems that the evil effects of 'poaching' have become somewhat of a trope in literature on the development industry.

Summing Up

Pay differentials, this huge 'elephant in the room' of development assistance, find its way into practically all aspects of the industry. It is pervasive and has perverse effects, and it is almost inevitable whenever professionals, technicians, and officials from the West and the Rest are brought together. It has a corrosive effect on the cooperation and partnerships that are supposed to be so important in the development business, and it produces an undercurrent that rankles one's sense of fairness, can destroy any desire to perform well, and definitely motivates people to move out of their own national environment. Despite the occasional research paper on the subject that bemoans the adverse consequences (usually concerned with poaching) it has been and continues to be little-discussed and a very inconvenient truth.

Most Westerners in development simply ignore the gaping salary divide, or at least keep quiet about it, perhaps letting it slumber in their pre-conscious, even if they sometimes hear the subject raised. But for those from the Rest, it is very much a conscious, ever-present issue, one that definitely rankles, and one that sours the atmosphere and permeates almost every corner of development partnerships.

References

Carr, S., & McWha-Hermann, I. (2016, April 18). Mind the gap in local and international aid workers' salaries ("How big is the gap?"). *The Conversation website*. Accessed June 20, 2022, from https://theconversation.com/mind-the-gap-in-local-and-international-aid-workers-salaries-47273

Docquier, F., & Rapoport, H. (2011, March). *Globalization, brain drain and development, IZA Discussion Paper No. 5590*. Accessed May 16, 2022, from http://ftp.iza.org/dp5590.pdf

Martin, D. (2016, January 23). Foreign aid fat cats are the best-paid in Whitehall and pocket nearly twice the salary of average workers. *Daily Mail*. Accessed May 16, 2022, from http://www.dailymail.co.uk/news/article-3412924/Foreign-aid-fat-cats-best-paid-Whitehall-pocket-nearly-twice-salary-average-workers.html#ixzz5B8nFi0kp

Mkenya Ujermumani Website. (2014, February 14). *GIZ aid workers threaten to down tools if forced to pay taxes*. Accessed June 18, 2022, from http://mkenyaujerumani.de/2014/02/14/giz-aid-workers-threaten-to-down-tools-if-forced-to-pay-taxes/

Schäfers, M. (2014, February 7). GIZ-Mitarbeiter müssen Steuern zahlen und wollen mehr Geld. *Frankfurter Allgemeine Zeitung*. Accessed May 16, 2022, from http://www.faz.net/aktuell/wirtschaft/wirtschaftspolitik/entwicklungshelfer-giz-mitarbeiter-muessen-steuern-zahlen-und-wollen-mehr-geld-12790553.html

SIDA Press Office. (2020, December). *Sida opens up JPO positions for applicants from partner countries*. SIDA Press Office. Accessed June 20, 2022, from https://www.sida.se/en/sida-opens-up-jpo-positions-for-applicants-from-partner-countries

The Capable Partnership Learning Agenda on Local Organization Capacity. (2013). *Executive summary to our report to USAID*. Accessed May 16, 2022, from https://issuu.com/localworks/docs/the_learning_agenda_on_local_capaci

U4 Anti-corruption Resource Center. (2013, December). *Transparency International, Salary top-ups and their impact on corruption.* Accessed May 16, 2022, from https://www.u4.no/publications/salary-top-ups-and-their-impact-on-corruption/pdf

Villarino, E. (2013, June 17). A monitoring and evaluation director in South Sudan. *Devex.* Accessed June 20, 2022, from https://www.devex.com/news/a-monitoring-and-evaluation-director-in-south-sudan-81244

World Bank Group. (2018). *Annual report 2017: Organizational information and lending data appendixes, annual remuneration disclosure notice, 70-72.* Accessed June 20, 2022, from https://openknowledge.worldbank.org/bitstream/handle/10986/27986/211119app.pdf

CHAPTER 18

The Rest Strikes Back

As we have shown in the previous chapters in Part II, recipient countries have been, and continue to be, struggling under unbalanced and asymmetrical relationships with donors. But over time, they have developed their own strategies and postures to confront these imbalances and realign them to fit domestic priorities and/or the interests of government bureaucrats and their networks of friends. These reactive and mostly uncooperative positions or postures are almost always ignored or discounted in written discourses about donor-recipient relations, but they can be found to operate in a host of situations, and they have often become longstanding and defining features of how recipient government institutions and officials react to donor impositions or how they take advantage of them. These can be called, collectively, ways that the Rest Strikes Back.

There are two main categories. First, there is what could be called clever manipulation of donors at strategic levels, of which there are at least three subcategories: using a donor's presence, however tangential, to legitimize certain policies and grand national schemes; letting donors take the lead in addressing intractable problems; and playing off donors against each other to gain the best terms. Secondly, there are a number of other postures or attitudes held by government officials that operate mainly at the program and project levels, such as leaving the donor to do the work; strangling access to information; pretending that donor ideas are already well in hand; leveraging access to powerful decision makers; asking the question

D. Sims, *Development Delusions and Contradictions*,
https://doi.org/10.1007/978-3-031-17770-5_18

"who is helping whom?"; and, finally, simply waiting out the donor (and ignoring its work and outputs). Each of these manipulations and postures are briefly described in this chapter.

Of course, these manipulations and postures are not found in all countries and all sectors. Less tend to be found in those countries whose economies are doing well and where donors have less of a footprint, and less in sectors where government policies and interventions are practical and realistic. But it is surprising how often the donor's foot soldiers run into these reactionary stances. And their true extent will never be known, since these ways that the Rest Strikes Back are definitely not subjects that anyone who makes his or her living out of development will easily agree to talk about, let alone investigate.

Clever Manipulations at Strategic Levels

Using a Donor to Legitimize Grand Development Policies

Recipient governments and their cheerleaders in the media take every opportunity to capitalize on the presence of donors in a sector or activity to confirm that there is widespread approval and even support of the government's approaches, however tangential the donor's actual involvement may be. Such strategies are employed to suggest donor endorsement of the ways government runs things, and they are particularly useful to legitimize prestige megaprojects, programs that deliver services to the better-off middle classes rather than the poor, and/or a plethora of wasteful and untargeted subsidy measures that are aimed at shoring up public support for the government. The fact that a donor is also engaged, however peripherally, is often trumpeted by association as affirmation of the legitimacy of wider policies.

This phenomenon is common at the macroeconomic level, where a state's supposedly wise and level-headed performance is affirmed by picking up and broadcasting any snippets of praise emanating from donor representatives (especially heavies such as the IMF and the World Bank) about such things as a small reduction in budget deficits, in a tiny shrinkage of the national debt overhang, in a reluctant currency devaluation, in the privatization of state enterprises, and the like. And there is much material to work with, since donors, in their diplomatic pronouncements about a country's economy, always temper any criticisms by first praising the government for any minor steps construed to be in the right direction.

At the sectoral and program levels, the phenomenon is also common. Donors may have been supporting with little success such programs as poverty reduction mechanisms, family planning programs, universal health insurance, or mainstreaming gender equality, and although governments may have only been lukewarm in their commitment, whenever possible this donor presence is underlined as proof that these governments are making great headway. The same occurs with enormous infrastructure projects—such as new industrial areas, low-income housing, or depressed area development—where some small component receives either technical assistance or loans through the activities of some donor. Such donor involvement can easily be conflated in the local media with wholesale support and can lend legitimacy to such large ventures. Occasionally, the donor is more directly complicit (with huge policy loans and/or massive technical assistance), but more often the donor's footprint is only minor or is aimed at correcting egregious aspects of these infrastructure boondoggles.

It is ironic that, whereas many donor initiatives may normally have a difficult time being recognized or even mentioned in host government media pronouncements (preferring to make it seem that efforts were 100 percent local), if these initiatives can be linked to a government's favorite development policies or programs, then these donor initiatives are likely to be given quite a lot of publicity.

Leaving Donors to Deal with the Difficult Problems

For certain intractable development arenas where, despite endless pronouncements by government leaders, there is little real commitment to tackle the problem, donors are welcome to be active, as long as they are careful not to criticize the client itself for inaction. This is a case of the host government exploiting a donor's presence to legitimize its inactions before its people. It is a little mentioned but particularly unseemly form of manipulation. It occurs in many development sectors: environmental protection, social safety nets, slum upgrading, SME support and job creation, etc., and it gives the government a free pass, so to speak, to do as little as possible in these areas. The strategy, from the recipient's point of view, can be paraphrased, "Oh, let Donor X appear to be handling the mess since it takes the pressure off us."

To illustrate how this kind of negative manipulation operates, take for example the upgrading of informal settlements and slum areas, where donors have a long history of engagement in many countries. They have sponsored academic and other studies that analyze this huge and growing problem, and both bilateral and multilateral donors have funded particular upgrading projects aimed at demonstrating how the lives of residents of these areas, almost always of the poorest segments of society, can be improved. The idea, carefully phrased in donor justifications, is that these deprived areas are growing very rapidly and that pilot or model upgrading projects can demonstrate how to tackle these effectively so that national programs can eventually be applied 'at scale.' Unfortunately, 'at scale' never seems to arrive, as the case of Egypt shows. For over two decades, GIZ has been financing small pilot upgrading projects in Cairo, where poorer informal neighborhoods (housing well over half the population) have been totally neglected. And recently, AFD joined GIZ in launching these small 'pocket' efforts, but collectively, donor involvement remains a drop in the bucket. And what has the government been doing? Neither local administrations nor the central government have taken serious interest. Instead, they simply 'engage' with donors and have created an Informal Settlements Development Fund, something that makes the *appearance* of having the issue in hand, but only looks at and removes the odd eyesore and dangerous slum. This is not to say that the government would have actually acted had there been no donor presence, but this presence certainly has made ignoring and dissimulating the issue much easier.

Playing Off Donors Against One Another

Governments and their ministries have over the years learned that donors are desperate to move their moneys in certain directions and that better terms might be offered by donors if there were even a hint that another donor just might step in. This is especially true these days with China and other new donors whose conditionality may be less intrusive than that of traditional donors. Systems for coordination among donors in particular countries are supposed to mitigate against this kind of competition (through development partner groups and through the sharing of country strategy documents), and much has been written about the need to avoid or at least reduce 'fragmentation.'[1] But even donors admit that the mess

[1] For a review of the growing problem of aid fragmentation, see Frot and Santiso (2021). For a theoretical discussion of donor motivations that lead to aid fragmentation, see Annen and Moers (2017).

of fragmentation and donor competition within particular countries remains and is even becoming worse (Chap. 3). It doesn't help that the involved sectoral ministry almost never decides to go with just one donor or a single, coordinated cartel of donors; instead, it loves to have several different donor projects running uncoordinated and in parallel, even those that duplicate each other, since this is perceived to expand the ministry's leverage and power.

Postures and Reactions at Project Levels

Here, we describe seven forms of obstructive postures that government recipients can and often exercise in response to overbearing donors at the project level. There could well be more:

Leveraging Access to Powerful Decision Makers

In a context of extremely rigid top-down government, where nothing gets decided except by the minister, permanent secretary, or other high-up chiefs, it is imperative that a donor (and/or his consultants) gain access to people at the top. But being able to meet with a president or prime minister or minister to get support for ongoing or new interventions can be problematic, since they are always surrounded by complexes of gatekeepers. The direct project counterpart (or designated focal point) may have this connective power if the donor is lucky, but often he is only a middle-level bureaucrat or professional who himself has difficulty in gaining such access. Thus, there is the need for the connected middleman who can easily set up these meetings (themselves probably ex-ministers or prominent university professors or both). Without access through these glorified fixers, a donor's programs may find more delays, more obfuscation, and more misunderstandings. The problem is that such conduits through influential middlemen often drag into the mix their specific personal interests, and these may distort the dialogue and even be inimical to what the donor is trying to achieve.

Letting the Donor Do All the Technical Work

Government departments and other entities that begrudgingly receive massive technical assistance or advisory services—usually performed by well-paid consultants—will often simply let the donor's team do the work with as little engagement as possible, either because they have better things to do or from some sense of pique. As a result, any exposure of local cadres to field methodologies, analytical approaches, or findings is minimal, and thus so is the transfer of technical skills and knowledge, however trumpeted by the donor as one of the benefits of such technical assistance. Such nonchalance extends to the final outputs of these kinds of advisory services, and as a result any lessons to be learned are studiously *not* learned, and final reports produced by these efforts are not read or circulated, but simply go on the proverbial shelf.

Curtailing Access to Information

Useful and accurate information is crucial for analyzing a development issue and for building up effective interventions, but this is extremely hard to come by in most donor-sponsored studies and projects. It may simply be that such information does not exist, but more often there are useful data sets and relevant studies that somehow are never made available. In many governments, there remains a perception that such information contains facts that foreigners shouldn't see and are treated almost as state secrets. And even where more liberal attitudes towards sharing knowledge prevail, making materials available is seen as losing power (since knowledge *is* power), and the easiest way to incur the wrath of one's boss is to let out some information without his or her express consent, something that is a priori not normally given. This leaves the donor team to carry out their own surveys (an activity often blocked or constrained by 'security' requirements) or to try to acquire the needed information from local consultants—or from previous efforts made by other donors and *their* consultants.

'We Already Do This' Posturing

Often, a donor initiative will suggest certain studies or a buildup of datasets that will illuminate a development problem and how to solve it. But unbeknownst to the donor, a raw nerve may be touched, since what is being suggested is something that the recipient agency or department should have already been, according to its own remit, an essential part of its structures or operations but which have been totally neglected, with important decisions having been made solely according to the whims of the boss(es). Instead of taking the opportunity of the donor presence to correct these deficiencies, the posture is often to claim that 'we already do this' to bury the issue, thus shielding the bosses from anything that could be perceived as criticism. This posturing can be found in many areas: Maintaining databases of towns with pockets of the extreme poor and destitute? We already do this. Inventories of polluting chemical workshops? We already have them. Monitoring leaks in potable water networks? We already have a unit for this. Ensuring basic workers' rights? We already have a commission that looks into this. And on and on. That what is proclaimed doesn't actually exist can be easily dissimulated.

Answering the Question: Who Is Helping Whom?

There is a widespread if naïve perception among donor staff that their projects are appreciated by beneficiaries, civil society, and government officials alike, since, after all, donor assistance supports agreed national objectives and the march towards prosperity and a green future. Thus, it follows that government employees involved in managing or assisting these initiatives should be enthusiastic parts of the team, ready to step in and help to complete any number of tasks that are above and beyond their normal duties. (These may involve, for example, hosting donor missions, arranging field trips, carrying out surveys, or attending donor-sponsored conferences and community meetings). However, various small perks aside, these officials may actually see little in the way of benefits flowing from this donor largess, and they know that the donor's staff and consultants are extremely well remunerated. Thus, they ask the questions: who is helping whom, where is the donor largess going, and what is in it for me? They can understandably be anything but cooperative in such an atmosphere, but donor types rarely understand this reluctance, since they assume that pretty much everyone has wholeheartedly bought into the specific intervention and its modalities. Instead, donor staff can be perplexed or even hurt by the realization that, in some countries and in some situations, there are counterparts who neither appreciate their efforts nor gladly bend over backward to help, and that they might even throw some spanners in the works.

Bashing a Donor's Consultants for Fun

Often, especially since the 2000s, in the spirit of 'ownership,' a donor will give a project's recipient agency (usually embodied in a PIU) considerable—even absolute—power over the consultant consortium who is designated to carry out most if not all project tasks (especially in projects requiring field studies, statistical analysis, infrastructure, and other design work). It is this agency that carries out procurement and contracts the consultant team, monitors its performance, and, most importantly, pays the consultant. Yet, it is the donor who sets the project goals and framework, prepares the project ToR, and okays the release of funds, so 'ownership' only extends so far. The national agency, while remaining subservient and cordial to the donor who funds everything, often takes out its frustrations on the 'soft target' consultant. The consultant becomes the whipping boy for any and all perceived failures and delays, being punished with information being withheld, reports and designs being rejected, and ToRs being combed through to find contractual ways to delay payments and force more work. It doesn't help that the very high remuneration of foreign consultants rankles (Chap. 17). Thus, the head of the agency—who often is clueless about the technical aspects of the work and is ill-informed—is in a perfect position to redress the inferiority generated by Western funding, to burnish his/her nationalist postures, and to score points with his superiors. Sometimes, his or her own ego is very much in play. The results can be and often are disastrous to the project.

This situation plays havoc with many development projects and can seriously damage a donor's overall country portfolio. And it should be underlined that, in spite of all the talk of 'ownership' and 'alignment,' in a huge portion of donor projects throughout the developing world, it is still the consultant consortium (usually with a foreign company in the lead) that does all the real work.

Just Waiting Them Out

Donor projects, people, and fashions come and go. Thus, over the long run, the whole development game can be perceived by locals as always being on eventual reset, and that patience is definitely a virtue. If a particular donor's approaches are unwelcome (but unavoidable), just wait a while, since they are likely to change or at least metamorphize into things that are more malleable. And more importantly, a donor's foreign staff will definitely change. If one has to put up with an arrogant, suspicious, and work-to-rule expatriate project manager, one knows for certain he will be gone in two to four years, if not less. The same can be said for an enthusiastic neophyte staffer assigned in-country. The same can also be said for the very ambitious task manager or project officer based in donor headquarters who goes on frequent missions and who drives his counterparts in the PIU mercilessly, expecting results (and on-schedule disbursements) at a snap of the finger.[2] In other words, all development assistance efforts are time bound, and eventually whatever or whoever is in place will be changed. It only requires patience, something that the government official or the local professional has in great abundance.

Why Are These Negative Stances and Postures so Popular? And What Are the Effects?

These manipulative strategies and defensive postures, while perhaps understandable and even in a certain way logical, almost always damage donor-sponsored interventions and the delivery of what are ostensibly mutually agreed results and outcomes. Manipulative strategies help recipient governments avoid confronting thorny economic and social problems and their embarrassments, and often these strategies extract what are considered clever concessions from donors. Furthermore, reactive postures delay project components and add to costs, and they also reduce the number and quality of project achievements. But more fundamentally, they undermine, in various ways, the mutual respect and partnership relations upon which the interventions were designed. Thus, it is the intangible aspects of donor-host relations—understanding the concepts and their modalities, faith in their positive effects, and support for replicability of the ideas—where the damage is most extensive. Put another way, these manipulations and negative reactions are symptoms of a widespread recipient malaise with donors and their activities. This leads to, at best, a feeble, begrudging acquiescence of donor-funded project specifics, and this makes what donor interventions aim to achieve anything but replicable or 'sustainable.' This is unless, of course, a donor comes in with tons more money to do much the same thing again, in which case the whole game starts over yet again.

What drives these oftentimes uncooperative postures? One factor is, obviously, the bitter taste produced by the ridiculously higher remuneration that donor staff and their consultants enjoy and the jealousies these

[2] The same cannot be said for the national professional employee in the donor's in-country office. But, although he/she may well understand what *should* be going on in a particular project or program, his/her position, vis-à-vis the international staffer, is usually so subservient that rarely can he/she influence things.

generate (Chap. 17). A second factor can be summed up under the phrase 'reactive nationalism,' something that is often stimulated when foreigners are observed poking their noses into almost everything and spewing out endless recommendations, especially when backed by arrogant displays of their superior resources and means. Such a reaction can be compounded by a latent country inferiority complex towards the West, something that is very much still alive in most developing countries and that produces an unfortunate form of defensiveness. In fact, it sometimes seems that it is a national duty to put forward the best possible face of a country to outsiders and, at the same time, to hide or at least dissimulate blemishes and embarrassments. Since development assistance—by definition—looks at these shortcomings, the stage is for postures and reactions that control what donor teams see and who they meet, that filter what information they can have, and that put tremendous spin on the policies that donors are meant to hear. And this defensive nationalism, be it postcolonial, rear-guard socialist, or simply second-rate capitalist, usually finds ready agreement and support among wide sections of a country's government, business, and professional elites. In other words, there are always points to be scored by suggesting that there are foreign impositions and meddling operating behind donor project facades.

A third factor could be termed the fallout from the relatively recent obsession in the development business of recipient 'ownership.' As we have already demonstrated in Chap. 16, the Effective Aid jamboree that started in the 2000s has led to a strange, almost schizophrenic situation where certain formal powers and responsibilities embodied in the architecture of program and project aid have been devolved to recipient actors, while dominance in design, disbursement, and control have remained firmly in donor hands. This has given considerable space to certain officials to play their reactive games, enhance their own powers, and nullify any project aspects that just might encroach upon these arrangements or call for reform of them. Again, it is the quality of donor programs and their intended outcomes that suffer.

What we have listed in this chapter are features of donor-recipient relations that, as far as is known, are practically never discussed in the copious literature on development cooperation. Is it that they are simply below anyone's radar? Is it that, because they mostly involve personal motivations and attitudes that depend on anecdotal sources, they thus do not lend themselves to anything like 'rigorous' analysis? Or is it the case that aspects of the development business are just too politically incorrect and, frankly, too embarrassing to be absorbed or even recognized by the industry?

To sum up, what is described in this chapter are some of the ways that developing countries use their few comparative advantages in the donor-recipient dance to reassert their nation's sovereignty and counter the donor steamroller. Unfortunately, these various strategies, mechanisms, and postures are almost always counterproductive. They further gum up the works, reproducing and compounding the misunderstandings, the delays, and the misalignment of what actually happens compared to what donor moneys are supposed to achieve. And as far as can be ascertained, they are deeply rooted and reproduce themselves time and again.

References

Annen, K., & Moers, L. (2017, October). Donor competition for aid impact, and aid fragmentation. *World Bank Economic Review, 31*(3). Accessed May 24, 2022, from https://elibrary.worldbank.org/doi/10.1093/wber/lhw019

Frot, E., & Santiso, J. (2021, January). *Crushed aid: Why is fragmentation a problem for international aid*. VOX-EU, CEPR. Accessed May 24, 2022, from https://voxeu.org/article/crushed-aid-why-fragmentation-problem-international-aid

CHAPTER 19

Blind Support for the Private Sector

For decades, one constant in most global development discourses has been that only by supporting the expansion and deepening the private sector can poorer economies grow and create jobs. It is probably the main article of faith shared across the development landscape—especially by the World Bank Group, the IMF, and the USAID, but also by other bilateral and multilateral agencies. One might have thought that 'unleashing the private sector' was such an accepted canon of development that it hardly needed repeating, but it seems the concept is ever in need of reaffirmation. Improving the business and investment climate with less red tape, better access to credit, transparent regulatory systems, revamped legislation, less onerous taxation, smooth market functioning, and clever incentive structures, all have been standard prescriptions, as have been the privatization of state enterprises and the selling of state assets.

Support to the private sector derives from a long-held faith in free markets which, if left to themselves—with a minimum of regulation to maintain strong competition and to protect the famous 'level playing field'—will deliver investments, increase productivity, generate good jobs, and result in efficient and rapid national growth. As the IFC (International Finance Corporation, 2020, 54) makes clear: "Promoting a more effective competition policy framework is key to enabling the private sector to fulfill its job-creating role. Competition and open markets have a positive effect on sustainable economic growth by driving investment and improvements in private sector competitiveness. Two mechanisms contribute to this effect.

D. Sims, *Development Delusions and Contradictions*,
https://doi.org/10.1007/978-3-031-17770-5_19

First, competition shifts market share toward more efficient producers. Second, it induces firms to become more efficient to survive."

It is no coincidence that the World Bank's Doing Business Index country rankings were until 2021 among the most followed of global indexes, and metrics such as private capital formation, exports, and levels of FDI are carefully monitored by mainstream economists as proxies for economic growth. Manifold are the number of ways corporate investments are encouraged and even directly financed by donor agencies, with a bewildering number of 'new' financing mechanisms constantly being cooked up by IFIs and those mesmerized by emerging and frontier markets. And if larger, more established firms are by far the main beneficiaries of these efforts, there is no lack of special financing vehicles for SMEs and budding young entrepreneurs. It has even become bedrock of development thinking that traditional public investments, combined with ODA, won't even begin to provide what is required for developing countries to tackle the woeful infrastructure deficits that are said to be strangling their growth. Thus, leveraging more private investment to levels never before seen—the 'billions into trillions' slogan—has come of age.

Some of this money and policy advice streaming from the West is not misplaced. Certainly, there are many countries—especially those whose economies are hamstrung by rigid bureaucratic rule, meddling government agencies, and predatory sectoral monopolies run by the ruler's buddies—where freer markets can help an economy to get moving. Most recipient governments have already enthusiastically accepted the theories that the private sector is the vanguard of development and has for years made reassuring noises to donors that there should be a business environment where all firms—big or small, connected or unconnected, high tech or traditional—can compete fairly in well-regulated but open and undistorted markets.

There are even some critics on the right who say that such support from the West either is insufficient to dynamize the private sector in the Rest or even perversely kills such dynamism. Such was the case made by Hubbard and Duggan (2009, 7) of the Columbia Business School. They saw that there is an "Aid Trap," where most of the donor financial support for the private sector either goes *through* recipient governments or is conditioned by overarching diplomatic partnerships. As such, there is a trap that "crowds out or corrupts the business sector" and that current means of helping promote private entrepreneurship are mostly counterproductive. For Hubbard and Duggan, the answer is to shift aid moneys towards massive lending directly to domestic private manufacturers, something akin to the postwar Marshall Plan in Europe. Such a radical approach has never been tried, but it shows that there are some extreme pro-business thinkers in the West who find current systems ineffective and even dangerous.

The unfortunate fact is that Western ideas of stimulating the private sector in the Rest run up against an inconvenient reality—that in almost all developing countries various capitalist classes are already firmly established and wield considerable political and economic power, that there are strong links between these capitalists and ruling regimes, and that these business ecosystems are very much characterized by a few dominant and well-connected players. There may be prominent businesses not directly enjoying favors from those in control, but these have their own networks for dealing with state bureaucracies and in protecting their market shares. Below this level, there are very few dynamic medium-sized enterprises and hardly any new ones coming up from the huge pool of small and informal businesses. Thus, there are no structural depth, such as feeder industries or forward and backward linkages to specialize and diversify industrial structures and expand overall productivity. The history of rising economies in the West in the nineteenth and twentieth centuries, as well as that of latecomers such as South Korea, Taiwan, and China, demonstrate the importance of integrating robust and competitive small and medium enterprises into national economic structures. Such smaller sized, more locally based enterprises have been adept at taking advantage of large pools of cheap labor and have been flexible enough to quickly adapt to changing market forces. But in most developing countries today, there is a 'missing middle' in the structure and performance of the private sector, something that explains much of the disappointing economic growth.[1] As we shall see, this lopsided reality has proven, with extremely rare exceptions, to be surprisingly resilient, and it is one that has repeatedly stymied the best intentions of donors.

[1] This conundrum in developing countries has been well summarized by Amr Adly in the Epilogue to his book (Adly, 2020), in reference to Egypt and other similar developing countries.

Crony and Dandy Capitalists, Economic Power, and the Missing Middle

The label 'crony capitalism' first appeared in the late 1970s to describe the particular form of government in the Philippines of Ferdinand Marcos, where a coterie of big businessmen surrounding the president received favors from the regime and, in turn, helped maintain and strengthen its power. This was not at all a unique case, and in the subsequent years, similar structures have been identified in many if not most developing countries. Big native capital has very comfortable relations with the ruling regime, business conglomerates exist that pivot around prominent personalities, and certain favored local firms seem to keep expanding and penetrating more and more markets. Sometimes, the most powerful of these enjoy long-standing relationships with global corporations and represent the main economic bridges to the outside world. Yes, some of these firms are efficient and productive, but many more owe their successes to their abilities to function in systems that are anything but level playing fields. And they are very tenacious, usually being intertwined with dominant political parties, with the military (very prominent in Thailand, Egypt, Myanmar, and Pakistan, for example), or with specific ethnic groups (such as Indians in South and East Africa, Syrians in West Africa, and Alawites in Syria).

The reality of this crony—or 'connected'—capitalism has been described in many ways in many countries in the decades since Marcos. For example, as one academic treatise states (Khatri & Ojha, 2016, x.): "Crony capitalism has taken deep roots in India. In some ways it can be perceived to be embedded in the basic premises of Indian economic philosophy. However, with the turn of the millennium it has gained a virulence which has transcended all regions, sectors, officials, the legislature, the executive, and the judiciary. Such cronyism ignores, nay negates, every requirement of objectivity let alone a modicum of transparency or accountability." Or, consider the words of an ex-advisor to Rwanda's Paul Kagame (Himbara, 2015): "Meanwhile, crony capitalism is on the rise. Crystal Ventures Ltd. (CVL), controlled by the investment arm of Kagame's ruling party, has become, in its own words, 'the biggest investment company in the country.' Its holdings include concrete products, construction, real estate development, telecommunications, agriculture, aviation, security services, printing and publishing, furniture trading, manufacturing, property management and engineering."[2] Then there is Botswana (Thapelo, 2017), where "asset stripping" of the state seems to be going on big-time, with crony businessmen being the main beneficiaries. Then there is Egypt, where a 2014 World Bank working paper (Diwan et al., 2014) found a very strong correlation between a firm's success in new ventures and the degree of its 'connections' with the (former) ruling National Democratic Party.[3] Also from Egypt, there is the extreme involvement of chummy military officers in an astounding array of economic activities which reached new heights after 2014, as has been thoroughly catalogued in a book published by the Carnegie Foundation (Sayigh, 2019). Finally, in China, among other kinds of cronyism, there is a particular type of 'forced cronyism,' where local authorities and the Chinese Communist Party sell assets and state land to private firms, but with purposely vague and inconclusive property rights in order to keep owners in thrall of certain public officials (Pei, 2016).

There is no grand theory of how crony capitalism works, but most definitions run along the following line: it is an economic system characterized by close, mutually advantageous relations between business leaders and higher government officials; personal relationships develop into networks, and both businesses and government officials will naturally turn to the more powerful people in these networks for support in their endeavors, especially in contexts where ground rules are vague, bypassed, or easily bent. These powerful people tend to form the hubs or pivots in networks, with economic and political power concentrated in small, interlocking groups.

Crony capitalism is normally much deeper than was the case of Ferdinand Marcos, an example where power was very much concentrated in a tight group of businessmen surrounding the ruler. It and its various networks can involve sets of businessmen within and across sectors on the one hand, and government officials at various levels on the other, interstitched with intermediaries who may themselves be active or retired government, banking, or military officials. Often, networks and intermediaries are essential to guide favored businesses through the myriad and inconsistent sets of rules and processes set up and maintained within large and

[2] The article states that employment in Rwanda's formal economy is only a little more than 300,000 in a country of 5.5 million economically active persons, and only 354 firms are significant taxpayers.

[3] Of course, this study would never have taken place had the National Democratic Party not been dissolved after the 2011 Egyptian uprising.

complex government bureaucracies. In fact, according to Amr Adly (2020), Egypt and other developing countries have a variant of the crony capitalist which could be called the 'dandy capitalist,' someone with no particular family or other strong links with a ruler, but who has created a well-known footprint in the economy (often initially by setting up foreign-facing agencies and by leveraging old family capital) and who, with various networks created along the way, has also reinforced ties and exchanged favors with state bureaucrats.

Government procurement systems, based on however well-designed principles of competition and transparency, are easily manipulated by these big players who have inside knowledge and extensive personal networks. And under these networks and their webs, oligopolies and cartels that exclude new entrants in particular sectors just get stronger and stronger. Sweetheart deals are the order of the day, and it is privileged access to ministers and other officials that represent the real skill sets of these big businessmen and their intermediaries. Whether it is import licenses and customs clearances, advantageous loans from state banks, access to public land or easy property registration and conveyance, permissions for acquisitions and mergers, approvals for franchises and new factories, or purchasing government assets, it is the big guys who time and again are given help to both protect their interests and expand them. They may be in manufacturing, imports, retailing, tourism, agriculture, banking, communications, or fintech (or more likely multiples of these), but the commonality is the ability to succeed through connections and exchanges of favors, usually built up carefully over time.

Even if government regulations are well intentioned (to curb actual abuses) and even if the initial lobbying by corporations was well intentioned (to reduce silly rules), this mixture of business and government through personal networks can make a mockery of these regulations and stifle competition, a collusive result sometimes called 'regulatory capture' by political entrepreneurs. Another kind of capture, especially prominent in countries where the state manages the exploitation of natural resources or controls other kinds of rents, has been called 'state capture,' a situation where influential or connected personalities manage to acquire state assets and natural resource exploitation at ridiculously low prices (Mulenga & Mulenga, 2018).

No matter how one classifies these mechanisms, they help explain the unfortunate phenomenon of the missing middle in many developing countries, where small and medium-sized enterprises find it difficult to expand and grow (or even become formal), being constrained or shut out by the privileged and connected big market players and by the lack of intermediary institutions (e.g. municipal, trade, or religious) that could provide conduits to larger markets. And because privileges and captured markets are so carefully protected and passed on generationally by established players, unless there is revolutionary change in the composition of the ruling coterie, one can expect more and more of the same. And even with abrupt regime change, the ability of former elites to make a rapid comeback is remarkable.

Donors and Connected Capitalists

Donor agencies, in their many efforts to support the private sector, find it convenient to ignore the reality of deep and widespread forms of crony and 'dandy' capitalism in many if not most developing countries. Instead, even without being conscious of it, they tend to support large and connected businesses whose main 'comparative advantage' is precisely in being part of these exclusive and privileged structures, those who enjoy very cordial relationships with the ruling military or civilian regime or those who have learned the intricacies of swimming in networks of government officials, intermediaries, and family connections.

Many are the ways donors engage with and support private business. Most obvious are the loans or equity coming from specialized donor institutions to local (and even international) firms operating in a particular developing country. These DFIs (private lending arms) are found in most donor countries. They tend to deal with larger, more respected firms that have plenty of recourse to local banks and other sources for loans, but who like the conditions, the hard currency, the subsidy element, and, yes, the prestige that these DFIs can offer. The World Bank Group's IFC is probably the biggest and best known, and it has been criticized for many of its loans going through dubious third-party lenders and for working excessively with large companies and wealthy individuals who hardly need its help.[4] A US Congressional Committee found that "The IFC's mechanism provides undisclosed levels of subsidy to firms selected on opaque, noncompetitive grounds, involving no input from beneficiary countries" (Kenny, 2019).

[4] A long catalogue of such IMF-funded projects can be found at the Bretton Woods Project (2013).

Most DFIs operate much as does the IFC, and in fact the IFC represents in many ways the industry standard for the donor world's private sector lending arms, something to be admired and emulated. Such admiration reached new heights in 2021 when the World Bank stubbornly—in spite of much criticism—clung to a new plan to use a significant chunk of the replenishments for its IDA, specifically for loans to the private sector. To open a path to use some of this money to help private corporations seemed to many as wrongheaded and hypocritical. As Charles Kenny (Kenny, 2021) remarked of the plan: "… there are better ways to spend it than on the 'Private Sector Window'—largely used as a slush fund to subsidize financially unattractive IFC projects to meet internal return benchmarks." Yet the doctrine of donors leveraging private sector investment seems unstoppable.

These private lending windows are only one aspect of donor support for the private sector. Virtually, every mainstream donor has an array of intervention and policy tools to support the private sector in one way or another. Prominent among them are credit and support for SMEs, almost always the larger, 'mid-cap' varieties who are bankable and whose clout is severalfold greater than the average small firm. These SME programs have, since the 2010s, become much beloved by multinational banks such as the EBRD and the EIB as well as a multitude of mainline donors, since they look good on their portfolios and can be conveniently implemented through fund managers and (conservative) local banks who very much like the transaction and other fees involved. Donors may also have technical assistance programs to improve the institutional infrastructure that private companies need (such as banks, judiciary, customs) and to help firm access credit, markets, and infrastructure services. Softer means of promoting private enterprise are also commonly practiced, such as sponsoring investment conferences and round tables that include prominent businessmen, supporting cozy bilateral trade delegations, aiding local business associations and industry federations, and so on. In addition, donors have been preaching for decades 'better markets' policy mantras such as the need for clear company and tax regulations, legal protections for registered private property, contract enforcement by the judiciary, and easy bankruptcy procedures. But this edifying advice has had little effect in most countries, and in any event, it doesn't begin to dismantle the thickets of special relations enjoyed by the big players who work to maintain dominance over markets and prevent others' entry into them, thus keeping the private sector 'middle' very hollow indeed.

Donors have preferred to ignore the inconvenient reality of patronage and privilege-driven oligopolies, cartels, and networks that exist in the background of the formal private sector, somehow assuming that various market reforms actually work, that 'level play field' advice actually sinks in, and that personal and family and crony connections are no longer a main factor in business success. Except for the odd research report, the bane of this widespread exclusionary capitalism is hardly mentioned by donors. One rare example was a 2014 World Bank report (World Bank, 2014) on Tunisian President Zine El Abidine Ben Ali's use of the levers of state power to enrich family and friends over many years (until he had to flee the country in 2011), but by the time of the report, he was very much an easy target. This report acknowledges that, except for blatant cases like Tunisia and oligarchs in the Ukraine and Russia, the subject of connected capitalists hardly surfaces in development literature. Moreover, it is only since the early 2000s that the phrase 'elite capture' was coined in the development industry, and this term (cooked up by the World Bank) seems to have been applied first to local-level elites capturing control of community development programs that are supposed to benefit the disadvantaged and poor (Roopanarine, 2013). Donors may also sometimes even query why there is no 'even playing field,' especially in job markets, but they stop short of reaching the conclusion that it is the pervasiveness of crony favoritism and connections that is behind it (Schiffbauer et al., 2015).

In other words, the wider sense of capture by business elites at higher levels and the cozy relations between big businessmen, political parties, banks, elites, and government (and often the military) somehow don't seem to factor into donor thinking. Yet the chumminess between connected businessmen, intermediaries, and government officials in the developing world has widespread negative effects on the economies of developing nations and *should be* a cause for concern, since this inevitably re-enforces economic inequality, privilege, and concentrations of power, and it restricts the growth of the myriad small enterprises that actually employ the large majority in any developing country.

Donors, particularly those with strong ideological underpinnings about the importance of free markets and the miracles of the private sector, cannot handle the fact of pervasive cronyism in its various forms. That free enterprise systems can become so distorted in so many countries and in so many ways is an inconvenient truth, and this fact alone could knock the theoretical props out from under a huge chunk of any donor country's foreign assistance budget. Sure, there is corruption (which donors have belatedly recognized and feebly fight), but the fact that recipient governments are so entwined with different forms of privileged networks should make donors shudder, since it is these governments that are the conduits of practically all donor largess.

Worse, could it be that donors, simply by always trumpeting the modern private sector and ignoring the whole cronyism-dandyism phenomena, are actually contributing to the tenacity of these systems? In other words, it seems that donor attempts at creating level playing fields have the perverse effect of reinforcing the very systems that make these playing fields anything but level. After all, connected businessmen are very aware of donor policies and are quick to project themselves to donors as the vanguard of modernization and as models of a brighter future for their countries. Gullible donors and their own corporate cheerleaders back home can then comfortably assume that there are dynamic development partners in place and that all that is needed is more and more of the same financial interventions and policy advice.

The donor-businessman nexus in developing countries is a subject that is rarely researched to any depth. Thus, a book by Sarah Smierciak (2022), who looks in detail at cronyism, elite capture, and complicity of international actors in Egypt, is certainly welcome. She recounts the growth and increasing complexity of business-state networks from 1991 to 2020, how channels of privilege were carved out (and how the non-privileged were excluded), and, most importantly, how this elite development was linked directly to opportunities created by massive assistance to Egypt international foreign financial and development players who were promoting market liberalization and a dynamic, globally linked private sector. The details are well worth reading. They include profiles of important businessmen, their networks, and quasi-government hats they sometimes wore. It was these elite personalities who monopolized channels of 'private sector' representation so important for international donors and that imparted a false guise of inclusivity. The author runs through a number of initiatives promoted and funded by Western governments over the period—such as USAID's private sector projects, PPPs, SME support, and privileged American trade agreements. And, crucially, she identifies the various platforms that enhanced big business collusion, such as federations of industries, chambers of commerce, economic think tanks, export councils, modernization centers, and the like.

How do these extensive and cozy relationships between private sector elites in the Rest and donor representatives establish themselves and grow?

On one level, it is understandable that donors are enamored with local businessmen. Generally, donors feel much more comfortable with the slick, Westernized businessman or manufacturer who exhibits a veneer of global high-tech or commercial savvy (and who speaks the same language and uses much the same codes and references) than they do with, say, a rural entrepreneur or small factory owner who doesn't even speak English. As an example, such a bias towards modern businesses was one of the reasons that the World Bank made such a mess in its design of the West Delta Irrigation Rehabilitation Project in Egypt in the 2000s.[5]

Westernized local businessmen may be part of family conglomerates, contractors, consultants, or former high government officials, and one of their most sought-after skills is personal access to the corridors of power (as in "Oh, minister so and so? Well, we went to university together and I can easily arrange a meeting, or even dinner if you want."). Thus often, without even knowing it, donor representatives, their consultants, and the home country businessmen they promote can easily become drawn into this comfortable world of elite business connections.

There are many ways that this meeting of like minds is reinforced. Donor in-country representatives often hobnob with local elites at various social and cultural events. This chumminess is reinforced by the phenomenon of business associations and chambers of commerce. One good example is the American Chamber of Commerce in Egypt which, since 1983, has been a wonderful platform for Egyptian and American corporate representatives to rub shoulders, make deals, track the latest tenders and mergers, and meet ministers, ambassadors, secretaries, and USAID officials. Of course, there is nothing inherently wrong with these extensive networks of business groups. But their main functions are very much the cementing of like interests and, through them, the reproduction of very chummy and elitist networks.

On a personal level, donor professional staff and their international consultants are often likely to engage with a country's upper middle classes and have lots of shared values. It is a comfortable meeting of like minds, both of which are desperate to ignore the gross inequities and inequalities that are plain to see out on the street and in the village. There are bonds

[5] Totally erroneous information about existing conditions—mainly provided by the few large businessmen with agro-business farms in the area, and spun together by the Bank's Public-Private Infrastructure Advisory Fund—led to a PPP irrigation project that was so irrelevant that it never even got off the ground (Sims, 2014, 88–92).

of sympathy and understanding between donor expatriates and their like-minded modern businessman counterparts, and the expatriate *wants* to believe that his counterpart/friend represents the trajectory of where the country should be going.

It wouldn't be so bad if this locked-in privilege and patronage, and the donors' implicit support for it, actually produced booming economies. Even in developing countries that can boast high GDP growth and in which there are 'vibrant' modern businesses and an array of corporate conglomerates, the depressing reality is that such formal private enterprises are only a modernist veneer and that their ability to generate jobs (any jobs, not just good jobs) is practically nil compared to the vast and ever-expanding pools of labor in these countries. This is the depressing reality, and it leads us to the subject of the next chapter, surplus labor and informality.

References

Adly, A. (2020). *Cleft capitalism: The social origins of failed market making in Egypt*. Stanford University Press.

Bretton Woods Project. (2013, February 12). *IFC investments rarely touch the poor*. Accessed May 10, 2022, from https://www.brettonwoodsproject.org/2013/02/art-572001/

Diwan, I., Keefer, P., & Schiffbauer, M. (2014). *On top of the pyramids: Cronyism and private sector growth in Egypt, Working Paper*. World Bank.

Himbara, D. (2015, January 16). Why I quit as Rwandan President Paul Kagame's economic advisor: His tyranny and lies. *Quartz Magazine*. Accessed May 10, 2022, from https://qz.com/327694/why-i-quit-as-rwandan-president-paul-kagames-economic-advisor-tyranny-and-lies/

Hubbard, R. G., & Duggan, W. (2009). *The aid trap: Hard truths about ending poverty*. Columbia University Press.

International Finance Corporation. (2020, December). *Country private sector diagnostic: Creating markets in Egypt*. Accessed May 10, 2022, from https://www.ifc.org/wps/wcm/connect/af513599-08b4-45a4-b346-1a44de58cda6/CPSD-Egypt.pdf?MOD=AJPERES&CVID=npT1-BJ

Kenny, G. (2019, May 6). Fighting crony capitalism at the World Bank. *The Hill*. Accessed May 10, 2022, from https://thehill.com/blogs/congress-blog/politics/442235-fighting-crony-capitalism-at-the-world-bank

Kenny, G. (2021, October 14). *Twitter thread*. Accessed May 10, 2022, from https://twitter.com/charlesjkenny/status/1448659039705964551

Khatri, N., & Ojha, A. (Eds.). (2016). *Crony capitalism in India: Establishing robust counteractive institutional frameworks*. Palgrave Macmillan.

Mulenga, C., & Mulenga, J. (2018, September). Demystifying the concept of state or regulatory capture from a theoretical public economics perspective. *African Journal of Political Science and International Relations, 12*(7), 132–141. Accessed May 10, 2022, from https://academicjournals.org/journal/AJPSIR/article-full-text-pdf/91C144D58697

Pei, M. (2016). *China's crony capitalism: The dynamics of regime decay*. Harvard University Press.

Roopanarine, L. (2013, November 13). Development jargon decoded: Elite capture. *The Guardian, Global development*. Accessed May 10, 2022, from https://www.theguardian.com/global-development/poverty-matters/2013/nov/13/development-jargon-decoded-elite-capture

Sayigh, Y. (2019). *Owners of the Republic: An anatomy of Egypt's military economy*. Carnegie Middle East Center. Accessed May 10, 2022, from https://carnegie-mec.org/2019/11/18/owners-of-republic-anatomy-of-egypt-s-military-economy-pub-80325

Schiffbauer, M., Sy, A., Hussain, S., Sahnoun, H., & Keefer, P. (2015). *Jobs or privileges: Unleashing the employment potential of the Middle East and North Africa. MENA development report*. World Bank. Accessed May 10, 2022, from https://openknowledge.worldbank.org/handle/10986/20591

Sims, D. (2014). *Egypt's desert dreams: Development or disaster?* AUC Press.

Smierciak, S. (2022). *Cronyism and elite capture in Egypt: From businessmen cabinet to military Inc*. Routledge.

Thapelo, T. (2017, July 31). Privatization war in Botswana: Rally against Crony Capitalism. *Weekend Post*. Accessed May 10, 2022, from https://www.weekendpost.co.bw/20797/opinions/privatization-war-in-botswana-rally-against-crony-capitalism/aa

World Bank. (2014, April 3). *All in the family: State capture in Tunisia – Questions and Answers*. Accessed May 10, 2022, from https://www.worldbank.org/en/news/feature/2014/04/03/all-in-the-family-state-capture-in-tunisia-question-and-answers

CHAPTER 20

Informality

Probably, the most intractable problem facing most developing countries is how to deal with their huge and growing informal activities, and it is these unregistered and/or extralegal activities that dominate economies. Informal businesses are said to make up over 80 percent of all establishments in a typical developing country, contribute up to 50 percent of its GDP (if at all measured), and employ (however marginally and underpaid) half, if not more, the labor force. It sounds staggering, and it is. At the same time, unregulated and extralegal informal housing—whether found in slums or spontaneous settlements surrounding larger cities and secondary towns and even swollen villages—accommodates 40 to 60 percent of a country's urban inhabitants, and sometimes much more.

These informal activities and enterprises are not being replaced by modern, regulated industries or absorbed and formalized, nor are they being replaced by affordable housing built by registered real estate companies (or built and subsidized by the state) at anything like even a fraction of the scale required. No informal processes are proving extremely resilient, providing the only real sponge for surplus labor and the only alternative to slums of despair. The formal, modern, and relatively capital-intensive economic sectors, even if expanding rapidly, have in most countries proven totally incapable of absorbing even a small fraction of the immense annual additions to the labor force or producing anything like the needed housing. And governments have been unable to provide useful incentives and

D. Sims, *Development Delusions and Contradictions*,
https://doi.org/10.1007/978-3-031-17770-5_20

relaxed regulatory environments that would encourage formalization of these activities.

This inability to incorporate informality into the formal structures and dynamics of a country's economy is not just a problem of leaving the disenfranchised majority behind, bad as this is. It means that opportunities for rapid economic growth, based on a country's real comparative advantages, are being missed.

In this chapter, we look at informality and how governments in the Rest and donor agencies have reacted. To do this, we quickly look at both the origins and growth of the two phenomena, their main characteristics, and the policies formulated to deal with them. It is intended to give the reader an understanding of how informality challenges both the legitimacy of governments in the Rest and the inability of donors, in their hubristic if relatively informed bubbles, to be more than marginally relevant.

How Did Informality Become so Massive in Developing Countries?

Laws and institutions in poor countries were either imposed (colonial) or imitated (postcolonial), in both cases producing the semblance of a rational, benevolent government and the rule of law, or of "acting like a state" (Andrews et al., 2013). This created a veneer of formality where laws and regulations were written and added to with a misplaced faith in the automatic enforcement of these rules by the weak institutions that were created in parallel. Only a small fraction of economic activities actually followed these rules, and those that did were mainly from elite, comprador, and upper-middle classes who could easily bend them to their will. So over time, alternative and parallel systems evolved, especially with the demographic explosion of the twentieth century. These included ways to confirm property ownership and its transfer, to skirt building controls, to create and operate businesses that avoided taxes, fees, and inspections, etc. And how was this done? Mainly by leveraging the weakest link—that of the underpaid government official whose 'entitlement' gave him means to extract payments to look the other way or otherwise ignore and bend the legal precepts and penalties ascribed by modernist laws, either because he never believed in their importance or simply because he saw in them income-generating potential. Most average citizens, having looked around at how connected players have jigged the system, despaired of these regulatory frameworks.

Even progressive social protection legislation—quite extensively adopted by developing countries over many decades—perversely pushed more and more workers and firms into informality (Levy, 2008). Most of this legislation was adopted from Western countries, but there was neither the means to enforce these precepts (basic labor rights, health insurance, retirement benefits, etc.) nor the budgets to pay for them.

In other words, the 'rule of law'—that of the famous neoliberal Holy Grail—became 'the rule by lots of laws and regulations applied arbitrarily, if at all' as a means of solidifying power and, parenthetically, as a means to pretend that the state is omnipotent. For the majority with no hope of connections with higher-ups, the solution was simply to remain as far as possible below the radar of officialdom. For many small businessmen or contractors/developers, or even small farmers, extractions (bribes) were far less costly and far less onerous than trying to play it straight. And over time, these alternative systems became entrenched and more and more sophisticated.

Western donors and academics have been tracking the informality phenomena in the Rest for some time and could be said to have monopolized the understanding of them. The concept of surplus labor and dual economies, where there is a small, regulated modern sector and a much larger but separate informal sector, was first postulated by Ranis and Fei in 1964 and elaborated in the early 1970s on studies in East Africa (Clement, 2015; Harris & Todaro, 1970). Given the obvious need to absorb those expanding labor forces, over decades donors redoubled their analytic work and advanced various prescriptions on how to formalize small and informal enterprises. The idea was that these enterprises needed to be recognized officially and to begin to behave like Western small businesses. Once 'regularized,' these micro and small enterprises could gain the bank credit, know-how, and technology they required to expand, raise their productivity, and, especially, generate lots of jobs. And, of course, they would then pay taxes. Prescriptions included reducing registration barriers and costs, providing tailored finance for small entrepreneurs, offering advice on small business management and marketing, and providing temporary tax incentives to sweeten going formal.

Over roughly the same period, the revelation that people were themselves carving out communities on urban fringes and building their own housing with virtually no outside help first appeared in studies in Latin

America in the late 1960s, and slowly a corpus of knowledge was assembled in the West that recognized that government systems for regulating the built environment were becoming less and less relevant. Donors and academics began to talk about lowering building standards and easing access to permits, creating small serviced plots of land for family-built housing, setting up mortgage finance systems that fit modest families, and preaching to formal developers that they had to go down market to target more than a country's haute bourgeoisie.

And how have recipient governments reacted to all of this knowledge being generated on informality? In most cases, they have politely nodded their heads in agreement and carried out some actions—especially if there is funding from donors involved—but few have adopted anything like transformative measures nor have they tried to understand these phenomena. Few are the countries that have relaxed building permit regimes, property registration requirements, or the plethora of stipulations regulating commerce and manufacturing to allow informal activities to easily fit in and grow. In effect, these developing countries seemed stuck in modernist postures that have relied on a compendium of accrued legislation in which informality plays no part.

Informality in Developing Countries: A Defining Feature?

The huge preponderance of informal activities in the Rest is something that rich countries, in their trajectories towards prosperity in the nineteenth and early twentieth centuries, simply didn't have to deal with, at least at anything like the depth and scale now experienced in the Rest. Thus, there were no policies, techniques, or tools to rely on as the phenomenon of massive informality became more and more of a reality in developing countries.

But one may say, Western economies and societies also had histories of dealing with extralegal practices and dubious financial dealings. Yes, there had always been informal practices (black, shadow, or grey economies, if you will), and history shows that regulation and formalization of these practices in the West were progressive and long. But the difference was that these controls and measures evolved in parallel with steady population growth and urbanization, in parallel with the enormous economic expansion and increasing prosperity, and also in parallel with the development of lending and regulatory institutions, commercial codes, legal frameworks, property regimes, forms of company organization, and relevant professional cadres.

There has not been much academic work on how informal businesses and SMEs grew and became formalized in the West. However, one 2010 study looked in detail at the financing sources of small firms and their growth in America and Western Europe, especially in the nineteenth and early twentieth centuries (Cull et al., 2005). It was a slowly evolving scene, and prominent were local banks (and local notaries in France and local credit cooperatives in Germany) who were able to offer services and loans that were tailored to and understood the needs of local small businesses as they formed and grew. Similarly, these local banks could also extend tailored loans for house construction and purchase. Thus, it was a situation of following and serving local market demand, unlike in developing countries today, where the source of small firm finance is extremely top-down and, one could say, 'supply driven' by the funds being injected into SME finance by donors and central banks.

This study by Cull et al. underlines the fact that small businesses and SMEs found in developing nations today have different motivations and face totally different financial and service environments than those that had been faced by growing businesses in the West. In other words, ways of trying to deal with informality in the Rest represent unchartered territory. Simply borrowing formats and mechanisms from the West—again and again—was never going to have much effect.

In the rest of this chapter, we take a look at the two main aspects of informality—informal employment and enterprises on the one hand, and informal housing and urban development on the other—to investigate how donors have been dealing with the informality phenomena, how recipient governments have begrudgingly followed along, and what have been the effects.

Informal Employment and Informal Enterprises

In 2015, the ILO described the informal economy as "referring to all economic activities by workers and economic units that are—in law or in practice—not covered or insufficiently covered by formal arrangements"(OECD/ILO, 2019, 155). Obviously, this is a regulatory definition that can vary considerably from one country or jurisdiction to another, and from one point in time to another.

Whatever the definition, it is commonly accepted that informal activities are extremely wide ranging and are mainly cash based. These activities include, at the lower end of the scale, individuals and their assistants (usually related, paid or unpaid) who are shopkeepers; stall and street vendors; petty wholesale and retail traders; own-account carpenters, plumbers, electricians, etc.; vehicle drivers and delivery boys; domestic servants; food caterers, etc. Moving up the scale a bit, one finds enterprises in fixed locations and that are mainly small, unregistered commercial, service, or manufacturing firms, including restaurants, repair workshops, retail stores, and small component manufacturers. These are normally characterized by low productivity and low skill levels of workers, partly due to lack of economies of scale. At the high end of informality are what could be called small- to medium-sized firms with say 10 to 50 workers. These may be 'mostly' formal, in that they have acquired as much official recognition as is necessary to operate (commercial registration, licenses, tax cards, etc.), but were they to be fully investigated, they would fall far short of formality in many ways.

Not only are definitions of the size and characteristics of the informal economy rather blurred, but also measuring the phenomenon is very problematic. Statistical offices in developing countries generate data from representative labor force surveys or representative household/enterprise surveys, combined with census data on establishments. But, besides the usual methodological and sampling problems, most surveys are mainly devised to collect information on a person's primary job only and tend to ignore unpaid family work, women's own account work at home, etc. Furthermore, survey reference periods are short and cannot encompass occasional or seasonable pursuits. Only specific and repeated (and expensive) sample surveys on a country's whole population of informal firms are likely to capture good data, and inevitably, these are very rare (Restrepo-Echavarria, 2015).

Still, however you look at the phenomenon, informal enterprises and informal employment are massive in most developing countries and are very much—with some exceptions—entwined with those on the lower ends of society. Furthermore, decades of measurements and studies show that not only informal enterprises and informal employment in most developing countries are extremely 'resilient,' but also the phenomenon is increasing. So why is this?

First, the situation in most developing economies is one of acute surplus labor, with scores if not hundreds of hopefuls lining up for each announced formal job. It is a situation of a small modern sector juxtaposed against huge traditional or informal economic sectors, with only tenuous interconnections. Inevitably, all sorts of barriers have grown up that restrict entry into the formal sector, and upward mobility, whatever one's qualifications and skills, is to most a myth. The concept of dual economies has been around since the 1970s, but it was first posited as a largely rural-urban dichotomy.[1] No more! Now, this dichotomy or dualism can be seen in all sorts of service, transport, and manufacturing industries anywhere in a country.

Third, a very sizable portion of any country's informal sector is made up of small businesses whose owners have made the conscious decision to remain informal, partly due to these dual-economy barriers, but also simply because they have made a rational choice to avoid the costs and hassles and the intrusions of the state. Such was the conclusion of one study in Indonesia, where it was found that, in spite of incentives and a national program of one-stop shops, many owners of informal enterprises did not register their businesses either because they had no desire to expand or borrow from formal financial sources or because they were avoiding taxes. This is a phenomenon that has been called 'rational exit' (Rothenberga et al., 2016). Similar rational exit paradigms could be said to operate in Pakistan, Bangladesh, India, Egypt, Nigeria, and other countries with large populations and entrenched informality.

How have donors (and their partners in the Rest) dealt with the large, complex, and growing phenomenon of informal economies? As always, there have been lots of noise and posturing, but basically there have been five approaches:

Microfinance to the Rescue?

Very small businesses (usually family affairs with one to three people involved), that struggle to increase pathetic and unstable incomes, can be considered the very bottom of a country's informal enterprise pyramid. These micro businesses can be in a variety of sectors and industries, ranging from agriculture, farming, or fishing to transportation, small shops or stalls, repair, food production, or artisanship. Some individuals may be

[1] Gustav Ranis at Yale was a long—if rather lonely—proponent of theories of labor surplus in developing countries (Fei & Ranis, 1964; Ranis, 2004).

entrepreneurs by choice, while others have become entrepreneurs through necessity.

The birth of 'modern' microfinance is said to have occurred in the mid-1970s in Bangladesh with the pioneering work of Muhammad Yunus. His Grameen Bank now works in over 80,000 villages and has more than six million borrowers. Although for once germination of the idea started in the Rest, very soon the West took notice and in practically no time microfinance had gone mainstream, with donors and INGOs leaping into the game, offering small loans for on-lending through an increasing array of local NGOs, microcredit financiers, and private foundations. And it seemed a win-win, since borrower default was rare (partly through borrower group guarantees), collateral was not required, and rural women were overwhelmingly the main borrowers. Innumerable case studies profiled successful examples of poor families who managed to increase income, better provide for their children, and acquire assets. The microfinance sector grew and grew, with more donors pumping funds into the system, with more local NGOs setting up microcredit arms, and with more recipient governments establishing microfinance departments and branches, writing microfinance laws and regulations, and sponsoring microfinance conferences, workshops, and training sessions.

Furthermore, good loan repayment allowed microcredit agencies to establish revolving funds for further on-lending, allowing these operations to claim (near) financial sustainability, an extremely rare phenomenon in the arsenal of poverty reduction methods. Thus, during the 1990s, many microfinance operations began to restructure themselves to attract commercial investors. The microfinance movement culminated with the year 2005 being declared the Year of Microfinance, and Mohammed Yunus and his Grameen Bank were awarded the Nobel Peace Prize in 2006.

It appears that microfinance is one rare example where both donors and recipient governments have come to agree wholeheartedly on something, where local 'ownership' is firmly in place, and where both can point to success in the struggle against extreme poverty. But is this the case? During the early rollout of microfinance initiatives and structures, there were some voices that questioned its success. Concerns centered around the almost usurious interest rates, loans being used for pure consumption, and families falling into endless debt cycles, but these questions were submerged or ignored. Starting in the early 2000s, sharper criticisms began to emerge, and an important marker of these was an anthology that appeared in 2007 (Dichter & Harper, 2007), and in 20 chapters by knowledgeable professionals both from the West and the Rest, the industry was carefully deconstructed as doing more harm than good. But it seems that these arguments had no effect on the global enthusiasm for microfinance, which continues unabated.

SME Finance and Support to the Rescue?

In most development literature, SMEs are considered an important if largely ignored element in a country's economic structure. They have been recognized as having been key in industrial and employment growth in Western countries (and also in lately developed countries in East Asia), so the logic is that they also should be key players in all developing countries. The problem is that these nations for the most part exhibit what is called 'the missing middle syndrome,' that is a lopsided situation where a small group of large, private companies and state-owned enterprises exist alongside a vast number of informal businesses, with a largely absent SME sector in between, as we have discussed in the previous chapter (Adly, 2019). Thus, most observers conclude that this missing middle must be corrected, and, to do this, efforts should concentrate on formalizing and strengthening at least some of the huge number of tiny enterprises so they can grow to occupy this missing space. Many programs have been rolled out that have tried to formalize very small enterprises, build trust between them and government, improve their operations and management, and, most importantly, provide them with access to financing, with a prime goal of creating jobs and hoovering up the many new entrants in the labor market. Sounds logical, doesn't it?

However, this stylized view is blurred by varying definitions and concepts of what constitutes an SME, with different organizations and countries constructing their own definitions, almost always based on simplistic labor head counts, sales, or assets. For example, Egypt defines SMEs as having more than 5 and fewer than 50 employees, and Vietnam considers SMEs to have between 10 and 300 employees. The World Bank defines SMEs as those enterprises with a maximum of 300 employees, $15 million in annual revenue, and $15 million in assets.

These definitions seem to stretch the concept, and the suspicion is that, by using high upper limits (in terms of number of employees or fixed capital or turnover), the inclusion of what are actually relatively large and comparatively modern enterprises into the SME category is ensured. These firms exhibit few characteristics of either informality or sponges for labor, but they are the most likely to benefit from the many incentives (tax breaks, subsidized finance, etc.) that governments, backed by donors, love to promote. If nothing else, it sounds very much like helping those who don't actually need help (Chap. 19). In any event, financing SMEs in the Rest has become a very big business.

Besides easy finance to existing and startup SMEs, many efforts aim at lowering the barriers for informal small enterprises to become formal. This usually means simplifying registration and licensing requirements and smoothing the process through one-stop shops, etc. Another tactic is to reduce and simplify taxes imposed on small firms who opt for formalizing (at least for an initial period, to get them on the books). Yet another is to include advice to formalizing SMEs on business development and management and on product development and marketing. This has created a field day for service NGOs and business advice consultants.

What is the record of all this extensive support for SME formalization and growth? One would have thought that donors and IFIs would have, long ago, seriously evaluated and re-evaluated the long-term impact of these various interventions in terms of increased firm sales, increased capital formation, adopting new and more productive technologies, improved management and entrepreneurship skills and savvy, and, *especially*, at creating more good jobs, lots and lots of them. After all, these are the repeated justifications for such interventions, but such evaluations are, as far as can be determined, surprisingly thin on the ground.

One informative 2017 World Bank publication carried out a review of what could be found in the literature and concluded: "While there is empirical evidence from analysis of datasets of SMEs on employment effects, findings from rigorous evaluations of targeted interventions designed to address finance constraints among SMEs is scarce. An Independent Evaluation Group (IEG) report on the World Bank Group's TSME portfolio in 2013 highlighted the lack of this rigorous evidence in literature and among WBG projects as one of the main findings. Several comprehensive meta evaluations find a small share of evaluations of the universe that have a specific objective of employment generation" (Kumar, 2017, 27). Such a conclusion on the scarcity of good evaluations of SME support programs in developing countries was also found in a literature review carried out by GIZ and the ILO in 2010 (De Kok et al., 2013).

One of the very few studies that tried to measure long-term job creation due to SME credit programs found that "evidence of actual impact is scarce, or mixed at best" (De Kok et al., 2013, 37). This rather depressing conclusion seems to be borne out in an evaluation of SME support programs in four Latin American countries where, although there were intermediate and short-term benefits, long-term benefits could only be clearly seen in terms of increased sales (and not increased employment) (Acevedo & Tan, 2010). Also, it seems that the popular strategy of lowering barriers to SME formalization has not been very effective, as highlighted by a review of Indonesia's one-stop shop program, which found that the program had no effect on firms' rates of informality and did not reduce the probability that workers were informally employed (Rothenberga et al., 2016, 96). There is some evidence that subsidized Business Development Services (BDS) and targeted technical advice have been successful in increasing informal SME performance, but again, things are not very clear. As one survey report put it: "There is significant funding of SME support programmes by multilateral development banks, international financial institutions, bilateral donors and governments. However, much of this support is focused on two areas: providing financial loans to SMEs, and advocating general reforms to the investment climate, which mainly benefit larger enterprises, including multinational companies, rather than SMEs" (Christian Aid, 2016, abstract).

What is going on? Perhaps, one explanation is that most of the support for SMEs is a kind of posturing that fits both sides. For the donors, it seems that anything like rigorous evaluations about job creation and other benefits can be conveniently sidelined or ignored so as not to compromise the continuation of significant credit outflows from IFIs and other donor institutions for SME financing. And for governments in the Rest and their high-level finance officials (whose prejudice against informal businesses is well known), this targeting approach allows them to continue their dreams of constructing a private sector that exhibits Western characteristics. Also, in spite of lots of cajoling on the part of donors to at least go partly down market and to include some traditional informal SMEs, this has been stubbornly resisted by those in government and banks who cherish bureaucratic regulations and requirements (and the rents these systems create). And who is going to shake up this situation? Certainly not the financial, banking, and fintech cadres who populate both the IFIs and their partner national banks, central banks, and ministries of finance and who share similar cultural affinities.

Training and Skill Development to the Rescue?

It has been a canon of development concepts that imparting practical skills and preparing youth for productive jobs will lead to more and better employment as well as more productive enterprises. Sometimes called Technical and Vocational Education and Training, TVET systems are many, aiming at unemployed school leavers, at increasing the employability of graduates, and at introducing new specialist skills for growing sectors such as information technology and green economy. The main thrust of TVET programs is to impart skills that supplement formal education and that allow trainees to be employed in large private sector firms. Rare are TVET programs that target young entrepreneurs and give them the business, management, and marketing skills needed to set up or expand their own businesses. And even rarer are TVET programs that specifically target workers and entrepreneurs in SMEs and informal businesses.

Digitalization, Financial Inclusion, and Fintech to the Rescue?

Large and expanding high-tech financial sectors have taken their aim at 'underbanked' SMEs as a growth market in developing countries. Financial and other products abound: full-service fintech companies, which offer unsecured credit, equity financing, venture capital, financial leasing for operating equipment and supply-chain financing, cloud computing, and big data technology. However, those being targeted by these services are almost always already formal, registered, and larger SMEs who had been poorly served by traditional banks and other lenders. So, this may be a growth market, but one that mainly benefits the thin ranks of larger companies who can take advantage of these new financial services and systems. And while smart phones, apps, and mobile banking (as in P-Mesa in Kenya) have attracted much interest as a way for small enterprises to function and expand, these have yet to show much transformative impact.

The startup ecosystem has recently emerged in developing countries and is much supported by Western businesses, donors, and social entrepreneurs. This has already become a crowded arena with angel investors, incubators, accelerators, co-working spaces, specialized funders, and pitching events, and it is capturing more and more interest. But will this help more traditional SMEs, especially those that are informal or semiformal? There are huge resource and cultural divides, which separate the startup world from that of the micro- and small-enterprise sector, and it could be said they are worlds apart.

The Chinese Approach as a Middle Road?

China appears to have offered an alternative (or at least a more relaxed) approach that allows for the inclusion of informal enterprises in its booming manufacturing economy. First, China has a relaxed classification and registration of what constitutes smaller/informal enterprises, called 'town and village enterprises' (TVEs), whereas the larger, more regulated, sector is under the heading of 'urban enterprises.' In 2006, TVEs accounted for 70% of the total industrial workforce in China (79.1 million workers). Not surprisingly, the average hourly compensation was reported at just $0.47 in TVEs compared to $1.47 in urban companies (Norfield, 2011). Secondly, China seems to have evolved ways to include informal trade and manufacturing enterprises as part of the larger economy. According to Robert Neuwirth, China's rise as a global center of manufacturing is owed, in part, to its willingness to include less-than-formal systems and enterprises in the mix (Neuwirth, 2011). For example, credit has been made easily available to TVE firms, either from state banks or, more often, directly from municipalities and their local lending arms. Also, in China, banks are much more flexible in extending credit to small and informal firms, allowing a firm's receivables and movable assets to be considered collateral. Furthermore, local governments in poorer provinces of China have unabashedly supported TVE firms as a way to stimulate local employment and to keep rural migrants from flooding the cities. Thirdly, China allows and even encourages informal or shady means of export, and unregulated Chinese goods are commonly found in markets in Africa, Latin America, and elsewhere (National Public Radio, 2011).

China's relaxed approach to semiformal manufacturing and trade has sometimes been called '*système D*,' derived from *se debrouiller*, meaning 'make do.' It is hard to know how this system really works in China and whether it could perhaps represent a better approach to stimulating the expansion of informal enterprises. Not only is information about the formal/informal business interface scanty in China, but also if true it could be attributed to China's particular history. Reforms that started in the 1980s led to the emergence of strong local banks and municipalities who charged ahead providing all kinds of credit to local SMEs, both formal and informal. This meshed well with the country's huge manufacturing expansion, with smaller firms quickly able to link into evolving supply chains. Plus, China's particular dualistic labor market (due to restrictions on family migration from the countryside) created a large and ready pool of cheap casual labor in larger cities into which informal firms could readily tap (Jutting & Xenogiani, 2007).

So, the idea that China's *debrouiller* approach might represent a middle road is still rather half baked. And it seems any 'making do' is, for most developing countries that are fixated on Western modernity, something that simply cannot be accommodated. This is, after all, the ultimate contradiction of informality: that accommodating it cannot be stomached by most governments and trying to rigidly formalize its dynamic simply kills it.

Informal Urbanization in the Rest

It is frequently pointed out that the world's population became half urban in 2007, with practically all of this growth taking place in developing countries. As usual, this imparts a hand-wringing narrative about slums, urban sprawl, wrenching poverty, environmental collapse, and urban congestion, something popularized and sensationalized by many (Davis, 2006). For donors as well as their developing country partners, this narrative is the backdrop that justifies an array of interventions, both those more traditional—such as more and better urban infrastructure, transport, upgrading of slums, and affordable housing—and more recently the need for urban resilience in the face of disasters and underlying climate change.

The 'elephant in the room' in this explosive growth of cities in the Rest is, without doubt, informality. Informal systems operate in land acquisition, subdivision, and development; in self-built housing; and in arrangements that underpin both the densification of existing slums and the creation of more. Furthermore, there are informal arrangements operating in traffic and transport, retail and wholesale trade, and a myriad of services. What complicates the scene is the fact that informal urban systems are intertwined with formal ones and cannot be considered as completely stand-alone phenomena. These informal systems are usually ignored or trivialized by modernist-obsessed governments, but at the same time they are nurtured by venal officialdom, usually at municipal and sub-municipal levels. And this informality is helped along by chronically dysfunctional property registration and taxation systems and by irrelevant and sclerotic legislative and institutional frameworks.

What have been the responses of governments in the Rest to the urban mess over six decades? Most governments have simply wished that slums, informal urban expansion, and extralegal housing would simply disappear, in spite of all the evidence to the contrary. Prohibitions against these informal phenomena have been enshrined and reinforced in legislation, but enforcement has been extremely lax, except in rigidly authoritarian/paternalistic states, such as in Iraq under Saddam Hussein and in China.

Policies and Mechanisms to Deal with Urban Informality

Over the years, a range of interventions have been championed to address the many challenges of urban informality. These have mostly originated with donors or Western academics, based on the analysis of what was, after all, a new field. As we shall see below, a range of fixes have been proposed over the decades to make cities in the Rest more functional, inclusive, and accommodating for the large majority. It is worthwhile to go rapidly through the four main approaches, because they illustrate both the contradictions inherent in host government attitudes towards informal urban development and the inability of Western donors, in their standard prescriptions, to factor in and accommodate the many ways the informality dynamic dominates.

1. *Slum eradication and resettlement*

   Eradicating slums and rehousing inhabitants have a long history that can be traced as far back as the early nineteenth century in Europe and North America. It is an expensive and complicated endeavor, one that stems from the perceived need to improve health and living conditions, and, at the same time, it is one frequently rooted in the desire to clean up a city's image and remove urban blight. And it is one that frequently runs roughshod over the interests of those it is supposed to help.

   These days, the idea of wholesale slum eradication and resettlement is generally considered a huge no-no by donor agencies, but with many governments in developing countries, it remains very much alive. Large involuntary resettlement schemes—usually involving relocation of families from slums to remote, cookie-cutter high rises—can still be found in Addis Ababa, Egypt, India, Kenya, Indonesia, Vietnam, and, especially, China. Donors tend to stay far away from these involuntary resettlement schemes, but this does not prevent them from engaging otherwise with the same government agencies that sponsor and fund such slum clearances.

2. In situ *slum and neighborhood upgrading*

   The idea of retaining most existing slum residents in place while undertaking various improvements—and thus preserving social structures and economic livelihoods—is something that gained credibility in the 1970s and 1980s as a better alternative to slum removal. Most of these projects confine themselves to improvements in public spaces, basic infrastructure, and social services, and they have steered away from the more complicated issues of home improvements and tenure security.

   While earlier slum and neighborhood upgrading efforts supported by donor agencies were mostly technical in nature, by the early 1990s, the concept of 'community participation' began to take hold. Soon, the idea of involving inhabitants and their 'natural' leaders in project scoping, design, monitoring, and even implementation had become a basic pillar of most donor-supported upgrading initiatives. Local and international NGOs began to play important roles in engaging with communities, and it seemed that strengthening community cohesion and agency became as important as physical improvements themselves. But while there were some positive impacts, community activities and support would normally fade away quickly once funding from donors dried up.

   Altogether, improvements in the livelihoods of slums across the Third World have been disappointingly meagre. Worse, underlying causes such as difficult land tenure configurations in informal settlements are hardly ever addressed, notwithstanding huge amounts of good advice generated by donors and academics. And the problem is getting much worse, as one 2019 paper on the issue remarked: "Across the developing world, over one billion people live in informal settlements, and this number is set to double in the next 15 years."[2]

3. *Sites and services: Harnessing the informal housing dynamic?*

   The idea of sites and services (S&S) is deceptively simple. There is a tremendous dynamic among households throughout most of the Third World that, if able to acquire a small plot of land, will build out housing units for themselves and, over time, add even more for their relatives or for rent/sale. This construction will rarely be instantaneous, as it will need to fit family finances and informal

[2] (Collier et al., 2019, 1) This is probably a gross underestimate of the size of existing informal settlements worldwide, but who knows?

means of credit, but in almost all cases, considerable family investments are made and the quality of construction can be remarkably good.

The idea of sites and services schemes was based on a recognition of this informal housing dynamic. Starting in the 1970s, the World Bank began to promote the S&S concept in various developing countries, closely followed by a handful of other donors. What were the results? Some schemes, since they had to be located on public land or cheap private land, were quite remote and remained largely unoccupied for years. Other schemes were prey to local crony interests and land fiddles. Plus, some projects were criticized for not accommodating the poorest families and being raided by the relatively better off. Even with all these problems, S&S schemes were in general successful, if usually much slower to mature than had been planned. But they remained mostly pilots and never had the intended effect of influencing government policies, something that would not only have solved acute urban housing problems at little or no drain on public finances, but also have been sustainable instruments for orderly urban expansions.

4. *Getting urban development standards right*

Most urban land use and construction standards used in developing countries have been copied from statutes common in the West, often based on colonial planning and subdivision laws. Not only were these standards often unsuitable to the climate and local norms, but they also raised plot and total housing costs dramatically, and land-hungry urban sprawl was one common consequence.

For decades, Western professionals and some donors had advised governments to relax these standards (at least for 'popular areas'), even showing how minor changes in legislation could vastly simplify planning regimes and the knock-on costs implied. Very few were the cases where this advice has been heeded, and officials seem to have a stubborn penchant for what they perceive as norms that will guarantee—in spite of all evidence to the contrary—the buildout of their cities into formats that would guarantee a modern, well-organized urban future. The detrimental effect of these high standards on house prices and thus housing affordability has been documented across the world, time and again, but it seems that these facts have had little influence.

Resolving the Informal Urbanization Conundrum

Looking at the means of dealing with informal urbanization, the future does not appear rosy. The immense and growing scale of urban problems makes almost all the donor prescriptions irrelevant that, even when successful, are little more than tiny 'islands of excellence' and more fodder for conferences and policy papers. The possibility of 'replicating' any of the recommended urban policies or interventions is, with rare exceptions, simply shrinking further and further away, and at the same time urban informality becomes more and more entrenched. It doesn't help that many aspects of informality are entwined with clientelist mechanisms of political control and regime patronage that are so common in developing countries (Sims, 2012, 20; Dorman & Stein, 2013).

Most governments in the Rest, though proclaiming wide-ranging pro-poor policies, maintain approaches to urban informality that reflect the dominant interests and values of the rising middle classes. It is instructive that, way back in the early 1970s, a Ford Foundation advisor to the Calcutta slum improvement program noted that extending anything like effective support to these slum communities needed to face up to the reality that "political attitudes were governed by middle class norms" and that these norms propped up both "bureaucratic and political opposition" to needed actions (Row, 1973). Fifty years later, and after thousands of pro-poor urban initiatives have been sprinkled around the globe, such opposition is still very much in evidence.

Conclusion: Informality Left to Fester and Huge Opportunities Lost

The depressing fact is that, after decades, the recommended approaches to counter, leverage, or formalize the phenomena of informality are not even palliatives. The fact that the impact of all these micro and SME and housing interventions is miniscule or nil and that the portion of a typical poor country's labor force working in informality and the percentage of families housed extralegally are *increasing*, somehow seems to be forgotten. Instead, donor agencies soldier on with more and more classic SME finance and support and with more schemes to 'formalize' the phenomenon away. At the same time, there are more attempts to provide alternatives to informal urbanization—'affordable' housing projects, subsidized mortgage schemes, and tiny islands of community-based slum upgrading.

In the process, to the extent that these approaches work at all, their selection and operational mechanisms tend to shift towards and target the upper-middle bands of household income distribution. It is the larger, more modern, and near-formal enterprise that benefits, and it is aspiring middle-class households that can find affordable housing units, leaving the lower strata to fester.

That massive informality is a phenomenon particular to developing countries, one that challenges the whole corpus of mainstream development thought (whether derived from Western experiences or claiming to fit Third World exigencies), cannot really be recognized. That informality is grounded in a myriad of social and personal networks that—in the face of ineffective if not predatory governments—are all that those who practice informality have going for them, and that this is a structural given somehow just cannot be accepted. That informality is the new social (dis) order of the Third World is an anathema to both Western donors and their modernist-obsessed partners in the Rest.

References

Acevedo, G. L., & Tan, H. W. (2010). *Impact evaluation of SME programs in Latin America and the Caribbean*. World Bank Group. Accessed June 22, 2022, from https://econpapers.repec.org/bookchap/wbkwbpubs/2298.htm

Adly, A. (2019, May 13). The Arab World must think big about its smallest businesses. *Bloomberg Opinion*. Accessed June 22, 2022, from https://www.bloomberg.com/opinion/articles/2019-05-13/the-arab-world-must-think-big-about-its-smallest-businesses

Andrews, M., Pritchett, L., & Woolcock, M. (2013). Looking like a state: Techniques of persistent failure in state capability for implementation. *Journal of Development Studies, 49*, 1.

Christian Aid, Church of Sweden, et al. (2016). *Supporting small businesses in developing countries: Which programmes work and why?* Accessed June 22, 20220, from http://curtisresearch.org/publications/supporting-small-businesses-in-developing-countries-which-programmes-work-and-why/

Clement, C. (2015). *The formal-informal economy dualism in a retrospective of economic thought since the 1940s. Schriftenreihe des Promotionsschwerpunkts Globalisierung und Beschäftigung, No. 43*. University of Hohenheim.

Collier, P., Glaeser, E., Venables, T., Blake, M., & Manwaring, P. (2019). *Informal settlements and housing markets*. LSE, International Growth Centre.

Cull, R., Davis, L. E., Lamoreaux, N. R., & Rosenthal, J.-L. (2005, October). *Historical financing of small- and medium-sized enterprises*. National Bureau of Economic Research, NBER Working Paper No. 11695.

Davis, M. (2006). *Planet of slums*. Verso.

De Kok, J., Deijl, C., & Veldhuis-Van Essen, C. (2013, April). *Is small still beautiful? Literature review of recent empirical evidence on the contribution of SMEs to employment creation*. GIZ and the ILO.

Dichter, T., & Harper, M. (Eds.). (2007). *What's wrong with microfinance?* Practical Action Publishing.

Dorman, W. J., & Stein, E. (2013). Informality versus the state? Islamists, informal Cairo and political integration by other means. *Turkish Journal of International Relations, 12*(4), 5–19.

Fei, J. C. H., & Ranis, G. (1964). *Development of the labor surplus economy: Theory and policy*. Economic Growth Center, Yale University.

Harris, J., & Todaro, M. (1970). Migration, unemployment and development: A two-sector analysis. *American Economic Review, 60*(1), 126–142.

Jutting, J., & Xenogiani, T. (2007, November). *Informal employment and internal migration: The case of China*. OECDO. Accessed June 22, 2022, from https://slideplayer.com/slide/8361611/

Kumar, R. (2017, July 17). *Targeted SME financing and employment effects: What do we know and what can we do differently*. World Bank, Jobs Working Paper No. 3 (draft date). Accessed June 22, 2022, from http://documents.worldbank.org/curated/en/577091496733563036/Targeted-SME-financing-and-employment-effects-what-do-we-know-and-what-can-we-do-differently

Levy, S. (2008). *Good intentions, bad outcomes: Social policy, informality, and economic growth in Mexico*. Brookings Institution Press.

National Public Radio. (2011, October 19). *The 'informal economy' driving world business*. Accessed June 22, 2022, from https://www.npr.org/2011/10/26/141503411/the-informal-economy-driving-world-business

Neuwirth, R. (2011). *Stealth of nations: The global rise of the informal economy*. Pantheon.

Norfield, T. (2011, June 4). What the 'China Price' really means. *The Economics of Imperialism blogspot*. Accessed June 22, 2022, from https://economicsofimperialism.blogspot.com/2011/06/what-china-price-really-means.html

OECD/ILO. (2019). *Tackling vulnerability in the informal economy*. Development Centre Studies, OECD. https://doi.org/10.1787/939b7bcd-en

Ranis, G. (2004, December). *Labor surplus economies*. Economic Growth Center, Yale University, Discussion Paper No. 900.

Restrepo-Echavarria, P. (2015, January 26). *Measuring underground economy can be done, but it is difficult*. Federal Reserve Bank of St. Louis. Accessed June 22,

2022, from https://www.stlouisfed.org/publications/regional-economist/january-2015/underground-economy

Rothenberga, A., Gaduhb, A., Burgera, N., Chazalic, C., Tjandraningsihc, I., Radikund, R., Suteraa, C., & Weilant, S. (2016). Rethinking Indonesia's informal sector. *World Development, 80*, 96–113.

Row, A. (1973). *An evaluation of the Calcutta planning and development project, cited and quoted in Thomas, Frederic (1997) Calcutta poor: Elegies on a city above pretense.* East Gate, pp. 81–82.

Sims, D. (2012). *Understanding Cairo: The logic of a city out of control.* AUC Press.

PART III

Conclusions

CHAPTER 21

Summing Up

This book has been an enquiry into the complex development industry, one that charts out the various ways it works and that uncovers its many weaknesses and contradictions. Such a critical view of the whole development industry will obviously not be welcome, but it is an approach that is long overdue. It shows in detail how the diverse ways that the industry operates—and the various donors who drive it—simply cannot be catalytic factors for development and, perversely, often have the opposite effect.

This chapter runs through some of the conclusions that can be extracted from this enquiry. Many observers with a critical eye on foreign assistance tend to focus on Western donors and, for diplomatic or ideological reasons, leave the recipient side of the equation pretty much alone. This book takes a more balanced view of how *both* sides have done their parts in making development cooperation such an ineffective mess. In other words, the structures and systems that have been created and expanded over decades have required the complicity of both sides in what could be called 'partnerships in dysfunction.'

The Dysfunction Is More Than the Sum of Its Parts

This book has looked at a number of facets or traits of the development industry, and these have been organized into themes that are taken up in individual chapters. The chapters of Part I have described and analyzed the donor, or Western, side of the equation, and the chapters of Part II have

D. Sims, *Development Delusions and Contradictions*,
https://doi.org/10.1007/978-3-031-17770-5_21

looked at how the recipient side (the Rest) reacts to and accommodates the donor flood. Focus on the driving motives that cluster around each side has been crucial in the analysis.

In this effort, it has been found that things cannot be neatly categorized and analyzed in isolation and that the cumulative negative results are more than the sum of the parts. The most prominent of what could be called 'unvirtuous circles' can be briefly summarized in a couple of paragraphs:

Donor agencies are always desperate to spend or at least commit their annual allocations, because if they do not, *their own* sources of funding might just dry up (Chap. 2). This behavior, which could be called an existential fear, has been a constant throughout the decades and, though sometimes criticized even by those within the industry, is never addressed. This 'moving the money' syndrome links to a number of other themes, in particular the incessant quest for new fields in which to intervene that are called 'product development' (Chap. 3), using the donors' faux techno-expertise (Chap. 6) to both package and justify these ventures. It is almost as if these incessant forays into new subjects and territories are necessary to distract observers from uncovering the embarrassing fact that decades of previous efforts have done little, either to build local capacities or to let the recipient side run even part of the show. Furthermore, increasingly elaborate systems of procurement have been constructed to acquire the many services that are essential for the development machine, these have led to a strange bureaucratic ecosystem controlling a large cast of service providers fighting for market share, and these providers have themselves become enthusiastic cheerleaders for ever more development business (Chap. 5).

Running directly counter to this Imperative to Spend is the fear of incurring the disfavor of the ultimate sources of funds, who are basically Western taxpayers, parliamentarians, and their various watchdogs. Thus, there is need for constant, pervasive, and squeaky-clean control of operations (Chap. 4). This need for 'no mud sticks on us' has created a pervasive tension that permeates the whole system and generates many of the chronic ills of donor operations (Chap. 7). And it contributes to the obsessive monitoring of partner government agencies throughout project cycles (Chaps. 14 and 16).

A certain Western superiority must be quietly maintained, part of which is a well-crafted techno-objectivity that conveniently avoids the messiness of politics and power and that provides a pseudo-scientific dissimilating veneer (again, Chap. 6). This trait, along with incessant product development (again, Chap. 3) and the cascade of donor fads and fashions (Chap. 10), is a prime reason the recipient is overloaded and kept its back foot, even to the extent of monopolizing the production of knowledge about the recipient's own economy and society (again, Chap. 14).

Allied to the above, there are what could be called the huge amount of 'easily observable outcomes' of the development industry, especially events and conferences (Chap. 8) and texts and documents (Chap. 9). These are ways that donors monopolize the discourse on development and global challenges and how they demonstrate their prowess. Added to this is the need for donors to project an obsession for constant reform and paradigm shifts, while in fact little ever changes (Chap. 12). In this, donors exhibit a remarkable herd instinct (Chap. 11) since, it seems, donors have also decided that there is safety in numbers.

An essential construct has been the industry-wide elaboration of partnerships with recipient governments, which has unleashed diplomatic dances to paper over what are inherent tensions between donors and recipients (Chap. 15). And donor obsession with 'ownership' has produced schizophrenic situations, with just enough rhetoric to seem politically correct (Chap. 17). And the development machine soldiers on, ignoring difficult contexts, especially outrageous pay differentials that make a mockery of pretended partnerships (Chap. 18). The recipient side, confronted with donor penetration into anything that might be construed as developmental, has its own ways of obfuscation, and these ways of striking back are overwhelmingly counterproductive (Chap. 18). These and other donor/recipient dances combine to reinforce the status-quo and, incidentally, the ability of pretty awful regimes to survive and prosper (Chap. 13).

Finally, donors, in their incessant support for the formal private sector and promoting of business-friendly environments (Chap. 19), have aided oligopolistic capitalist elites, totally missing small and informal enterprises and informal workers—except in terms of rhetoric—which are by far the biggest shows in town (Chap. 20).

Most of these contradictory traits and interlocking failures have been around for decades, are deeply embedded, and are—especially in the last two decades—getting worse. Attempts to reform development institutions and to reformulate aid delivery mechanisms never seem to succeed and, perversely, simply add to the confusion.

From this investigation of the development industry and its pathologies, it is possible to draw out a number of conclusions, as follows.

The Development Industry Cannot Function Even as Donors Themselves Would Wish

It is impressive the number of ways that donors, in their control mechanisms, operational structures, procurement modalities, imperative for partners, and metrics for success, have generated outcomes that are mostly irrelevant (and are becoming more and more so). The resulting aid delivery systems stumble along, made almost unworkable by these largely self-imposed structural conditions. Prime among these is what could be called the half-way, schizophrenic world of 'partnership' between donors and recipient governments. These partnerships are almost always contentious and two-faced, and they have been made even more so by donor's half-way embrace of 'country ownership,' which makes project design and execution more and more difficult. In spite of elaborate diplomatic window dressing, this ownership only extends so far and is constantly countered by the donor's obsessive need for control, not to mention its hubristic, masters-of-the-universe managerialism.

Another serious fault could be called mission creep, part of the phenomenon of excessive 'product development.' This has complicated management efforts, added more niche functions, required ever-expanding mobilization of tailored expertise, and required more product justification gymnastics, and it has erased any advantages of concentrating on core competencies that donors might have had.

There are also a number of pathological ills that bedevil donor operations and that never seem to get fixed: (1) so-called independent evaluations and lessons that are hardly ever learned; (2) institutional amnesia and reinventing of the wheel; (3) systemic delays throughout program and project cycles; (4) lost good work and practical, field-based knowledge; (5) donor elitism and privileged, uninformed bubbles; and (6) distorted remuneration levels. Some of these ills have been half-heartedly criticized at one time or the other, but all contribute to making what donors wish well-nigh impossible.

The Development Industry Is Locked into an Increasingly Self-Referential 'Processism'

Donors have collectively raised formulaic processes to ever greater heights. This could be called a 'processism' that permeates more and more donor bureaucratic structures, especially in procurement systems and in donor obsessions to project the kind of sanitized images that they wish the world (and each other) to see.

Requirements for bidding and winning contracts have become particularly bureaucratic and dumbed down. On both the donor and contractor sides, this has produced evermore make-work and more experts whose expertise is limited to these processes and metrics. This has created a wonderful field day for outsourced make-work and has carved out a whole submarket for those who excel in formulaic box ticking. Huge amounts of time and effort must be wasted in writing proposals, tracking funding sources, processing applications, and monitoring funding flows. In other words, who has time for the real work? Internalized learning processes were never that great, but now there is simply so much process-oriented make-work in the industry that any understanding about what matters in development is simply drowned out. And it doesn't help that the fiction of a cohesive 'development community' permeates most discourses, restricting real debate and criticism to the remote margins.

The Development Industry Is Evermore Anchored in the West

Throughout this book, there are numerous points where it is underlined that the development industry remains firmly anchored in rich countries, in terms of institutions, players, loci, research, and its service providers. There is nothing particularly revealing in this, but with all the verbiage about re-centering, localization, and country ownership, one would have thought that by now there would be more relocation of development ideas, discourses, and management into the countries of the Rest. But no, such development space remains almost completely outside the countries that are, after all, the focus of the whole show. And it seems that there is little criticism or even recognition of this from within the industry itself, despite feeble donor efforts to help grow local research and higher education capacities and in sponsoring national/regional policy platforms. Apparently, it is as if Western donors see no contradiction in keeping the high ground very much to themselves.

Anchoring the development of the Rest in the West occurs in many ways. In addition to having donor agency policy-making, program formulation, and project management almost totally rooted in their Western headquarters, there has been considerable movement over the last several decades of highly qualified professionals of Third World origin into both middle and upper levels of these agencies. The recognition, salaries, and perks that Western development institutions can offer these professionals are very attractive. Plus, having clever and skilled people as technical staff or managers imparts a kind of extra legitimacy on donors (especially multilateral development banks).

A parallel phenomenon exists in international development research, which has also been dominated by scholars based in Western academic and research institutions, far removed from the objects of study. Even today, international development journals publish contributions by scholars overwhelmingly based in the West.

This tendency for development delivery systems and the discourses, research, and dialogues surrounding them to remain stubbornly anchored in the West are much more than the facile calling for development aid being in need of de-colonialization. This current fashion is the most recent manifestation of a tradition of dismissing Western attempts to help the Rest as nothing more than a continuation of hegemonic colonial practices.[1] But today, the development world is far beyond the plunder and extraction models of colonial empires. It is a world whose complexities are evermore driven by subtle marriages of global corporate interests, market imperatives that the development industry has created, and active collusion by regimes in the Rest and their corporate elites. This has made the old dichotomy of colonial powers versus subject races seem almost quaint.

The Development Industry Creates a Symbiotic Dependency

Over the years, many have criticized how the development business puts poor countries into positions of chronic dependence on Western donors and Western largess. Countries in the Rest have weak capacities and cannot raise sufficient revenues, nor can they regulate their economies, enforce legislation and contracts, or fairly adjudicate conflicting interests.

[1] There is a long tradition of postcolonial writing about development, with prominent examples including Eduardo Galeano (1997) and Arturo Escobar (2011).

Nor can poverty be properly addressed, since governments can't even identify who is really poor and thus can't reach them even should they wish to. Unfortunately, transfers from rich countries to poor countries make things worse by undermining the development of local state capacity, and, over time, it creates a mentality of dependency on donor grants and credits (Deaton, 2013, Chap. 7).

For very poor, fragile, and small countries, dependency is stark and ever present. But what about larger, middle-income countries, where various forms of external assistance only represent a small fraction of state budgets? Surely these nations should by now have escaped the dependency trap and have put themselves to work to develop and strengthen autonomous development paths, leveraging donor aid when it serves their own interests but keeping their own priorities paramount. Unfortunately, even in these countries, there are strong if subtle forms of dependency operating, especially in letting donors tackle the difficult tasks and, at the same time, extracting a maximum of legitimacy out of the presence of donors. This works in many ways. First, when it comes to difficult and intransigent issues—such as alleviating poverty through effective social safety nets, struggling with slums and informal settlements, combatting pollution and environmental degradation, or helping small enterprises to expand and formalize—recipient governments will let the donor be very active—as long as they gain most of the credit in the eyes of their citizens. Secondly, at all levels, recipient governments (and their allied elites) have become very clever at manipulating the donor obsession with partnerships and donor rhetoric about country ownership. Thus, they have a wonderful opportunity to leverage the lukewarm praise of the IMF, World Bank, and other donors to show their citizens that their development policies are on the right track. All recipient governments do this, but it is particularly true for ineffective and authoritarian governments whose main preoccupation is simply regime and elite survival and who can easily control local media.

In fact, one could say that there is a cozy symbiosis that operates between donor agencies and host governments. A bit of obsessive state control, combined with a veneer of diplomatic donor approbation of a government's development stances, goes a long way towards maintaining regime stability. Sure, there are contentious moments and maneuvering from time to time between individual donors and such governments, but these can usually be easily smoothed over by the partnership imperative. This binding together of 'giver' and 'taker' is self-reinforcing and has been called "the hamster-wheel syndrome," where incentives drive everyone to buy into a system that simply needs to keep the wheel going (Holcombe & Howard, 2019, 14).

Hardly ever do donors play hardball. And, crucially, 'partner' governments in even the weakest, least-developed countries know this very well. In fact, governments in the Rest have become adept at playing donors like a fiddle, saying the right things but reforming just enough to keep the donor largess (and the pleasing ornaments that are attached) continuing to flow. Fundamentally, these are symbiotic relationships that allow many regimes in the Rest to continue to maintain a legitimacy they should never have had.

Donor Overload Permeates Host Countries, Something Donors Cannot See

Development assistance flows to individual developing countries can be huge and diverse. Were these donor funds carefully coordinated and well directed towards important development sectors, perhaps this crushing overload would not be so pervasive, but such is definitely not the case. Donors are always keen to expand their portfolios, and donor project activities and initiatives can spread over the whole of a country's development landscape. The sheer volume and complexity of 'stuff' that recipient governments, their local authorities, and their agencies must deal with can be more than challenging.

Most recipient governments have tried to track this flood of development aid activities, mainly through ministries or departments of international cooperation. But, faced with the avalanche, their ability to coordinate donor-recipient relations has been negligible, especially in environments where their own ministries are competing, compartmentalized, and 'siloed.' After all, a minister's or under-secretary's worth and power are often measured by the number of donors collected under his or her wing.

Thus, without doubt, donor overload is much more than a simple issue of demands on scarce bureaucratic capacities or 'increased transaction costs,' something that has been often pointed out in the development literature. The donor blithely assumes, since its intervention has been determined to be good for the country, that this should be sufficient motivation for everyone involved. That such an assumption might be wrong, and that poorly paid nationals, sensitive to foreign penetrations, have a whole other world of motivations driving their behavior, is rarely considered.

What is probably worse, donors generate much—sometimes most—of what is currently known about a developing country, and even in larger countries, this production of various sorts of knowledge about a society or an economy seems steered in certain directions that reflect donor interests and preoccupations. It is shocking that knowledge writ large—as an embodiment of what a country is and where it is going—is so determined by outside forces.

Overall, it appears that donors simply cannot see that collectively they represent what could be called a large bull in a small china shop, and that their presence in the Rest has multiple effects that, cumulatively, can lead to outcomes that nullify and pervert the very development aims that they so loudly proclaim. The tiny bits of donor self-criticism about mission overload and poaching talent hardly scratch the surface. If one-tenth of the efforts spent by donors in analyzing and objectivizing countries in the Rest were to be redirected at analyzing their own impacts and pernicious effects, maybe things would change. But the endless tsunami of self-glorification and group think found in the development industry won't allow this.

Donor-Recipient Partnerships Are Rife with Tensions and Obstructionist Undercurrents

If one reads standard donor descriptions of what they do and what they accomplish, one comes away with the impression that partnerships between like-minded actors are the overarching principles of donor-recipient relations. But these well-crafted texts—in beautifully laid-out brochures, on clever websites, and in elegant policy documents—obscure a reality that everyone dealing in the business knows very well, but rarely articulates—that these 'partnerships' are almost always characterized by hard and often contentious negotiations and maneuvers during formulation and on foot-dragging and obfuscation after agreements are signed.

Both sides will marshal negotiating capital and may argue over the wording of draft financial agreements, but the signing (and the accompanying photo-ops) will be forced through, leaving tensions to bubble back up during implementation. Sometimes called the 'development dance,' these contentious relations delay the business of development, add costs to donor programs, make planning for the future difficult, and bring in a lot of confusing political posturing and unnecessary technical baggage.

Worse, this 'development dance' is repeated and repeated every time another project or initiative is added to a particular donor's all-important country portfolio. It is as if nothing is ever learned.

From the recipient side, there is an undercurrent of nationalistic frustration at the unequal state of affairs where donors, with their ample resources and funds, tend to dictate terms that the recipient can rarely refuse, particularly with grant funding. This uncomfortable position often leads to subtle forms of pushing back, and there are a number of weapons that can be used to assert either a country's perception of sovereignty, its development priorities, or, more probably, the interests of powerful government bureaucrats and their networks of friends in the private sector, the military, and the security apparatuses (sometimes confounded all together).

The first tactic is *playing off donors*, a well-honed approach with origins during the Cold War. Donors are desperate to move their moneys in certain directions, and better terms might be offered if there is a threat that another donor might just step in. Donors have built up systems for coordination among themselves that are supposed to mitigate this kind of competition, but even donors admit that these rarely work. This creates wonderful opportunities for the recipient regime to extract concessions and advance its own pet agendas.

The second tactic is the recipient's ability to *leverage access to powerful decision makers*, a necessity in the many situations where nothing gets decided except at the level of minister or permanent secretary (or, for crucial issues, a president or prime minister), all of whom are surrounded by thickets of gatekeepers. Thus, there is an imperative for a donor to gain access to people at the top, a need which can often be exploited by recipients. And if bad feelings between a donor agency and its counterparts have reached toxic levels, there is another ploy in the recipient's arsenal—simply to wait and put things on hold. The one thing the government official certainly has is time on his side.

The third ploy is to simply *let the donor do the work*. Government departments and other entities who begrudgingly receive technical assistance will often simply stand back and let the donor's team undertake all the effort, presumably due to some sense of pique (or misplaced sense of power). As a result, any exposure of local cadres to the methodologies or findings of this work is minimal, and thus so is the transfer of skills, however trumpeted by the donor sponsors as the main benefit of such technical assistance.

Another ploy is to *suppress the flow of information*. This simply may be that such information does not exist, but more often useful data sets and relevant studies do exist in some form but somehow are never made available. Moreover, such information is seen as losing power, and the easiest way to incur the wrath of a boss is to let out some data without his or her express consent. This leaves the donor team with no recourse but to carry out their own surveys or to try to acquire the needed information from local consultants or from previous efforts made by *other* donors.

Finally, there is a confusion over *who is helping whom*. Donors assume that their projects are universally appreciated by 'beneficiaries' and government officials alike, since after all these are construed as helping grand national or sectoral objectives. Thus, government employees involved in managing or assisting these initiatives are presumed to be enthusiastic parts of the team, ready to step in and help to complete any number of extra tasks. However, various small perks aside, these officials may actually see little in the way of benefits flowing from this donor largess. They know that the donor's staff and consultants are shockingly well remunerated, and often they are asked to do things that are far beyond their normal duties. So, they ask the logical question of who is helping whom, and they can be anything but cooperative.

In effect, these are understandable ways that developing countries use their few comparative advantages in the donor-recipient dance to reassert their nation's sovereignty, keep foreign fingers at arm's length, or otherwise counter the donor steamroller. Unfortunately, these various behaviors are hardly helpful ingredients for the effective delivery of development aid. In fact, most of these could be said to further gum up the workings of the development industry, reproducing and compounding misunderstandings, delays, and misalignment between what donor money is supposed to do and what actually happens.

Among Donors, Is There an Undercurrent of Malaise and a Need to Seek Legitimacy?

Something coming out of this romp through the development industry is the feeling that, fundamentally, there is a malaise in donor establishments and an uncomfortable realization, never expressed, that what they do is mostly irrelevant posturing. Donors must constantly present themselves as being engaged and effective, and they need to constantly reaffirm their legitimacy as catalysts for change. This expresses itself in many ways:

The first of these exercises is found in countless forms of what can be called isomorphic mimicry. In other words, donors exhibit a serious case of herd instinct, with almost all donors conforming to the fads and fashions that periodically sweep the business. This can also be seen in the common use of elaborate sets of buzzwords and codes—whether for project justifications and indicators or for more lofty policy discussions. This can be seen as a kind of donor instinct for self-justification, as in 'We must be doing something right since everybody else is on the same page' (and by repeating that page endlessly).

The second of these exercises in legitimacy, and linked to the first, is the rollout by donors of evermore what has been called 'easily observable outcomes.' These are the production of immense volumes of texts that few if anyone ever read, as well as the sponsoring of countless events that, whether in real space or on video, put most attendees to sleep. Why are these elaborate frivolities so common, given that they rarely relate to the donor core competency of transferring funds to developing countries? One is that they are ideal forums for donor self-referential aggrandizement. But more importantly, they project the aura of selfless engagement in the various problems of our time (including the SDGs and, especially, climate change), lifting their organizations up into the concerned stratosphere, far from the humdrum and contentious realities of project and program implementation. Evidently, it allows a certain moral superiority and an institutional virtuousness that, among other things, ensures a prosperous future for development players.

The third of these exercises in legitimacy is the imperative for donors to impart lots of advice, the donor logic being "We must show we know what is going on, right? Thus, we must be showing we have solutions for practically anything." So, there is an imperative to roll out recommendations, the more the better, even if most haven't a prayer of being implemented in the contexts towards which they are aimed.

Finally, as we have observed throughout this tracking of the industry, it seems that donors, practically without exception, are seeking legitimacy by aping many of the symbols and traits of corporate behavior. This can be seen in the importance put on branding and imaging, in the rise and importance of communications departments, and in the borrowing of analytical techniques and vocabularies from the business world. This is ironic, since what donors fundamentally do—spend budgetary allocations that come from public purses—couldn't be farther away from objectives of private enterprise, which is to make money. Yet there is a certain seductive logic in mimicking the corporate dynamism, since this is something that donor agencies very much wish to exhibit. But when one thinks of it, any parallel with the corporate world simply doesn't hold; development agencies never go bust and hardly ever change fundamentally, whereas of the companies that appeared on the *Fortune 500* 50 years ago, only half are still in existence. Evidently, this doesn't bother donors, since dressing up with the *appearances* of the corporate world is sufficient to assuage feelings of insecurity.

Stepping back and looking at these desperate attempts to reaffirm legitimacy, it is difficult not to conclude that, in their heart of hearts, donors know that they are marginal or even irrelevant. But this big malaise is something that must be hidden at all costs, and comfort must be found in mimicking each other, in projecting self-confident success and corporate prowess, in generating copious amounts of inspirational noise, and in dispensing a lot of advice that few want.

Informality Is the Joker in the Pack

An enormous problem facing many developing countries is how to deal with their huge and growing informal economies. These informal activities are not withering away to be steadily replaced by modern, regulated industries and mortgage-financed housing. No, they are proving extremely resilient, providing the only sponge for surplus labor and the only hope for the majority seeking even remotely affordable housing.

Most laws and institutions found in the Rest today were either imposed (colonial) or imitated (postcolonial), in both cases aping and reproducing the semblance of rational government and the rule of law. This created a kind of veneer of formality, but only a small fraction of economic actors actually followed these rules or had the wherewithal to bend them to their will. In other words, the 'rule of law' became what could be called the 'rule of lots of laws applied very selectively if at all.' The results have been cumbersome, arbitrary, and byzantine systems that empower government officials and connected businessmen to bend stipulations, shortcut procedures, or ignore them entirely. It has become a matter of who you know or are related to, and for the majority with no connections, the solution is to remain below the radar of officialdom as far as possible.

For decades, donors have recognized problems associated with widespread informality, and they see informal systems as putting a drag on economic development and undermining anything like well-functioning and legitimate government.[2] Given the enormous problem of employing new entries into national labor forces, over the decades, donors have focused considerable analytic work and adopted various prescriptions on how to formalize small and informal enterprises. At the same time, recognizing that government systems for regulating the built environment were becoming more and more irrelevant, donors began to talk about lowering building standards, easing access to permits, introducing mortgage finance, and delivering registered land for modest family-built housing.

How have recipient governments reacted to these ideas? In most cases, they have politely nodded their heads in agreement and carried out some actions—especially if there was donor funding behind them—but they have never accepted anything like the fundamental reforms needed to accommodate at least some of the informal dynamic. Recipient governments in most cases seemed stuck in modernist postures of legitimacy in which informality plays no part. And donors have simply continued to repeat their same tiny programs and their polite policy advice, never making their funding conditional on realistic policies towards informality being adopted. In the meantime, the inefficient and confusing mix of formal, semiformal, and informal activities has become evermore the defining characteristic of many if not most developing countries.

What the Donor World Is Best at: Self-Promotion and Self-Perpetuation

Among the takeaways that can be gleaned from this book, there is one conclusion that stands out. The numerous donor agencies and associated development structures have serious staying power; they never go out of business, and over decades virtually all have been successful in increasing their funding, expanding their portfolios, and getting their fingers into almost everything to do with countries in the Rest. There may be noisy pronouncements about the need for more effective systems, there may be new conduits for specialized aid, there may be more spin-off institutions and platforms, and there may be loud reform campaigns, but never do donors simply fold up shop. Not a bad feat, something unheard of in the

[2] In 2007, the World Bank published a long, plaintive analysis of informality in Latin America and complained about how state-society interactions surrounding informal systems 'ultimately constitute an indictment of the overall effectiveness and legitimacy of the state' and it 'crystallizes in a dysfunctional underlying social contract' (Perry et al., 2007, 215).

wider world, where the idea of 'creative destruction' is supposed to be one of the driving forces of late global capitalism.

In other words, we are looking at a particular ecosystem of institutions formed around unique streams of external public funding, and it seems that all system components are motivated, above everything else, by the need to "Carry On Carrying On" (Wrong, 2009, 189). Surprisingly, this overriding penchant for self-preservation has only rarely been mentioned by commentators, and then only on the margin.

In effect, a monster has been created that feeds on itself and has generated built-in systems for self-protection and self-reproduction. Justifications to keep going are found both at the humdrum program and sectoral levels and also at the lofty policy and strategy levels. The argument is helped by constant repetition of how global issues are becoming more complex and how there are always new challenges on the rise, and thus 'our' development work is never done. Together, all of this represents mission creep on a colossal scale. You can almost hear Western development players of all types rubbing their hands with glee: More fields to conquer, more financial wizardry to concoct, more expertise to manufacture.

One important contribution to industry perpetuation is what could be called the acute careerism of top management in donor agencies (and also in ancillaries like INGOs, large consulting firms, and meta-development institutions). To survive and prosper, such managers must be loyal 'corporatists' who talk the talk and whose career interests are aligned with bureaucratic structures and the building of little kingdoms within these. Although these insular, bureaucratic 'silos' are often criticized, they are exactly the kind of vertical lifts that careerists like and build.

Another mechanism of perpetuation is the Donor World's ability to generate tiny bits of self-criticism, which feed conveniently into the need for more diligence, reform, and even 'reinvention.' This book has catalogued many examples of this soft mea culpa spun out by some of those in the industry or on its fringes, and these are ways to conveniently deflect concerns, as in: "Oh, don't worry, we have already looked at the problem, have learned our lessons, and have created (our own) frameworks, dialogues, strategies, platforms, and action plans to deal with them." But for all their talk about reform, change, and reinventing themselves, donors tend to plod on, over years and even decades, doing pretty much what they have always done, underwhelming results not-withstanding. A case of *plus ça change* if ever there was one.

Development Pathways Beyond the Development Industry?

For developing countries, there is of course a much bigger world beyond the confines of the development industry, and there are more important paths that poor countries can use for their own economic advancement. After all, especially in terms of capital flows, development assistance is a minor factor. At the top of this list of paths is for poorer countries to drastically improve their own resource mobilization, especially improving both tax and nontax revenues. Also, developing countries also need to stamp out illicit personal wealth outflows, usually gained by sheer robbery. And they need to enhance foreign direct investment and do a better job at leveraging international credit. And, of course, better mobilization of the huge remittances from expatriate workers would help. Plus, developing countries need to make a common and forceful stand for the reform of the terms of international trade and intellectual property rights to better reflect their own interests. Finally, there is the need to revisit the successful Asian export-based manufacturing growth model, at least for some countries with plentiful cheap and skilled labor (Hulme, 2016, 55–82).

The problem with all of these paths towards sustained and autonomous development is that the discourses and policy considerations that swirl around them are already almost completely monopolized by Western donor institutions. Thus, there is a strong undercurrent, where however relevant policy advice from donors might be (and sometimes it is), it is based on mind sets that are completely in lockstep with the donor's need to spend, on donor superiority, or simply on Western worldviews. Moreover, they are colored by the technocratic, anti-political analytics that donors are so careful to promote and, we might add, by more than a little arrogance.

The Original Sin

As we have seen, the development industry is riddled with many contradictions that produce behaviors and outcomes that are at best mediocre and that are sometimes completely counterproductive. But for each fault and each contradiction, there is no easy way out, and this is due to the interlocking nature of the 'unvirtuous circles' that dominate. There may be some easily identifiable faults and worthless people and useless institutions, but it is the system itself that makes even good and admirable aspects so insignificant. Each element in the system is acting according to internal logics that make stimulating 'development' in the Rest, however defined, almost always impossible.

It could be said that the first contradiction, the Original Sin, from which all other contradictions flow, is to think that outsiders can do what country insiders can't or won't. Never has a country developed out of the charity or good intentions of another country. It is not that good intentions are bad, but when they hide so many self-interests and carry such absurdist and arrogant baggage, they become so.

References

Deaton, A. (2013). *The great escape: Health, wealth and the origins of inequality*. Princeton.

Escobar, A. (2011). *Encountering development: The making and unmaking of the third world*. Princeton University Press.

Galeano, E. (1997). *Open veins of Latin America: Five centuries of the pillage of a continent, translated from the Spanish by Cedric Belfrage*. Monthly Review Press.

Holcombe, S., & Howard, M. (2019). Good intentions and the reality of development practice. In S. Holcombe & M. Howard (Eds.), *Practicing development: Upending assumptions for positive change*. Kumarian Press.

Hulme, D. (2016). *Should rich nations help the poor?* (p. 10233). Polity Press.

Perry, G. E., Maloney, W. F., Arias, O. S., Fajnzylber, P., Mason, A. D., & Saavedra-Chanduvi, J. (2007). *Informality: Exit and exclusion*. The World Bank.

Wrong, M. (2009). *It's our turn to eat: The story of a Kenyan whistleblower*. The Fourth Estate.

CHAPTER 22

Peering into the Future

What are the prospects for the development industry? Some stubborn optimists say that it will be transformed by adherence to the aspirational SDGs and will have a coordinated, effective, and glorious future. Others see a robust future for humanitarian aid but a dwindling of mainstream development cooperation. Others have said that development cooperation is largely irrelevant and will slowly be replaced by commercial loans and other types of international financing. Still others think that donors should concentrate exclusively on health, education, and other basics.

Whatever the views of the industry's future, the current state of most countries that are the objects of its efforts does not present a pretty picture, especially those in sub-Saharan Africa and parts of Asia, the Middle East, and Latin America. For most developing countries, there is what could be called development status, a kind of depressingly familiar story of difficult external contexts combined with depressing realities on the ground—persistently awful governments, predatory elites, stubbornly rising state debt, expanding informality, and rising inequality. Thus, there is one thing that is sure: the theoretical need for development assistance will certainly continue unabated. And the development industry will make every effort to leverage these realities to continue to justify and expand itself. After all, UN demographers project that the 6.5 billion people in developing countries in 2020 will increase to 8.4 billion by 2050, over which period the population of all advanced countries is expected to remain stuck at a paltry 1.3 billion.[1]

[1] China is considered to stay part of the developing world (UN Department of Economic and Social Affairs, 2019).

D. Sims, *Development Delusions and Contradictions*,
https://doi.org/10.1007/978-3-031-17770-5_22

So, donors have their work cut out. Yet there are several trends that appear to threaten any hope for anything like more effective 'delivery' of assistance by donors. These include (1) increasing budgetary constraints in donor countries; (2) interventions that more than ever are beholden to Western domestic business, diplomatic, or trade priorities; (3) evermore pressures to concentrate on self-serving Western issues such as reducing carbon emissions, promoting green economies, and limiting migration; (4) a continuing fragmented and contentious understanding of what constitutes effective development cooperation; (5) consistently poor governance in partner countries and, for most, increasingly autocratic styles of government; and (6) an increasing need to work in failed states and fragile and conflict-affected situations, where 'development' per se reverts to nothing more than crisis management and humanitarian band-aids.

How might the development industry meet the many challenges and unknowns it faces? Some optimists inside the development bubble (or hovering just outside it) have said that widely coordinated efforts are making aid more effective and that the industry has entered what could be called the 'stage of sustainable development.' And there are also those who have said that the Covid-19 pandemic will force all development players to put their shoulders together and Build Back Better. Plus, there is endless hype about smart cities, interconnected digital economies, clever startup ecosystems, inclusive finance mechanisms, and lots of 'leapfrogging' technologies. Are these hopes the best that can be articulated to make development cooperation and the industry that supports it more relevant in the future?

What can be predicted with near-total confidence is that, say for at least the next 20 or 30 years, things in the development industry will remain, unfortunately, roughly as they are now. As has been pointed out throughout this book, nothing has changed fundamentally, new paradigms, new fads, and new players not-withstanding. Yes, appearances of change and shifts are prominently displayed, but most of this is just superficial fluff, and there is little on the horizon to be optimistic about.

In fact, this is a main takeaway. As was said in the previous chapter, the only thing development players and institutions are consistently good at is in ensuring their own perpetuation. This is their existential obsession, how to process aid allocations, endowments, and replenishments year after year, budget after budget, carefully pretending that the money is well spent, well monitored, and disbursed more or less on time, so that the next cycle's allocations will be protected from the hovering anti-aid types who try to cut off these flows at the source. Thus, the watchword is always to remain in control of these flows and always to keep the pump of bite-sized initiatives primed. The result is an industry that muscles through obstacles, sidestepping obviously dysfunctional and recalcitrant governments, continuing to maintain the fiction of supposed partnerships, creating more obtuse bureaucracies to handle all this, and continuing to pretend to have an important say in things that should have been left well alone.

Ideas for Change

There is no lack of ideas for changing or reinventing the ways foreign aid should be organized and managed to be more effective. It is almost an industry in itself. Such ideas have been kicking around for decades, but they seem to have accelerated since around the start of the twenty-first century. They have come from a profusion of development gurus and 'top scholars' such as Nancy Birdsall, Craig Burnside, Esther Duflo, Abhijit Banerjee, Lant Pritchett, Steven Radelet, William Easterly, Michael Woolcock, Jeffrey Sachs, David Dollar, Paul Collier, David Booth, and Ruth Levine, to name just a few (Easterly, 2008). These ideas include bigger institutional clout—such as making bilateral aid agencies bigger and more independent.[2] Other ideas are more operational, such as a focus on social safety nets, fine-tuning conditionality, generalizing the use of randomized control trials and cash transfers, expansion of competitive marketplaces for aid, enforcing rigorous and independent evaluation modalities, plus using advanced purchase commitments, 'aid vouchers,' and even 'cash on delivery.' Others look at alternative means of financial conveyance, such as replacing donors with private nonprofit companies or self-governing implementing agencies.

Still other ideas see solutions resting mainly on changes in attitudes and on a large dose of modesty. In fact, one academic's call for better, more effective development aid boiled down to a simple formula: 'avoid hubris' (McMillan, 2008, 506). Other attitudinal approaches to reform of the aid system were put forward in a 2019 anthology, and some good points were made about contradictions in the development world, its top-down technical fixes, and the self-interested motivations that drive much of it

[2] Some would even see the creation of a mega global public investment facility that pools increased contributions from all donor countries (Glennie, 2021).

(Holcombe & Howard, 2019). However, the authors advanced 'new directions' that relied mainly on personal ethics. They called on development practitioners to have more empathy towards the poor and listen to community voices, to instill in young professionals in the Rest an ethical dimension to challenge rampant corruption, to work towards the devolution of authority to local and civil society levels, to move towards greater transparency and accountability, and to instill passionate and committed leadership. In other words, they called on practitioners to "move towards development practice that honors participation, ownership, capacity building, agency, conservation of the environment, and social transformation" (Holcombe & Howard, 2019, 5). These are admirable attitudes, but they represent a kind of moralistic wishful thinking that has been around for some time and that hardly can be expected to upend the development world in the twenty-first century.

In almost all of these 'reformist' ideas for change and improvement, it is assumed that one must work under existing major development frameworks and overarching institutional structures. Most tellingly, little or nothing is said about the need for a rethinking of the penchant for headlong spending on the part of donors. In other words, it seems that Moving the Money is as sacrosanct as ever.

Could Less Be More? And Could Aid Be Shrunk?

The history of thinking on development includes a few rare examples of those who see that development assistance from the West has negatives that far outweigh the positives, and that the Rest would be better without it. For decades, Marxist and dependencia theorists such as Samir Amin and Arturo Escobar have, in one way or another, seen the need of a decoupling from the West and its penetrating, self-serving capitalism, of which development assistance is an important part. More in the mainstream, one could say that there are two 'rejectionist' pillars: Radicals on the left who champion social justice embedded in community empowerment as the fundamental path, and radicals on the right, who see market-based solutions and better business practices as alternative ways for countries to move forward (Gulrajani, 2011). For example, in 2006, William Easterly put forward that what was needed in development was more emphasis on searching than on planning, implying alternative financing paradigms based on real demand from societies in developing countries (Easterly, 2006). And there is of course P. T. Bauer who, way back in 1972, simply rejected foreign assistance as pernicious and market distorting (Bauer, 1976), and it could be said that Dambisa Moyo was advocating the same in 2009, since in her view international commercial borrowing was a better alternative than foreign aid to finance development (in Africa at least) (Moyo, 2009). And there have been a tiny number of more modest proposals to at least limit aid volumes.[3]

Unfortunately, it seems that none of these rejectionist stances have moved beyond simple statements and on to how developing countries could be weaned off (or wean themselves off) development assistance. One commentator, Thomas Dichter, understood that it was the spending obsession of the development industry itself that was the core problem, and in 2003, he presented "The Case for a Radical Reduction in Development Assistance," in which he states (Dichter, 2003, 288):

> Development assistance has largely failed to work because it cannot work. This is so because of human nature, the complexity of the development world's problems and, most important, the inevitable structural distortions and contradictions within the development assistance industry. To put it another way, the organizational imperatives of the industry have generally worked against our ability to act on what we do understand about real development, rendering us not only ineffective but harmful as well.

He concludes: "The best service we development professionals can now render to developing countries is for most of us to fade away quietly and allow the era of externally provided development assistance to come to a close" (Dichter, 2003, 294).

Another commentator, Lindsay Whitfield, pursued a similar 'less is more' line of thinking (Whitfield, 2009). After reviewing the deplorable state of global foreign assistance, its inability to reform itself or become more effective, and the distorting effects of aid dependence, he called for aid practices to be simplified and become more humble, honest, and pragmatic. "Foreign aid should stop trying to develop other countries' economies and societies, and start supporting countries to solve specific problems or constraints" (Whitfield, 2009, 14–15). To do this, Whitfield advances five recommendations for donors: (1) pull back, loosen ties, and reduce the intensity of engagement; (2) reduce the number of donor agencies

[3] Modest proposals include putting a ceiling on aid flows. Adrian Wood at Oxford suggested that all ODA be limited to some percentage of an African government's tax revenues (Birdsall, 2008).

operating in a particular country;[4] (3) stop expanding aid bureaucracies and reduce the size of donor organizations (starting with the World Bank); (4) limit donor agencies so they specialize in what they do best (and only undertake technical assistance that is very long term); and (5) reduce the sectors of donor intervention and the number of a donor's projects in a country (Whitfield, 2009, 15–18).

This was great conceptual advice from both Dichter and Whitfield, but neither elaborated on how such downsizing or 'fading away' of development assistance might be set in motion. As far as is known, no one has come up with even remotely practical ideas or campaigns for curtailing the development juggernaut. In fact, even the concept of the need to reduce foreign aid levels as a talking point hardly exists. (This fact should raise alarm bells, but evidently it doesn't.) The ground conditions that determine foreign aid operations and funding are for the most part seen as immutable facts.

Let us take a moment to run through what might be practical approaches, recognizing that the key would be to tackle the problem at its roots. In other words, ways would need to be found to somehow reduce or nullify the imperative for donor institutions to spend regular budgetary allocations, thus disconnecting them from the Move the Money syndrome that grinds the whole industry on and on. Only then could there be some hope and space for basic restructuring that would eventually find ways to support what countries and localities really need.

Any new paradigm would need somehow to be based on principles that each developing country must find their own way and must rely on its own endogenous management. It would also require that any reformed financial assistance would need to be totally 'demand driven' by the countries themselves, with donor as simply passive actors. And donor institutions would have to play tough. If a country wastes or diverts funds under the new system, it simply wouldn't get any more. In other words, if the recipient screws up, so be it, and, yes, there would need to be strict policing. It would imply true ownership, including the ownership of failure.

There are various mechanisms that might be considered. One would be to hold or park annual aid allocations to specific countries in escrow accounts, to be used when these countries can come up with their own

[4] For example, Whitfield sees no need for the European Commission to have an aid program while individual European nations each have their own programs in parallel (Whitfield, 2009, 15).

ideas and projects that pass muster. Implementation modalities would be however the country chooses, including using their own money to hire international expertise. Another idea would be to set up and finance large endowments in the name of national governments (or local NGOs or municipal administrations), with the beneficiary institution free to use the investment proceeds as they wish. Yet another idea would be for donors only to advance concessional credit to countries (no more grants), with the cost of any project preparation tacked on to the loan repayment. Another idea would be to simply erase financial support to formal private companies in the Rest, since they should be able to find market-based credit (in other words, bye-bye to the IFC and dozens of other donor private lending windows).

Other mechanisms, some of which have been suggested in the past, might be considered again. One would be limiting grant aid to humanitarian responses. Another would be to only lend for general budget support, which would obviate the need for almost all project- and program-based assistance (although such has been tried with disastrous results in the 1990s and 2000s). Another idea would be for each donor agency to drastically reduce the production of easily observable outcomes (events and texts), or at least require that donors publish the full budgets for these outcomes (Chaps. 9 and 10). Other approaches would be to severely limit development programs to certain countries and certain sectors, although this too hasn't worked well in the past.

Overall, the aim of these Less-Is-More mechanisms would be not only to reduce the ponderous weight of the development industry on recipient countries and on the whole development debate, but also to wean countries off the underlying paternalism and dependency and the many business-as-usual symbiotic relationships that reinforce them.

Could Any of These Less-Is-More Mechanisms Be Made to Work?

Answering this question exposes what could be called a real Catch-22 dilemma, and it puts in stark relief the self-reinforcing nature of the development establishment and the industry it has created.

First, a 'prisoner's dilemma' would kick in big time. There are maybe 30 rich sovereign countries that have serious aid funding programs, each of which is usually managed through multiple agencies. Then there are private foundations and charities, and there are also numerous IFIs. None of these various donors is going to agree to curtail its own funding dramatically unless all other donors agree to do the same. Each donor would want to maneuver to keep going, propelled by their managerial elites and by serious interest groups back home. Who would make them toe the line? Is this finally a real role for the United Nations? Forget it! It would require a level of ironclad international agreements that even a hypothetical world government would find hard to impose and police.

What about donors simply waiting for good ideas on how to spur development or relieve poverty to bubble up from developing countries themselves? As has been pointed out in Chap. 16, past attempts by donors to set up even limited 'demand-driven' schemes (based on proposals generated from government units, NGOs, and communities) have devolved into hopelessly bureaucratic exercises. On a larger scale, any of these funding requests would need to be screened and scored and then monitored closely, requiring much the same tedious procedures and assessments and micromanagement by donors that already gum up the works. In other words, 'demand driven' would remain just another hollow phrase, with donors imposing the same result frameworks, indicators, and evaluations that have already dumbed down the whole industry. Worse, the same commercial self-interests of development industry stalwarts would creep back in.

And what donor countries would agree to put huge sums of money aside every year into escrow accounts? It wouldn't take long for domestic politics to eventually axe any such schemes. As has been pointed out in various studies, in all Western countries, there are formidable pro-aid constituencies, alliances, and lobbies that have grown to have considerable political and media clout (Lancaster, 2007).

What about limiting or restricting the scope of aid programs, such as only funding 'good' countries or limiting the scope to specific sectors or programs that are considered benign?[5] But how do you measure good or benign (or screwed up, for that matter)? The development industry has shown impressive agility at justifying practically anything, and it would be necessary to have an independent super assessment body to counter this, one that would somehow be immune to both international and domestic

[5] The Millennium Challenge Corporation (set up in the USA in 2004) was aimed at focusing only on well-behaved receiving countries (based on 16 criteria!), but its record to date has been less than impressive.

politics. Even if this were possible, the immense power inherent in such an institution would attract some pretty nasty players.

Finally, no matter what Less-Is-More schemes might be thought up, truly formidable opposition would inevitably crop up from those inside the development industry. Many government and civil society organizations and armies of businesses, academics, and professionals live very comfortably off the industry, and practically all of these are located in the West. Each would claim that they are 'doing good' and have supreme and well-honed skills to confirm this. No matter how well a new paradigm might be constructed, it would be attacked in many ways, with backdoor self-interest and sheer arrogance dominating and with donor agencies themselves leading the charge.

Development Cooperation Is Trapped in Its Own Survival Instinct

This little exercise—of exploring how less would be more—goes to show how the supertanker of development cannot be made to deviate from its self-serving, ineffective, and oftentimes harmful path. The West and its varied institutions remain very much on top of the whole industry, and consciously or not, the international cooperation system helps perpetuate this ascendency. Foreign assistance needs to be seen as a phenomenon that, although unique in terms of resources (funded by rich countries to help other countries), it is very much entwined in the economies and politics of the West. The abiding irony is that wholesale reform of aid institutions and the development industry can only happen by and in the West. In other words, You Have to Change the West to Help the Rest. Good luck!

References

Bauer, P. T. (1976). *Dissent on development: Studies and debates in development economics (1972)* (Revised Edition). Harvard University Press.

Birdsall, N. (2008, September 8). *Adrian Wood's FT proposal to cap aid in Africa sets off lively debate – Here's what I and others think.* Center for Global Development Blog Post. Accessed September 30, 2022, from https://www.cgdev.org/blog/adrian-woods-ft-proposal-cap-aid-africa-sets-lively-debate-heres-what-i-and-others-think

Dichter, T. (2003). *Despite good intentions: Why development assistance to the third world has failed.* University of Massachusetts Press.

Easterly, W. (2006). *The White Man's burden: Why the west's efforts to aid the rest have done so much ill and so little good* (Vol. 367, p. 2060). Oxford University Press.

Easterly, W. (Ed.). (2008). *Reinventing foreign aid*. MIT Press.

Glennie, J. (2021). *The future of aid: Global public investment*. Routledge.

Gulrajani, L. (2011). Transcending the great foreign aid debate: Managerialism, radicalism, and the search for aid effectiveness. *Third World Quarterly, 32*(2), 199–216.

Holcombe, S., & Howard, M. (Eds.). (2019). *Practicing development: Upending assumptions for positive change*. Kumarian Press.

Lancaster, C. (2007). *Foreign aid: Diplomacy, development, domestic politics*. University of Chicago Press.

McMillan, J. (2008). Avoid hubris: And other lessons for reformers. In W. Easterly (Ed.), *Reinventing foreign aid*. MIT Press.

Moyo, D. (2009). *Dead aid: Why aid is not working and how there is a better way for Africa*. Penguin Books.

UN Department of Economic and Social Affairs. (2019). *World Population Prospects 2019, (medium variant projections)*. Accessed from https://en.wikipedia.org/wiki/Projections_of_population_growth

Whitfield, L. (2009). *Reframing the aid debate: Why aid isn't working and how it should be changed*. Danish Institute for International Studies, DIIS Working Paper 34.

Index[1]

[1] Note: Page numbers followed by 'n' refer to notes.

D. Sims, *Development Delusions and Contradictions*,
https://doi.org/10.1007/978-3-031-17770-5

G

H

I

V

W

X

Y

Z

CPSIA information can be obtained
at www.ICGtesting.com
Printed in the USA
LVHW080738250123
737903LV00005B/230

9 783031 177699